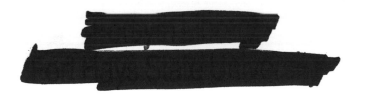

ALSO BY HARVEY J. KAYE

The British Marxist Historians
The Powers of the Past
The Education of Desire
"Why Do Ruling Classes Fear History?" and Other Questions
Thomas Paine: Firebrand of the Revolution
Are We Good Citizens?

EDITOR

History, Classes, and Nation-States: Selected Writings of V. G. Kiernan
The Face of the Crowd: Selected Essays of George Rudé
Poets, Politics, and the People: Selected Essays of V. G. Kiernan
E. P. Thompson: Critical Perspectives (with Keith McClelland)
The American Radical (with Mari Jo Buhle and Paul Buhle)
Imperialism and Its Contradictions: Selected Essays of V. G. Kiernan

THOMAS PAINE

AND THE PROMISE

OF AMERICA

THOMAS PAINE

AND THE PROMISE

OF AMERICA

HARVEY J. KAYE

📖 HILL AND WANG

A DIVISION OF FARRAR, STRAUS AND GIROUX

NEW YORK

Hill and Wang
A division of Farrar, Straus and Giroux
19 Union Square West, New York 10003

Distributed in Canada by Douglas & McIntyre Ltd.
Printed in the United States of America
First edition, 2005

Library of Congress Cataloging-in-Publication Data
Kaye, Harvey J.
    Thomas Paine and the promise of America / by Harvey J. Kaye.— 1st ed.
        p.   cm.
    Includes bibliographical references and index.
    ISBN-13: 978-0-8090-8970-3
    ISBN-10: 0-8090-8970-X (hardcover : alk. paper)
    1. Paine, Thomas, 1737–1809—Influence.   2. United States—Politics and
government.   3. Political culture—United States—History.   I. Title.

JC177.A4K39 2005
320.51'092—dc22   2004025565

Designed by Jonathan D. Lippincott

www.fsgbooks.com

3   5   7   9   10   8   6   4

For Lorna's parents,
Ann and Lorimer Stewart

CONTENTS

THOMAS PAINE

AND THE PROMISE

OF AMERICA

INTRODUCTION

On July 17, 1980, Ronald Reagan stood before the Republican National Convention and the American people to accept his party's nomination for president of the United States. Most of what he said that evening was to be expected from a Republican. He spoke of the nation's past and its "shared values." He attacked the incumbent Carter administration and promised to lower taxes, limit government, and expand national defense. And invoking God, he invited Americans to join him in a "crusade to make America great again." But Reagan had much more than restoration in mind. He intended to transform American political life and discourse. He had constructed a new Republican alliance—a New Right—of corporate elites, Christian evangelicals, conservative and neoconservative intellectuals, and a host of right-wing interest groups in hopes of undoing the liberal politics and programs of the past forty years, reversing the cultural changes and developments of the 1960s, and establishing a new national governing consensus.

His ambitions were well known, but that night Reagan startled many by calling forth the revolutionary Thomas Paine and quoting Paine's words of 1776, from the pamphlet *Common Sense*: "We have it in our power to begin the world over again."[1]

American politicians have always drawn upon the words and deeds of the Founders to bolster their own positions. Nevertheless, in quoting Paine, Reagan broke emphatically with long-standing conservative practice. Paine was not like George Washington, Benjamin Franklin, Thomas Jefferson, or John Adams. Paine had never really been admitted to the most select ranks of the Founding Fathers. Recent presidents, mostly Democrats, had referred to him, but even the liberals had generally refrained from quoting Paine the revolutionary. When they called upon his life and labors, they usually conjured up Paine the patriot, citing the line with which, during the darkest days of the war for independence, he opened the first of his *American Crisis* papers: "These are the times that try men's souls." Conservatives certainly were not supposed to openly speak favorably of Paine, and for two hundred years they had not. Conservatives had despised Paine and scorned his memory. And one can understand why. Endowing American experience with democratic impulses and aspirations, Paine had turned Americans into radicals—and we have remained radicals at heart ever since.

Contributing fundamentally to the American Revolution, the French Revolution, and the struggles of British workers in the Industrial Revolution, Thomas Paine was one of the most remarkable political writers of the modern world and the greatest radical of a radical age. Yet this son of an English artisan did not become a radical until his arrival in America in late 1774 at the age of thirty-seven. Even then he had never expected such things to happen. But struck by America's startling contradictions, magnificent possibilities, and wonderful energies, and moved by the spirit and determination of its people to resist British authority, he dedicated himself to the American cause, and through his pamphlet *Common Sense* and the *American Crisis* papers, he emboldened Americans to turn their colonial rebellion into a revolutionary war, defined the new nation in a democratically expansive and progressive fashion, and articulated an American identity charged with exceptional purpose and promise.

Five feet ten inches tall, with a full head of dark hair and striking blue eyes, Paine was inquisitive, gregarious, and compassionate, yet strong-willed, combative, and ever ready to argue about and fight for the good and the right. A workingman before an intellectual and author, he developed his revolutionary beliefs and ideas not simply from scholarly study (though he read voraciously) but all the more from experience—experience that convinced him that the so-called lower orders, not just the high-born and propertied, had the capacity both to comprehend the world and to govern it. And addressing his arguments to those who traditionally had been excluded from political debate and deliberation, he helped to transform the very idea of politics and the political nation.

At war's end Paine was a popular hero, known by all as "Common Sense." Joel Barlow, American diplomat and poet, who had served as a chaplain to the Continental Army, wrote: "without the pen of Paine, the sword of Washington would have been wielded in vain." And yet Paine was not finished. To him, America possessed extraordinary political, economic, and cultural potential. But he did not see that potential as belonging to Americans alone. He comprehended the nation's history in universal terms, the actions of his fellow citizens-to-be filled with world-historic significance: "The sun never shined on a cause of greater worth. 'Tis not the affair of a city, a county, a province, or a kingdom; but of a continent—of at least one eighth part of the habitable globe. 'Tis not the concern of a day, a year, or an age; posterity are virtually involved in the contest, and will be more or less affected even to the end of time, by the proceedings now."[2]

America's struggle had turned Paine into an inveterate champion of liberty, equality, and democracy and after the war he went on to apply his revolutionary pen to struggles in Britain and France. In *Rights of Man* he defended the French Revolution of 1789 against conservative attack, challenged Britain's monarchical and aristocratic polity and social order, and outlined a series of public welfare initiatives to address the material inequalities that made life oppressive for working people and the poor. In *The Age of Reason* he criticized organized religion, the claims of biblical scripture, and the power of churches and clerics. And in *Agrarian Justice* he proposed a democratic system of addressing poverty that would entail taxing the landed rich to provide grants or "stakes" for young people and pensions for the elderly.

Reared an Englishman, adopted by America, and honored as a Frenchman, Paine often called himself a "citizen of the world." But the United States always remained paramount in his thoughts and evident in his labors, and his later writings continued to shape the young nation's events and developments. And yet as great as his contributions were, they were not always appreciated, and his affections were not always reciprocated. Paine's democratic arguments, style, and appeal—as well as his social background, confidence, and single-mindedness—antagonized many among the powerful, propertied, prestigious, and pious and made him enemies even within the ranks of his fellow patriots.

Elites and aspiring elites feared the power of Paine's pen and the radical implications of his arguments. In reaction, they and their heirs sought to disparage his character, suppress his memory, and limit the influence of his ideas. And according to most accounts, they succeeded. For much of the nineteenth century and well into the twentieth, Paine's pivotal role in the making of the United States was effectively erased in the official telling. Writing in the 1880s, Theodore Roosevelt believed he could characterize Paine, with impunity, as a "filthy little atheist" (though Paine was neither filthy, nor little, nor an atheist). Not only in the highest circles but also in various popular quarters, particularly among the religiously devout, Paine's name persistently conjured up the worst images, leading generations of historians and biographers to assume that memory of Paine's contributions to American history had been lost. In the early 1940s the historian Dixon Wecter observed, "To trace the curve of Paine's reputation is to learn something about hero-worship in reverse." And as recently as 1995 Gordon Wood, one of the foremost scholars of the American Revolution, could state that Paine "seems destined to remain a misfit, an outsider."[3]

Yet those accounts were wrong. Paine had died, but neither his memory nor his legacy ever expired. His contributions were too fundamental and his vision of America's meaning and possibilities too firmly imbued in the dynamic of political life and culture to be so easily shed or suppressed. At times of crisis, when the Republic itself seemed in jeopardy, Americans almost instinctively would turn to Paine and his words. Even those who apparently disdained him and what he represented could not fail to draw on elements of his vision. Moreover, there were those who would not allow Paine and his arguments to be forgotten.

Contrary to the ambitions of the governing elites, as well as the presumptions of historians and biographers, Paine remained a powerful presence in American political and intellectual life. Recognizing the persistent and developing contradictions between the nation's ideals and reality, diverse Americans—native-born and immigrant—struggled to defend, extend, and deepen freedom, equality, and democracy. Rebels, reformers, and critics such as Frances Wright, William Lloyd Garrison, Elizabeth Cady Stanton, Ernestine Rose, Susan B. Anthony, Walt Whitman, Herman Melville, Abraham Lincoln, Albert Parsons, Mark Twain, Emma Goldman, Eugene Debs, Alfred Bingham, Franklin

Roosevelt, A. J. Muste, Saul Alinsky, C. Wright Mills, and innumerable others right down to the present generation rediscovered Paine's career and work and drew ideas, inspiration, and encouragement from them. Some honored him in their own memorials. Many more honored him all the more by adopting his arguments and words as their own. Workingmen's advocates, abolitionists, freethinkers, suffragists, anarchists, populists, socialists, progressives, labor and community organizers, peace activists, and liberals have garnered political and intellectual energy from Paine, renewed his presence in American life, and served as the prophetic memory of his radical vision of America.

Ironically perhaps, in these years of conservative ascendance and the retreat of liberalism and the left, we have witnessed an amazing resurgence of interest in Paine, extending across American public culture. New biographies (including works for children and young adults), collections of his writings, and exegeses of his thought have been published. Older works have been reissued. Professors from the humanities to the social sciences have added Paine's texts to their course syllabi and, armed with the latest historical, social, and literary theories, contributed original interpretations of his work.

Moreover, with only a few major exceptions the new scholarship has been overwhelmingly appreciative. Whereas academics used to ponder whether to pay Paine much heed, today they debate where to position him in the history of political thought. Protagonists have variously portrayed him as a liberal, republican, populist, libertarian, utilitarian, social democrat, and radical or revolutionary democrat— affirming J.G.A. Pocock's observation that Paine is "difficult to fit into any kind of category."[4]

Still, as much as they have differed in theory, intellectuals have shared in asking how Paine, a man of such humble background, could have made so much history with his pen. How could he, an immigrant, have articulated a vision that Americans found so gripping? And explicitly or implicitly, they also have raised the question of why Americans continue to find his words so engaging.

Simultaneously, Paine has achieved a new status in public history and memory and has come to be admired and celebrated almost

universally. Nothing more firmly registered the change than the decision in October 1992 by Congress to authorize the erection of a monument to Paine in the nation's capital. Initiated by the Thomas Paine National Historical Association, the lobbying campaign involved securing the endorsements of civic organizations, public figures, and historians and, most crucially, mobilizing truly bipartisan congressional support—Democratic and Republican, from the liberal Ted Kennedy to the conservative Jesse Helms.

Paine also started receiving ever-greater notice in popular histories of America and the Revolution. The Newseum, which opened in Washington, D.C., in 1997, recognized him as a pioneer of American journalism and a crusader in the fight for a free press. The producers of C-Span's *American Writers: A Journey Through History* devoted an entire three-hour episode to him. The History Channel broke new ground in its series *The Founding Fathers* by treating him as one of that select number. And the national television news anchor Peter Jennings gave special attention to Paine and the folks at the Thomas Paine National Historical Association in his coproduced series and work *In Search of America*.

References to Paine and his writings have begun to pop up everywhere, in magazine articles, television programs, Hollywood films, and even the work of contemporary musical artists, from classical to punk rock. Cable television talk-show host Chris Matthews referred to Paine as one of his favorite figures, whose "big ideas have changed history." And while Paine's image may not have become iconic, the editors of *American Greats* have enshrined his pamphlet *Common Sense* as popular Americana, alongside the baseball diamond, the Brooklyn Bridge, the Coca-Cola recipe, and the Chevrolet Corvette. His presence has expanded with the growth of cyberspace. Media critic Jon Katz enthusiastically dubbed him the "moral father of the Internet":

> Nearly two centuries after his death, in a form Paine couldn't have imagined but would have plunged into with joyous passion, the Internet is, in many ways, the embodiment of everything he believed . . . It's easy to imagine him fitting right into the new culture, issuing fervent harangues from http://www.commonsense.com. He would be a cyber provocateur, a Net fiend, perpetually enmeshed in bitter disputes with adversaries in government, corporations, churches.[5]

Paine has achieved near-celebrity status. And while academics have been squabbling over his place in the history of ideas, politicians and public intellectuals have been fighting over his political legacy. Liberals and radicals have continued to muster his memory. Inspired by his pamphleteering, young leftists launched the Open Magazine Pamphlet Series in reaction to the 1991 Gulf War and went on to deliver a noted set of broadsides on social justice and the environment by prominent progressive intellectuals. In New York City pirate radio's "DJ Thomas Paine" organized underground broadcasting folk to pursue a First Amendment lawsuit against Federal Communications Commission regulations and corporate domination of the nation's airwaves. A national disabilities rights group titled its newsletter *Common Sense*. In Texas, Mexican American community leaders cited Paine in their efforts to get their fellow Latinos to register and vote. A team of liberal writers launched the online opinion journal *TomPaine.com* in 1999 "to enrich the national debate on controversial public issues by featuring the ideas, opinions, and analyses too often overlooked by the mainstream media." Even more recently, columnist Christopher Hitchens announced, "I've always been a Painite." *Harper's Magazine* publisher Lewis Lapham bemoaned Paine's absence from the contemporary political scene. Famed attorney and author Alan Dershowitz mobilized Paine in defense of the separation of church and state. And as part of his unsuccessful bid for the 2004 Democratic presidential nomination, former Vermont governor Howard Dean issued *Common Sense for a New Century*, modeled on Paine's revolutionary essay.

Making the new attention to Paine all the more ironic, conservatives too have glommed on to him—seemingly with greater ardor. President George H. W. Bush followed Reagan's lead and quoted Paine on various occasions, most strikingly at the outset of the Gulf War in January 1991, when he announced that the United States and its allies had commenced air attacks against Iraq. Right-wing activists have harnessed Paine's lines to decry the nation's "moral decay," denounce plans for campaign finance reform, promote the idea of term limits for elected officials, lobby for school vouchers, and oppose the welfare state. Christian Coalition leader Ralph Reed appreciatively acknowledged how Paine quoted "extensively" from the Bible in making the "case for revolution." Richard Brookhiser, senior editor at *The National Review* and the author of several Founders' biographies, wrote of Paine, "May we always honor him." California Republican state senator Raymond Haynes made Paine's memory a personal cause after discovering that high school students in his district could not adequately explain his role in American history. A New York chapter of the Libertarian Party named itself after Paine. And the greatest enthusiasm in Congress for a Paine monument reportedly came from the ranks of Republicans.[6]

Left and right alike have depicted Paine as an opponent of the concentration of power and authority. Yet whereas the left usually has resurrected him in favor of challenges to increasing corporate power, the right has most often done so in support of campaigns against the growing power of government. In 1995 North Carolina liberals established the Common Sense Foundation "to realize Thomas Paine's vision of a society where the poor are not oppressed, the rich are not privileged," and soon after libertarians set up the Thomas Paine Fund "to restore liberty . . . and make the cause of America the cause of all mankind once again!" Cohorts of the very far right have also tried to claim Paine. But they did not go unanswered. In response to the rise of right-wing militias and the horrific 1995 Oklahoma City bombing, editorial writers used Paine's words to condemn those who would resort to extremism and violence.

The Age of Reason made Paine anathema to nineteenth-century Christians, and their ministers portrayed him as the Antichrist. Today not only do liberal clergy quote him in their sermons (the Unitarian Universalists have posthumously listed him as one of their own number and named one of their congregations after him), but so too do various Protestant evangelicals.

Paine's new popularity left and, especially, right has been astonishing, leading one Paine biographer, Jack Fruchtman, to muse, "Who owns Tom Paine?" The very extent of it has made it seem as if it had never been otherwise. Reporting on a campaign to have a marble statue of suffragists Susan B. Anthony, Elizabeth Cady Stanton, and Lucretia Osborne Mott moved into the Capitol Rotunda, a Washington-based journalist wrote, "Imagine a statue of Benjamin Franklin shoved into a broom closet in the White House. Or a portrait of Thomas Paine tucked behind a door. That would never happen." And in Columbus, Ohio, a reporter noted without reservation: "Some politicians evoke Abraham Lincoln or Thomas Paine to express Middle America's ideal of honesty and patriotism."[7]

Paine's attraction is undoubtedly related to the general renewal of interest Americans have shown in the American Revolution and the

Founding Era (journalistically referred to as "Founding Fathers Fever" or "Founders Chic"). A flood of new political and military histories, biographies, anthologies, scholarly monographs, and novels has appeared. Documentaries, docudramas, and even a Hollywood epic have been produced. Not only have Washington, Franklin, Jefferson, and Adams (both John and Abigail) received fresh scrutiny, but so have Madison, Monroe, Hamilton, Burr, and numerous lesser figures (not to mention Benedict Arnold). And yet in this context the fascination for Paine actually becomes all the more remarkable. Compared to the broadly enthusiastic press accorded Paine, the Founding Fathers have received rather mixed reviews.

While conservative scholars, pundits, and publicists have continued to defend and promote the Founders collectively as heroes and models, radical historians have revealed them to be less than the high-minded, public-spirited, freedom-loving, and democratic figures we have believed. As Gordon Wood has lamented, "Not so long ago, the generation that fought the Revolution and created the Constitution was thought to be the greatest generation in American history . . . But not anymore . . . in fact, they are being held responsible for nearly everything that is now deemed wrong with American culture and society." Though Wood was reacting most immediately to one particular historian's description of the Founders as "political bosses, bootleggers, financial tricksters, and slavers," he had in mind an entire genre of work, and he expressed the sentiments of many both in and outside of the historical profession.[8]

The new revisionist scholarship, moreover, has spilled into the nation's public conversation. It has not toppled Founders from their pedestals, but it has tarnished reputations, especially those of the slaveholders among them. At least one public school dropped George Washington as its name in favor of a deserving African American figure. And Jefferson became the subject of heated exchanges from seminar rooms to talk-radio shows, following the release of DNA studies supposedly confirming that he had fathered children in the course of a lengthy affair with the slave Sally Hemings. Even conservatives have contributed to the debunking by boosting certain of the Founders, most especially those who expressed grave reservations about, or even outright hostility toward, democracy, such as John Adams and Alexander Hamilton, at the decided expense of others, particularly the more professedly radical Jefferson.

Of course, both glorifying and debunking the Founders represent attempts to reconnect with them. But saying that simply begs the questions, why have we become so intent on doing so, and why specifically with Paine?

Historically, we have turned to our revolutionary past at times of national crisis and upheaval, when the very purpose and promise of the nation were at risk or in doubt. Facing wars, depressions, and other travails and traumas, we have sought consolation, guidance, inspiration, and validation. Some of us have wanted to converse with the Founders and others to argue or do battle with them. All of which is to be expected in a nation of grand political acts and texts. As one historian has noted: "The Founders have come to symbolize more than just their own accomplishments and beliefs. What did [they] really stand for? This is another way of asking, What is America? What does it mean to be an American?"[9]

In recent years we have faced events and developments that once again have led us to ask ourselves, What does it mean to be an American? Commitment to the "American creed of liberty, equality, democracy," the "melting-pot theory of national identity," and the idea of American exceptionalism endures. We continue to comprehend our national experience as entailing the advancement of those ideals and practices. And we still want that history taught to our children. Nevertheless, globalization, immigration, ethnic diversification, expanding corporate power, intensifying class inequalities, political alienation, the enervation of civic life, and domestic and international terrorism have instigated real anxiety and trepidation about the nation's future and the political alternatives available. In the 1990s those very concerns fomented "culture wars" and a discourse of social and political crisis reflected in works with titles like *The Disuniting of America*; *America: What Went Wrong?*; *One World, Ready or Not*; *Democracy on Trial*; *The End of Democracy?*; *The Triumph of Meanness*; *The Twilight of Common Dreams*; *Bowling Alone*; and *Is America Breaking Apart?*[10]

In the wake of September 11, 2001, and the outpouring of patriotism that followed, many of those titles no longer seem relevant. The Islamic terrorists' attacks on America and the nation's ensuing wars in Afghanistan and Iraq dramatically refashioned the prevailing sense of crisis and danger. But they did not resolve the critical questions of American identity and meaning. Not at all—they simply posed them anew and in a more urgent manner.

We sense that America's purpose and promise are in jeopardy, and we wonder what we can *and* should do. Like other generations confronting national crises and emergencies, we have quite naturally looked back to the Revolution and the Founders in search of answers and directions. As John Dos Passos wrote in 1941, "In times of change and danger when there is a quicksand of fear under men's reasoning, a sense of continuity with generations gone before can stretch like a lifeline across the scary present." And like our predecessors we have fought about what we have discovered there because the very meaning and direction of America are at stake.[11]

Still, why have we become so eager to reconnect specifically with Paine? Perhaps because when compared to the other Founders, he has come to look so good. He was no slaveholder or exploiter of humanity. Nor did he seek material advantage by his patriotism. But that explains his popularity in an essentially negative manner. Besides, as admirable as Paine was, the answer lies not in his life alone. It also has to do with our own historical and political longings. However conservative the times appear, we Americans remain—with all our faults and failings—resolutely democratic in bearing and aspiration. When we rummage through our revolutionary heritage, we instinctively look for democratic hopes and possibilities. And there we find no Founder more committed to the progress of freedom, equality, and democracy than Paine. Moreover, we discover that no writer of our revolutionary past speaks to us more clearly and forcefully than Paine. In spite of what might have seemed a long estrangement, we recognize Paine and feel a certain intimacy with his words.

But do we fully appreciate the endowments Paine provided us? Do we understand how his conception of America's purpose and promise has shaped our sense of ourselves as a people? Do we grasp why his words in particular seem so familiar and resonate so strongly *after more than 225 years*? Might we engage his arguments to address the difficulties and challenges we face?

I offer this book in response to American anxiety and aspiration. I take seriously our worries about the nation's prospects; our desires to reconnect with the Revolution and those who made it; and especially our urge to link up with Paine. In the spirit of Neil Postman's suggestion that we "build a bridge to the eighteenth century," I seek to cultivate the conversation between past and present in order that we might more critically and democratically make the future. As he asked: "What else is history for if not to remind us of our better dreams?"[12]

One might read the present volume as merely another effort to secure Paine's well-deserved place among the foremost Founders. But this work is not simply an attempt to do justice to Paine. It is about the democratic currents that have run through American experience—currents that Paine did so much to bring forth, that later generations did so much to sustain, and that we continue to feel. It is about appreciating our own democratic anxieties and aspirations and recognizing what they are about. In other words, it is about Paine *and* the promise of America.

Nobody can "own" Paine—if for no other reason than that the Englishman William Cobbett actually lost his remains long ago, after illegally removing them from their resting place in New Rochelle, New York, shipping them back to Britain, and storing them for a projected monumental reinterment. Yet we should not fail to contest Paine's memory and legacy, for not all readings of history are valid and some are more valid than others. Furthermore, what we make of the past will determine what we seek to make of the present and future. Paine's texts may be selectively read and variably interpreted, but as much as those on the political right can quote and try to command him, Paine himself was no conservative. He was a radical, a revolutionary democrat. He fought to liberate men and women from the authoritarianism of states, classes, and churches and to empower them to think for and govern themselves.[13]

While I dispute conservatives' renditions of Paine, I do concur with the right on at least one thing. We do need to better appreciate America's history and heritage. As Republican William Bennett wrote in introducing *Our Sacred Honor: Words of Advice from the Founders*: "We need to engage in a relearning—to borrow novelist Tom Wolfe's phrase, 'a great relearning.' We also need to restore this nation's sense of greatness, to learn once again about the great deeds and the great men and women of our past so that we might move forward." At the same time, I expect that Bennett's and my own understandings of the nation's greatness differ.[14]

Democratic energies and hopes may seem to be in recession, yet our own efforts to re-engage Paine reveal that such impulses and aspirations persist. Indeed, when we read or hear his radical arguments and sense they were already there in our minds and imaginations, it's because they probably were.

1

A FREEBORN BRITON

On January 10, 1776, *Common Sense,* an unsigned forty-seven-page pamphlet, appeared in Philadelphia and redefined what the American colonists were fighting for. A conflict over taxes, parliamentary authority, and the place of the colonies in the British Empire became a war for independence, a struggle to create a democratic republic, and the fundamental act in the making of an American nation-state and a new age of human history.

Looking back, the American Revolution seems to have been inevitable. In the wake of Britain's triumph in the Seven Years' War (1756–63)—known in America as the French and Indian Wars—the British government had sought to secure its empire and more firmly assert dominion over its American colonies. Parliament enacted a string of revenue-raising laws and regulations, including the Sugar Act, Stamp Act, Quartering Act, Declaratory Act, and Townshend Acts. But Americans, rejecting Parliament's right to legislate for them, resisted. They decried tyranny, demonstrated in the streets, and organized boycotts and movements such as the nonimportation associations and Sons of Liberty. Their defiance made each ensuing British initiative essentially unworkable. Yet repeatedly, after repealing its latest law or tax, Parliament imposed a new one, instigating fresh protests. Confrontations occasionally turned violent, as in the Boston Massacre of 1770. Resistance escalated. Bostonians staged their Tea Party in December 1773. And Britain reacted with the Coercive or Intolerable Acts. A Continental Congress convened in September 1774, and in April 1775 armed conflict broke out at Lexington and Concord. By the time a Second Continental Congress established an American army under George Washington, resistance had become rebellion, rebellion became revolution, and in July 1776 the thirteen colonies became the United States of America.

Yet neither the Americans who would remain loyal to Britain, nor those who would lead the patriot cause, had initially envisioned revolution. Even as Americans defied the British government's authority, they voiced fealty to the Crown, appreciation for Britain's constitution, attachment to the empire, and pride in being British. They protested—and felt empowered if not compelled to protest—because they were Britons, possessed, they believed, of the rights of freeborn Britons.

The imperial political climate soon changed, yet Americans' sense of identity did not. The Boston jurist James Otis insisted, "Every British subject born on the continent of America . . . is entitled to all the natural, essential, inherent and inseparable rights of our fellow subjects in Great Britain." Thus, he averred, Americans could not be "taxed without their own consent." Willing to challenge the legitimacy of the government's actions, Otis would still conclude: "We love, esteem, and reverence our mother country, and adore our King." Not one American in a hundred, he claimed, "does not think himself under the best national civil institution in the world." Similarly, Francis Hopkinson of New Jersey, who would later sign the Declaration of Independence, avowed, "Are we not one nation and one people? We in America are in all respects Englishmen, notwithstanding that the Atlantic rolls in waves between us and the throne to which we all owe our allegiance."[1]

Even the Boston radical Joseph Warren, who would die just a few months later at Bunker Hill, maintained that "an independence on Great Britain is not our aim. No, our wish is, that Britain and the Colonies may like oak and ivy, grow and increase in strength together." As late as November 1775 Thomas Jefferson wrote that "there is not in the British Empire a man who more cordially loves a union with Great Britain than I do." And George Washington continued to toast George III at dinners with his officers.[2]

Common Sense changed all that. Proffering a vision of free people governing themselves, it rhetorically turned the world upside down, making the discourse of the day before sound irrelevant. Almost six months were to pass before Congress would act in favor of separation, yet Americans no longer argued about the colonial relationship, the authority of Parliament, and their rights as British subjects. Rather, they debated a break with Britain, the formation of new governments, and what it meant to be an American.

Common Sense shocked people and drove many of them to reaffirm their British ties. Yet it inspired many more to declare for independence. In a letter to the *Pennsylvania Evening Post*, a Connecticut reader communicated his gratitude to the unidentified pamphleteer, writing, "Your production may justly be compared to a land-flood that sweeps all before it. We were blind, but on reading these enlightening words the scales have fallen from our eyes." A Marylander wrote, "If you know the author of *Common Sense* tell him he has done wonders," and a New Yorker declared, "This animated piece dispels, with irresistible energy, the prejudice of the mind against the doctrine of independence, and pours in upon it such an inundation of light and truth, as will produce an instantaneous and marvellous change in the temper—in the views and feelings of an American." Representing New Hampshire in the Continental Congress, Josiah Bartlett noted that *Common Sense* was "greedily bought up and read by all ranks of people." And George Washington informed his secretary Colonel Joseph Reed that it was "working a powerful change there in the minds of men."[3]

Noting that "I can hardly refrain from adoring him. He deserves a statue of Gold," a Rhode Islander impatiently inquired, "Who is the author of *Common Sense*?" And having earlier confessed to her husband John that she was "charmed by the Sentiments of Common Sense," Abigail Adams similarly asked, "Who is the writer . . . ?"[4]

Though only a very few actually knew the name of the author, many imagined they did. General Horatio Gates wrote his comrade General Charles Lee: "*Common Sense*—it is an excellent performance—I think our friend Franklin has been principally concern'd in the Composition."[5] Others nominated the likes of John Adams, Thomas Jefferson, and Samuel Adams. In spite of how the pamphlet differed fundamentally in content, language, and tone from all hitherto published pieces, almost everyone assumed a leading figure of the

American political elite had written it, presumably a radical member of Congress. But they assumed wrongly.

The man who wrote *Common Sense* was Thomas Paine, an unknown, recently arrived thirty-nine-year-old English immigrant of working-class background. Anything but elite, Paine's life and career before coming to America had included corsetmaking, privateering, tax collecting, preaching, teaching, labor campaigning, and shopkeeping, punctuated by bouts of poverty, the loss of two wives, political defeat, business bankruptcy, and dismissal from government service (twice).

Had they known all that, Americans might have responded differently. But perhaps only an Englishman such as Paine could have disabused Americans of their lingering affections for Britain. Perhaps only an immigrant could have convinced them of their own grand possibilities. And perhaps only an artisan could have propelled them to take radical-democratic action. In turn, perhaps only America and its people could have made Paine a revolutionary and caused him to write, "We have it in our power to begin the world over again."

Paine was born January 29, 1737, in Thetford, England, to Joseph Pain and his wife, the former Frances Cocke. Joseph was eleven years younger than Frances. But more significant were their class and religious differences. Joseph was a corsetmaker and a Quaker. Frances, the daughter of a prominent local lawyer, was an Anglican. And early on young Thomas Paine would become sensitive to inequality and the possibility of reversals.[6]

The England in which Paine grew up seemed orderly and stable compared with the England of the past. In the 1640s a civil war between the Crown and Parliament had culminated in the beheading of the king, the abolition of the monarchy, the House of Lords, and the Church of England, and the establishment of a Puritan-dominated republic or "Commonwealth." A wider revolution also threatened when popular political and religious movements took seriously the parliamentarians' oratory about the "rights of freeborn Englishmen" and called for a more egalitarian and democratic Albion. Levellers demanded political equality and manhood suffrage. Diggers called for sharing the land and set about collectively occupying parcels of it.

Ranters denied sin and hell and spoke of liberation and free love. And Baptists and Quakers challenged traditional Christian hierarchy and authority. The radicals were suppressed and the republic itself collapsed, but their struggles and dreams still made the propertied nervous and the common folk troublesome.

While kingship, lords, and church were restored in 1660, in 1688 the Glorious Revolution refashioned the Crown as a constitutional monarchy and initiated the ascendance of the Whig oligarchy, a ruling class of landed aristocrats and London financial interests. Governing in the name of preserving Englishmen's "ancient liberties," the Whigs promoted the interests of property and Anglican Protestantism while limiting royal and churchly absolutism. The Tory opposition venerated the monarchy and the church, yet it was no less eager to protect property and those who owned it. And in any case Whigs and Tories alike viewed the spoils of offices and titles—status, income, and influence—as ultimately more important than principles. In 1714 the originally German Hanoverians replaced the originally Scottish Stuarts on the throne, but the Whig regime persisted.

Orderly and stable, England was not static. Its rulers undertook or oversaw new kinds of revolution—the forging of a nation-state, the building of an overseas empire, the development of capitalism and industry—and transformed the country into the world's foremost military and commercial power. They would not go unchallenged, but in almost every instance they would prevail. With Wales already incorporated and Ireland conquered, they tied Scotland to England by the 1707 Act of Union, creating "one united kingdom of Great Britain." Thereafter they enlarged the empire, especially in North America and the Caribbean. And the British people expected they would extend it still further.

Hanoverian England differed from the absolute monarchies and seigneurial lands of contemporary Europe. The English toasted their own uniqueness and boasted not just of their military and commercial prowess but also of their "liberties," by which—along with "security of property"—they had in mind:

Freedom from absolutism . . . freedom from arbitrary arrest, trial by jury, equality before the law, the freedom of home from arbitrary entrance and search, some limited liberty of thought,

of speech and of conscience, the vicarious participation in liberty . . . afforded by the right of parliamentary opposition and
by elections and election tumults . . . as well as freedom to
travel, trade, and sell one's own labour.[7]

Furthermore, although only Anglican men of property had full civil
and political rights—most significantly, voting, holding public office,
and attending university—the Toleration Act of 1689 accorded freedom of worship to Protestant Dissenters.

Meanwhile, inequalities intensified. The Whigs continued to control Parliament, the Lords by inheritance and the Commons by patronage. Many towns had no representation, and men without property, or
at least an annual income of £40, were excluded from the franchise. At
best only one out of every five Englishmen could vote.

Capitalism advanced. Aristocrats and gentry enclosed fields previously available for common uses, dispossessed smallholders, and carried on the "primitive accumulation of capital" that financed Britain's
Industrial Revolution. Merchants and shop owners abandoned customary methods of regulating commerce and labor. And political economy superseded the traditional moral economy, subjecting people to
the vagaries of the market and creating a growing class of poor, propertyless workers.

A new political revolution never threatened, but English working
people believed they had a right to express their grievances and regularly did so through swift communal actions directed against property
and its symbols, giving them the reputation of an "ungovernable
people." Still, England's governors managed their power and authority
resolutely. When necessary they resorted to force. More often they secured their rule through other means. Nationalism and Protestantism
played significant roles, but "the law" served as the foremost vehicle
for controlling the common folk. "Liberty" and "property" became England's watchwords, and the most potent fiction was that all freeborn
English were equal before the law. While the law set limits to the ambitions and predations of the powerful, it was crafted to instill respect
for authority and the sanctity of property in those who possessed neither. Failing respect, fear would suffice. The number of offenses pun-
ishable by death—which included the most minor of crimes, such as

petty theft—increased from 50 to 250 in the course of the eighteenth century. Neither age nor sex disqualified one from hanging.

Situated seventy-five miles northeast of London, Thetford was a market town of two thousand people. Dominated by the wealthy Duke of Grafton and his family, the local economy remained agricultural, yet it included a diverse community of artisans, to which Paine's father belonged. Beneath the artisans the laboring poor struggled to make a living and, further down the social scale, a swelling number of paupers struggled to survive.

Blatant displays of the nation's inequalities, criminal court sessions were held in Thetford every March, during which time the town's population ballooned and routine life gave way to a bizarre carnival of theatricals, amusements, trials, verdicts, and executions. Most of those sentenced to hang had been convicted of stealing and, overwhelmingly, were of the lower classes. Gallows Hill itself could be seen from the Paine home, and its grisly images must have made a lasting impression on the young Thomas.

Paine's own family made him skeptical of authority, both political and religious. Joseph's brethren in the Society of Friends had ostracized him for marrying Frances Cocke in a Church of England ceremony. But he never ceased to consider himself a Quaker, and he imbued his son with Quaker ideas and values. A "tolerated" religious minority, the Quakers were still looked upon with suspicion and had yet to achieve civil and political equality. They rejected the formalization of religion and priestly authority, refused to pay tithes, practiced pacifism, and called upon men and women to discover the "divine spark" with which God had endowed them. Seeing one another as brothers and sisters, they also felt responsible for one another's welfare and took care of the poorer members of their communities themselves. Though never truly a Quaker (for he was no pacifist), the mature Thomas would often identify himself as one and—impressed by their lives—he would oppose hierarchies, support freedom of worship and separation of church and state, and advocate public ways of addressing poverty.

While Paine's father instilled Quaker values, his mother raised him in the church, making sure he learned the Bible and Anglican catechism. Yet years later Paine would claim that even as he memorized lengthy passages of scripture, he began to have serious doubts about

Christianity. He wrote that a sermon on *"redemption by the death of the Son of God"* had "revolted" him: "it was making God Almighty act like a passionate man who killed His son when he could not revenge Himself in any other way, and as I was sure a man would be hanged who did such a thing, I could not see for what purpose they preached such sermons." And convinced that God was "too good" to "do such an action," Paine came to believe that "any system of religion that has anything in it that shocks the mind of a child cannot be a true system."[8]

With financial assistance from an aunt, Paine's parents enrolled him in Thetford Grammar School. He most liked science and poetry, both of which became lifetime avocations. In particular, he relished the works of Shakespeare and the seventeenth-century writers John Milton and John Bunyan (which no doubt nourished his later political and religious radicalism). Though the school offered Latin, his father forbade him from learning it, for as a Quaker Joseph believed that Latin, the official language of states and churches, functioned to obscure the exercise of authority from the people. And the ban probably served Paine well, for it later helped to keep him from fancifying his prose and alienating working people.

Like many English boys, Paine "ached to go to sea," but his parents had other plans for him. On his turning thirteen, they withdrew him from school and apprenticed him to his father to learn corsetmaking or, as it was also called, staymaking, for it entailed the making of whalebone stays for the woolen-cloth corsets of upper-class women. Laborious work, it demanded skill, concentration, and endurance. But Paine learned more than a craft in his father's workshop. Likely Joseph also filled their many hours together with Quaker historical memories of the revolutionary 1640s and 1650s.[9]

Thetford presented a declining market for corsetmakers, compelling the younger Paine to leave for London in 1756 to work as a journeyman. Yet even the capital's opportunities and excitements did not satisfy him. Twice he enlisted for service aboard a privateer. The first time his father dissuaded him, probably saving his life, for the ship onto which Paine had signed suffered horrific losses. The second time he sailed.

Nineteen years old, healthy, strong, and skilled, Paine joined the crew of the *King of Prussia* in January 1757. Commissioned by the Crown to capture or, if necessary, sink enemy vessels, the captain and crew of a privateer were entitled to keep the seized vessels' contents and divvy up the money garnered at auction. We don't know exactly what motivated Paine to sign up. Adventure, patriotism, and profit were equally powerful recruiters. But there were also powerful disincentives. Disease and death stalked the ships, and life at sea mirrored the oppression and exploitation of the larger world. Whatever actually led him to sail, he would learn a great deal, both about seamanship and about life, for the tides and currents of the Atlantic carried not only dangers and threats but also many a radical notion. Paine later admiringly recalled the comradeship of his fellow seamen—usually a multinational or even multiracial lot—and how experienced sailors took it upon themselves to "instruct the landmen in the common work of the ship." He also must have found impressive their bravery, egalitarianism, solidarity, and defiant stance before the elements, the enemy, and when their sense of fairness and justice was violated, their own officers.[10]

During the eight months Paine spent "between the devil and the deep blue sea," the *King of Prussia* pursued several successful engagements. Still, after it was over Paine did not sign on for a second cruise. A veteran of naval combat but sound, whole, and £30 richer (a small fortune for someone of his age and background), he left the ship in late summer and returned to London, keen to learn and to make something more of himself.

Eighteenth-century Britain was the "birthplace of the modern." Even the French *philosophes* envied the nation's advances in politics, letters, and science. "To enlighten" became the great metaphor of the age, and at the heart of Britain's empire and Enlightenment stood its capital, London, a metropolis of six hundred thousand. Its streets and shops teemed with diverse peoples and goods, and its expanding middle and artisan classes supported a thriving culture of theaters, debating clubs, periodicals, booksellers, and lectures. Paine immersed himself in it. He passed hours in the bookshops and avidly attended talks on an array of scientific subjects. His favorite lecturers—such as the spectacle maker and mathematician Benjamin Martin and the painter and astronomer James Ferguson (both of whom he befriended)—were most often self-taught, skilled artisans. And also like Paine, those who frequented their presentations were usually lower-middle-class Dissenters eager for self-improvement.[11]

Paine's new comrades questioned the order of the universe and the order of society. Clearly shaping Paine's own views, the natural philosophy of Sir Isaac Newton emerged as the foremost current of thought. Newtonians held that God the Creator had provided a "natural order" to the universe, the laws of which could be discovered and progressively applied through scientific inquiry and reason. They also supposed that such laws governed the social world and that knowledge of them could guide the reform of political and social life.

Paine always said he had little interest in politics as a young man. But the contradictions he encountered in the capital—the rich getting richer and proud talk of English liberties even as working people and the poor suffered destitution and state violence—apparently made deep impressions. And in London's artisan-intellectual community he became not only more aware of middle- and lower-class resentment of aristocratic privilege but also quite familiar with the radical ideas of the day, including the republican-inspired arguments of the "Real Whigs" and the liberal philosophy of John Locke. The former, nostalgic for the seventeenth-century commonwealth, yet worshipful of the supposedly balanced government of King, Lords, and Commons, decried the Crown's and its ministers' patronage system, abuses of power, and the corruption of Britain's constitution and liberties. The latter, while stressing the sanctity of property, discounted divine right in favor of natural rights and proposed that in the "social compact" between the king and his subjects, legitimacy sprang from consent and the people retained the right to rebel against unlawful or oppressive authority.[12]

In these circles, Paine also became attuned to the latest thinking in logic and communication, which was undergoing drastic revision in light of the scientific revolution. The new theory of rhetoric—which Paine would so effectively employ—rejected the traditional preference for flowery and elegant style over substance as well as the traditional equation of grandiloquence and eloquence. Instead, it advocated "drawing arguments directly from the facts of the case" and urged speakers and writers to cultivate simplicity, brevity, and "plainness of style."[13]

Yet Paine could afford to remain a "student" for only so long, and in 1758 he finally moved to Sandwich to set up shop as a master staymaker. Though he may already have become a religious skeptic, he also involved himself in the local Methodist movement and occasionally preached at its gatherings, experiences that surely encouraged his emergent belief in the potential of the common people and shaped his own rhetorical verbal skills. Begun by the brothers John and Charles Wesley as a mission to reinvigorate the Christian spirit of the common people and bring them back into the church, Methodism which would eventually become an alternative to both Anglicanism and Calvinism—was growing rapidly in the mid-eighteenth century, especially among the lower classes, for it offered hope of redemption during an age of mounting insecurities. Affirming that every individual could be saved, it proclaimed that salvation depended on individual choice and action and that to be a good Christian one not only had to discover God but also do good works and tend to the welfare of others. Methodism clearly demanded self-discipline, however, built around congregations, it also afforded community, mutual assistance, and opportunities for self-governance. And by promoting Bible study, it also advanced reading, writing, and public speaking among the otherwise illiterate and voiceless, including women.[14]

It may well have been at a Methodist gathering that Paine met his first love, Mary Lambert, a young woman who worked as a maid in the home of a prominent local family. Courting in the spring and summer of 1759, they married in the autumn and soon afterward Mary became pregnant. But the couple's happiness did not last long, for Paine's business failed and both Mary and the baby died in childbirth. In ensuing years Paine would speak little of his losses. Yet he would forever despise regimes that accepted poverty as part of the natural order of things, and he developed a special sympathy for women and the subordination they suffered.[15]

Returning to Thetford alone and penniless, Paine looked into government employment as an excise officer (the occupation of Mary's late father), and by way of family contacts in the Duke of Grafton's household, he received tutoring for the entrance exams and influential help in overcoming the bureaucratic hurdles. His first appointment came in 1762, and two years later he was promoted to a station officer's post on the North Sea coast, where, in addition to his regular tasks, he had the dangerous duty of watching out for smuggling activity by patrolling the shore on horseback. He enjoyed the job but was dismissed in the summer of 1765, specifically for "stamping" goods he had not actually inspected (a not uncommon practice, given the low wages, heavy duties, and unpopularity of excisemen).

Unwilling to accept his fate and believing he had suffered a grave injustice, Paine returned to London and with the requisite humility and deference petitioned the Excise Commission for reinstatement. In fact, he may have been innocent. His supervisor, William Swallow, may actually have framed Paine in an attempt to cover up his own corruption, for the Excise Commission discharged Swallow only weeks after Paine. It is even possible that Paine knew of Swallow's dirty dealing but given the system of authority felt incapable of doing anything about it.[16]

Whatever the case, Paine was reinstated. And yet unable to immediately secure a new posting, he was forced to eke out a bare living by teaching in schools for working-class children. Still, the delay in London allowed him to renew his friendships in the city's intellectual community, which fortuitously led to his meeting the renowned American writer and scientist Benjamin Franklin.

Living again in London also afforded Paine further lessons in British popular politics, for economic depression in the 1760s had fomented a wave of industrial disputes and crowd actions, including rallies in support of John Wilkes. A member of Parliament and the publisher of the North Briton, Wilkes was being prosecuted—or as many thought, persecuted—by the government for printing "seditious libel against George III and his ministers." A wit and a scoundrel, Wilkes had no reservations about exploiting popular sympathies. Nevertheless, those who took to the streets shouting "Wilkes and Liberty!" saw his case as an ominous example of government menacing the rights of a freeborn Englishman. Paine could not have failed to notice working people's nascent radicalism.[17]

Finally, in 1768 the Excise Commission assigned Paine to Lewes, on the Sussex coast. Not only did the posting promise to rescue him from dire poverty, but its location must have seemed inviting. A town of four thousand people, Lewes had several Dissenting churches and was known for its republican political tradition. Arriving there, Paine soon found residence with Samuel Ollive, a tobacconist and local constable, who took an immediate liking to his new lodger. Self-assured and sociable, Paine himself happily joined in community life, winning election to the town council and serving on a local Church of England committee responsible for supervising the disbursement of the parish taxes and aid to the poor.

In Lewes, as well, Paine enthusiastically participated in the Headstrong Club, a drinking, dining, and discussion group that met regularly at the local White Hart. Here he began to openly express his political views and soon gained a reputation as a superb debater. A lifelong friend, Thomas Clio Rickman would later recall that Paine was "at this time a Whig, and notorious for that quality which has been defined perseverance in a good cause and obstinacy in a bad one. He was tenacious of his opinions, which were bold, acute, and independent, and which he maintained with ardour, elegance, and argument." And—though Paine himself would always insist that he had published nothing before coming to America—he may have taken to penning articles under pseudonyms. He definitely composed pieces for the Headstrong entourage, one of which, "The Trial of Farmer Shorter's Dog Porter," satirically challenged the prevailing power structure and belief in the inevitability of gross social inequalities.[18]

In July 1769 Samuel Ollive died, and at his widow's invitation Paine took over the tobacco shop. Also with her encouragement, he drew closer to the Ollives' daughter Elizabeth. And in March 1771—apparently motivated by friendship more than by love—he married her. The marriage would not last.

Increasingly resentful of their impoverished circumstances, excise officers in the Sussex area banded together in 1772 to formally request a salary boost from Parliament, and given his rising reputation as a wordsmith, they commissioned Paine to write their petition. Accepting the task, he carefully prepared *The Case of the Officers of Excise*. While clearly presenting the needs of the men and their families, Paine did not yet demonstrate his extraordinary literary skills. But he began to reveal feelings and thoughts that would become all the more evident in and critical to his later works, such as a disdain for excessive wealth, a compassion for the poor, and a recognition of the critical connection between affluence and distress.[19]

Almost every one of the nation's excise officers signed on to the effort and paid a small subscription to send Paine to London, where he spent the winter months of 1772–73 lobbying Parliament. In the end, however, his mission accomplished nothing material. Making it all the worse, his long absence from Lewes cost Paine everything. The shop failed for lack of attention, the Excise Commission sacked him for abandoning his post, and his marriage collapsed.

With nothing left in Lewes, Paine cleared up his affairs and returned to the capital. The only obvious good that had come from his winter-long campaign—other than a sobering immersion in British politics—was that it afforded him a chance to reconnect with Franklin, who was now the official representative of the rebellious colonies. And in the late summer of 1774, Paine sought him out to talk about America. Hearing of Paine's defeat and debacle, the elder Franklin readily sympathized, for he too had recently suffered public abuse from King George's government on account of actions pursued in favor of those he represented. Not surprisingly, he encouraged Paine to emigrate and promised him a note of introduction.

That September Paine departed for America, outfitted with Franklin's letter. Directed to Franklin's son-in-law, Richard Bache, an insurance underwriter in Philadelphia, and to Franklin's son, William, then Royal Governor of New Jersey, it read:

> The bearer, Mr. Thomas Pain, is very well recommended to me as an ingenious worthy young man . . . If you can put him in a way of obtaining employment as a clerk, or assistant tutor in a school, or assistant surveyor (of all of which I think him very capable) so that he may procure a subsistence at least, til he can make acquaintance and obtain a knowledge of the country you will do well and much oblige your affectionate father.

Though Franklin did not express great expectations, he no doubt hoped Paine could somehow serve the American cause. Paine had suffered a series of failures and scandals, but he had acquired skills and knowledge, tested his courage and intellect, made friends and contacts, and developed an intolerance of hypocrisy, injustice, and inequality along with a budding sense of working people's political potential. Whatever Franklin actually expected, he would in time take great pride in having played a pivotal role in Paine's coming to America, referring to Paine as his "adopted political son." As Paine prepared to cross the Atlantic, however, neither man suspected the revolutionary consequences of Paine's encounter with America.[20]

Britain's American colonies were flourishing, dynamic, rambunctious, and rebellious. The colonial economy had soared to two-fifths the size of Britain's. The total population had grown rapidly, reaching almost three million. And though the vast majority lived in the countryside—with many colonists looking westward for new opportunities—Boston, New York, Philadelphia, and Charleston had become prosperous and relatively sophisticated regional capitals.

British imperial controls did give the colonies some political cohesiveness, but as Franklin had observed, real unity seemed out of the question, for the thirteen provinces "are not only under different governors, but have different forms of government, different laws, different interests, and some of them different religious persuasions and different manners."[21]

Moreover, waves of immigrants made America ever more diverse, as Scots, Scots-Irish, Irish, Welsh, Germans, Dutch, French, Swedes, and enslaved Africans joined English colonists and American Indians. And ethnic diversity brought religious diversity, as Lutherans, Calvinists, Mennonites, and Moravians—as well as smaller numbers of Catholics and Jews—joined Anglicans, Congregationalists, Presbyterians, Baptists, and Quakers. In fact, by the 1770s two-thirds of the white population belonged to the Dissenting tradition (though many of them, to no church in particular), and while religious toleration varied from colony to colony, the Church of England never secured the authority it held at home (not even in the southern colonies, where it was the officially established church) and a midcentury wave of revivalism, a first "Great Awakening," made pluralism and enthusiasm all the more characteristic of American spiritual life.

At the same time both Evangelical Protestantism and Enlightenment thought shaped colonial culture, and though these two intellectual traditions competed for hearts, minds, and souls, they were not necessarily antithetical. Both strove to "remove barriers to sight" and "bring light out of darkness." Both rejected "inherited wisdom as the basis of knowledge" and encouraged the questioning of—if not resistance to—authority: "New Light" Congregationalists versus "Old" in New England; "New Side" Presbyterians versus "Old" in the middle colonies; Presbyterians, Baptists, and Methodists versus the Anglican establishment in Virginia; Reason versus Tradition among the "enlightened." And both optimistically anticipated great transformations ordained by Providence.

Like their British cousins, colonials celebrated their liberties—arguably, they had even more reason to do so—and the lower classes, even if excluded from high political debate, effectively registered their own views and set limits to the power of the governing classes through the British tradition of crowd actions. Still, socially and politically, America differed significantly from Britain. As much as rich gentlemen "lorded it" over others on both sides of the Atlantic, actual aristocrats were a rare breed in the colonies. Though class inequality was widening, colonists generally lived materially better than the average Briton, and far fewer of them suffered real poverty. And while the same franchise qualifications applied as in Britain, the colonies were far more democratic places. More than half of all the white men possessed sufficient property to vote; they governed themselves through elected assemblies (subject to the veto power of royal governors); and they enjoyed the freest press of the eighteenth century.

Nevertheless, as exceptional as America seemed, fundamental inequalities structured colonial life—and as much as the colonials prided themselves on their liberties, their economies depended upon denying freedom to others. All women, regardless of class and marital status, suffered patriarchal restrictions and political exclusion. Poor immigrants gained passage to America by subjecting themselves to several years of indentured servitude, a "much harsher, more brutal, and more humiliating status than it was in England." And even more cruelly, a vicious trade brought Africans to America to work as slaves, with their numbers totaling half a million by the 1770s. (The vast majority of them toiled in the southern colonies, where they represented 30 percent of the population in Maryland, 40 percent in Virginia, and the actual majority in South Carolina.)[22]

While colonists may have assumed the inevitability, if not legitimacy, of such hierarchies and practices, social tensions and antagonisms intensified. Servants and slaves alike made their masters

nervous with their persistent rebelliousness. And—determined to resist European territorial expansion as best they could—American Indian peoples living in the interior to the west added all the more to the
colonists' worries.

Class inequality and contentiousness characterized relations
among free white colonials as well. Unhappy reminders of Britain,
landlordism, and tenantry spread in the colonial countryside. Frontier
families felt especially threatened by the propertied of the coastal
cities—feelings exacerbated in certain places by religious differences.
And in the 1760s armed rural conflicts broke out in the Carolinas,
Pennsylvania, New Jersey, New York, and Vermont.

Upper and lower classes confronted each other in the cities as
well. Wealthy merchants—upon whose transactions practically every
other class depended—made their fortunes on transatlantic commerce and, together with southern planters and northern landlords,
constituted provincial ruling elites that dominated colonial assemblies. And somewhat beneath but closely connected to them stood an
intellectual elite of lawyers and prominent Protestant clergy.

The urban majority, however, was made up of the working classes—
artisans and laborers. The master artisans or "mechanics" had their own
shops and hired journeymen and apprentices. Literate and often interested in science and public affairs, they aspired to material independence and community respect gained through hard work, sobriety, thrift,
and self-improvement. And yet as much as they stressed individual initiative and responsibility, they readily bonded together in clubs and mutual aid societies and did not hesitate to stand up collectively to
authority and seek a greater role in determining colonial developments.
Meanwhile, propertyless laborers—sailors, dockworkers, hired servants, and the unskilled—increased in number, well aware that they
lacked the rights of the propertied and that the rich grew richer.

Rural and urban gentry alike looked down upon and viewed the
working classes with scorn. Though their personal attitudes would
change somewhat by the 1770s, planter George Washington had referred to smallholding farmers as the "grazing multitude," lawyer John
Adams had spoken of working people as "the common Herd of
Mankind," and New York attorney and businessman Gouverneur Morris
had described them as "poor reptiles." Naturally, farmers and workers

saw themselves otherwise, and their rising sense of injustice and readiness to express it made colonial elites not only disdainful but also anxious.[23]

Not all white colonials were British, or even of British descent, but they shared a sense of "Britishness"—most fundamentally the belief that their "liberties" distinguished them from other peoples—and that identity bound them to the empire. Their distance from Britain may even have made the colonials fonder subjects than the British themselves. And yet in the wake of Britain's greatest eighteenth-century triumph, the very demands of the British Empire would wear at the colonists' ties to it.

Victory over France in the Seven Years' War exhausted the British treasury and forced the government to raise taxes and seek additional sources of income. Given the circumstances, it seemed only logical to George III and his successive ministers in Parliament that colonists should bear the costs of colonial security. But the colonists disagreed, feeling they had already paid for British supremacy in North America with their blood. Nevertheless, the government enacted fresh taxes and new schemes to more effectively regulate commerce to Britain's advantage. And, to reduce defense costs and protect the Indians, it laid down the Proclamation Line of 1763, an official boundary to restrict western expansion. In doing so, it instigated a series of imperial crises and accomplished what the colonists on their own could not have achieved, uniting them in rebellion.

More than a matter of paying taxes, the fight between the government and the colonists had to do with the "right" of the former to tax the latter. The government presumed that the constitution authorized Parliament to make laws for the colonies in all cases whatsoever (for all freeborn Britons were understood to be virtually "represented," whether or not they actually voted for members of the Commons). But the colonials presumed otherwise, believing that Parliament had violated their rights by legislating for them without their consent—or as it would forever be remembered, "No taxation without representation!"

Still—quite crucially—the rebellion was directed against the government and Parliament, not the king and the constitution. Notably, in the Anglo-American mind George III stood above the crimes perpetrated by his ministers and—even though Real Whig and Lockean

ideas had greater followings in America than in Britain—colonial leaders refrained from advocating republicanism and the end of monarchy.
Citing the prosecution of Wilkes and other "ministerial schemes,"
American Whigs condemned the government as tyrannical and corrupt and voiced alarm that its tyranny and corruption might spread to
America. Some even accused it of planning to "enslave" America. But
sincerely or pragmatically, they continued to celebrate the constitution, and whether it was because of attachment to the Crown, the
poor record of ancient and modern republics, or republicanism's democratic implications, limited monarchy remained the publicly favored
form of government—with Loyalists vehemently calling to account
those who spoke otherwise.

By 1775 the constitutional fight between the government and the
colonists had reached a stalemate. But stalemates do not necessarily
give way to revolutions. So long as Americans continued to think and
operate in terms of King, Constitution, and Mother Country, they
would remain British subjects.

Moreover, as much as rebellion was in the air, even radical American Whigs worried about rousing the ever-attentive and already-
agitated working classes. Yet their very own words were serving to
refashion Whig theory. Whereas the Real Whigs saw "the people" serving vigilantly as a "check on governmental power," American radicals
began to speak of "the people" as the real source of power, and of the
"active consent of the governed" as "the only true foundation of government." Tapping into popular inclinations, the latter's arguments
had the effect of further licensing working people to harass officials,
enforce boycotts, occasionally riot, and even press for more democratic polities. As the historian Carl Becker once put it, the question of
"home rule" increasingly entailed the question of "who should rule at
home."[24]

In time the radicals would come to appreciate that popular mobilization strengthened their own hand; but hearing nervous complaints
about "anarchy" amid the cries against British tyranny, they also knew
that "the people" required deft handling. In June 1775 merchant Elbridge Gerry reported to his fellow Continental Congressmen that in
Massachusetts "the people are fully possessed of their dignity from the
frequent delineation of their rights, which have been published to

defeat the ministerial party in their attempt to impress them with high notions of government. They now feel rather too much their own importance, and it requires great skill to produce such subordination as is necessary."[25]

Paine landed in Philadelphia on November 30, 1774. The voyage had been awful. Typhus had struck down passengers and crew alike, and Paine himself had to be carried ashore on a stretcher and spend several weeks recuperating. But he was fortunate, and not just for having survived the journey. In contrast to most of his fellow passengers, he came as a free man.[26]

Once recovered, Paine explored his new home and met with Richard Bache, who promised to help him find employment and introduce him to the city's leading figures. Heavily involved in the triangular trade of the Atlantic world, Philadelphia had emerged as British North America's largest city, busiest port, and unofficial capital. Its prosperity and diversity impressed Paine immensely. Founded by Quaker William Penn, the Pennsylvania colony served as a haven for the Society of Friends and clearly reflected its heritage. Philadelphia's population of thirty thousand included native and immigrant English Quakers, Anglicans and Catholics, German Lutherans and Mennonites, Scotch-Irish Presbyterians, and Jews. And the city sustained a remarkable assortment of periodicals, debating clubs, booksellers, and scientific lectures.

As he had in London, Paine was soon browsing the bookstores, and in one of them he found not only good reading but also an unexpected opportunity. The owner, Robert Aitken, on inquiring about his interests and hearing of his literary efforts, asked to see some of his work. Paine gladly returned the next day with samples. After looking through them—and perhaps aware of Paine's association with Franklin—Aitken surprised Paine by offering him the editorship of *The Pennsylvania Magazine*, a periodical Aitken planned to copublish with John Witherspoon, the president of the College of New Jersey (later renamed Princeton).

Philadelphia's political scene thrilled Paine. Only weeks before his arrival in the city, the First Continental Congress had resolved to ban the import and consumption of British goods (as well as the export of selected American goods) and to create a Continental Association to institute the ban, all of which had led to the formation of enforcement committees throughout the colonies. In Philadelphia itself, where the merchant elite had long controlled commercial and public affairs, Paine actually witnessed something of a "mechanics' revolution." Artisans—Paine's own people—had not only militantly supported the boycott but also, in alliance with the city's radicals, run their own slate of political candidates and successfully challenged merchants for control of the Committee of Observation and Inspection. At the same time, poorer mechanics and laborers also became politically active. Having enlisted in Philadelphia's militia, they created their own Committee of Privates, through which they demanded the right both to elect their own officers and, regardless of their incomes, to vote in city elections.[27]

Thirty-eight years old and in America only a few weeks, Paine had a new career as a journalist. In addition to fulfilling his editorial duties, he contributed essays, poems, and scientific reports both to the magazine and to other local periodicals (penned, as was customary, under pseudonyms). And like many a fortunate immigrant before and since, he wrote as if reborn, his words manifesting a phenomenal sense of renewal, elation, and possibility. With England's poor and his own rough experiences still fresh in his mind, he started to outline a proposal for a system of public assistance. But he decided against publication, probably in view of Americans' higher living standards and the relative absence of poverty. Indeed, he quickly took to speaking of America in the most exceptional terms. "Degeneracy is here almost a useless word," he wrote. "Those who are conversant with Europe would be tempted to believe that even the air of the Atlantic disagrees with the constitution of foreign vices; if they survive the voyage, they either expire on their arrival, or linger away in an incurable consumption. There is a happy something which disarms them of all their power both of infection and attraction." America's resources, energies, and movements excited and inspired Paine, and he quickly came to believe that America's future held in store unimaginable greatness. Looking around him, he also spied the real engine of the greatness. "Our happiness will always depend upon ourselves," he declared, unofficially anointing himself an American as he did so.[28]

But as exultant as America made Paine, its very promise and possibilities compelled him to confront its contradictions. Able to see the

Philadelphia slave market through the windows of his lodgings, he was particularly disturbed by the paradox of white indentured servitude and black bondage in the midst of a thriving and liberty-loving people: "That some desperate wretches should be willing to steal and enslave men by violence and murder for gain, is rather lamentable than strange. But that many civilized, nay, Christianized people should approve, and be concerned in the savage practice, is surprising." Thus, in March 1775 he vigorously called for the abolition of slavery. He chastised those who quoted "sacred scriptures" to defend that "wicked practice"; scolded those who had the audacity to "complain so loudly of [British] attempts to enslave them, while they hold so many hundreds of thousands in slavery"; and insisted upon America's responsibility to support the slaves following their emancipation. And when Franklin returned to Philadelphia and established the first American Anti-Slavery Society not long after, Paine became a founding member.[29]

While Paine criticized imperial power, he continued to favor reconciliation between America and Britain—that is, until the Battles of Lexington and Concord on April 19, 1775, which left ninety-five Americans dead or wounded. A few years hence he would look back and recall:

> I happened to come to America a few months before the breaking out of hostilities. I found the disposition of the people such, that they might have been led by a thread and governed by a reed. Their suspicion was quick and penetrating, but their attachment to Britain was obstinate, and it was at that time a kind of treason to speak against it. They disliked the ministry, but they esteemed the nation. Their idea of grievance operated without resentment, and their single object was reconciliation . . . I had no thoughts of independence or of arms. The world could not have persuaded me that I should be either a soldier or an author . . . But when the country, into which I had just set foot, was set on fire about my ears, it was time to stir. It was time for every man to stir.[30]

Lexington and Concord made Paine a patriot and a radical. In May he lambasted kingly and lordly arrogance, writing, "When I reflect on the pompous titles bestowed on unworthy men, I feel an indignity that instructs me to despise absurdity. The *Honorable* plunderer of his country, or the *Right Honorable* murderer of mankind, create such a contrast of ideas as exhibit a monster rather than a man." In July, he asserted the legitimacy of violence in defense of liberty, and linking religious freedom and political freedom, he urged mobilization: "As the union between spiritual freedom and political liberty seems nearly inseparable, it is our duty to defend both."[31]

In September Paine published the song "The Liberty Tree," the last stanza of which portrayed King and Parliament together attacking American liberty:

> But hear, O ye swains ('tis a tale most profane),
>   How all the tyrannical powers,
> Kings, Commons, and Lords, are uniting amain
>   To cut down this guardian of ours.
> From the East to the West blow the trumpet to arms,
>   Thro' the land let the sound of it flee:
> Let the far and the near all unite with a cheer,
>   In defense of our Liberty Tree.[32]

And in October he condemned Britain's treatment of Africans, Asians, and American Indians and hoped for the most radical consequence of a "divinely-ordained" separation:

> Call it independence or what you will, if it is the cause of God and humanity it will go on. And when the Almighty shall have blest us, and made us a people *dependent only upon him*, then may our first gratitude be shown by an act of continental legislation, which shall put a stop to the importation of Negroes for sale, soften the hard fate of those already here, and in time procure their freedom.[33]

The Pennsylvania Magazine prospered under Paine's editorship. Subscriptions increased from six hundred to fifteen hundred, making it the best-selling magazine in America. Paine's own writings had begun to garner critical attention, and he had met many a Philadelphian. However, his relations with his bosses soured during the summer of 1775, and in early autumn he resigned. He had antagonized Witherspoon by having the audacity to edit Witherspoon's words, leading Witherspoon to fabricate a rumor that Paine drank heavily, a slur that would follow Paine to the grave and beyond. He did drink (mostly wine and brandy) but not at all to the extent Witherspoon and later adversaries would allege. Simple salary questions divided Paine and Aitken. And yet something more powerful had motivated Paine's departure. He had resolved to devote all his time to writing a pamphlet in support of the American cause.

The Continental Army had engaged British forces. Americans had begun to take charge of their own political affairs. But what exactly was America's cause? Radicals in the Continental Congress had privately raised the question of independence. However, the majority of delegates would not entertain it. Publicly, even the former continued to deny that they sought separation, suggesting that they intended only to reorganize the imperial relationship. And yet most colonials seemed to think even the latter idea too extreme an aim.

Nevertheless, Paine sensed that the time for revolutionary action had arrived. He did not believe that Americans' pronouncements of affection for King, Constitution, and Mother Country truly represented their sentiments. What he saw and heard convinced him that although Americans did not openly favor either independence or republicanism, they actually yearned for separation and a chance to create a new kind of political order for themselves. America had transformed Paine. He would now transform America.

2

AN AMERICAN REVOLUTIONARY

The lawyers, merchants, landowners, and planters who debated in the Continental Congress and the colonial assemblies argued spiritedly and often radically. The classes they represented would effectively direct the American Revolution. Yet if history had had to wait solely upon their deliberations, the rebellion might never have become a war for independence. Even if it had, by the time they got around to proclaiming the United States of America, it might well have been too late. And likely it would never have become the world-history-shaping event that it did.

America's working classes—farmers, mechanics, laborers, seamen, servants, and slaves—would make the American Revolution a revolution. They would not all realize their dreams, but they would power the struggle, materially, martially, and politically, indeed, at a most crucial moment, literally. The Declaration of Independence, though drafted by a Virginia aristocrat and edited by a committee of colonial gentlemen, issued from the force of *Common Sense*, authored by an immigrant workingman who would proudly describe himself as a "farmer of thoughts."[1]

"The cause of America made me an author," Thomas Paine said. It also made him a revolutionary. Emerging from the working classes, he had come to believe that they too, not just the titled and propertied, could live as citizens, not merely subjects. What he discovered and witnessed in America—especially the mobilization of mechanics and laborers and the formation of committees to enforce colonial resolutions—convinced him of it: "I was struck with the order and decorum with which everything was conducted; and impressed with the idea, that a little more than what society naturally performed, was all the government that was necessary, and that monarchy and aristocracy were frauds and impositions upon mankind."[2]

Paine saw all of history turning on the outcome of the American colonies' conflict with Britain. Yet he worried that Americans themselves might not adequately perceive what was at stake. "The independence of America would have added but little to her own happiness, and been of no benefit to the world," Paine wrote, "if her government had been formed on the *corrupt models of the old world*. It was the opportunity of *beginning the world anew* . . . of bringing forward a *new system* of government in which the rights of *all* men should be preserved that gave *value* to independence."[3]

Paine's originality in *Common Sense* remains a contentious question. Some scholars have presented Paine as a truly innovative political thinker. A greater number, deferring to the assertion by the ever-envious John Adams that Paine merely restated what Adams and others had previously advanced in the Continental Congress, have found Paine's originality not in his ideas but in his craft as a writer. They variously celebrate Paine for developing a radically new literary style, creating a new political grammar, and bequeathing so many "memorable lines" to American letters. And still a few others, while acknowledging Paine's momentous influence, have denied him credit for anything really novel at all.[4]

Paine himself—for all his reputed bravado and boastfulness—never professed to have invented either a new set of political principles or a new political rhetoric. He had no doubt about the importance of his labors and did not hesitate to remind others of them, claiming "the honest pride" of "ranking myself among the founders of a new Independent World." But he repeatedly averred that the originality lay within Americans themselves. In contrast to revolutions elsewhere, "here the value and quality of liberty, the nature of government, and the dignity of man, were known and understood, and the attachment of the Americans to these principles produced the Revolution, as a natural and almost unavoidable consequence." He would probably have agreed with the Vermont minister who said, "*Paine*, and other writers upon American politics met with amazing success: Not because they taught the people principles, which they did not before understand, but because they placed the principles which they had learned of them, in a very clear and striking light, on a most critical and important occasion."[5]

Paine underestimated his own originality, but he grasped the originality of American life. And inspired by it, he would make Americans aware of themselves *as* Americans, a people possessed of exceptional purpose and promise and capable of creating a free, equal, and democratic nation-state that would become "an example to the world."

Paine knew about American reticence. He had encountered it firsthand, even among radicals like the prominent young Philadelphia physician Benjamin Rush. Rush—who had sought out Paine's acquaintance after reading Paine's abolitionist article, "African Slavery in America"—had earned his own political reputation by producing a controversial antislavery pamphlet and several articles boosting the colonials' cause. Rush himself would later claim that even before Paine had thought of doing so, he had thought of writing in favor of independence, but he would also admit that unlike Paine he had dreaded the possible consequences.[6]

In July 1776 Rush would sign the Declaration, but in the summer of 1775 he proved hesitant. He was not alone—and his hesitation was not necessarily a matter of loyalty to Britain. Anxieties fettered the imagination of even the most disenchanted Americans. How could the colonies defeat Britain, the greatest of all military powers? How could they govern themselves without the Crown or the constitution? How could they survive without the security and commerce of the British Empire?

Rush's own apprehensions, however, did not keep him from encouraging Paine. As Rush unashamedly recollected, "I suggested to [Paine] that he had nothing to fear from the popular odium to which such a publication might expose him, for he could live anywhere, but that my profession and connections, which tied me to Philadelphia, where a great majority of the citizens and some of my friends were hostile to a separation . . . forbad me to come forward as a pioneer in that important controversy."[7]

According to Rush, Paine "seized the idea with avidity." Paine had never lacked grit—and he likely had had enough run-ins with English upper-class folk to look beyond Rush's insulting approach. (Still, Paine might have been thinking of more than London financiers when he later observed, "The more men have to lose, the less willing are they to venture. The rich are in general slaves to fear.") Rush cautioned Paine that "there were two words which he should avoid by every means as necessary to his own safety and that of the public—*independence* and *republicanism*."[8]

That autumn Paine devoted himself to preparing his pamphlet. History beckoned; he could not delay. He had to disabuse Americans of their lingering British attachments, cultivate in them a vision of their possibilities, and get them to believe they could actually beat the British. He held nothing back. He summoned forth memories of Britain and impressions of America. He marshaled scripture, history, natural philosophy, and political theory. He bound his rage, hopes, and aspirations with those of his fellow citizens-to-be. He invoked the powers of reason, passion, and Providence. And he poured it all into less than fifty pages.

Political writers traditionally composed their pieces with their educated peers in mind. But Paine, an artisan by upbringing and an intellectual by effort, formulated his arguments so everyone could understand them. In later years he would reflect on the difference: "I dwell not upon the vapors of the imagination . . . I bring reason to your ears, and, in language as plain as A, B, C, hold up truth to your eyes." Identifying with working people, he wrote so they in turn would identify with him. He kept his words and sentences "short and accessible," avoided scholarly quotations and foreign phrases, and said what he had to say in a plain yet passionate fashion. His style was bold, lucid, and lively, at times "vulgar," at others "lyrical."[9]

Working long and hard, Paine completed his manuscript in December. Rush, after proposing the title, helped him find a publisher willing to print it. And on January 10, 1776, *Common Sense* "burst from the press with an effect which has rarely been produced by types and paper in any age or country." In just two weeks the first thousand sold out. With or without permission, presses around the colonies ran off new printings, including a German translation. Newspapers ran excerpts from its pages. In mid-February, Paine himself released a new edition. Supply could not keep up with demand.[10]

Since 1763 American pamphleteers had issued hundreds of works. But whereas the most notable of these was read by tens of thousands, *Common Sense* was read by hundreds of thousands. Within just a few months 150,000 copies of one or another edition were distributed in America alone. The equivalent sales today would be fifteen million, making it, proportionally, the nation's greatest best-seller ever. By one estimation, half a million copies were sold in the course of the Revolution. Plus, copies were shared, and those who could not read it heard it read aloud in homes, taverns, workshops, and fields.

Common Sense was like nothing published before. Paine did not simply protest British policies and taxes. He completely recast the conflict. For a start, he directly connected the king to the British government's criminal and murderous actions. Yet he made clear that the problem was not the current king or government but the very structure and character of Britain's political and social order. The British constitution was not a fount of liberty but one of corruption and tyranny. Monarchy and aristocracy ensured not stability and order but civil strife and anarchy. The empire granted not peace and prosperity but war and hardship. The colonists were not even Britons but Americans, fighting not for British rights but for human rights. Thus, separation would be not a desperate, criminal, or treasonous act but an inspired, moral, and patriotic one.

Paine called upon Americans to make a true revolution of their struggles. Ignoring Rush's warning, he clearly spelled out both independence and republicanism. Moreover, he radically articulated the ideal of self-government they signified and positively identified the Revolution with democracy. (But knowing the sheer horror that "democracy" would strike in the hearts of the elite, he never used the word itself in the pamphlet.)

Even before addressing independence, even before arraigning Crown, Constitution, and Empire, Paine told a story of the "origin and design of government" that spoke directly to American experiences, sentiments, and values. In words that would forever delight libertarians and anarchists, he distinguished between society and government and maintained that "society in every state is a blessing, but government, even in its best state, is but a necessary evil." Yet Paine was neither a libertarian nor an anarchist or for that matter a Lockean liberal. He was a revolutionary democrat, and contrary to the commonly accepted view, his tale was rendered not so much as a diatribe against government, at least not all forms of government, as a narrative of democratic beginnings and commitments.[11]

Paine depicted a "small number of persons" who—representing "the first people of any country, or of the world"—live in a "state of natural liberty." For both practical and moral reasons, "society will be their first thought." But as in Eden, "virtue" does not remain constant and they necessarily agree to establish "some form of government to supply the defect." Still, they do not set up just any form of government; they create what Paine would call in his later writings a "simple democracy": "Some convenient tree will afford them a State House, under the branches of which the whole colony may assemble to deliberate on public matters . . . In this first parliament every man by natural right will have a seat."[12]

The "colony's" growth compels its citizens to delegate civic responsibilities and, eventually, to "divide the whole into convenient parts" and choose "representatives." Yet they do not relinquish their freedom or abandon their democratic principles. To prevent the alienation of electors from the elected, they make sure to hold elections often. And by way of this "frequent interchange," Paine affirmed, they "mutually and naturally support each other, and on this . . . depends *the strength of government, and the happiness of the governed.*"[13]

Having presented his democratic allegory, Paine abruptly introduced the "much boasted Constitution of England," making it appear, by contrast, all the more "imperfect" and oppressive. He outlined its three constituent parts, "monarchical tyranny in the person of the king . . . aristocratical tyranny in the persons of the peers . . . republican materials in the persons of the Commons"; delineated its much lauded "checks and balances," noting how they imply that the king is not to be trusted yet still empower him with final authority; and he summed it all up as a "mere absurdity," a "house divided against itself." Alluding to England's revolutions of the seventeenth century, he acknowledged that British kings were no longer "absolute" but pointed out that *it is wholly owing to the constitution of the people, and not to the constitution of the government* that the crown is not as oppressive in England as in Turkey."[14]

Paine revealed the origins of monarchy to be anything but divine, natural, or honorable. He recounted the biblical story of the Jews who, in envy of the heathens, repudiated God's wishes and requested *"a king to judge us like all other nations."* And he left no doubt as to its implications: "That the Almighty hath here entered his protest against monarchical government is true, or the scripture is false."[15]

Observing that "hereditary succession" merely compounded the "evil of monarchy," Paine wisecracked that "one of the strongest natural proofs of the folly of hereditary right in kings, is that nature disapproves it, otherwise she would not so frequently turn it into ridicule, by giving mankind an *ass for a lion*." In any case, it was unacceptable, "for all men being originally equals, no one by birth could have a right to set up his own family in perpetual preference to all others," and nobody can "give away the right of posterity."[16]

Paine also ridiculed the fabled history of English royalty: "A French bastard [William the Conqueror] landing with an armed banditti and establishing himself king of England against the consent of the natives, is in plain terms a very paltry rascally original." And charging monarchy with having "laid (not this or that kingdom only) but the world in blood and ashes," he confidently warranted that "of more worth is one honest man to society, and in the sight of God, than all the crowned ruffians that ever lived."[17]

Paine then turned to the question of America and its future. Spurning talk of reconciliation, he issued a bracing call to arms: "The sun never shined on a cause of greater worth." To those who cited the commercial necessity of staying linked to Britain, Paine retorted that America will "always have a market while eating is the custom of Europe." Similarly, he dismissed the need for and importance of Britain's military protection. In the past England had defended the colonies when it was in England's interest to do so. In the future, comity among America's trading partners would obviate the need for further defense. "France and Spain never were, nor perhaps ever will be, our enemies as *Americans*," Paine concluded, "but as our being the *subjects of Great Britain*."[18]

To the seemingly more sentimental folk who would say, "Britain is the parent country," Paine rejoined, "Then the more shame upon her conduct. Even brutes do not devour their young, nor savages make war upon their families." But again, he recast the question: "Europe, and not England, is the parent country of America. This new world hath been the asylum for the persecuted lovers of civil and religious liberty from *every part* of Europe." Valuing ethnic diversity as no pamphleteer before him had, Paine gladdened many an American Celt, German, Hollander, Frenchman, and Scandinavian by announcing that "we claim brotherhood with every European Christian, and triumph in the generosity of the sentiment." America, he hinted, was destined for a more universal brotherhood than ever before realized.[19]

And to those who fantasized Britain and America together constituting a power that "might bid defiance to the world," Paine replied, "What have we to do with setting the world at defiance?" Appealing to Americans' commercial ambitions, urban and rural, he began to elaborate the theory that democracies would promote peace—"Our plan is commerce, and that, well attended to, will secure us the peace and friendship of all Europe"—and to conceive the United States' original foreign policy goal of avoiding entangling alliances: "As Europe is our market for trade, we ought to form no partial connection with any part of it. It is the true interest of America to steer clear of European connections."[20]

More poetically, Paine wrote, "Every thing that is right and reasonable pleads for separation. The blood of the slain, the weeping voice of nature cries 'TIS TIME TO PART." And heartening many a Protestant Dissenter, he preached:

Even the distance at which the Almighty hath placed England and America is a strong and natural proof that the authority of one over the other, was never the design of heaven. The time likewise at which the continent was discovered, adds weight to the argument, and the manner in which it was peopled, encreases the force of it. The Reformation was preceded by the discovery of America: As if the Almighty graciously meant to open a sanctuary to the persecuted in future years.[21]

Paine scorned those who could "espouse reconciliation" in the face of evil and brutality. And of those who could "still shake hands with the murderers" of men, women and children, he pronounced, "you [are] unworthy the name of husband, father, friend, or lover, and whatever may be your rank or title in life, you have the heart of a coward, and the spirit of a sycophant." He explained that he did not "mean . . . to exhibit horror for the purpose of provoking revenge, but to awaken us from fatal and unmanly slumbers." For Americans had to act right away: "The present winter is worth an age if rightly employed, but if lost or neglected the whole continent will partake of the misfortune."[22]

Comprehending that for lack of a plan "men do not see their way out," Paine sketched a *federalist*, *republican*, and *liberal-democratic* plan of government that built upon existing arrangements and redeemed the democratic story with which he had opened the pamphlet. The national "Continental Congress" and the provincial assemblies alike were to be unicameral, to meet annually, and to be headed by elected presidents (not "governors"). The business of the assemblies was to be "wholly domestic and subject to the authority of . . . Congress." And to ensure provincial equality, each colony was to send to Congress no less than thirty elected delegates (each representing a distinct district), and at every session the delegates were to elect a new president from their own number, with the presidency rotating through the different colonies. Finally, Congress was to have a "large and equal representation," consisting of no fewer than 390 members, three-fifths of whom would constitute a majority and be required to pass a new law.[23]

Republicanism to Paine, as he would later explain, meant not a "*particular form* of government" but a government constituted for "*respublica* . . . or the public good," as opposed to one that served "despotic" ends. And he understood the particular form of government he advanced as *representative democracy*: "By ingrafting representation upon democracy, we arrive at a system of government capable of embracing and confederating all the various interests and every extent of territory and population."[24]

The America Paine portrayed was not thirteen separate entities but a single nation-state. Deeply concerned that the tenuous colonial alliance might fall apart, he was the first to propose the idea of convening a conference to frame a "Continental Charter." And—making it all the more original—his democratic commitments and sensibilities led him to insist that the conference be "impowered by the people." This charter, or constitution, would not only unify Americans in a "continental government" but also, by encompassing something of a Bill of Rights, guarantee their "freedom and property" and "above all things, the free exercise of religion, according to the dictates of conscience."[25]

Confronting the bigotry of the age, Paine extolled America's religious pluralism: "I fully and conscientiously believe, that it is the will of the Almighty that there should be a diversity of religious opinions among us." And challenging the established orders in Congregational-dominated New England and the Anglican-dominated South, he moved the separation of church and state: "As to religion, I hold it to be the indispensable duty of government to protect all conscientious professors thereof, and I know of no other business which government has to do therewith."[26]

Anticipating the query "But where is the king of America?" Paine preemptively shot back, "I'll tell you, Friend, he reigns above, and doth not make havoc of mankind like the royal brute of Great Britain." Then, without pause, he projected an American Independence Day filled with splendid democratic ritual:

> [L]et a day be solemnly set apart for proclaiming the charter; let it be brought forth placed on the divine law, the Word of God; let a crown be placed thereon, by which the world may know, that so far as we approve of monarchy, that in America the law is king. But lest any ill should afterwards arise, let the crown at the conclusion of the ceremony be demolished, and scattered among the people whose right it is.[27]

Declaring that "a government of our own is our natural right," Paine showed Americans they could obtain it. "'Tis not in numbers but in unity that our great strength lies," he wrote, "yet our present numbers are sufficient to repel the force of all the world . . . No country on the globe is so happily situated, or so internally capable of raising a fleet as America . . . In almost every article of defense we abound." His pen seemingly swaggered on every line.[28]

Finally, Paine reiterated the need for swift and concerted action. Americans had to seize the day. The opportunities were enormous and the circumstances propitious. Failure to act forthwith could be disastrous. Earlier, he had cautioned that hesitation would not only increase Britain's chances of conquering America but would also leave the door open to a politics of the "desperate and discontented," which might tragically restore kingly rule and "sweep away the liberties of the continent like a deluge." He now warned as well that "it might be impossible to form the Continent into one government half a century hence. The vast variety of interests . . . would create confusion. Colony would be against colony." And as long as Americans remained "subjects of Britain," other European powers would treat them as nothing but "Rebels," undeserving of diplomatic recognition, unworthy of support. "Nothing," he concluded, "can settle our affairs so expeditiously as an open and determined DECLARATION FOR INDEPENDENCE."[29]

In both content and form, Paine crafted *Common Sense* as a manifesto for a *democratic* America. He did not specify qualifications for citizenship or suffrage, yet he evidently had in mind a broad, egalitarian male franchise. Developing a more democratic language of politics and advancing a more inclusive conception of "the people" than had ever prevailed, he wrote not only to recruit working people to the cause of independence but also to empower them to restructure the political and social order. Sadly, he failed to incorporate his abolitionist views into the pamphlet (presumably worrying that doing so might split the colonial alliance, and possibly believing an independent America would liberate the slaves sooner than a colonial one).[30]

Nevertheless, Paine's vision of American democracy was expansive and potentially unlimited. America would provide a model for the world and a refuge for those who sought freedom: "O! ye that love mankind! Ye that dare oppose, not only tyranny, but the tyrant, stand forth! Every spot of the world is overrun with oppression. Freedom hath been hunted round the globe. Asia and Africa have long expelled her. Europe regards her like a stranger, and England hath given her warning to depart. O! receive the fugitive, and prepare in time an asylum for mankind." And in the millennial tones of both Evangelicalism and Enlightenment thought, Paine prophesied that the American Revolution would initiate a *universal* transformation: "The cause of America is in a great measure the cause of all mankind . . . We have it in our power to begin the world over again. The birth-day of a new world is at hand."[31]

Whatever its originality in idea and language, *Common Sense* was radically original in appeal and consequence. Whether it changed people's minds or freed them to speak their minds, it pushed them—not all of them, but vast numbers of them—to revolution. It probably helped that they presumed a prominent Whig had written it. Timing also helped. Just as the pamphlet came out, the text of the King's October speech to Parliament arrived in Philadelphia. Therein George III described America's rebellion as a war for independence and declared Britain's intention to crush it. Ironically, his words enhanced Paine's. Hurriedly, Continental Congressmen bought copies of *Common Sense* and sent them off to family and friends—to spread its message, test the waters, and warn their kith and kin.[32]

Common Sense thrilled the radical Whigs. When suddenly called home on military business in mid-January, South Carolina delegate Christopher Gadsden carried copies with him, prepared to move for independence in the Provincial Congress meeting in Charleston. On February 9 he marched in carrying a bright yellow flag bearing the image of a coiled snake and the words "Don't Tread on Me," and the following day he read aloud from Paine's pamphlet. Shocked by its language, his colleagues shouted him down, calling him and the author traitors. South Carolina's planters clearly would not yet hear of revolution. But minds would change, and in April—after many of them had actually studied Paine's words—they too would move in favor of separation.[33]

Common Sense gave dramatic new meaning and momentum to the American cause. From Boston, Deacon Palmer let John Adams know that "no pages was ever more rapturously read, nor more generally approved. People speak of it in rapturous praise." From New York, Hugh

Hughes reported to Samuel Adams that "it is certain there never was anything printed here within these thirty years or since I been in this place that has been more universally approved or admired." North Carolina delegate John Penn informed his colleagues in the Continental Congress that in the course of his journey home he "heard nothing praised . . . but Common sense and Independence." Similar news came in from every corner of the colonies. Edmund Randolph of Virginia would later recall how Paine's arguments "insinuated" themselves "into the hearts of the people," both "learned" and "unlearned," and "public sentiment, which a few weeks before had shuddered at the tremendous obstacles with which independence was environed, overleaped every barrier."[34]

Of course, *Common Sense* inflamed Loyalists. Assuming that a Whig leader had written it, they read it as confirmation of their worst nightmares. Liberty required order, they believed, and order required deference; the America envisioned by the anonymous author promised not freedom but anarchy and, inevitably, "democratic tyranny." They reacted energetically in their own letters and pamphlets, the most notable of the latter being *The True Interest of America Impartially Stated* by Charles Inglis, a prominent Anglican minister, and *Plain Truth* by James Chalmers, a Scottish-born Maryland landowner. Urging reconciliation, the Tory essayists earnestly defended monarchy and the constitution. They predicted that independence and republicanism would engender civil war, economic catastrophe, and the dissolution of property, and they warned that in the absence of British power and protection, foreign powers would seek dominion over America. They countered Paine carefully, logically, and in the very ways Paine himself had expected; but their works didn't stand a chance against his and the popular fervor for revolution it and mounting British belligerency were whipping up.[35]

Common Sense made many a moderate and conservative Whig feverish. Elias Boudinot of New Jersey, who would serve as a colonel in Washington's army, referred to its author as a "Crack Brain Zealot for Democracy." Virginia plantation owner Colonel Landon Carter recorded that "*Common Sense* . . . is quite scandalous & disgraces the American cause much," for it advanced "new and dangerous doctrines to the peace and happiness of every society." Dr. William Smith, an

Anglican churchman and provost of the College of Philadelphia, who supported the American cause but drew the line at independence, responded to Paine that spring in a series of widely noted letters to the city's newspapers, written under the pseudonym "Cato." Advocating a settlement on "constitutional principles," he vigorously attacked the pamphlet and its author.[36]

Paine's egalitarian and democratic spirit also troubled certain radicals, most formidably John Adams. Adams welcomed Paine's call for independence and republicanism, but he was convinced that Paine had gone too far. Adams distrusted "the people," worshiped the English constitution, and suspected anyone who would elevate the former and denigrate the latter. And in years to come, he would grow to despise and envy Paine. Having heard from his wife Abigail that she adored *Common Sense* and wanted eagerly to know the author's identity, Adams honestly replied that, contrary to what a lot of people thought, he himself "could not have written any Thing in so manly and striking a style." However, he went on, "this Writer seems to have very inadequate Ideas of what is proper and necessary to be done, in order to form Constitutions." Through the rest of his life, Adams would never stop railing against Paine, that "profligate and impious . . . *Star of Disaster*" whose writing was "suitable for an Emigrant from New Gate [an English prison]." Adams would even come to refer to *Common Sense* as "a poor, ignorant, Malicious, short-sighted Crapulous Mass" and agonize over the supposed fact that "History is to ascribe the American Revolution to Thomas Pain [sic]."[37]

Jealousy aside, what really bothered Adams was what Paine's radicalism threatened to unleash. The mysterious pamphleteer had not only "charmed" his wife; he also apparently had turned her into a feminist democrat. "In the new Code of Laws which I suppose it will be necessary for you to make," Abigail wrote, "I desire you would Remember the Ladies." She even threatened insurrection: "Do not put such unlimited power into the hands of the Husbands. Remember all Men would be tyrants if they could. If perticuliar [sic] care and attention is not paid to the Ladies we are determined to foment a Rebelion [sic], and will not hold ourselves bound by any Laws in which we have no voice, or Representation." To which Adams answered: "We have been told that our Struggle has loosened the bands of Government every where. That Children and Apprentices were disobedient—that schools and Colleges were grown turbulent—that Indians slighted their guardians and Negroes grew insolent to the Masters. But your Letter was the first Intimation that another Tribe more numerous and powerful than all the rest were grown discontented."[38]

Common Sense had tapped Americans' democratic yearnings, and Adams didn't like it. Frightened by Paine's politics of the people, Adams also feared Paine's plan for government. He quickly published his own pamphlet, *Thoughts on Government*, in which, utterly rejecting Paine's "single assembly," he laid out his own model. Replete with "checks and balances," it involved a bicameral legislature whose annually elected members would be drawn from "the most wise and good"; a separate executive, chosen by the legislature and titled "governor", and an independent judiciary, who "should hold estates for life in their offices." Adams was no democrat, and in contrast to Paine, he spoke mostly of the "colonies," not of continental unity.[39]

Adams, however, did reveal a contradiction in Paine's reasoning, that is, between Paine's acknowledgment that people are not saints and his plan for a government without institutional checks and balances. But Paine himself thought he had resolved the contradiction. He had immense confidence that Americans could create a constitution—a liberal-democratic constitution—that would both establish democracy *and* secure their rights. And he believed that through a representative system, frequent elections, and constitutionally assured freedoms, citizens could develop and, when necessary, correct their government.

In the Adams-Paine exchange we see the beginnings of the perennial contest in American political culture between those who would try to set limits to the expansion of democracy and those who would seek to extend and deepen it. And yet while scholars have long acclaimed Adams as an intellectual benefactor of the constitutional reformation of the American colonies and the later framing of the United States Constitution, they have given less attention to how Paine endowed the process (beyond noting the obvious influence *Common Sense* had on Pennsylvania's unique revolutionary-era democratic constitution and unicameral legislature). They have generally undervalued Paine's pioneering arguments regarding popular empowerment of constitutions, the need to affirm citizens' rights in *written* constitutions, the importance of separating church and state, and the establishment of a federal system. In fact, while they have recognized the unidentified author of the pamphlet *Four Letters on Interesting Subjects* as a progenitor of the idea that legitimate constitutions are framed by the people—"We the People"—only very recently have they come to acknowledge that its author, and the author of the words, "All constitutions should be contained in some written Charter; but *that* Charter should be the act of *all* and not *one man*," was Paine.[40]

Intending *Four Letters* at least in part as a reply to Adams's *Thoughts on Government*, Paine critically, yet not adamantly, addressed the matter of bicameral versus unicameral legislatures. He strongly favored the latter, but—deferring to the importance of setting up a government that would naturally inhibit political divisions of interest, and conceding that different colonies might experiment with different models—he presented his case without dwelling on it. Rather, he moved on to his real concern, rights *and* democracy. He indicated the necessity of constitutionally limiting the legislature's authority. He repeated the imperative of a constitution "guaranteeing," not "granting," the "great rights" like "liberty of conscience" and "security of person against unjust imprisonments." He highlighted the rights of Indians to their lands. And he underscored the "ancient" democratic institution of trial by jury. He also provided that a constitution must both "fix the manner in which officers of government shall be chosen" and specify the authorities and terms of such officers, as well as those of "delegates for Congress" (all of whom, he suggested, should be subject to term limits). Lastly, he considered a means of "preserving" the constitution by way of periodical review and democratic amendment.[41]

Adams had good reason to be alarmed. Paine had infused the making of an independent America with radical-democratic significance and fired the imaginations of working people. From Boston to Charleston, they made his arguments their own. They lifted their drinks to its still-unknown author and to the now-clarified American cause, titling both "Common Sense." Adams's own Philadelphia barber told him that he and his fellows had begun to enthusiastically toast—in words straight out of *Common Sense*—"the free and independent States of America." In New York, the Mechanics Committee commanded printer Samuel

Loudon to reveal the name of the author of *The Deceiver Unmasked; or Loyalty and Interest United: In Answer to a Pamphlet Entitled Common Sense*, a work hostile to Paine's that he was soon to publish. When Loudon refused, committee members rushed to his shop to confiscate the print run, and the following night a crowd of workingmen burned the entire stock. Other cities witnessed comparable events in defense of "Common Sense."[42]

Just weeks after Paine's pamphlet appeared, a letter to the *Pennsylvania Packet* noted the independence movement's class character: "surely thousands and tens of thousands of common farmers and tradesmen must be better reasoners than some of our untrammeled *juris consultores*, who to this hour feel a reluctance to part with the abominable chain." The same was observed in New England. James Warren communicated to Adams that the ordinary colonist could not understand why "the dictates of common sense have not had the same influence upon the enlarged minds of their superiors that they feel on their own." The pamphlet stirred not only Anglo-Americans: referring to the impact of a German translation on Philadelphia's largest immigrant community, a gentleman of the city exclaimed that it "Works on the Minds of those People amazingly."[43]

Reading *Common Sense* excited country as much as city folk. Virginia's smallholding and poorer farmers, who were fed up with the colony's gentry-dominated politics, suddenly saw the prospect of independence as an opportunity to create a new, more democratic political order. Requested to choose delegates for a convention to be held that spring to decide on a new government, the freeholders of Buckingham County sent theirs off declaring: "We ask for a full representation, [with] free and frequent elections." The echo of Paine was distinct.[44]

Paine's appreciation of America's religious pluralism and the need to divorce church and state, along with his skillful articulation of Bible story, American history, and providential intent, also appealed to many of Virginia's smallholders, the great majority of whom were Presbyterians, Baptists, and Methodists who strongly resented the power and authority of the colony's Anglican establishment. Paine converted them to independence and republicanism, and they made him one of their heroes. And in Virginia at least, such mobilizations from below "forced" the gentry to face the fact that, having undermined the colonial regime, they probably could contain the disorder and threat of class anarchy only by actually taking charge of the effort to establish an independent republican government.[45]

Though *Common Sense* did not bear his signature, Paine became known as its author soon enough. And while he relished the attention it brought him, he sought no material rewards. He had specifically stipulated that all his royalties should go to Washington's army to purchase mittens for the troops.

Meanwhile, Paine continued to write. Along with answering Adams in *Four Letters*, he pursued a heated and much-followed debate with the moderate Whig "Cato" (William Smith) by way of another set of letters he published as "The Forester." In addition to expanding upon points he made in *Common Sense*, Paine challenged the legitimacy of the conservative-dominated Pennsylvania Assembly. He pulled no punches, resorting at times to "personal" attacks against his equally pseudonymous antagonist. Yet he repeatedly returned to the themes of independence and republicanism.[46]

Possessed of grave reservations about the popular politics and democratic aspirations of the working classes, the elites themselves continued to fret about independence and republicanism. Ultimately, however, most figured they would be better trying to lead the struggle than resist it. In the words of the New York lawyer Robert Livingston, they recognized the popular enthusiasm as a "stream which it is impossible to stem."[47]

Thus, that spring, with pressure building from below, local councils and provincial assemblies began to pass resolutions declaring for independence and instructing their delegates at Philadelphia to follow suit. The town of Canterbury, Connecticut, entered its resolve by "unanimously adopting the principles contained in Thomas Paine's *Common Sense*." And in May the Continental Congress passed a resolution requesting the respective colonies to create new governments.[48]

On July 4, 1776, an independent United States of America proclaimed that "all men are created equal . . . endowed by their Creator with certain unalienable Rights, that among these are Life, Liberty, and the pursuit of Happiness." Within days the thirty-nine-year-old Paine enlisted in the military to serve as personal secretary to General Daniel Roberdeau, commander of the Associators, a militia unit set to depart for north Jersey to bolster Washington's army against the British forces landing on Staten Island. As they headed out, their spirits were high, but on arriving at their positions, Paine and his comrades were astounded by what they saw across the water. Whereas Washington had only 19,000 relatively inexperienced men, the British had 73 ships, 13,000 sailors, and 32,000 well-equipped soldiers commanded by General Sir William Howe. Roberdeau and Paine had to work hard to prevent desertions.

In September, at the end of the Associators' enlistment period, the militia unit broke up without having seen any action. But securing a transfer to the Continental Army, Paine remained at the front to serve as aide to General Nathanael Greene, whose troops held the Palisades on the Jersey side of the Hudson River. And from the heights overlooking New York, Paine gathered intelligence and provided accounts of the fighting to Philadelphia's newspapers.

Things did not go well. By early November the British had driven Washington and his men out of New York and into full-scale retreat across New Jersey. What survived of the American army disintegrated further as more and more men slipped away from their units with each passing day. It looked as if the fledgling United States was doomed. Holding up with his men on the Pennsylvania side of the Delaware River, Washington wrote to a cousin of their urgent need to recruit fresh forces, stating, "If this fails, I think the game will be pretty well up."[49]

Defeatism spread. Congress abandoned Philadelphia, expecting the British to take the city. Tories rejoiced, imagining the war would soon be over. The revolutionary cause seemed hopeless. But Paine would not entertain defeat. On a drumhead, by campfire's light, he penned words that would resound through the generations:

These are the times that try men's souls: The summer soldier and the sunshine patriot will, in this crisis, shrink from the service of his country; but he that stands it now, deserves the love and thanks of man and woman. Tyranny, like hell, is not easily conquered; yet we have this consolation with us, that the harder the conflict, the more glorious the triumph. What we obtain too cheap, we esteem too lightly—'Tis dearness only that gives everything its value.

Securing Greene's permission, Paine hurriedly made his way to Philadelphia to finish the new work and arrange for its printing. He found the city in turmoil, but he knew what he had to do. And on December 19 he published *The American Crisis*. Bearing the signature "Common Sense," it quickly sold in the many tens of thousands (though once again Paine relinquished any claim to royalties).[50]

Less than a year before, Paine had turned Americans into revolutionaries. He now reminded them of their revolutionary hopes and aspirations. But most immediately he enabled Washington to turn the tide of battle, for the *Crisis* served both to recruit militiamen back to their units and to persuade locals to volunteer aid and assistance. Washington himself recognized the inspirational power of Paine's newest work and as part of the preparations for his now-famous Christmas Night attack on Britain's Hessian mercenaries occupying Trenton, he ordered his officers to read it to their troops. No summer soldiers or sunshine patriots, the ill-clad and freezing Americans listened to Paine's words, marched to the river's edge, loaded themselves into open boats, and crossed back over the icy and treacherous Delaware to face the enemy. The next morning they surprised the Hessians, captured the town, and marched on to Princeton and another victory.[51]

The American Crisis recharged the revolutionary cause. Paine reassured Americans that "God Almighty will not give up a people to military destruction . . . who have so earnestly . . . sought to avoid the calamities of war, by every decent method which wisdom can invent." And offering an eyewitness account of the retreat from New York, he commended American soldiers for their "manly and martial spirit" and celebrated Washington for his bearing and leadership. He also mocked Howe for his blunders and lashed out at the Loyalists. But most strenuously he challenged Americans to fight: "I call not upon a few, but upon all . . . Say not that thousands are gone, turn out your tens of thousands; throw not the burden of the day upon

Providence, but 'show your faith by your works,' that God may bless you." And conjuring up images of Joan of Arc, he appealed not just to the menfolk: "Would that heaven might inspire some Jersey maid to spirit up her countrymen, and save her fair fellow sufferers from ravage and ravishment."[52]

Committing all his energies to the Revolution, Paine went on to serve as secretary to the Committee on Foreign Affairs (1777–79), Clerk of the Pennsylvania Assembly (1779–81), and a member of a diplomatic mission seeking additional aid from America's ally, France (1781). As well, he briefly returned to military duty with General Greene at the front in the winter of 1777–78, made a series of arduous and exhausting journeys (including a forced evacuation of Philadelphia in 1777), and—while en route to France in 1781—found himself back in naval combat aboard the American gunboat *Alliance*, an engagement that included his dueling with the enemy captain. Yet his greatest contributions continued to come as a pamphleteer.

To rally the troops and citizenry, instill them with courage and determination, and convince them to make further sacrifices and stay united, Paine issued sixteen *American Crisis* papers and a host of other pamphlets and public letters between 1776 and 1783. Ringing with the patriotic arguments of *Common Sense* and exuding the same vehemence, confidence, and verve, these new pages redeemed the vision of America as a nation gifted with a special mission. And just as they had with the lines of *Common Sense*, Americans recited to each other those of the *Crisis* series. New Englanders even heard members of the clergy preach Paine's words from their pulpits in support of both the American war against Britain and the Christian war against sin.[53]

Stating it for all to hear—"Let them call me rebel"—Paine proceeded to portray the British in the most villainous of terms, comparing them to Satan and describing King George as a "monster" and Lord Richard Howe, their commander in chief, as a "degenerate." American Loyalists fared no better. Paine labeled Tories "traitors," the "foulest fiend on earth," and eager to expose them, tax them, and even dispossess them of their holdings, he advised Congress to institute an "oath" of allegiance to America.[54]

A brilliant propagandist, Paine discussed battlefield setbacks in terms of the fresh opportunities they afforded. On one occasion, his doing so may have saved Washington's command. In the winter of 1777–78, after inflicting a series of losses on the Americans, the British occupied Philadelphia, forcing Washington and his already weakened army to hold up at Valley Forge under the worst of conditions. Paine, hearing that members of Congress had begun to question Washington's leadership, penned the fifth *Crisis*, berating the decision-making of the British commander, General Howe, and essentially showing Washington to be the smarter strategist and tactician. On yet another occasion, Paine distinguished between Britain's rulers and commoners and audaciously threatened to foment popular revolution in Britain itself.[55]

Over and over again Paine roused Americans to renew the struggle: "Those who expect to reap the blessings of freedom, must like men, undergo the fatigues of supporting it." He reminded them of the righteousness of their cause and praised them for their world-historic accomplishments. If only "the mist of antiquity be cleared away, and men and things be viewed as they really were," he proudly wrote, Americans' ranking above the supposedly superior Europeans ancient and contemporary would be plain, for "had it not been for America, there had been no such thing as freedom left throughout the whole universe." Americans, he affirmed, had every reason to hope and to fight. "I look through the present trouble to a time of tranquility," Paine predicted, "when we shall have it in our power to set an example to the world."[56]

The theme of American identity, nationalism, and solidarity pervaded Paine's wartime writings. He persistently worried about the country's fragile unity, and a major dispute over the future of the western territories gave substance to his fears. The Articles of Confederation adopted by Congress in 1777 clearly favored states like Virginia that held expansionary claims to western lands, instigating Maryland, one of the "locked-in" states, to resist ratification. Unwilling to sit by and watch the country splinter, Paine applied himself to preparing and releasing a special pamphlet, *Public Good*, in which he proposed that the territories be treated as *national* property, and he presciently discussed the possibility of their eventual admission as new states. Haunted by the possibility of the confederation breaking up, he again pushed for a "Continental convention" to create a United States constitution and a stronger federation.[57]

Paine worried not only about recruiting soldiers but also about equipping them, for fiscal woes persistently plagued the government, seriously jeopardizing the war effort. In 1780, when the tide once again seemed to turn against the Americans, he called upon the rich to advance the necessary funds. And though hardly rich himself, to set a good example he personally donated $500. But the real problem was that the Articles of Confederation made Congress financially dependent on the states, and any changes to the document required approval by all of them.

When Congress requested a change in 1781 that would have permitted it to impose an import duty, Paine dedicated one of the *Crisis* papers to urging its acceptance. And soon afterward, appreciating how Paine's writings had helped to maintain troop morale and rally support for the army (and recognizing that Paine needed an income), Washington arranged a secret commission for him to continue to cultivate sympathy for Congress's need to raise revenue. While most states agreed to the new duty, Rhode Island—concerned about an encroachment on states' rights and the impact such a tax would have on its trading economy—did not, which led Paine to pen a series of public letters directed specifically to Rhode Islanders. Explaining the necessity of the duty, he implored them to see themselves as Americans above all else. In this instance, however, his arguments did not win out.[58]

The war demanded solidarity, and postrevolutionary prospects required unity, but Paine did not expect, imagine, or desire uniformity. He applauded America's diversity and pluralism and conceived of the United States as a political laboratory: "We are a people upon experiments, and though under one continental government, have the happy opportunity of trying variety in order to discover the best." He firmly believed that American history would be progressive in every way, and he was fully prepared to make the case, against the dire prognoses of the propertied elites, that the growth of democracy would spur, not deter, economic development.[59]

In the summer of 1776 the Pennsylvania radicals with whom Paine had been allied before heading off to military duty had captured control of the state's political convention. Determined to empower western farmers and Philadelphia artisans, they drew up the most

democratic of the original state constitutions. Following Paine's sketch
in *Common Sense* and ignoring the principles of separation of powers
and checks and balances, they provided for a one-house legislature,
annual elections, voting and office-holding rights for all taxpaying
men, and term limits. (The drafters even entertained setting limits to
the accumulation of property!) As expected, however, members of the
wealthier classes fought against the constitution; and while Paine at
first tried to stay out of the contest, he naturally sided with the radicals
and in March 1777 helped to organize the pro-constitutionalist Whig
Society.

In late 1778, after the British withdrew from Philadelphia to shift
their military efforts to the southern colonies (where they believed the
greater numbers of Loyalists would rush to support them), Paine himself championed the radical-democratic Pennsylvania Constitution in
"A Serious Address to the People of Pennsylvania on the Present Situation of Their Affairs." Presenting his case in the form of letters to the
Pennsylvania Packet, he pressed the connection between democracy
and material prosperity, basing his brief on the assumption that the
state—*and* the United States—needed people, working people, to im-
migrate. "The true policy of constructing constitutions in a young country, is to calculate for population," he wrote. "The strength, the riches,
the defence of a State rest upon it." Democracy, he contended, would
draw people to Pennsylvania, where democracy would favor rich and
poor alike: "As a rich man, I would vote for an open constitution, as the
political means not only of continuing me so, but of encreasing my
wealth; and as a poor man I would likewise vote for it, for the satisfaction I should enjoy from it, and the chance of rising under it."[60]

Here as well, Paine set out a series of powerful propositions on
freedom, equality, and democracy. Registering that "the toleration act
in England, which *granted* liberty of conscience . . . was looked upon
as the perfection of religious liberty," he proudly maintained that
"America is the only country in the world that has learned how to treat
religion," for "in America we consider the assumption of such power as
a species of tyrannic arrogance, and do not *grant* liberty of conscience
as a *favor* but *confirm* it as a *right*." At the same time, he never lost
sight of the dangers of class. Admonishing his fellow citizens—the well
off, in particular—not to forget that "in all countries where the freedom of the poor has been taken away, in whole or in part, that the

freedom of the rich lost its defence," he insisted that "freedom must have all or none, and she must have them equally."[61]

Paine was not naïve. He knew freedom could be dangerous, but he pointed out that "if dangerous in the hands of the poor from ignorance, it is at least equally dangerous in the hands of the rich from influence." Dismissing neither possibility, he suggested ways of addressing them. To prevent ignorance he recommended education. And to prevent political corruption he again demanded democracy: "numerous electors, composed as they naturally will be, of men of all conditions, from rich to poor."[62]

On October 19, 1781, the Americans and their French allies defeated the British at Yorktown, effectively ending the war. Eighteen months later, in April 1783, Britain and America signed the Treaty of Paris. And on April 19, eight years to the day after the Battles of Lexington and Concord, Paine issued *Crisis XIII*, leading off with "The times that tried men's souls are over." He reveled in the triumph and swelled with pride in the Revolution and the nation it had wrought.[63]

Nevertheless, Paine remained anxious: "It would be a circumstance ever to be lamented and never to be forgotten, were a single blot, from any cause whatever, suffered to fall on a revolution, which to the end of time must be an honor to the age that accomplished it." Perhaps he was thinking of slavery. Definitely he had in mind the troubled status of the American confederation. "I ever feel myself hurt when I hear the union, that great palladium of our liberty and safety, the least irreverently spoken of. It is the most sacred thing in the constitution of America," he declared, "and that which every man should be most proud and tender of. Our citizenship in the United States is our national character . . . Our great title is AMERICANS."[64]

Devoting the final *Crisis* to promoting the "Union of the States," Paine exhorted his fellow citizens to appreciate, embrace, and strengthen it. Yet his concerns extended beyond that of maintaining a hard-won independence, however fundamental. They had to do with America realizing its purpose and promise and inspiring the world in the process. It was, he proclaimed, "to see it in our power to make a world happy—to teach mankind the art of being so—to exhibit, on the theatre of the universe a character hitherto unknown."[65]

3

A CITIZEN OF THE WORLD

"We see with other eyes; we hear with other ears; and think with other thoughts, than those we formerly used," Thomas Paine proudly wrote in 1782.[1] The American Revolution had created a republic, turned subjects into citizens, and undermined traditional relations of authority and deference. Americans—white Americans, at least—were eager to exercise their rights and reap the benefits of independence. Dreams abounded.

Nevertheless, America was still marked by terrible contradictions—inequalities of property and wealth and the powers and privileges they afforded, state religious establishments and discriminations, the status of women, and worst of all, slavery. The Revolution made them appear all the more contradictory and afforded a set of ideals that would empower struggles to overcome them, but it did not resolve them. Fundamental questions presented themselves to the people who were set "upon experiments." What did "all men are created equal" mean, and who possessed "unalienable Rights"? What kind of nation would America become? Where would the United States stand in a world of monarchies and empires? Would the United States even survive as a nation?

There were those—mostly of the better-off sort—who were eager to proclaim the Revolution, not just the war, over and done. Though to some it might on occasion have seemed otherwise, Paine definitely was not among them. He recognized America's contradictions and what justice demanded. He remained a revolutionary democrat.

Worried about foreign threats and the solidarity of the confederation, however, he was convinced that the further realization of America's purpose and promise first required securing the Revolution and the nation it had forged. He had envisioned independence freeing Americans to govern themselves and liberating farmers, artisans, and merchants to improve and expand agriculture, manufacturing, and commerce. But in that vision the progress of democracy and prosperity depended on the progress of each, and both depended on the making of a coherent and vigorous nation-state. To more effectively ensure Americans' freedom and rights and to advance the nation's political and economic development, Paine repeated his call for a constitutional convention to strengthen the federation and central government.

As Paine saw it, American unity and vitality were themselves revolutionary imperatives—but not just for Americans. More than anyone, he had promoted the idea of American exceptionality and the originality of 1776. And as peace approached, he reiterated it. In *Letter to the Abbé Raynal*, published in 1782 and widely distributed in the United States and Europe, he thoroughly rejected the assertions of the French historian Guillaume Raynal that America's rebellion differed little from rebellions of the past and that it had more to do with tax rates than political principles. While noting that "it is yet too soon to write the history of the Revolution," Paine responded to Raynal's *Révolution d'Amérique* with his own narrative and once again avouched the uniqueness of the Revolution:

> A union so extensive, continued and determined, suffering with patience and never in despair, could not have been produced by common causes. It must be something capable of reaching the whole soul of man and arming it with perpetual energy. It is in vain to look for precedents among the revolutions of former ages . . . The spring, the progress, the object, the consequences, nay, the men, their habits of thinking, and all the circumstances of the country, are different.

Yet as much as Paine preached American exceptionality, he did not believe in American exclusivity. He continued to insist that the Revolution had initiated a new epoch of history for all peoples. When he wrote in *Common Sense*, "The cause of America is in a great measure the cause of all mankind" and "We have it in our power to begin the world over again," he meant it. The American Revolution made Paine not only a patriot and a radical but also a "citizen of the world" and a member of the international "Republic of Letters." He had come to understand the world in cosmopolitan, not narrowly nationalistic, terms.[2]

The story is told of a gathering at which Paine, on hearing his mentor Benjamin Franklin say, "Where liberty is, there is my country," cried out, "Where liberty is not, there is my country." Though the United States motivated both men's exclamations, Paine's promised fresh campaigns. All along Paine had pictured America as an asylum of freedom and a model to the world. In *Letter to the Abbé Raynal* he proffered a more assertive role: "The true idea of a great nation, is that which promotes and extends the principles of universal society." He was not proposing military interventions. Observing that "there is a greater fitness in mankind to extend and complete the civilization of nations" and that America's victory had "exploded the notion of going to war for the sake of profit," he insisted Americans could expand freedom peacefully through "commerce, letters, and science."[3]

Paine wanted to help build America and advance universal society, and he would, but not exactly as he had intended. Venturing to Europe only a few years after the war, he would encounter new political upheavals and recommit himself to making the age in which he lived an age of revolution. Inspired by America, he would write new pamphlets—defending revolution in France and trying to foment it in Britain, challenging religious authority and scripture, and pioneering social democracy. He would face tragedies and horrors and suffer disappointments and persecutions. Yet his writings would provide hope and ideas to generations of European radicals and working people. Moreover, his arguments would resound back across the Atlantic to encourage new popular movements for freedom, equality, and democracy and to further shape the development of the new American nation.

Following Yorktown, Paine felt anxious not only about America's future but also about his own. He had given his greatest writings free to the cause and now found himself, at forty-six years old, without property or income. Fearing a return to poverty, he petitioned Congress for a pension in recognition of his wartime labors. Those labors had made him a popular hero and literally bound his identity to the making of the nation. On July 4, 1780, the Philadelphia radicals who had recently established the University of Pennsylvania awarded him an honorary master of arts degree. In a more popular vein, Jeremiah Greenman, a working-class youth who had enlisted in 1775 as a common soldier and risen to first lieutenant and regimental adjutant of the Rhode Island Continentals, recorded in his diary for July 4, 1783, "This day had all the officers of the Regement to dine with me, after dinner drank the following Toasts, with a Discharge of a Volley of Musquets at the end of each—1st The Day, 2nd The United States & their congress, 3rd the Genl. & Army of the United States, 4th the Congress of the year 1776 & common Sence."[4]

Paine, however, had made enemies, even among the patriot elite, especially among the richer and more conservative elements. He had challenged slavery, defined the Revolution as a democratic struggle, campaigned for the radical Pennsylvania Constitution, assailed war profiteers, and called for states such as Virginia to cede their western land claims to the nation. One incident cost Paine dearly. While serving as secretary to the Committee on Foreign Affairs, he had publicly pursued a case against one of America's agents to France, Silas Deane, for his "crooked dealings." Deane was definitely guilty, yet Paine went after him so zealously that he indiscreetly revealed diplomatic secrets that were embarrassing to the French government (whose aid America desperately needed). Paine lost his government post and made many of Deane's rich and important friends his lifelong adversaries. Franklin's daughter, Sarah Bache, who herself resented Paine's role in the Deane affair, wrote to her father from Philadelphia in 1781 to declare, "There never was a man less beloved in a place than Paine is in this, having at different times disputed with everybody. The most rational thing he could have done would have been to have died the instant he had finished his *Common Sense*, for he never again will have it in his power to leave the world with so much credit."[5]

The hostility toward Paine reflected not only political and personal antagonisms but also social prejudice. A wealthy New York lawyer and friend of Deane, Gouverneur Morris—who would remark that "there never was, and never will be a civilized Society without an Aristocracy"—probably registered the nastiness of many of his class when in Congress he described Paine as "a mere adventurer *from England*, without fortune, without family or connexions, ignorant even of grammar." Paine's democratic bearing and pen must really have unnerved Morris and his ilk; and while such enemies might be to Paine's credit, they could make his life miserable.[6]

Of course, Paine also had made influential friends, such as Benjamin Franklin, Thomas Jefferson, and George Washington, and when Paine's request to Congress encountered objections, efforts on his behalf were made in various state assemblies. In spite of Washington's endorsement, prominent Virginians would not forget Paine's call for their state to give up its western lands, and they prevented Virginia from bestowing anything on him. Then there was talk in Congress of having Paine write a history of the Revolution, a project Paine had long imagined pursuing. Yet he himself rejected the commission when Congress failed to clarify the salary. Eventually, however, Pennsylvania made him a gift of $500, New York provided a farm confiscated from a Tory landowner in New Rochelle, and in 1785 Congress authorized a grant of $3,000. Though these endowments did not make him rich, they afforded him some security and made it possible for him to work on a new venture.[7]

While he was petitioning Congress, Paine withdrew from politics to pursue his original passion, science and technology. During the war he had carried out various experiments. He now undertook a major engineering project, one that could truly help to unify a nation: the design and construction of a new kind of bridge. Bridges of the time were made of wood and could not effectively endure the impact of winter ice. Paine conceived of an iron bridge, consisting of a single long arch instead of piers.

Still, Paine could not stay out of the fray for long. In early 1786 he intervened directly in the controversy over Philadelphia's Bank of North America, the first bank in the country. In the face of postwar recession and increasing indebtedness, especially among farmers, radicals had called for withdrawal of the bank's charter, attributing the people's economic woes to the concentration of financial power the bank represented. Paine, however, opposed termination, enraging longtime friends and associates, who accused him of selling out to the city's mercantile and financial interests, which almost unanimously favored the bank's survival. But Paine had not sold out. Convinced that America's future depended on sound monetary policies, infrastructural improvements, and the expansion of commerce and industry, he saw the bank and its endeavors as crucial to the nation's development. Arguably, the bank question was not even a class question, for Philadelphia's artisans had split on the issue.[8]

The controversy did lead Paine to reconsider his commitment to single-chamber legislatures, especially when the antibank forces prevailed in the Pennsylvania Assembly and repealed the bank's charter. Paine saw it as sad evidence of disunity and the dangerous rise of political parties and factions, which, he worried, might lead to the triumph of a single faction and even possibly to one-party rule and dictatorship. Holding to the republican ideal that politics need not—and should not—degenerate into parties and factions, Paine now leaned in favor of bicameralism as a means of creating political balance and curbing such developments. To his eventual satisfaction, however, the pro-bank forces won the Pennsylvania elections of 1786 and restored the charter the following spring.

Providing Paine with pressing evidence of the need for banking institutions, his bridge project was on the verge of collapse for lack of capital. His design had garnered real interest, yet the likely construction cost had intimidated individual investors. He had no choice but to follow Franklin's recommendation and seek funds in Paris and London. Departing Philadelphia in April 1787, Paine fully expected to return the following winter.[9]

The France and Britain to which Paine traveled were themselves caught up in revolutionary developments. In France the old regime of royal power and aristocratic privilege persisted but faced intensifying crises. Supporting America's war for independence had bankrupted the French government. Popular anger and resentment grew as the peasant, middle, and working classes suffered ever more burdensome taxes. And the nobles actively resisted reforms that threatened their own incomes. Events would soon compel King Louis XVI to convene the long-dormant Estates-General in vain hopes of avoiding a catastrophe.

A different story was unfolding across the Channel. In spite of the loss of the thirteen colonies, George III continued to reign, and Britain sustained its commercial supremacy and economic development. However, the advance of capitalism and industrial revolution entailed increasing exploitation, inequality, and poverty and engendered a new dynamic of class struggle, which made Britain's rulers all the more nervous and watchful. Common people still spoke of Englishmen's rights, but they began to talk of political change and democracy as well.

Reformers and radicals in both France and Britain warmly greeted Paine. In Paris he found himself in circles that included figures such as the philosopher the Marquis de Condorcet and the Marquis de Lafayette, who as a young man had volunteered himself to the American cause and fought heroically as one of Washington's generals. Men such as these shared a commitment to Enlightenment ideals and a belief that humanity and society could be improved through the application of reason and the extension of freedom. Paine also regularly visited with Jefferson, now American minister to France, to discuss European politics and America's newly proposed constitution (which, with reservations, both clearly welcomed). Arriving in London, Paine was granted membership in the Society for Constitutional Information, a middle-class organization promoting the cause of parliamentary reform. And when Britain seemed poised for yet another war with France, he wrote *Prospects on the Rubicon*, arguing for peace on the grounds that while war would enrich some, it would merely generate further misery for working people and the poor.[10]

Paine would spend two years traveling back and forth between Paris and London in search of support for his bridge. While he succeeded in securing official endorsements, he failed to line up the necessary investors and, though he would never completely abandon the project, events drew him back into politics.[11]

What ultimately turned Paine's attention away from his bridge project was the outbreak of revolution in France. On July 14, 1789, Parisian crowds stormed the Bastille, an old prison and fortress. Within days peasants attacked the landed estates of the aristocracy.

And in August a new Constituent Assembly abolished the remnants of feudalism and promulgated the "Declaration of the Rights of Man and of Citizens," establishing civil equality, freedom of conscience and religion, and the principle of popular sovereignty. Now commander of the National Guard, Lafayette personally invited Paine back to Paris to witness developments. Though Lafayette and his political associates were not democrats, they refashioned the government as a constitutional monarchy, leading Paine to believe that the principles of the American Revolution were taking hold and might be realized with limited violence. He wrote enthusiastically to Washington, "A share in two revolutions is living to some purpose," and began to take notes in favor of writing a new book.[12]

Paine was not the only one provoked to pick up his pen. French events had reinvigorated British radicalism and deeply disturbed the political establishment. Fearing the possibility of a new British revolution, Edmund Burke, the renowned Irish-born writer and member of Parliament (who had been an early friend to America's cause), authored an all-out literary assault on the Revolution of 1789. In *Reflections on the Revolution in France*, Burke denounced the revolutionaries and celebrated Britain's constitution and political system. Rejecting the spread of reason and equality, he praised tradition and hierarchy. Maintaining that history tested institutions and that later generations were essentially bound to follow the precedents and compacts of their ancestors, he contended that monarchy and aristocracy deserved respect and deference. And directing his words to the British upper classes, while referring to the common people as the "swinish multitude," he registered his disdain for popular politics and warned that revolution invited not progress but chaos, violence, and tyranny.[13]

Published in November 1790, Burke's *Reflections* became a tremendous literary success and would come to be seen as the first great treatise of modern political conservatism. It sold twenty thousand copies within a year and incited forty-five major literary replies, including *Letters to the Right Hon. Edmund Burke* (1791) by the Unitarian scientist Joseph Priestley, *Inquiry Concerning Political Justice* (1793) by the radical philosopher William Godwin, and *A Vindication of the Rights of Men* (1790) and *A Vindication of the Rights of Woman* (1792) by the pioneering feminist Mary Wollstonecraft. But the most powerful of the replies—titled simply *Rights of Man*—came from Paine.[14]

Burke's words infuriated Paine. They struck him as an attack on America as much as on the French Revolution. Now back in London, Paine applied himself to refuting Burke. But, on one very crucial point Paine wished to prove his antagonist right. Impressed by Burke's anxious perceptions, Paine hoped to make revolution in Britain a reality. Noting Burke's class allegiances ("He pities the plumage but forgets the dying bird"), Paine presented his own arguments, just as he had in 1776, so everyone would understand them, particularly working people. And indeed they did.[15]

Rights of Man would become a two-part work. In the first part, which appeared in 1791, Paine challenged Burke's account of the Revolution, rearticulated "Englishmen's rights" to encompass civil equality and political democracy, and effectively declared the British state illegitimate. Conceding the danger of "mobs," Paine attributed their actions to the brutality of aristocratic societies, especially their cruel forms of punishment. Rejecting Burke's thesis that generations were obliged to defer to their ancestors, he upheld the "rights of the *living*" and insisted that generations cannot "bind" future generations: "Every age and generation must be free to act for itself, *in all cases*, as the ages and generations which preceded it." And countering Burke's propositions about the "ancient" origins of rights, he retorted that Burke did "not go far enough into antiquity," for the "natural rights of man" went all the way back to "creation" and remained in every generation "equal" and "universal" among men. Divinely ordained, natural rights might be suppressed, but they could not be forfeited or alienated.[16]

Paine expressed tremendous confidence in the "genius and talents" of common people, if only governments would engage them: "There is existing in man, a mass of sense lying in a dormant state, and which, unless something excites it to action, will descend with him . . . to the grave. As it is to the advantage of society that the whole of its faculties should be employed, the construction of government ought to be such as to bring forward, by quiet and regular operation, all that extent of capacity which never fails to appear in revolutions."[17]

Paine evidently had the United States in his thoughts when he wrote *Rights of Man*. In 1789 he had confessed, "I wish most anxiously to see my much loved America—it is the country from whence all reformations must spring." Dedicating his new work to the nation's first president, George Washington, Paine actually repeated many of his arguments from *Common Sense*. He ridiculed the British Constitution and hereditary power and privilege, boosted republican democracy, and held that in contrast to war-mongering monarchical states, democratic republics were peace-loving. Moreover, he demanded recognition of the "universal right of conscience" and separation of church and state.[18]

Discussing the origins of the French Revolution, Paine highlighted the influence of the American Revolution. Its principles became known, he pointed out, not simply through reportage and the publication of documents like the Declaration of Independence (he modestly did not cite *Common Sense*); they also spread by way of France's troops having served in America, that "school of Freedom" where they "learned the practice as well as the principles of it by heart." First America, now France: Paine perceived the "principle of [American] government—the '*equal Rights of Man*'"—"making a rapid progress in the world."[19]

In fact, Paine optimistically concluded with a vision of a peaceful and progressive Europe in which newly established republican governments would join together in a confederation both to advance republicanism and to replace the traditional and unstable international system with a system of collective security:

> From what we now see, nothing of reform on the political world ought to be held improbable. It is an age of revolutions, in which every thing may be looked for. The intrigue of courts, by which the system of war is kept up, may provoke a confederation of nations to abolish it: and an European Congress, to patronize the progress of free government and promote the civilization of nations with each other is an event nearer in probability, than once were the revolutions and alliance of France and America.[20]

The first part of *Rights of Man* appeared in February 1791. Its reception was as revolutionary as its content. Within weeks it had sold fifty thousand copies. It elated radicals and fired the democratic spirit of working people—many of whom were religious Dissenters, who could personally relate to Paine's words, "Toleration is not the *opposite* of intoleration, but is the *counterfeit* of it. Both are despotisms. The one assumes to itself the right of withholding liberty of conscience, and the other of granting it." Corresponding societies composed of "tradesmen, mechanics and shopkeepers," mushroomed in cities around the country.[21]

Translations of *Rights of Man* soon appeared, and Paine became one of Europe's best-known writers. Though the British government hesitated to take legal action, for fear of generating even more support for Paine, it secretly targeted him for attack. Its skullduggery included hiring George Chalmers, a Scottish civil servant, to produce a scurrilous biography of Paine under the pseudonym Francis Oldys.[22]

Meanwhile, Paine finished the second part of *Rights of Man*. Dedicating it to Lafayette, he called for France to pursue the projected spring military campaign against Prussia and Austria as a revolutionary war; that is, as a war of liberation to "terminate in the extinction of German despotism, and in establishing the freedom of all Germany." For as Paine explained, "When France shall be surrounded with revolutions, she will be in peace and safety." Not solely concerned with France, he went on to state, "When all the governments of Europe shall be established on the representative system, nations will become acquainted, and the animosities and prejudices fomented by the intrigues and artifice of courts will cease. The oppressed soldier will become a free man; and the tortured sailor, no longer dragged through the streets like a felon, will pursue his mercantile voyage in safety."[23]

America, as it would always be for Paine, remained his revolutionary Archimedean point: "What Archimedes said of the mechanical powers, may be applied to reason and liberty: '*Had we,*' said he, '*a place to stand upon, we might raise the world.*' The Revolution in America presented in politics what was only theory in mechanics." Paine once again celebrated America's original struggle and extraordinary endowments and predicted that by way of representative democracy, "what Athens was in miniature, America will be in magnitude." Furthermore, he maintained, America had "made a stand, not for herself only, but for the world," and it was now up to others to advance the cause: "If universal peace, civilization, and commerce, are ever to be the happy lot of man, it cannot be accomplished but by a revolution in the system of governments." Seeing no contradiction between his commitment to America and the cause of mankind, he declared that "my country is the world and my religion is to do good."[24]

Observing that monarchy and aristocracy entailed "excess and inequality of taxation" and threw the "great mass of the community . . . into poverty and discontent," Paine added the question of class to his brief. "When, in countries that are called civilized, we see age going to the work-house, and youth to the gallows, something," Paine declared, "must be wrong in the system of government." And he bluntly asked, "Why is it that scarcely any are executed but the poor?"[25]

According to Paine, America demonstrated that nations might be otherwise. For there "the poor are not oppressed, the rich are not privileged." He portrayed the United States in the most idealistic, if not utopian terms:

> If there is a country in the world where concord, according to common calculation, would be least expected, it is America. Made up, as it is, of people from different nations, accustomed to different forms and habits of government, speaking different languages, and more different in their modes of worship, it would appear that the union of such a people was impracticable; but by the simple operation of constructing government on the principles of society and the rights of man, every difficulty retires, and all the parts are brought into cordial unison.[26]

Paine did more than censure Britain's political order. Reviving the plan he had begun to formulate years earlier but had set aside in his encounter with America, he extended his radical-democratic thinking by outlining a series of welfare programs that a revolutionary change in government would afford. Along with suggesting a progressive estate tax to limit accumulation of property, he recommended raising the incomes of the poor by remitting their taxes and augmenting the sums, distributing special relief for families with children, creating a system of social security for the elderly, instituting public funding of education through a voucher system, providing financial support for newly married couples and new mothers, and establishing employment centers for the jobless. He also rendered a most appealing image of the good society:

When it shall be said in any country in the world, "My poor are happy; neither ignorance nor distress is to be found among them; my jails are empty of prisoners, my streets of beggars; the aged are not in want, the taxes are not oppressive; the rational world is my friend, because I am a friend of happiness": when these things can be said, then may that country boast of its constitution and its government.[27]

Even as Paine pushed radicalism in a *social*-democratic direction, he proclaimed, "I have been an advocate for commerce, because I am a friend to its effects." It may seem odd to many of us today, but like many eighteenth-century radicals confronting the legacies of absolutism, Paine comprehended "political liberty and economic liberty" as mutually interdependent and imagined that economic freedom served to assure equality of opportunity *and* results. Witnessing monarchical regimes taxing the productive classes, transferring wealth to parasitic royals and aristocrats, and punishing working people and the poor, he personally had come to view nondemocratic governments, not markets, as the fundamental cause of social inequality and oppression. Consequently, he proposed the liberation of the market and expansion of commercial activity.[28]

Commerce was, for Paine, "a pacific system, operating to unite mankind by rendering nations, as well as individuals, useful to each other . . . If commerce were permitted to act to the universal extent it is capable of, it would extirpate the system of war, and produce a revolution in the uncivilized state of governments." As much as he appreciated the manifold potential of free markets, however, he did not hold that equality and democracy must necessarily defer to the imperatives of commerce and trade. And as his revolutionary proposal for welfare-state policies attests, he increasingly realized that the democratic governments for which he fought would have to *politically* address inequality and poverty.[29]

Recalling the idea of a confederation of republican nations with which he closed the first part of *Rights of Man*, Paine went on to envision an Anglo-Dutch-French coalition for peace, and presuming America's cooperation (effectively revising his idea that the United States should avoid foreign entanglements), he suggested that the re-

spective allies might agree to reduce the numbers of their naval war-
ships and get others to do the same. He also foresaw the coalition suppressing piracy and pressuring Spain into granting the "independence
of South America."[30]

Everything depended on the spread of republican democracy, a
prospect Paine was certain of. Having previously referred to the times
as an "age of revolution," he now wrote, "The insulted German and the
enslaved Spaniard, the Russ and the Pole are beginning to think. The
present age will hereafter merit to be called the Age of Reason."
And once more he returned to the matter that had disturbed his child-
hood. Condemning the politicization of faith and celebrating religious
diversity ("Why may we not suppose that the great Father of all is
pleased with variety of devotion; and that the greatest offense we can
act is that by which we seek to torment and render each other miserable?"), he postulated that *every religion is good that teaches man to
be good.*"[31]

The second part of *Rights of Man* appeared in February 1792. Its
reception vastly exceeded that of the first. In Britain alone it sold two
hundred thousand copies in the first year after publication. Paine literally "gave to English people . . . a new rhetoric of radical egalitarianism, which touched the deepest responses of the 'free-born Englishman'
and which penetrated the sub-political attitudes of the urban working
people." Paine's name "became a household word," and there were
"few places in the British Isles where his book had not penetrated."
Agitation for democracy expanded and intensified. In Ireland nationalists and republicans revered Paine and popular musicians honored
him with a hornpipe melody, "The Rights of Man." Paine's revolutionary reputation soared internationally, and his revolutionary words, in
English and foreign translation, reverberated around the shores of the
Atlantic world, powerfully so in America.[32]

The British government responded by intensifying its antiradical
campaigns. Paine's supporters rallied, but so too did their antagonists.
The government spied on Paine's every move, distributed anti-Painite
literature, and incited "Church and King" mobs, which took to burning
effigies of Paine and physically attacking the homes and persons of the
democratic movement's leaders. In May 1792 the government issued
a proclamation "against wicked and seditious writings," along with a

summons for Paine to appear in court. Though the hearing was postponed, harassment and repression continued.

Defiantly, Paine penned another, shorter pamphlet, *Letter Addressed to the Addressers on the Late Proclamation*, which blatantly called for a constitutional convention and the establishment of a British republic. Therein he responded not only to the government but also to the self-styled Friends of the People, a newly organized middle-class political society whose members—in fear of the people—had issued a plea for "temperate and moderate reform." Expressing his scorn for the gentlemen's presumptuousness and lack of integrity, he noted (in words that would be harnessed to a quite different cause generations later in the United States), "Those words, 'temperate and moderate,' are words either of political cowardice, or of cunning, or seduction. A thing, moderately good, is not so good as it ought to be. *Moderation in temper is always a virtue; but moderation in principle, is a species of vice.*"[33]

Not unexpectedly, on the evening of September 13 Paine heard from the poet William Blake that the authorities planned to arrest him that evening. Heeding Blake's warning, he fled to Dover, just one step ahead of the authorities, and escaped early next morning by boat to Calais, never again to return to Britain.

Though it had driven Paine out of the country and outlawed *Rights of Man*, the British government was not satisfied. That December it prosecuted him in absentia for "seditious libel." The defense attorney Thomas Erskine argued for Paine's innocence in terms of "liberty of the press." Still, the government's handpicked jury found him guilty as charged. Crowds expressed their displeasure, but to no avail. The government suppressed the radical cause, making the 1790s a decade of repression. A republican and democratic revolution would never come to Britain. Driven underground for a generation, however, radicalism and the working-class struggle for democracy would reemerge to commence a slow yet steady transformation of the British polity, and Paine's *Rights of Man* would be esteemed as a foundation text of that movement.[34]

Arriving at Calais, Paine received a glorious welcome. Only weeks earlier the French government had granted him honorary citizenship, along with a number of other foreigners, and Calais had subsequently elected him its representative to the new National Convention. Exhilarated by the reception, he seemed oblivious to the troubles that lay ahead.

In the fifteen months that had passed since Paine's last stay in Paris, much had changed. France had entered into war against Austria and Prussia, and the war was going badly. Louis XVI had been imprisoned for colluding with the enemy. The constitutional monarchists were utterly disgraced, and Lafayette had defected to the Austrians. In August 1792 the sans-culottes, the urban artisan and working classes, had staged a violent insurrection, and in September enemy forces had entered French territory, inciting mobs to storm the country's prisons and massacre more than a thousand inmates suspected of being counterrevolutionaries. Republicanism was in ascendance, but the republicans themselves had split into moderate and radical factions, Girondins and Jacobins respectively. The former gentlemen preferred formal deliberation, stood firmly for private property and the idea of a free market, and drew their support from the more affluent citizenry. The latter favored acting swiftly to establish a political democracy, took a more flexible stance on property and the market, and drew their support from the sans-culottes.

Paine arrived in Paris just in time to join his fellow Convention delegates in abolishing the monarchy and declaring France a republic. He was eager to participate in the country's revolutionary politics, but it was guaranteed to be difficult. He had not witnessed the recent mob violence and knew little of either the fear that gripped the nation or the deepening divisions among the republicans. He spoke little French and still tended to see things in terms of his American experience. And his old antagonist, the reactionary Gouverneur Morris, was now America's minister to France.

Paine developed a coterie of English, Irish, and American radicals resident in the capital and made friends in both factions of the Convention, including one of the foremost Jacobins, their greatest orator, Parisian lawyer Georges Danton. Paine himself was quickly honored with an appointment to the committee assigned the responsibility of drafting a new constitution. Nevertheless, for personal and ideological reasons, he was soon branded an ally of the Girondins. Knowing English, their leaders had made his acquaintance during his previous stays in Paris, and their commitments to private property and a free market, as well as their pronounced aspirations to spread republicanism in Europe, appealed to him. But what really ended up identifying Paine as a moderate was his stance on the issue of what the French nation should do with the imprisoned Louis XVI.[35]

While leading Jacobins sought a speedy execution, some Girondins argued that with the monarchy abolished they needed to take no further action. The majority of delegates stood somewhere in the middle. But the uncovering of secret papers, showing the king had eagerly and continually corresponded and conspired with France's enemies, strengthened the case for his execution.

Paine had championed the struggle against monarchy and was ready to see Louis tried and punished, but—abhorring capital punishment—he opposed sentencing him to death. Paine also knew Americans had not forgotten that it was Louis's government that had aided their revolution and he worried that an execution might alienate the United States just when France needed its support.

Once the Convention had resolved to try the former king, Paine, fully expecting a guilty verdict, used the time afforded to vigorously campaign against the death penalty. Addressing his fellow delegates, he proposed that they exile Louis and his family to America and, to avoid the moral and political corruption characteristic of monarchical regimes, set an example to the world by abolishing the death penalty altogether:

> Monarchical governments have trained the human race, and inured it to the sanguinary arts and refinements of punishment; and it is exactly the same punishment, which has so long shocked the sight, and tormented the patience of the people, that now, in their turn, they practise in revenge on their oppressors. But it becomes us to be strictly on our guard against the abomination and perversity of monarchical examples; as France has been the first of European nations to abolish royalty, let her also be the first to abolish the punishment of Death, and to find out a milder and more effectual substitute.

Paine persuaded many, but not enough. In mid-January 1793 he joined a near-unanimous Convention in finding Louis guilty, but then voted no as the delegates decided by a slim majority for a sentence of death. Again he rose to speak against carrying out the execution. Yet all he accomplished was to incense many a Jacobin, including Maximilian Robespierre, who was on his way to commanding the revolution. Within days after the vote, Louis was taken to the guillotine and beheaded.[36]

That winter France enlarged its circle of enemies by declaring war on England and Holland. Conditions rapidly worsened. Peasants rebelled. Food shortages ensued. The sans-culottes returned to the streets. And the Girondins and Jacobins commenced a deadly power struggle. Discouraged, Paine withdrew from the Convention. He even wrote to Thomas Jefferson, now secretary of state, of plans to return to the United States. But fearing capture at sea by the British, Paine did not follow through on them.[37]

By summer's end the Jacobins had established a dictatorship. They ordered a total mobilization of the citizenry and, with one million men under arms, finally turned the tide of war, suppressed provincial uprisings, and stabilized the economy. But they also commenced a ruthless campaign to eliminate "enemies" at home. Prosecuting the Girondin leadership and ordering their executions, the Jacobins initiated their infamous Terror.

Knowing they would come for him as well, Paine, now fifty-six years old, devoted his energies to a long-intended work on religion. He had reflected critically on religion all his life and in his maturity had arrived at deism. Deists believed in God as the first cause of the universe, the Creator, whose Creation, in its perfection, did not require ensuing interventions. With roots in the prior century, deism developed in eighteenth-century England among the elite and educated as a religious expression of the Enlightenment and natural philosophy. Though it remains unclear exactly when Paine himself became a deist, he recalled that in the course of the American Revolution he "saw the exceeding probability that a revolution in the system of government would be followed by a revolution in the system of religion."[38]

Paine concentrated on the issue of religion not only because he became all the more anxious about his own mortality but also because he felt compelled to respond to the Jacobins' offensive against the Catholic Church. Anticlerical campaigns had always been a part of the revolutionary movement, yet the Jacobins made "dechristianization" official state policy. Eventually, they would close the churches of Paris and establish the "Cult of the Supreme Being" as the state religion. Though Paine probably welcomed the scaling down of the Catholic Church, as an ardent believer in freedom of religion and the separation of church and state, he opposed policies that would make religion either an arm or an enemy of the state. Also, it greatly concerned him that dechristianization might sacrifice religion's better values, "of morality, of humanity, and of the theology that is true."[39]

Still hopeful about the course of world history, Paine titled his work *The Age of Reason* and dedicated it to the American people. Though he would end up writing and publishing it in two stages, his objectives remained the same in both parts and, as he later put it, in what they always had been and always would be:

> My motive and object in all my political works . . . have been to rescue man from tyranny and false systems and false principles of government and enable him to be free, and establish government for himself . . . And my motive and object in all my publications on religious subjects . . . have been to bring man to a right reason that God has given him; to impress on him the great principles of divine morality, justice, mercy, and a benevolent disposition to all men and to all creatures; and to excite in him a spirit of trust, confidence and consolation in his Creator, unshackled by the fable and fiction of books, by whatever invented name they may be called.[40]

Mounting a direct assault on organized religion and biblical scripture, Paine announced that "all national institutions of churches, whether Jewish, Christian or Turkish, appear to me no other than human inventions, set up to terrify and enslave mankind, and monopolize power and profit." And intent upon revealing the contents of the Bible to be no more than a grand "mythology" imposed on humanity by priests and clerics, he denied that the Bible was the word of God and proceeded to render a critical examination and debunking of the Old and New Testaments from Adam and Eve to Jesus Christ.[41]

Paine dubbed Christianity a "species of Atheism—a sort of religious denial of God," for it "professes to believe in a man rather than in

God." Appreciatively acknowledging that Jesus Christ was a "virtuous and an amiable man" and that the "morality that he preached and practised was of the most benevolent kind," Paine portrayed Jesus "the person," as a preacher of the "equality of man" and a "reformer and revolutionist." Nevertheless, Paine absolutely rejected the story of "miraculous conception . . . resurrection . . . and ascendance," noting that it is "altogether the work of other people" and "has every mark of fraud and imposition stamped upon it." He then reviewed the Old Testament and concluded that "when I see throughout the greater part of this book scarcely anything but a history of grossest vices and a collection of the most paltry and contemptible tales, I cannot dishonor my Creator by calling it by his name."[42]

Though he had often quoted scripture for revolutionary purposes and with great effect, Paine now had nothing good to say of the Bible, and in the second part of the work he extended his hostile exegesis. He denied the Bible's authenticity, scorned it for the cruelties it related, and belittled the morality it contained. Yet contrary to antagonists' claims, past and present, he was no atheist. He actually produced *The Age of Reason* both as a sincere profession of faith and as an angry answer to the atheism that he believed motivated the Jacobins' dechristianization campaigns. Anticipating the charges to be made against him—"Infidelity does not consist in believing, or in disbelieving; it consists in professing to believe what he does not believe"—Paine avowed: "I believe in one God, and no more; and I hope for happiness beyond this life . . . I believe in the equality of man; and I believe that religious duties consist in doing justice, loving mercy, and endeavouring to make our fellow-creatures happy. I do not believe . . . in the creed of any church I know of. My own mind is my own church."[43]

Paine reminded readers that the "True Revelation" was the Creation itself. "THE WORD OF GOD IS THE CREATION WE BEHOLD and it is in *this word*, which no human invention can counterfeit or alter, that God speaketh universally to man," he declared. The path to understanding God's revelation, he directed, lay through reason and natural philosophy, "embracing the whole circle of science." Moreover, the Creation itself presented a compelling morality, for its magnificence and bountifulness attested to God's generosity and essentially obliged humans to serve God by "imitating" God's benevolence and goodness. Paine imagined the "Almighty Lecturer" saying, "I have made an earth for man to dwell upon, and I have rendered the starry heavens, to teach him science and the arts. He can now provide for his own comfort, AND LEARN FROM MY MUNIFICENCE TO ALL, TO BE KIND TO EACH OTHER."[44]

The Age of Reason became an international best-seller, read both by the propertied and by the working classes. And as was the case with *Rights of Man*, Britain's secular and religious rulers rightly saw it as a threat to their hegemony. While the government tried to suppress sale of the work by prosecuting those who distributed it, clergy high and low across the country vehemently, often venomously, replied to Paine in print and sermon. Some, such as Richard Watson, the bishop of Llandaff, seriously answered Paine's arguments, but most simply portrayed Paine's ideas as vile and vicious and their author as an infidel or agent of the devil (which actually served to heighten interest in Paine's work).[45]

Arguably, Paine's great mischief—as ever—was to democratize ideas that had previously circulated only among the higher social ranks by making them understandable and accessible to laboring folk. But in contrast to Paine's previous works, *The Age of Reason* shocked and offended far more people than those it inspired and "converted." While it would come to serve as a manifesto or "bible" for deists and later generations of freethinkers, it would forever remain Paine's most controversial work, especially in the United States, rendering his having dedicated it to his fellow Americans particularly ironic.[46]

In late November 1793 Robespierre called for action against "foreign conspirators" in France, and a few weeks later, on Christmas Eve, the police arrested Paine and escorted him to the Luxembourg Prison. Paine naturally sought the aid of the American minister Gouverneur Morris, but after making some inquiries Morris failed to act effectively. Given France's need for American support, he probably could have secured Paine's release had he wished to. But with little personal desire to see Paine free (or for that matter, alive), and no doubt figuring it would please both the British and his fellow American conservatives at home, Morris deferred quite happily to the French government's position that the United States had no right to interfere, for Paine was an Englishman.

Though death threatened, the daily regimen at the Luxembourg was at first not so terrible. Prisoners could receive newspapers and mingle with fellow inmates. But as the Terror escalated in the spring of 1794, Paine and his comrades found themselves shut off from the outside world. Still, they could probably gather what was happening, for when the Jacobins inevitably turned on one another, the vanquished—including Paine's friend Danton—arrived at the Luxembourg en route to the guillotine. That summer the Terror intensified still further, with an estimated 2,600 people executed in Paris alone.[47]

In July, Paine collapsed with a fever that almost killed him. But tended to by his cellmates, he survived the illness. Quite "miraculously" he also escaped the executioner's blade. On July 24 the public prosecutor scheduled Paine for execution. Next morning, as was the practice, prison officers passed through the Luxembourg's corridors to mark the still-closed doors of those due to be collected later for execution. It happened that on the previous evening, Paine's cellmates had asked permission to keep their cell door open so that a breeze might enter and cool their feverish patient. Thus, in error, the officers placed their chalk mark on the wrong side of their door, which happened to be closed when the guards later came to collect the Terror's next victims. The guards walked right on past the cell. Then on July 27, before the authorities could correct their mistake, Robespierre was overthrown and dispatched to the guillotine.

The Jacobin regime fell with Robespierre's head, yet Paine remained a prisoner. Fortunately, the United States government soon replaced Morris with James Monroe, who had long admired the imprisoned pamphleteer. Claiming Paine as an American citizen, Monroe pressed for his release, which finally came on November 5, 1794. Though the days of the Terror were over, revolutionary turmoil did not come to a halt. A new government, the Directory, would be established in 1795. Suppressing revolts from all sides, and spreading the ideals of the Revolution through military victories beyond France's borders, the Directory would hold power until 1799, when a military coup would overthrow it and pave the way for Napoleon's ascendance.[48]

On securing Paine's freedom, Monroe took the severely debilitated revolutionary back to his official residence, where he and his wife could tend to him. Paine would live with the Monroes for almost two years, and though he recovered slowly, he did not stay quiet. Reinstated to the Convention, he was soon speaking out against a newly proposed French constitution that reversed the democratic advances promised in the suspended Constitution of 1793.

In July 1795 Paine published *Dissertation on First Principles of Government*, fervently reaffirming his commitment to republican democracy. While he granted that "property will ever be unequal," he argued against the right of any regime to divide the citizenry into civil or political ranks by wealth and rejected the notion that owning property afforded any entitlements. Furthermore, he demanded the establishment of universal manhood suffrage. And laying down that "the only ground upon which exclusion from the right of voting is consistent with justice would be to inflict it as a punishment for a certain time upon those who should propose to take away that right from others," he proclaimed. "The right of voting for representatives is the primary right by which others are protected."[49]

When, regardless of his complaints, the government proceeded with its constitutional plans, Paine withdrew from the Convention and went to work on finishing the second part of *The Age of Reason*. That autumn he again fell seriously ill, and rumors flew around the Atlantic that he had passed away. But Mrs. Monroe nursed him back to health.

Back on his feet, Paine immediately set himself to writing a series of new pieces, including the highly original *Agrarian Justice*. He had come to see all the more clearly that inequality and poverty were the consequences not simply of exploitative systems of taxation and government expenditure but also of economic power and the payment of inadequate wages. "Civilization," he wrote, "has operated two ways: to make one part of society more affluent, and the other more wretched, than would have been the lot of either in a natural state . . . [T]he accumulation of personal property is, in many instances, the effect of paying too little for the labor that produced it; the consequence of which is that the working hand perishes in old age, and the employer abounds in affluence."[50]

Paine refused to blame the poor for the economic circumstances to which they were reduced, for "poverty is a thing created by . . . civilized life," which, he believed, did not exist "in the natural state." In the face of increasing disparities, he grew increasingly impatient: "The present state of civilization is as odious as it is unjust. It is absolutely the opposite of what it should be, and . . . a revolution should be made in it." And even more strenuously than he had in *Rights of Man*, Paine propounded that society had an obligation to address material inequality and poverty through a system of public welfare. This "ought to be considered as one of the first objects of reformed legislation," he insisted, and its aim should be to "preserve the benefits of what is called civilized life, and to remedy at the same time the evil which it has produced."[51]

Paine had been led to write *Agrarian Justice* by Bishop Richard Watson's sermon "The Wisdom and Goodness of God, in having made both rich and poor," which Watson had included in his reply to *The Age of Reason*. "It is wrong to say God made both *rich* and *poor*," Paine responded. "He made only *male* and *female*; and He gave them the earth for their inheritance." Paine then held that since God had provided the land as a collective endowment for humanity, those who had come to possess the land as private property owed those who had been *dis*possessed of it—"on every principle of justice, of gratitude, and of civilization"—an annual ground rent. Specifically, he delineated a limited redistribution of income by way of a tax on landed wealth and property:

> To create a national fund, out of which there shall be paid to every person, when arrived at the age of twenty-one years, the sum of fifteen pounds sterling, as a compensation in part, for the loss of his or her natural inheritance, by the introduction of the system of landed property: And also, the sum of ten pounds per annum, during life, to every person now living, of the age of fifty years, and to all others as they shall arrive at that age.

And notably, Paine did not limit the initial stake or later payments to men.[52]

Paine also made it clear that he was not proposing a charity but rather was advocating the "right" of the dispossessed to "compensation." And he then enunciated an important democratic principle and practice, namely that "the payments [are to] be made to every person, rich or poor. It is best to make it so, to prevent invidious distinctions." Those who "do not choose to receive it," he added, "can throw it into the common fund."[53]

While Paine called for a "revolution in the state of civilization," he was not a socialist. He did not suggest redistributing or recollectivizing the land. He did not contest the right of the propertied to hold their property. Nor did he long to restore some lost "golden age." The progress of "civilization" had created inequality and poverty, yet it had also materially improved life. Not only was the natural state clearly "without those advantages which flow from agriculture, art, science and manufactures," but "it is never possible to go from the civilized to the natural state." There was no turning back the historical clock.[54]

In the late spring of 1796 Paine also penned *Letter to George Washington*. In it he vented his lingering anger at Washington for both his failure to push for Paine's release from prison and for his support for Jay's Treaty of 1794, a pact establishing close commercial ties between the supposedly neutral United States and Great Britain. To Paine and others the treaty appeared to be what it was in fact, a betrayal of France, America's original ally.[55]

Paine denounced Washington as "treacherous in friendship . . . and a hypocrite in public life." He lambasted him both for his principles, or lack thereof, and for his behavior, as general, politician, and statesman. And he unsparingly portrayed him as both ambitious and incompetent. "You slept away your time in the field," Paine charged, "till the finances of the country were completely exhausted, and you have but little share in the glory of the final event. It is time, Sir, to speak the undisguised language of historical truth."[56]

Monroe tried to dissuade his houseguest from posting the piece to America, but after some hesitation, Paine sent it. He may or may not have been justified in doing so (we still do not actually know if Gouverneur Morris ever directly informed Washington of Paine's predicament); yet as Monroe foresaw, the *Letter*, which was published and widely excerpted back in the United States, created a furor. A beloved figure to most Americans, Washington—who did not himself directly respond to Paine's piece—appeared to them as standing above the political turmoil and the battles that had broken out in partisan 1790s America.

Paine stayed on in France for another five years, defending the original ideals of the Revolution, serving as a friend to exiled British and Irish republicans, and promoting deism. But he became less and less consequential a figure. More and more often he spoke longingly of the United States. He still feared British capture, but when his old friend Jefferson defeated John Adams in the presidential election of 1800, Paine thought seriously about attempting the transatlantic voyage, especially after Jefferson himself wrote and offered passage on an American naval vessel. Finally, in August 1802, with peace between Britain and France, Paine sailed for America. Though he left behind a continent still ruled, brutishly so, by monarchs and aristocrats, he had definitely helped to plant the tree of liberty in Europe for future generations.

Returning to the country he admired, loved, and considered his home, Paine, now almost sixty-six years old, would receive at best, a mixed reception. While he would be publicly and privately feted in certain quarters, he would endure vicious scorn, insult, and abuse in many others. America had witnessed dramatic conflicts and changes during Paine's fifteen-year absence. The debate over ratification of the U.S. Constitution had generated a heated confrontation between Federalists and Anti-Federalists. Ensuing fights over the character and direction of America's development as a nation had led to the formation of the fiercely opposed Federalist and Republican parties. Rebellions had threatened, and authoritarianism, too. Though Paine was physically removed from these events, his writings had found their way back to America, and predictably, while radicals and working people had continued to celebrate Paine and draw inspiration from his words, many among the powerful and the propertied had grown to despise him all the more. But he had antagonized far more than those who expected or longed to constitute America's governing class. His radical pronouncements on Christianity and the Bible had outraged many others, including those whom Paine had once stirred and empowered with his vision of an independent America. The man whom they saw as the champion of republicanism increasingly became in their eyes the champion of infidelity.

Paine knew enough not to expect universal adoration, but he was not prepared for the hostility he encountered. Nevertheless, he remained in America—warmly received by some, despised by many, and increasingly ignored by most. He continued to write, at times quite effectively and at others rather prophetically, as for example when he returned to the prospect of a system of collective security and essentially proposed that the United States participate in forming an "Association of Nations for the Rights and Commerce of Nations." But Paine became a relatively minor figure in public life, and for some years in the wake of his passing in 1809, it would seem that the only people sustaining his public memory were those who spurned him.[57]

How could the once-so-popular revolutionary have become so marginal if not hated a figure in the nation he had done so much to bring into being? Those who have wondered at Paine's "fall from grace" have rightly attributed most of his public difficulties in the 1800s to his militant deism, which clearly ran against the spiritual grain of an America caught up in the beginnings of the Second Great Awakening. Yet they all too often have wrongly projected Paine's marginality in those years back into the America of the 1790s. In doing so, they have seriously undervalued his contributions to the movements and nation-building developments of Federalist and Jeffersonian America and, in turn, have ended up exaggerating the religious issue as the explanation for his uneven reception and later marginality. To better understand Paine's controversial return to America and the ensuing story of his memory and legacy—not to mention the progress of American democracy—we must understand what happened while he was away. And oddly enough, to understand what happened during his absence, we must better understand his actual presence.

4

THE AGE OF PAINE

In March 1801, only a fortnight after taking office as president, Thomas Jefferson wrote to Thomas Paine in response to Paine's restated desire to return to the United States. Reaffirming his comradely affection, Jefferson offered his old friend passage home on an American warship. It was an act of some political courage. Jefferson had to have figured that the letter would become public knowledge and—given Paine's controversial image, as well as the Federalists' readiness to pounce on the new president for any perceptible indiscretion—a matter of some consequence.[1]

Jefferson's antagonists did not disappoint him. When his letter turned up in the press in mid-July, they let loose with a series of nasty tirades. The Federalist editors of the *Gazette of the United States* eagerly made known their outrage on discovering that Jefferson had written "*a very affectionate letter* to that living opprobrium of humanity, TOM PAINE, the infamous scavenger of all the filth which could be raked from dirty paths which have been hitherto trodden by all the revilers of Christianity." Boston's *Mercury and New-England Palladium* labeled Paine a "lying, drunken, brutal infidel," while the *Port Folio* of Philadelphia exclaimed, "that the loathsome Thomas Paine, a drunken atheist, and the scavenger of faction, is invited to return in a national ship . . . [is] an insult to the moral sense of the nation."[2]

Nevertheless, when Paine arrived home in 1802—having declined the president's offer to sail on an American naval vessel—Jefferson

hosted him at the White House and Monticello. Jefferson clearly admired Paine. "No writer has exceeded Paine in ease and familiarity of
style, in perspicuity of expression, happiness of elucidation, and in
simple and unassuming language," Jefferson, an extraordinary author
himself, conceded. An avid designer, he also applauded Paine's technological inventiveness. Moreover, he evidently appreciated what
America owed Paine and surely sensed how Paine's thinking had
shaped his own. It was not only the Declaration of Independence that
reflected Paine's influence. Jefferson's later work did as well, as in "the
earth belongs to the living," his oft-repeated answer to the question
"whether one generation has a right to bind another," and his first inaugural address, declaring "peace, commerce, and honest friendship
with all nations, entangling alliances with none" and anointing America the "world's best hope."[3]

Jefferson probably felt a further debt to Paine. He apparently understood how much the Republican movement had depended on
Paine's pen and the diverse folk inspired by it. In the spring of 1791
Jefferson had hailed the first part of *Rights of Man*. Then serving as
secretary of state, he saw in it an antidote to the rise of antirepublican
sentiments expressed in writings like *Discourses on Davila*, a series of
newspaper essays penned anonymously by Vice President John Adams
warning against the dangers of democratic politics and praising aristocratic government. In a note Jefferson sent to the printers who were to
issue the American edition of Paine's work—a note that created something of a scandal when the printers included it as a foreword—he
stated: "I am extremely pleased to find [*Rights of Man*] will be
reprinted here, and that something is at length to be publicly said
against the political heresies which have sprung up among us. I have
no doubt our citizens will rally a second time round the standard of
Common sense."[4]

Jefferson seems also to have recognized at the time how Paine's
new pamphlet and possible future labors could enhance his and James
Madison's efforts to organize an opposition to the congressional and
cabinet Federalists led by Adams and Alexander Hamilton, the secretary of the Treasury. In July 1791, just returned from the northeast
with Madison, ostensibly "botanizing" but actually recruiting political
allies, Jefferson happily reported to Paine that *Rights of Man* "has been

much read here, with avidity and pleasure." And having persuaded naval veteran and poet Philip Freneau to come to Philadelphia to start a newspaper, he was now touting Paine as a candidate for postmaster general, presumably hoping to bring him, too, to the capital to work on behalf of the new party.[5]

A year later Jefferson worried no less about Federalist proclivities. On receiving copies of the second part of *Rights of Man*, he lamented to Paine in correspondence, "Would you believe it possible that in this country there should be high and important characters who need your lessons in republicanism, and who do not heed them? It is but too true that we have a sect preaching up and panting after an English constitution of kings, lords, and commons, and whose heads are itching for crowns, coronets and mitres." Still, again citing the value and appeal of Paine's labors, Jefferson remained optimistic. "Our people, my good friend," he wrote, "are firm and unanimous in their principles of republicanism, and there is no better proof of it than that they love what you write and read it with delight. The printers season every newspaper with extracts from your last, as they did before . . . Go on then in doing with your pen what in other times was done with the sword."[6]

Jefferson never formally acknowledged Paine's part in the creation of the Republican movement, yet we can hear him doing essentially that in his letter of 1801 offering Paine transport home. "I am in hopes you will find us returned generally to sentiments worthy of former times," he stated. "In these it will be your glory to have steadily laboured and with as much effect as any man living. That you may long live to continue your useful labours and to reap the reward in the thankfulness of nations is my sincere prayer. Accept assurance of my high esteem and affectionate attachment."[7]

Attending closely, we can also better grasp what agitated the Federalists about Jefferson's invitation. It had to do not only with how much they despised Paine and wanted to embarrass the president, but all the more with their fear that Jefferson was finally bringing Paine back to promote the Republicans' cause. If Jefferson does not provide sufficient testimony to Paine's role in fomenting the Republican movement and what Jefferson himself would call the "Revolution of 1800," then we should listen to the man he defeated for the presidency. Ever envious of Paine's talents and presumed place in history, outraged by his democratic ideals and appeal, and still bitter about the election, John Adams hated Paine. Yet whereas jealousy might have silenced others, it did not keep Adams from unashamedly speaking his mind. In 1805 he wrote to a friend:

> I am willing you should call this the Age of Frivolity, as you do; and would not object if you had named it the Age of Folly, Vice, Frenzy, Fury, Brutality, Demons, Buonoparte, Tom Paine, or the Age of the burning Brand from the bottomless Pit; or anything but the Age of Reason. I know not whether any man in the world has had more influence on its inhabitants or affairs for the last thirty years than Tom Paine. There can be no severer satyr on the age. For such a mongrel between pigs and puppy, begotten by a wild boar on a bitch wolf, never before in any age of the world was suffered by the poltroonery of mankind to run through such a career of mischief. Call it then the Age of Paine.[8]

Paine's response to his Federalist assailants included mockingly claiming membership: "If . . . by *Federalist* is to be understood one who was for cementing the Union by a general government operating over all the States . . . *I ought to stand first on the list of Federalists*, for the proposition for establishing a general government over the Union, came originally from me."[9]

Of course, in contrast to Paine, most of the elite figures who had gathered in the Constitutional Convention of 1787, though republican, were not democrats. Shocked and distressed by the rambunctiousness of the citizenry, the emergence of "demagogic" leaders in the state legislatures (often men of humbler means and education), and even more by Shays's Rebellion of farmers in western Massachusetts, they sought not only to address the weaknesses that threatened the confederation but also to temper the energies that endangered the deferential political order they projected for postrevolutionary America. The constitution they fashioned fortified the union, yet—along with accepting the persistence of slavery—it favored the power of the propertied and limited that of the popular classes.[10]

Still, the framers subscribed to the principle of popular sovereignty and knew that America's democratic impulse represented too great a force to ignore or completely suppress. Variously motivated by principle and pressure from below, they provided the most democratic national constitution theretofore seen and invited generations of struggle over who constituted "We the People" and how much "We" would actually rule.

Such struggles made the 1790s as dramatic as the 1780s. Having secured the Constitution's ratification over Anti-Federalist opposition, the Federalist elite fractured. And in spite of professed antipathies to factionalism, two parties, the Federalists and the Republicans, emerged, each advancing a distinct conception of America's future. Headed by Adams and Hamilton, the Federalists held sway in the new national government. Though they would become personal enemies, both leaders revered the British Constitution, understood politics in terms of "the few and the many," and believed government should constrain the inclinations of the latter. Hamilton further admired Britain's economic and military might and aspired to turn the United States into a nation rivaling the powers of Europe. As Treasury secretary, he formulated a series of major initiatives to further strengthen the central government and promote commerce and manufacturing in concert with an ascendant class of merchants, financiers, and industrialists. Unsurprisingly, the Federalists garnered their greatest support in New England and the Northeast, especially among the upper classes.[11]

Led by Jefferson and Madison, the Republicans formed their party in reaction to the Federalists. Madison had fought for the Constitution, and Jefferson had greeted its adoption, yet these sons of Virginia's planter class inherited Anti-Federalist anxieties about concentrated state power and the advent of an American aristocracy—anxieties exacerbated by Adams's sympathies and Hamilton's schemes. Seeing Britain as corrupt and its power corrupting of others, they distrusted the Federalists' Anglophilia and scorned Hamilton's vision of an industrializing America. They imagined the United States remaining predominantly agrarian, and Jefferson in particular pictured a republic of independent, commercially and publicly minded yeomen farmers, expanding westward and growing economically by exporting its bounties to the world.[12]

Though rhetorically more democratic, Jefferson and Madison were no more eager than the Federalists to actually mobilize "the people."

Jefferson disdained the urban working classes; Madison preferred property qualifications for the right to vote; and both understood politics in elitist terms—Jefferson himself would envision America developing a "natural aristocracy," an educated and meritocratic governing class. Yet the Republican movement, originally finding its most solid support in the South and West, increasingly reached across sectional and class lines to become the party of "democracy."[13]

Federalists and Republicans alike perceived American politics in relation to the conflicts across the Atlantic. Americans had enthusiastically welcomed the French Revolution as the promised extension of their own struggle against tyranny. But as it grew more radical and violent, and as Britain joined the anti-French coalition, public opinion split along party lines. The Federalists vehemently turned against the Revolution, pushed for ties with Britain, and branded as "Jacobin" any expression of pro-French sentiment. Eventually, with the outbreak of an undeclared war with France during Adams's presidency (1797–1801), they saw all Republican challenges as evidence of Jacobinism and by way of the Alien and Sedition Acts of 1798 resorted to authoritarian measures to silence their critics. The Republicans, however, continued to defend the French Revolution. Recalling French support for American independence, as well as dreading the consequences of too great a connection with Britain, they urged loyalty to France.

While the Federalists dominated national office, the Republicans grew in strength and finally triumphed in the presidential election of 1800. How they did has fascinated students of American politics, for "one of the most curious anomalies in American history was the way southern aristocrats assumed leadership of a Republican party that in the north was composed mostly of unaristocratic sorts—common farmers, artisans, manufacturers, and hustling entrepreneurs." Equally anomalous, the party faithful included evangelicals *and* deists. Stressing the brilliance and acumen of Jefferson and Madison, traditional accounts have portrayed the Republican movement as their "top-down creation." Yet they have never truly explained how the Virginians, given their agrarianism and reservations about popular politics, managed to gather to their banner groups that had previously lined up with the Federalists.[14]

Eschewing the preoccupation with "national celebrities," recent scholarship has uncovered how "pressure from below . . . helped force an epochal shift in American politics." And as one historian presents the argument, the Republican insurgency owed precious little to Jefferson and Madison. Northern Republicanism [at least] is better seen as a popular movement, as the aggregation of many local challenges to Federalist gentlemen by ambitious democrats. In national politics northern Republicans cooperated with Jefferson and Madison, but they rarely relied upon their writings."[15]

Historians have continued to aver that Republicanism entailed more than a shared hostility to Federalism: "The Jeffersonians coalesced around a set of ideas—radical notions about how society should be reorganized . . . Their common vision about the reform of politics and the liberation of the human spirit made a national democratic party possible in the 1790s." But torn between the genius of Jefferson and the genius of the people, most have persistently ignored what both Jefferson and the people appreciated—that the making of the Republican movement depended fundamentally on the writings of Paine.[16]

In the 1770s Paine had articulated American longings and imbued American experience with revolutionary meaning. In the early 1790s he reminded Americans of their nation's exceptional purpose and promise. From *Common Sense* to *Rights of Man* he cultivated a vision of a democratic and prosperous United States, an America in which political and economic development advanced together, an America serving as an asylum to mankind and a model to the world. Paine's vision differed significantly from Hamilton's and Jefferson's. Like Hamilton, Paine foresaw an increasingly industrial nation; however, whereas Hamilton wanted to fabricate a new aristocracy of wealth, Paine offered a picture of American economic life in which agriculture, commerce, and industry progressed through the investments, improvements, and innovations of farmers, smaller merchants and manufacturers, and artisans. Like Jefferson, Paine presumed an America characterized by limited government and westward expansion. Yet more than Jefferson, he imagined republican government fostering national development and enhancing citizens' lives, and through both the style and the content of his writing, he expressed far greater confidence in the democratic potential of working people.[17]

Paine wrote both parts of *Rights of Man* with the United States in mind, and both found their way home to invigorate fresh political campaigns. Celebrating America and the extension of the struggle for liberty, equality, and democracy to France, his lines once again captured the imagination of Americans—not just radical politicians and writers, but also enterprising merchants and manufacturers; hardworking farmers, artisans, and laborers; settlers hurriedly pushing across the Appalachians; immigrants arriving from the British Isles and Europe; and religious evangelicals and liberals still subject to state religious establishments.

America in the early 1790s witnessed a "veritable Paine revival." *Rights of Man* became a phenomenal success in the United States. Responding to demand, printers issued at least twelve editions of part one, nine of part two, and several more of the combined text. Copies sold totaled somewhere between fifty and one hundred thousand. Additionally many Americans received copies lent by friends, borrowed them from the new and popular circulating libraries, or read portions excerpted in the press. It has been estimated that "as many people read *Rights of Man* as read *Common Sense*."[18]

Thrilled by Paine's new pamphlet, the New York newspaperman Thomas Greenleaf exclaimed, "Every American should be possessed of Paine's works," and publishers in Albany quickly helped out by producing the first of several American versions of Paine's "collected writings." In Virginia, gentlemen purchased such volumes for their personal libraries. In Kentucky, where Paine had remained popular right through the 1780s—for many saw his *Public Good* as having paved the way for the territory's eventual statehood—he became the "most widely read author" among townsfolk and farmers alike, as he did in the Cumberland region of Tennessee, where book buying for many represented a real financial challenge.[19]

In the 1770s Paine had led Americans to see their revolution in more than merely political and economic terms and in the 1780s men such as the playwright William Dunlap, the artist Charles Wilson Peale, the editor and grammarian Noah Webster, and the poets Joel Barlow and Philip Freneau, along with hosts of others had set out to create an original American culture. Webster, who had idolized Paine ever since his first reading of *Common Sense* as a Yale undergraduate in 1776, spoke for many of his generation when in 1783 he asserted, "America must be as independent in *literature* as she is in politics."[20]

In the 1790s Paine's writings energized a new kind of "intellectual" activism. In every corner of the nation Republican editors attended to and reproduced his words. John Bradford, the publisher of the *Kentucky Gazette*, like so many of his colleagues, punctuated the latest news from Philadelphia, London, and revolutionary France with excerpts from *Rights of Man* and advertised nearby the works of Paine and other radicals available through the bookstore he operated out of his print shop.[21]

Newspapers—whose numbers doubled to nearly two hundred—were decidedly partisan enterprises. Editorials and reportage alike were tailored to shape public opinion. The Federalists took the lead in the "newspaper wars" in 1789, when Boston merchant John Fenno established the *Gazette of the United States* in the capital and, with Hamilton and Adams's support, turned it into the party's semiofficial national organ. But the Republicans soon found their own press voices in Philadelphia, when Benjamin Franklin Bache started up the *Aurora General Advertiser* in 1790 and Philip Freneau, the *National Gazette* in 1791.[22]

When Jefferson wrote to Paine, "The printers season every newspaper with extracts from your last," he did not exaggerate. Bache inherited not only his grandfather's name and printing presses but also his republican spirit and affection for Paine. Producing the first American edition of *Rights of Man* in his shop and serializing the text in his newspaper, he became the leading distributor of Paine's works and during the next few years made the *Aurora* the Federalists' leading antagonist.[23]

In May 1791 Bache published Freneau's "Lines Occasioned by Reading Mr. Paine's Rights of Man," a poem honoring Paine and American republicanism:

> Roused by the REASON of his manly page,
> Once more shall PAINE a listening world engage:
> In raising up *mankind*, he pulls down kings . . .

So shall our nation, form'd on Virtue's plan,
Remain the guardian of the Rights of Man,
A vast Republic, famed through every clime,
Without a king, to see the end of time.

And that autumn, at the urging of Jefferson and Madison, who sorely needed a *national* Republican journal, Freneau launched the *National Gazette* and prominently featured Paine's work in its pages.[24]

Outfitted with Paine's arguments, Republican newspapermen attacked the Federalists for their "monarchical and aristocratic" ambitions and pretensions. But *Rights of Man* spurred more than criticism. Recalling the spirit of the American Revolution, impressed by developments in Britain and France, and impatient with Jefferson and Madison's elitism and reticence, Republican editors began to publish calls for popular political action in America. Taking issue with the Federalist view that "the care of the state should be the exclusive business of the officers of government," and defending Paine in the process, the pseudonymous "Mirabeau" (after the French revolutionary) wrote in the *Aurora* in December 1792:

It is well enough in England to run down the rights of man, because the author of those inimitable pamphlets was a staymaker; but in the United States all such proscriptions of certain classes of citizens, or occupations, should be avoided; for liberty will never be safe or durable in a republic till every citizen thinks it as much his duty to take care of the state, as to take care of his family, and until an indifference to any public question shall be considered a public offence.

In the words of a correspondent to the *National Gazette*, every citizen "ought to be a politician in a degree." As such, they not only should stand ready to check government policies, but also to deliberate and determine them. And as the editor of the *Newark Gazette* made clear, "It must be the mechanics and farmers, or the poorer class of people (as they are generally called) that must support the freedom of America."[25]

Men as diverse as Abraham Bishop, Jedidiah Peck, William Manning, and Matthew Lyon responded to and carried forth Paine's message. The son of a prominent New Haven family, Abraham Bishop, who was educated at Yale and trained in the law, defied expectations to become the most celebrated (or notorious) Republican in Federalist-dominated Connecticut. He cheered the French Revolution, opposed slavery, defended black rebellion in St. Domingue (Haiti), lambasted the Federalists as "aristocrats," blamed the woes of the world on the "great men" of the upper classes, and challenged his state's Congregationalist "Standing Order." Ardently believing in the American Revolution's ideals, he proudly invoked Paine's words in his pursuit of class *and* racial equality.[26]

A revolutionary war veteran, artisan, farmer, itinerant preacher, and populist democrat, Jedidiah Peck, who had taught himself to read, first entered politics in the frontier region of central New York as a Federalist. After winning election to an associate judgeship, however, he found that his views and attitudes conflicted with those of the state party's leaders. Hoping to ignite a rebellion from below among the Federalists, he penned a volume's worth of newspaper pieces that—collected and published in 1796 as *The Political Wars of Otsego*—registered his passion both for the Bible and for Paine's political writings. In doing so, Peck made himself some dangerous enemies; but while he failed to instigate any popular insurgencies, he succeeded in developing a local following that would eventually send him, as a Republican, to the New York Assembly, where he would gain fame as a political reformer and a proponent of public education.[27]

A farmer and tavernkeeper in western Massachusetts, William Manning was another revolutionary war veteran who had closely read both the Bible and Paine's works. Although he sympathized with Shays's cause, Manning's concern for the new nation's stability had made him a supporter of the Constitution. And yet in light of the Federalists' class-biased policies and programs and their increasingly evident presumptions that the "few alone were fit to rule," he came to believe that the elites had been deceiving working Americans. Directing himself to "farmers, mechanics, and laborers," he wrote "The Key of Liberty," in which, referring to *Rights of Man*, he proposed a "Laboring Society" that he hoped would counter and in time bring an end to the power of the few. Unfortunately, he failed to actually publish the manuscript.[28]

Born in Ireland in 1749, Matthew Lyon had come to America in 1764 as an indentured servant and, after securing his freedom, had moved to Vermont in the early 1770s with his wife and family. Serving with Ethan Allen and the Green Mountain Boys during the Revolution, he supported Vermont's democratic constitution of 1777 (which was apparently inspired by Paine's arguments in *Common Sense*) and after the war succeeded in making a small fortune by investing in land, lumbering, and iron manufacturing. But his own material and political ambitions conflicted with those of Vermont's lawyerly elite of college-educated judges and attorneys, men who presumed themselves the "natural" governing class and would soon form the core of the state's Federalist party.[29]

A "self-made man" who would not defer to those who thought themselves his social "betters," Lyon saw his antagonists as a new "aristocracy" and became ever more determined to challenge their ascendance. Running unsuccessfully for Congress in 1791 and again in 1793, he responded to his second defeat by setting up a weekly Republican newspaper titled the *Farmers' Library*, the very first issue of which opened with Paine's speech to the French National Assembly supporting the trial of Louis XVI. Regularly citing Paine's example as a nemesis of tyranny and a champion of democracy and the common man, Lyon appealed to middle- and laboring-class men to oppose the power of the elite with their votes. And in 1797 he would terrify his Federalist enemies by winning election to Congress.[30]

Though their lives differed dramatically, Bishop, Peck, Manning, and Lyon all opposed hierarchy and authority, shared a commitment to equality and democracy, and in their respective engagements pushed Paine's arguments in new directions. And others, both native and foreign born, vigorously joined them in doing so.

Tens of thousands of immigrants settled in the United States in the 1790s, including many a veteran of the British and Irish republican struggles. *Rights of Man* had fired their political aspirations and their expectations of the United States as a land of liberty and opportunity. As one of their collective biographers has noted, "These radicals brought with them a peculiarly Painite political discourse that combined, without strain, egalitarianism, advocacy of commercial development, and a vision of unlimited progress." While American realities

disillusioned some, many remained steadfast. Eager to realize the
America Paine had extolled, they would also reinforce the cosmopolitan character of American Republicanism by highlighting its connection to the republican causes across the Atlantic.[31]

The émigré radicals from the British Isles arrived in two waves
(and it would not be the last time that immigrants would enliven
American democratic activism). While most of the English, Scottish,
and Welsh came early, driven into exile by the British government's
suppression of dissent in 1793–94, most of the Irish would arrive later,
following the suppression of the 1798 Rebellion. Given the material
demands of emigration, those who sought refuge in the United
States—including the well-known English Unitarian scientist Joseph
Priestley—were predominantly professionals and smaller merchants
and producers. While they would pursue various careers in America,
many entered journalism and—indicating their importance to the Republican movement—they would edit nearly fifty newspapers in the
course of the 1790s and early 1800s. The most notable among the
newspapermen, Irishman William Duane, would work with Benjamin
Franklin Bache and take over as editor of the *Aurora* in 1798.

As in the times that tried men's souls, Paine's words spoke most
critically to the working classes. Urban artisans had stood firmly with
the original Federalists on the Constitution, but the artisans' egalitarian and democratic sensibilities, heightened by their reading of
Rights of Man, now propelled them into the Republican movement.
Festivities sponsored by mechanics' societies and city militias always
included toasts to their heroes, and Paine stood near the top of the list.
In 1792 the Tammany Society of New York, a fraternal order with
a majority of artisan members, joyously drank to "The Clarion of
Freedom—Thomas Paine" and the "Citizen of the World, Thomas
Paine."[32]

Paine never publicly called for African American slaves to rise up,
but he did contemplate such initiatives, and his ideas—perhaps
known to some of the twelve thousand slaves brought to Virginia by
refugee French planters escaping Haiti—may actually have found
their way into their quarters as well. It is not very hard to imagine the
courageous and liberty-loving Gabriel, a literate slave and skilled artisan who in 1800 would organize a slave rebellion in Richmond (where

white artisans were staunch Republicans), deriving encouragement from the words of *Rights of Man*.[33]

From Boston to Charleston, and from New York to Lexington, Kentucky, Republican fervor expressed itself in 1793–94 in the formation of thirty-five Democratic-Republican societies (with several more following in the next few years). Their sudden appearance and rapid growth horrified the Federalists, who saw them as French inspired and dangerously subversive of constitutional order. Yet as much as the intensifying radicalism of the French Revolution played a part, the societies were modeled at least equally on republican clubs in Britain and, if not more so, on the Sons of Liberty and the Correspondence Committees from America's own revolutionary tradition.[34]

Varying regionally, the societies, whose respective memberships ranged from 25 to upward of 250, drew together a diverse assortment of native and immigrant "merchants, political leaders, landowners, slaveowners, professionals, small tradesmen, mechanics, seamen, and laborers." Their leaders were usually men of local prominence, but the greatest participation came from the working classes, and while the leaders were also often deists, the societies included many a devout Christian. The very first group, organized in April 1793, was the German Republican Society of Philadelphia, whose initial circular effectively declared the philosophy of all of them: "In a republican government it is the duty incumbent on every citizen to afford his assistance, either by taking part in its immediate administration, or by his advice and watchfulness, that its principles may remain uncorrupt; for the spirit of liberty, like every virtue of the mind, is to be kept alive only by constant action."[35]

In decided contrast to the Federalists, who denigrated democracy, the Democratic societies, following Paine, proclaimed it both the very meaning of America *and* a universal possibility. The societies were conceived as patriotic organizations, committed to defending the ideals and victories of the American Revolution and supporting their spread overseas. In a joint meeting of the two Philadelphia societies on May 1, 1794, the eight hundred folk who gathered enthusiastically saluted democratic internationalism:

The Democratic and Republican Societies of the United States—
May they preserve and disseminate their principles, undaunted

by the frowns of power, uncontaminated by the luxury of aristocracy, until the Rights of Man shall become the supreme law of every land, and their separate fraternities be absorbed in one great democratic society comprehending the human race.[36]

Though radical, the societies were not revolutionary organizations. They espoused "freedom of speech, press and assembly" and cultivated the arts of debate and deliberation. Advocating the interests of working people, they campaigned for public education and criminal justice reforms, especially regarding the treatment of debtors and the poor. And those of Kentucky, North Carolina, and Vermont lobbied as well for national expansion—into the Mississippi valley, down into Florida, and north into Canada.

The societies would essentially serve as an incubator for the Republican Party. Yet as much as Jefferson and Madison might have privately welcomed their appearance, they never publicly endorsed them. The societies' first historian rightly contended that Paine "deserves the credit for fathering them," and the societies themselves "sang his praises, toasted his name, and distributed his *Rights* with missionary ardor."[37]

Paine's arguments moved secular *and* religious democrats. In 1776 *Common Sense* had recruited Protestant dissenters to the Revolution and turned Paine into one of their heroes. In the early 1790s his *Rights of Man* reaffirmed the promise of democracy and religious liberty and helped to join the evangelicals to the Republican movement.[38]

In Virginia, Jefferson and Madison addressed the dissenters' raised expectations during and after the war by pressing for freedom of worship and disestablishment of the Anglican Church, both of which were fully accomplished in 1786. Working closely not only with rationalists and liberals, such as themselves, but also with non-Anglican Christians, they made future political allies of Presbyterians, Baptists, and Methodists, the latter two of which were the fastest-growing American denominations.[39]

Jefferson and Madison's chief religious supporter was the Reverend John Leland, an energetic Baptist revivalist and a crusader for the separation of church and state. With victory in Virginia and, later, the addition to the U.S. Constitution of the Bill of Rights, Leland headed to New England, where Congregational "establishments" persisted both in Connecticut and in his own home state of Massachusetts (and would survive until 1818 and 1833, respectively). His sermons and writings, such as *The Rights of Conscience Inalienable*, reflected his Democratic-Republican politics and his study of Jefferson, Madison, and Paine. Utterly rejecting the idea of a "Christian nation," he was fully prepared to cooperate with deists against other Christians to abolish the prevailing ties between churches and state governments. Venerating the cause of 1776, Leland spoke like a true Painite when he said, "The revolution of America has been an event which . . . has promised more for the cause of humanity, and the rights of man, than any revolution that can be named."[40]

Ironically, in light of the later controversy over *The Age of Reason*, Paine's political writings infused certain currents of American Protestantism—and the Second Great Awakening itself—with democratic spirit and energy. In Virginia, James O'Kelly, an Irish-born Methodist preacher who had read Paine while fighting the British in the Revolution, applied the teachings of *Common Sense* and *The American Crisis* to questions of church governance and practice. After welcoming the postwar creation of an American Methodist Church independent of the British, O'Kelly grew increasingly anxious about the episcopal authority established under Bishop Francis Asbury. And in 1794, after repeatedly challenging Asbury's "ecclesiastical monarchy" in favor of a more "representative" leadership structure, he and thirty of his fellow Virginia and North Carolina ministers, along with thousands of their congregants, declared their independence and formed the "Republican Methodist Church."[41]

Animated by the experience of earlier evangelicals and steeped in revolutionary ideas of freedom and equality, religious radicals set out to reconstruct—or "restore"—American Christianity. They rejected clerical authority and churchly hierarchy as vestiges of monarchy and aristocracy and, like Paine and Jefferson, refused to defer to tradition. Denying the supposed superiority of formally educated theologians, they took seriously the spiritual enthusiasms of common folk, encouraged them to trust their own readings of the Bible, and countenanced lay preaching. With verve and determination they created not just churches but also movements.[42]

One of the most fascinating of those figures was the itinerant preacher Lorenzo Dow. Born in 1777 to a family of Connecticut Congregationalists, Dow rejected Calvinism for Methodism and at nineteen left home to "convert" the nation. His preaching was said to be mesmerizing and to have incited the "jerks" or "jerking exercises" among the vast numbers who would gather to hear him. Tall and thin, with long hair and a beard, and possessed of a strong but high-pitched voice, he referred to himself as a "cosmopolite," though others called him "Crazy Dow." Nevertheless, his calling took him up and down and back and forth across the country, and he eventually became not only the most traveled but also the most popular preacher of his day. (Only George Washington may have had more baby boys named after him than Dow in the early nineteenth century.) Speaking of sin and class inequality in the same breath, Dow would quote Paine directly when sermonizing.[43]

In the mid-1790s a series of political, diplomatic, and literary events made the contest between Republicans and Federalists all the more rancorous and bristling. During the summer of 1794 several thousand Pennsylvania farmers, who found it commercially convenient and profitable to distill much of their grain into spirits, rose up in angry opposition to the federal excise tax on whiskey that Congress had imposed as part of Hamilton's financial plans. Washington responded by raising and assuming personal command of an army of fifteen thousand men to subdue the rebels, who dispersed even before the expedition arrived on the scene.[44]

Though the short-lived "Whiskey Rebellion" presented little real threat to the union, it shook up Washington and the Federalists, for it came in the wake of the explosive spread of the Democratic societies and further news of revolutionary terror in France. The Federalists, however, turned things to their own advantage. Asserting a connection between the insurrection and the societies and depicting the rebels as "Vendeites" (referring to a recent and rather bloody peasant uprising in France), they denounced their actions as an effort to violently impose the "principles of Thomas Paine's *Rights of Man*." Washington himself held the societies responsible for the rebellion and publicly vilified their members as "incendiaries of public peace and order." Such attacks delivered a serious blow to the Republicans, and though the Democratic societies survived, they never regained their original momentum.[45]

In 1795 Federalists and Republicans confronted each other over the direction of American foreign affairs. With Britain attacking American shipping and its troops still occupying forts in America's Northwest Territories, Washington had dispatched Chief Justice John Jay to London in 1794 to negotiate. Jay returned with an agreement that promised to improve relations and establish close commercial ties between the two countries, while maintaining American neutrality. Yet the Republicans opposed the terms of Jay's Treaty, perceiving them injurious to France and as binding the United States to British interests. They fought its ratification in Congress and their supporters staged riotous street protests. The Senate, however, ratified the pact, rendering yet another blow to the Republican movement.

These years also saw the publication of the two parts of Paine's *The Age of Reason*, which, like *Rights of Man* before it, became an American best-seller and an inspiration to many an American radical. And yet in contrast to the *Rights of Man*, the new work ultimately had the effect of strengthening the forces of American conservatism even more than those of radical Republicanism. Its very success would serve to consolidate an already developing alliance between the Federalists and the Calvinist clergy, especially the Congregational and Presbyterian ministry of New England, who read Paine's treatise on religion as both an attack on Christianity and proof of the connection between democracy and infidelity. Moreover, the work would make Paine anathema to those who had long considered him one of their champions.[46]

America was a nation of Protestants, but deism was by no means an alien ideology. Many of the nation's original Founders subscribed to some version of religious rationalism, including Benjamin Franklin, Thomas Jefferson, George Washington, and John Adams. Yet whereas such men held their beliefs quietly—either because they felt organized religion was essential to maintaining morality and order, or because they feared the animosity that public revelation might entail—Paine came out in *The Age of Reason* as a militant. Here too he was neither alone, nor even the first. Ten years earlier the Vermont revolutionary Ethan Allen, leader of the Green Mountain Boys, had published a deist text, *Reason the Only Oracle of Man*. But whereas Allen's rather dreary book had sold only two hundred copies, Paine's lively and accessible work generated twenty-one American editions and dozens of replies.[47]

To Federalists, Paine was already the chief villain of Republicanism. *The Age of Reason* made him the Antichrist, not simply because of its "theology"—for there were actually quite a few closeted rationalists among the Federalist elite—but all the more because it threatened to further disrupt the Federalists' desired political and social order. Though not as much as they themselves thought, they did have reason to worry. Reaching into every region of the country, Paine's new work made deism a prominent topic in newspapers and magazines, taverns and meetinghouses, and rendered accessible to working people ideas long restricted to elite circles. In Vermont, where Paine's writings were already extremely popular and Democratic societies remained active, a Christian missionary reported that "*The Age of Reason* is greedily received."[48]

Other deist books, such as *Ruins: or a Survey of the Revolutions of Empires* by the French exile Constantin-François Volney, gained a wide readership and with *The Age of Reason* further stimulated organizing efforts among the deists. The ranks of the militants included such figures as Philip Freneau, Joel Barlow, William Dunlap, and John Fitch (inventor of the steamboat), but the movement's leading activist was Elihu Palmer, a former Calvinist minister who had turned Baptist, then Universalist, and finally deist. A member of both the Tammany and the Democratic societies, Palmer—who never allowed his loss of eyesight in Philadelphia's yellow fever epidemic of 1793 to deter him—founded the Deistical Society of New York in 1795 and attracted native-born and immigrant, upper- and working-class "congregants." Soon groups of deists in Newburgh, Philadelphia, and Baltimore were creating their own societies.[49]

Congregational ministers were already made anxious by the mushrooming of Baptist, Methodist, and Universalist churches, the further emptying of their own churches due to emigrations west, a rising chorus of anticlericalism, calls for disestablishment, and the emergence of Unitarianism within their own ranks. They felt all the more under siege in the face of popular deism, which, as far as they were concerned, was nothing more than atheism. And yet the clerics' greatest fright may have come when "republican religion" flared up in the nation's colleges, the training grounds of America's foremost preachers, teachers, and statesmen. Of his time at Yale in the mid-1790s, famed Congregational revivalist Lyman Beecher would recount, "That was the day of the infidelity of the Tom Paine school. Boys that dressed flax in the barn, as I used to, read Tom Paine and believed him." Renowned for his readiness to confront "infidel" tendencies (which to orthodox Calvinists included both deism *and* the new religious radicalism), Timothy Dwight, the college's new president, swiftly responded with an aggressive program of lectures and sermons.[50]

At Harvard deism became so popular that college authorities felt compelled to provide every student with a copy of *Apology for the Bible*, Bishop Watson's famed reply to *The Age of Reason*. At the Presbyterians' College of New Jersey in Princeton, "infidelity" was also said to be "spreading its dominion far and wide" and demanding a reaction. And still farther south, Paine-inspired activities were reported at Virginia's College of William and Mary and the new University of North Carolina. Only at William and Mary, a recognized bastion of Republicanism—where syllabi included Paine's *Rights of Man* and *Dissertation on First Principles of Government*—was deism apparently accompanied by political radicalism, yet Federalists everywhere imagined the worst.[51]

In Kentucky, where Republicanism predominated in politics, a heated fight broke out within the state's elite between rationalist Unitarians and Calvinist Presbyterians for command of the publicly supported Transylvania Seminary (soon to be chartered as a university). It started when several members of the board, including John Breckenridge and John Bradford, both founders of Lexington's Democratic society, secured appointment of the English émigré radical Harry Toulmin as the school's president. Further rankling the Presbyterians, students had taken to reading Paine's and other infidels' deistical writings along with his political works. With power seesawing between the two factions, the contest for control would continue well into the 1820s (at which time the latter conclusively prevailed with the backing of Baptists and Methodists).[52]

Whereas in New England replies to Paine's "blasphemy" came mostly from the Congregationalists, in Virginia they emanated particularly from Baptist and Presbyterian churchmen, presumably motivated not only by Christian outrage but also by a feeling that the very man who had first rallied them to revolution—with passages from the Bible—had now betrayed them. Though *The Age of Reason* did not necessarily alienate them from the Republican movement, it severed their attachment to Paine and made him the object of evangelical scorn for generations to come.[53]

Laying the basis for Federalist victories over Jefferson and the Republicans in both 1796 and 1798, Federalist politicians and editors and New England Calvinist clerics reacted to the crises by joining forces to confront their mutual Republican enemies. As powerful as the Federalists would become, however, those electoral triumphs would be their last at the national level.

The newspaper wars grew ever more furious. Continuing to promote Paine's words and writings, including his new pamphlet *Agrarian Justice*—which engendered a lively and critical debate on the social consequences of commercial expansion and no doubt riled the Federalists even more—Bache and his fellow Republican editors struck ever harder at the Federalists and their allies. Their favorite targets were Alexander Hamilton and that "friend of monarchic and aristocratic government" John Adams, especially after Adams emerged as the Federalists' presidential candidate. But they also now went after the president himself, printing, for example, Paine's scathing *Letter to George Washington*.[54]

Federalist newspapermen like John Fenno and Noah Webster (the latter of whom had abandoned his Painite views in light of the French Terror and the imprisonment of Paine himself) responded to their "Jacobin" foes with their own broadsides. Yet no one responded more vociferously and viciously than the English émigré William Cobbett who, though he would become a devotee of Paine later in life, sided with the Federalists in the 1790s. Sounding more like an English Tory than an American conservative—he even criticized his Federalist comrades when they failed to properly support British interests—Cobbett would publish two journals, the *Political Censor* and *Porcupine's Gazette*, plus seventeen of his own pamphlets. Writing as "Peter Porcupine," he laid into Republicans like Jefferson, Bache, and the late Benjamin Franklin. But he directed some of his harshest invective at Paine. Comparing Paine to Judas Iscariot, Cobbett predicted that "men will learn to express all that is base, malignant, treacherous, unnatural, and blasphemous, by the single monosyllable, Paine." Eventually the war of words between Federalist and Republican pressmen would turn truly violent, when Federalist ruffians physically attacked Benjamin Franklin Bache on the street and, later, him and his family at their home.[55]

Yale graduate Thomas Robbins, the son of a Congregational minister, wrote in his diary for May 2, 1797, "The world [is] coming either to Christianity or infidelity." Seeing the contest between Federalists and Republicans as a fight not simply for political power but also for America's moral order, Federalist-aligned clergymen, led by Timothy Dwight, "the Pope of Connecticut," threw themselves into the fray and earnestly incorporated anti-Republicanism into their sermons and pronouncements. To orthodox Calvinists like Dwight, democracy and deism meant pretty much the same thing. Believing in a predetermined division of the Elect and the Damned, they naturally opposed the egalitarianism and progressivism of those like Paine, who, trusting in the essential goodness of human nature and the possibility of human and social betterment, preached "salvation within history," not beyond it.[56]

Adams's presidency witnessed escalating war fever, xenophobia, thuggery, and the suppression of dissent. Relations with France steadily deteriorated in 1797, and following the diplomatic debacle known as the XYZ Affair, the United States entered into the so-called Quasi-War, operating, in effect, as an unofficial ally of the British. At the same time the number of Irish political refugees and immigrants increased significantly, especially in the wake of the failed Irish Rebellion of 1798.

Worried about a full-scale war with France and a fresh influx of radical republicans, Federalist elements began to call for strengthening the nation's military, restricting immigration and naturalization, and limit-

ing freedom of speech and the press. Acknowledging the political importance of the clergy to Federalist politics and hoping to rally the
people to his administration, Adams soon announced a national day of
"solemn humiliation, fasting and prayer" for May 9, 1798. Everyone expected that the occasion would elicit sermons attacking not only
France but also American democrats and deists. Yet speaking at
Boston's New North Church, the Reverend Jedidiah Morse would go
well beyond the expected. He used the occasion to expose a purported
grand conspiracy that threatened America with "fraud, violence, cruelty, debauchery" and, ultimately, the destruction of its government and
churches. Deriving the outlines of the plot from *Proofs of a Conspiracy*,
a recent book by the Edinburgh University professor John Robison,
Morse revealed that the conspirators behind this fantastically "deep-
laid plan" were the Bavarian Illuminati, a secret offshoot of the Free-
masons. Claiming that their intrigues had brought about the French
Revolution and France's ensuing military victories, he chillingly warned
that the Illuminati already had "secretly extended [their] branches
through a great part of Europe, and even into America." Linking Paine
to the conspiracy's progress, he asserted that "there can be little doubt
that *The Age of Reason* and the other works of that unprincipled author,
as they proceeded from the fountain head of *Illumination*, and have
been so industriously and extensively circulated in this country, were
written and sent to America expressly in aid of this demoralizing plan."
To thwart the Illuminati's schemes, Morse implored faith in and energetic support for the Adams administration and religious institutions.[57]

Accepting the veracity—or at least the political utility—of Morse's
claims, Federalist presses and pulpits resounded histrionically with
demands for action abroad and at home. Some would even take to
publishing and repeating the scurrilous rumor that Paine had connived
with the French to stage an invasion of the United States.[58]

Adams resisted the pressure to pursue outright war with the
French, but he was persuaded not only to expand America's military
forces and build up the nation's coastal defenses but also to take measures against aliens and dissidents in the United States. The Federalist-
dominated Congress readily approved expenditures on men and
matériel and in June and July it passed a series of laws directed against
immigrants, foreigners, and American democrats. Notably, though the

Federalists had supported immigration in the 1780s, they now no longer did. The Naturalization Act of 1798 extended the period of residence required of immigrants for citizenship from five to fourteen years. The Alien Enemies Act licensed the president in time of war to round up subjects of the enemy nation and hold them or remove them from the country. And the far more outrageous Alien Act further authorized the president—in time of war or peace—to deport from the country any foreigner he considered "dangerous to the peace and safety of the United States." Lastly but most crucially, the Sedition Act essentially made it a crime to criticize the government, by outlawing the issuing of "any false, scandalous, and malicious writing or writings against the Government . . . or either House of Congress, with intent to defame . . . or bring them into contempt or disrepute."[59]

While nobody suffered expulsion under the Alien Act, its passage persuaded many a Frenchman to preemptively pack up and leave. The Federalists did, however, put the Sedition Act to use against their own enemies. They prosecuted the editors of the *Aurora*, first Bache—who, along with his Federalist counterpart, John Fenno, would pass away suddenly in a yellow fever epidemic in September 1798—and then Bache's successor, William Duane, whom they succeeded in packing off to prison, along with a goodly number of other Republican printers and pamphleteers. They also indicted and secured the convictions of the renegade New York Federalist-turned-Republican Jedidiah Peck, for circulating a petition demanding repeal of the acts; the troublesome Republican congressman from Vermont Matthew Lyon, for having "libeled" President Adams by referring to his "continual grasping for power" and "unbounded thirst for ridiculous pomp, foolish adulation, or selfish avarice"; and the Massachusetts laborer, Revolutionary War veteran, and popular itinerant democratic speaker David Brown, for inciting sedition. Brown had decried the oppression of working people, the greed of the governing elite, *and* the protection that the Sedition Act afforded the latter class. Eager to silence him, the Federalists claimed that his visit to the town of Dedham had led local Republicans to protest government policies by erecting a liberty pole; and hostile witnesses further testified that Brown had had the audacity to speak openly and favorably of *The Age of Reason*. Bache, Duane, Peck, Lyon, Brown, and others—the Federalists clearly had *Painite* Republicans in their sights.[60]

As much as the Federalists wanted a deferential, or at least passive, citizenry, they got something else. Their increasing expenditures on the military, which necessarily entailed higher taxes, irritated many. Their authoritarian initiatives, as well as the presumptions and practices of their clerical allies, antagonized many more. And while the Federalists may have aimed the Naturalization Act at the "wild Irish," they hit the growing German and other immigrant-ethnic communities as well, making themselves all the more unpopular. With their editorial ranks replenished by Irish radicals, the Republicans, in spite of the persecution they encountered, did not retreat. They even remained capable of poetic whimsy, as in the verse published in the 1799 New Year's edition of Hartford's *American Mercury* criticizing the Federalists:

> Strange this! This [the Revolution] no sooner's done,
> Than *Whig terms* out of fashion run,
> Dame *Liberty* and *Rights of Man*
> Are slid down hill with *Thomas Paine*.
> *Democracy* and *civil Level*
> Are swiftly packing to the Devil.[61]

As resentment toward Adams and his party grew, the Federalists themselves split into factions, each pushing its own candidate for the presidency. Meanwhile Republicanism experienced new vigor and popularity, and in the "Revolution of 1800" Jefferson's Republican Party captured the presidency and both houses of Congress.

Imagining Jacobins and infidels ruling the nation, Federalists feared the worst from a Jefferson presidency. But as much as Jefferson wanted to secure Republicanism, he also wanted to bring an end to the dangerous divisions between the parties. As president, he would prove to be no revolutionary, and aside from welcoming Paine home to the United States, he and his administration would keep a critical distance from the radicals who had done so much to bring about and advance the Republican movement. Though on his return Paine would have some influence with the president, it would have to do mostly with efforts to purchase Louisiana from the French. Jeffersonian Republicanism in office would eschew the egalitarian, democratic, and cosmopolitan spirit of the Painite tradition. Still, the Republican ascendance did represent a critical democratic advance. It not only involved the defeat of the politics of deference and authoritarianism, and the peaceful transfer of power from one party to another; it also served to reaffirm the progressive ideals of the American Revolution, however exclusive they remained in practice.[62]

Paine remained a radical and was forever confident of America's prospects and possibilities. In late 1802, in a public letter addressed to his fellow "Citizens of the United States," he observed that "there is too much common sense and independence in America to be long the dupe of any faction, foreign or domestic." Though angered by the Federalists and their supporters, he continued to believe in the democratic goodness of American working people:

> There is in America, more than in any other country, a large body of people who attend quietly to their farms, or follow their several occupations; who pay no regard to the clamors of anonymous scribblers, who think for themselves, and judge of government, not by the fury of newspaper writers, but by the prudent frugality of its measures, and the encouragement it gives to the improvement and prosperity of the country . . . When this body moves, all the little barkings of scribbling and witless curs pass for nothing.[63]

Paine continued to write and enjoy many a good time in the company of fellow democrats and deists. Yet his last years were personally trying and disappointing. Federalists high and low continued to hound him. In New Rochelle, where he went to live on the confiscated farm granted to him after the Revolutionary War, the local community, dominated by former Tories, would even find it possible to deny him the right to vote, on the false grounds that due to his service in the French Revolution he was no longer a U.S. citizen. And when debilitating illness forced him to move down to New York City, clergymen would show up at his quarters—and as death approached, even at his bedside—to harass him with dire warnings of what awaited should he refuse to recant his infidelity and return to Christianity. Nevertheless, Paine gave them no satisfaction. Determined to meet the Creator on his own terms, he held firmly to his beliefs.[64]

Paine died on June 8, 1809. Refused a place in the Quaker cemetery, he was buried on his own property in New Rochelle. Very few attended the funeral. No public dignitaries were present. The Frenchwoman Madame Marguerite de Bonneville, who had accompanied Paine back to America with her sons and tended him through his illnesses and final days, would recall:

> Contemplating who it was, what man it was, that we were committing to an obscure grave on an open and disregarded bit of land, I could not help feeling most acutely. Before the earth was thrown down upon the coffin, I, placing myself at the east of the grave, said to my son Benjamin, "stand you there, at the other end, as a witness for grateful America. Looking round me, and beholding the small group of spectators, I exclaimed, as the earth was tumbled into the grave, "Oh! Mr. Paine! My son stands here as testimony of the gratitude of America, and I, for France!" This was the funeral ceremony of this great politician and philosopher![65]

Indeed, for some years it would seem that Paine and his role in the making of the United States would forever be ignored, his name banished from official remembrance of the American Revolution, and his memory, like his remains, lost to posterity. When people spoke publicly of him, they did so with disdain more often than admiration. Caught up in a Second Great Awakening, most Americans found his religious arguments detestable. And the nation's governing elites, fearing association with that "lying, drunken, brutal infidel" of Federalist and clerical tales—and in any case, little interested in dramatically extending and deepening American rights—would readily cooperate in suppressing or marginalizing the story of his radical life and labors.

Yet Paine and his contributions would not be forgotten. Within a generation Americans would come forth who would refuse not only to permit his name to go publicly unremembered, but also, and more important, to allow his vision of America's purpose and promise to go unredeemed. Caught up in the continuing struggle for freedom, equality, and democracy, they would harness Paine's words and articulate them anew. As Adams truly feared, the Age of Paine had really only just begun.

5

FREEDOM MUST HAVE ALL OR NONE

Four months after Union forces defeated Robert E. Lee's Confederate army at Gettysburg, Abraham Lincoln traveled to Pennsylvania for the dedication of the battlefield cemetery. As he was not invited as the principal speaker, the president kept his remarks brief. But the words he offered on November 19, 1863, would take their place in American memory not far from the Declaration of Independence: "Four score and seven years ago our fathers brought forth on this continent, a new nation, conceived in Liberty, and dedicated to the proposition that all men are created equal."[1]

Lincoln had often expressed his reverence for the Founders in his speeches, but the Gettysburg Address transcended his earlier orations. Linking the struggles of the 1860s to those of the 1770s, Lincoln presented the Civil War as a second American Revolution and called upon his fellow citizens to dedicate themselves to the "great task" of assuring "that this nation, under God, shall have a new birth of freedom—and that government of the people, by the people, for the people, shall not perish from the earth." We do not know if the president intended his evocation of the "fathers" to include Thomas Paine, but we have good reason to think he did.[2]

For fifty years American statesmen had rarely acknowledged Paine in public. When they recalled the American Revolution and the Founders, they regularly did so in support of the status quo, and Paine obviously did not suit that purpose. In 1825, at the cornerstone-laying ceremony for the Bunker Hill Monument, Daniel Webster, the great Federalist and, later, Whig orator, delivered a speech that set the standard for commemorative rhetoric. As Lincoln would, he spoke most venerably of the Founders, but whereas Lincoln would present the Revolution as yet to be completed, Webster presented it as already accomplished: "We can win no laurels in a war for independence. Earlier and worthier hands have gathered them all . . . there remains to us a great duty of defence and preservation." Lincoln would evoke the promise of 1776 to challenge the order of things; Webster, like so many others of his ilk, did so to legitimate it.[3]

To the powerful, propertied, and prominent, the Revolution was over. While they would celebrate the lives of Washington, Franklin, Jefferson, Adams, and Hamilton—clearly some more than others, depending on the region of the country and the occasion—they would never celebrate Paine. When they did speak of him, it was almost always in a derisive fashion, regularly repeating the same old slurs—"infidel," "liar," "drunk."

Still, Paine was not forgotten. The radical democratic impulse he had sensed and literally inscribed in American experience continued to shape understandings and longings and to propel Americans to social and political action. When confronting the nation's contradictions, diverse radicals, reformers, and critics would rediscover Paine and his work. Inspired and encouraged by them, they would advance their own conceptions of America's revolutionary heritage and what it demanded and contest the accelerating class inequality and oppression of capitalism, the persistence of slavery, the denial of the equal rights of women, and the cultural authority of the clergy, making the first half of the nineteenth century an age of "militant democracy." At the same time, writers—including Emerson, Whitman, and Melville, as well as the more popular George Lippard—would absorb Paine's arguments and cultivate both American letters and the nation's democratic sensibilities. Lincoln himself—born in 1809, the year Paine died—did not start out a political radical. But by the time he arrived at Gettysburg, he had become a revolutionary, and though he made no particular reference to Paine, it seems he too carried Paine's ideas with him.[4]

Scholars now accept the originally controversial claims of Lincoln's law partner, William Herndon, that while the young Lincoln was trying to establish himself at New Salem in the 1830s, he not only studiously worked to improve his grammar but also avidly read *The Age of Reason* and took to professing religious liberalism, to the point of writing a deist treatise of his own (which his friends considerately tossed into a stove to protect the aspiring politician's reputation). Where historians continue to disagree is over the question of whether Lincoln eventually abandoned freethought or simply held on to it privately. Yet either way—deist or Christian—Lincoln himself apparently saw that challenging scripture could have disastrous consequences, as he nearly discovered firsthand when his opponent in the 1846 race for Congress, the renowned circuit-riding Methodist preacher Peter Cartwright, accused him of "infidelity." Lincoln would succeed in discounting the charges and winning the seat, but the incident must have firmly impressed upon him the imperative of avoiding favorable reference to freethought and its saints. He would never join a church, but neither would he ever again speak publicly of deism or Paine. Of course, this does not mean Lincoln stopped thinking about them.[5]

Oddly, while historians and biographers have come to acknowledge the influence of Paine's religious arguments on Lincoln's thinking, they have failed to consider his influence on his political arguments. But according to Herndon's New Salem informants, the young Lincoln enthusiastically read not only *The Age of Reason*, but also *Common Sense*. And the chief editor of Lincoln's *Collected Works*, Roy Basler—though he never pursued the question at length—observed that Paine may well have been Lincoln's "favorite author" and that Lincoln's private engagement with Paine, not the legendary "instruction of a frontier schoolmaster," probably provided the future president with his "most important literary education," as well as the model of "eloquence" that would later characterize his own compositions. Moreover, Basler averred, "no other writer of the eighteenth century, with the exception of Jefferson, parallels more closely the temper or gist of Lincoln's later thought."[6]

Though Lincoln the public figure never quoted Paine's work, we do find a certain correspondence between his words and Paine's—and if Lincoln's memory was as good as reported, he likely could recall exact lines from *Common Sense*. Equally well versed in the Bible, both men wrote of "a house divided against itself." Where Paine insisted that *"the time hath found us,"* Lincoln declared, "Fellow-citizens, *We* cannot escape history." Paine portrayed America as the only remaining hope for the salvation of the world; Lincoln proclaimed America "the last, best hope of earth." Paine wrote the "birthday of a new world is at hand", Lincoln spoke of a "new birth of freedom."[7]

Furthermore, like Paine, Lincoln firmly subscribed to the liberating power of reason. And like Paine, Lincoln projected America both as a land of opportunity and as an asylum for mankind—the American people constituted and steadily reconstituted by the arrival of people from diverse European backgrounds. Without question, Lincoln embraced and acclaimed the Declaration of Independence above all. But he may well have read it through the lens of *Common Sense*, as many of the radical figures of his day did. Indeed, we can hear Paine's most powerful arguments echoing through Lincoln's speeches: that people had a "natural love of liberty" and the oppressed had a right to revolution; that American "reverence for the law" could serve as the nation's "political religion"; and that the solidarity of the Union must take precedence because only as one nation could the United States go on to realize the exceptional purpose and promise assigned to it by Providence and demonstrate to the world that men could establish and maintain self-governing nation-states of liberty, equality, and democracy.[8]

Finally, like Paine, Lincoln believed strongly in the dignity of free labor. In 1858 he wrote, "As I would not be a *slave*, so I would not be a *master*. This expresses my idea of democracy. Whatever differs from this, to the extent of the difference, is not democracy." Lincoln gathered what Paine had: "Freedom must have all or none, and she must have them equally."[9]

From Jefferson to Lincoln, the United States witnessed extraordinary developments. By way of purchase, annexation, acquisition, and war, the national territory stretched across the continent. Through natural increase and immigration, the country's population quintupled. Roads, steamboats, canals, and railways connected America's regions to one another and the world. Though punctuated by "panics," economic growth proceeded at a phenomenal pace, and the market subsumed and drove agriculture and manufacturing. Americans pushed into the Midwest to farm the land. Cotton took hold in the South and soon reached beyond the Mississippi. Factories mushroomed in the burgeoning cities and towns of the North.[10]

America became more democratic and pluralistic. By the 1830s many states had fully extended the suffrage to white workingmen. The last of the religious establishments had been terminated in New England. And bonded servitude and slavery had come to an end in the North. Moreover, while the Second Great Awakening roused the spirit of Protestants, and Methodist and Baptist numbers exploded, new sects emerged and new arrivals multiplied the numbers of Catholics and, to a lesser extent, Jews. Traveling around the United States in 1831, the young French aristocrat Alexis de Tocqueville, who would return home to write *Democracy in America*, found the country fascinating for its "equality of conditions," its democratic polity and the bearing of its citizens, and its religious fervor alongside its tolerance.[11]

Compared to Europe, America was everything Tocqueville said it was. Nevertheless, contradictions old and new challenged, if not denied, America's proclaimed ideals. Class inequalities widened, possibly more in his day than ever before or since. The advance of commerce, industrialization, and urbanization benefited those who could take advantage of the new opportunities; yet for all too many workers the accumulation of capital meant low wages, the loss of autonomy, long hours, and abysmal living conditions. The ranks of the poor swelled, and so, too, did the number of individuals imprisoned for failure to repay debts. Still more brutally, slavery spread with the spread of cotton. The importation of Africans was halted in 1808, but the South's domestic trade in black people flourished. Settling the West, Americans devastated native peoples. Even as white workingmen secured the vote, barriers were erected to deny women and free black men their rights as citizens. And Protestant clerics, in alignment with powerful and propertied folk, continued to dominate much of American culture and education.

Some saw portents of social breakdown, most others saw wondrous possibilities, but in all quarters there were calls for action. Intellectuals, religious and secular, critically applied their pens and voices in support of repairing, perfecting, advancing, resisting, or transforming parts, if not all, of the social order. Americans and newcomers organized religious revivals, utopian communities, reform campaigns, political parties, and labor unions. In the 1830s the Whig political party would take the place of the Federalists, and the Republicans under Andrew Jackson would become known as Democrats. A generation later the slavery question would lead to the dissolution of the former and the fracturing of the latter. Along the way third parties would arise and disappear. And as civil war approached, the divided Democrats would face a new party, the Republicans. Meanwhile, political, business, and clerical elites sought to hold the evolving national and regional orders together even as they endeavored to secure advantage, profit, and station. And with good reason they all worried about the collective aspirations of the laboring classes and the appeals and movements that might inspire them.

Though elites denied Paine a place in "official" commemorations of the Revolution, Americans never actually abandoned his memory, not even, as has been long supposed, during the 1810s. For a start, conservatives themselves found Paine—that is, their fabricated image of him—too ideologically valuable to let go of. The English émigré journalist James Cheetham rendered them great assistance in that respect. Driven out of the Republican movement for his renegade behavior, Cheetham produced a vengeful work, *The Life of Thomas Paine*, within only months of Paine's passing. He presented Paine as a "vain . . . intemperate . . . dirty . . . hypocritical . . . friendless . . . parasitical . . . unpatriotic . . . wretched . . . copier of ideas . . . and atheist" and salaciously claimed that Paine had "seduced and abandoned" Madame de Bonneville, his friend, housekeeper, and nurse. She successfully sued Cheetham for libel, but those who hated Paine and what he stood for cared little about Cheetham's veracity, and his book supplied anti-Paine invective to generations of conservatives to come. Empowered by Cheetham, preachers made up their own tales of Paine's life and the dire consequences of subscribing to his ideas. They propagated fantastic stories of Paine's "deathbed agonies" and of how *The Age of Reason* had incited lust, adultery, and suicide, bringing disease and natural disasters to those communities exposed to its teachings. On the secular side, lecturers and writers, scholarly and popular, continually repeated the personal slurs and dismissed Paine's writings as either unoriginal or encouraging of anarchy.[12]

However, Paine's memory and legacy also lived on in favorable ways. *The Age of Reason* had repulsed the populist evangelicals who had so admired Paine, and at revivalist camp meetings folks sang hymns that included verses like:

> The *world*, the *Devil* and *Tom Paine*
> Have try'd their force, but all in vain,
> They can't prevail, the reason is,
> The Lord Defends the Methodist.

Yet Paine's religious writings did not necessarily lead them to abandon Paine's democratic ideals or, for that matter, his words. Challenging the class divisions of church and society, the peripatetic Methodist preacher Lorenzo Dow—without ever mentioning Paine himself—used Paine's arguments and lines to write his *Analects Upon the Rights of Man* in 1812. As well, Elias Smith, James O'Kelly, Barton Stone, and Alexander Campbell, the founders of the fast-growing "Christian restorationist movement," had all encountered Paine's political writings and, apparently, been heartened by them as they "came out," respectively, from the Baptist, Methodist, and Presbyterian churches to create more egalitarian congregations. Though he did not cite its author, Smith published a lengthy extract from *Common Sense* in 1813 in his widely circulated newspaper, *Herald of Gospel Liberty*. Letters to newspapers showed that the Christian faithful in Kentucky continued to read Paine, for they noted how Paine himself had depended on scripture when penning his call for independence. And had Lincoln known of it, he might well have answered Peter Cartwright's accusation of infidelity by pointing out that the preacher himself had not hesitated to quote Paine—"These are the times that try men's souls"—as he converted Illinoisans to Methodism.[13]

The deist movement had faded away by 1810, but "natural religion" did not completely disappear, as Christian missionaries discovered when sailors in New York responded to the handing-out of Bibles by whipping out editions of Paine and other deist authors. Moreover, the radical Quaker leader Elias Hicks, who had befriended Paine in New York, absorbed ideas from *The Age of Reason*, as did the foremost "prophet" of the Universalists, Hosea Ballou. While most deists presumably remained churchless, numbers joined the Unitarian and Universalist congregations (the former appealing more to middle- and upper-class New Englanders and the latter to working people). Both churches publicly distanced themselves from Paine, but orthodox clergy still branded them as "infidel" for their liberal theologies.[14]

Paine's memory and legacy survived, as well, in a generation of radical republicans and democrats, many of whom would pass these ideas on to their children. Charles Pinckney Sumner, the son of a Revolutionary War hero, read Paine while at Harvard in the mid-1790s. In contrast to so many of his classmates, however, he remained devoted to Paine's arguments on the "rights of man." Translating them into personal support for the Haitian Revolution and emancipation in the United States, he also made every effort to cultivate them in his son, Charles Sumner. And he apparently succeeded, for the younger Sumner would become a leading antislavery activist and represent Massachusetts in the U.S. Senate as a Radical Republican. Meanwhile, lower down the social ladder, the New York carpenter Walter Whitman—who proudly noted he actually had met Paine—impressed Painite ideas on his own son, Walt, who would make himself America's great poet of democracy.[15]

As "Peter Porcupine," Englishman William Cobbett was the journalistic scourge of Republicans in the 1790s. But on his return to Britain in 1800, he became a leading voice in English radical politics and, when faced with renewed government repression in 1817, sought refuge back in the Republican-governed United States. Now committed to redeeming the revolutionary pamphleteer rather than to burying him, Cobbett, intending to raise a monument to Paine, had his coffin dug up and shipped back to England when he finally went home in 1819.[16]

Cobbett's "theft" infuriated American radicals, but those who wished to honor Paine would not need his bones to do so. America would soon witness the energetic revival of his memory and legacy. And even though Paine's physical remains had been removed to England, many a radical Briton would journey to America in pursuit of his spirit, the most prominent among them the Welsh industrialist, philanthropist, and utopian socialist Robert Owen.[17]

Owen's story—how he had worked his way up from laboring in factories to managing and owning them—was well known. But Owen owed his fame not so much to the fact that he had accumulated a fortune as to how he had transformed his Scottish textile mill and the town of New Lanark in the process. Raising wages and reducing hours, banning child labor and establishing schools, opening shops and building new housing, he had turned a dreadful factory and industrial village into a model workplace and community while keeping the operation profitable.

Subscribing to Paine's proposition that "we have it in our power to begin the world over again," the fifty-three-year-old Owen developed an even grander vision of social change and looked to America as the place to start realizing it. Specifically, he planned to create a "socialist" community in Indiana that would show the world how—through education and rational organization—cooperation could replace competition, sharing could replace private property, and mutualism could replace individualism. Various philosophers had influenced him. And while Paine was no socialist, his writings had made Owen a deist and nourished his optimism that people could improve themselves materially, socially, and morally if freed from oppressive institutions.[18]

Arriving in the United States in 1824, Owen gave a series of speeches promoting his venture, including two to Congress, before heading west to the settlement he had named New Harmony. Almost overnight the community attracted eight hundred members—intellectuals, technicians, and working families (as well as a number of crooks and parasites)—and instigated other Owenist experiments around the country. Elated by developments, taken with America, and eager to proclaim the commencement of a "new moral world," Owen stood before the New Harmonites on July 4, 1826—the fiftieth anniversary of the founding of the nation—and delivered his "Declaration of Mental Independence," wherein he promised to fight the "TRINITY OF EVILS . . . PRIVATE OR INDIVIDUAL PROPERTY—ABSURD AND IRRATIONAL SYSTEMS OF RELIGION—AND MARRIAGE FOUNDED ON INDIVIDUAL PROPERTY [AND] IRRATIONAL SYSTEMS OF RELIGION." Attacking the most sacred institutions, he thrilled some and shocked many more.[19]

New Harmony would fail within a couple of years, but not simply on account of Owen's ideological audacity. While the community's schools and clinics made it a fine place to live, poor planning, lack of discipline, the diversity of the residents, the absence of a shared ethos, and most crucially, the inability of the community's enterprises to turn a profit all contributed to its ruin. Owen himself, though forced to abandon his dream, did not give up his ambition to liberate people from "Ignorance, Superstition, and Hypocrisy." He continued to advocate deism and, upon returning to England, devoted himself to the development of working-class cooperative enterprises. Moreover, New Harmony's failure would do little either to dissuade other communitarians from trying to build utopia in America or to deter other freethinkers from seeking to advance the "age of reason."[20]

In fact, Robert Owen's own career in America was not fully over. On a return visit in 1828, he instigated a face-to-face debate on the veracity of scripture and the value of religion with the populist evangelical and cofounder of the Disciples of Christ, Alexander Campbell, who himself had come from Ireland to the United States as a young man in 1809. Held in Cincinnati in April 1829, the debate extended over eight days and drew more than a thousand people each day. The actual exchange was of little theological value, for the two men argued right past each other; the assembled folk, who accorded Campbell the victory, must have found both men variously entertaining and tiresome. But historians have viewed the event as an extraordinary confrontation between religious skepticism and evangelicalism. Still, what made the event truly remarkable was that it involved not one but two figures who carried Paine's arguments with them. Both men cherished the American Revolution as the commencement of a new age of history and possibility, attacked ecclesiastical aristocracies and authorities, and opposed any connection between church and state. And more than Owen's addresses ever did, Campbell's sermons exuded the *democratic* perspectives of *Common Sense* and *Rights of Man*.[21]

The remaking of an American *movement* of freethinkers really began in New York. On January 29, 1825, forty of Paine's old friends—American and British, a mix of professionals and artisans such as the Revolutionary War veteran John Fellows, attorney Thomas Hartwell, and shoemakers William Carver and Benjamin Offen—met at Harmony Hall in New York to remember Paine on his birthday. Supported by two new American anthologies, *The Theological Works of Thomas Paine* and *The Political Writings of Thomas Paine*, their gathering served to catalyze interest and effort and soon a full-scale revival of "infidel" activity was under way, including societies, educational institutes, periodicals, and programs of lectures and debates.[22]

Like the Christian revivalists whose endeavors had instigated their own, the freethinkers had "missionaries." Setting out from Virginia in the mid-1820s, Anne Royall, the young widow of a Revolutionary War officer and Paine admirer, traveled the United States expounding Paine's deist arguments and writing articles on her sojourns. She suffered physical attack and civil prosecution, but she persisted, and upon settling in Washington in the 1830s, she would apply her pen to various reform efforts. Her mottos were "Free thought, free speech and a free press" and "Good works instead of long prayers."[23]

Far more famous, or infamous, was the immigrant Scottish feminist Frances "Fanny" Wright. Born in 1800 and orphaned as a child, Wright inherited her radicalism from her parents—her father had distributed Paine's *Rights of Man* in Britain during the dangerous 1790s—and her wealth from an uncle killed in military service. She would apply both to combating tyrannies of class, race, gender, and religion.[24]

Wright had first visited the United States in 1818 and warmly praised its development and prospects in *Views of Society and Manners in America*, a book that brought her to the attention of various European notables, including the now-sixty-four-year-old veteran of the American and French Revolutions, the old friend of Jefferson and Paine, the Marquis de Lafayette. Wright and Lafayette grew quite close, and when he set off on a triumphal return tour of America in 1824, she followed.[25]

Once again excited by America, Wright nonetheless recognized that she had sorely underestimated the evils of southern slavery. Impressed by Owen's plans for New Harmony, she organized Nashoba, a cooperative plantation in Tennessee with an interracial workforce of freemen and slaves that she hoped would serve as a model for the peaceful abolition of slavery. Her plan involved the whites teaching literacy and technical skills to the slaves, with the plantation's profits going to a fund to purchase the slaves' freedom. Like New Harmony, however, Nashoba failed. Wright herself invested heavily and labored strenuously to make the project succeed—so strenuously, she collapsed of fatigue and had to withdraw from the settlement to recover. Her absence—and the ensuing mismanagement, conflicts, and revelations of free love and sex among the community's residents—led to Nashoba's demise in 1827. Dissolving the enterprise, Wright personally escorted the slaves to freedom in Haiti. Still, she did not eschew radicalism but teamed up with Robert Dale Owen, Owen's son and the publisher of the New Harmony newspaper, the *Free Enquirer*.[26]

In 1829 Wright and Dale Owen relocated to New York and threw themselves into both the freethought movement and workingmen's politics. Purchasing an old church, they set up a "Hall of Science" dedicated to "the sectarian faith . . . and universal knowledge." On its premises—in whose windows they prominently displayed portraits of Paine and other deist heroes—Wright and Dale Owen produced the *Free Enquirer*, sold freethinker literature, and conducted a deist Sunday school and lecture series on science and other subjects.

The first woman in America to formally address a gathering of men *and* women outside of a church, Wright herself was an extremely popular speaker. A striking presence, she drew huge crowds of admirers and the curious, not just in New York but everywhere she took her message. Denouncing the designs of a "crafty priesthood and a monied aristocracy," she urged her listeners to renew and extend America's revolutionary heritage. A disciple of both Paine and Mary Wollstonecraft, she spoke of the needs of the working classes, advocated the sexual equality of women and the transformation of marriage, and called for universal public education free of clerical control and sway. Clergymen and other conservatives reacted vehemently, labeling Wright the "Red Harlot of Infidelity" and a "female Thomas Paine."[27]

In the late 1820s and 1830s, under names such as the Society of Deists, the Society of Free Enquirers, and the Moral Philanthropists, freethinkers gathered and organized in New York, Boston, Philadelphia, Baltimore, Providence, Wilmington, Rochester, Pittsburgh, Cleveland, Cincinnati, St. Louis, and a good number of smaller cities and towns, from West Avon, Massachusetts, to Galena, Illinois. The movement encompassed deists, agnostics, and atheists. All, however, shared a commitment to the further separation of church and state, the dissolution of the cultural hegemony of the clergy, and the advancement of reason and science. No less than the Second Great Awakening, the resurgence of freethought represented a critical response to the irrationality and injustice of the market revolution. The movement attracted folks of various ranks but especially "small master and journeyman artisans—shoemakers, printers, stonecutters and assorted others."[28]

The freethinkers' societies sponsored activities from lectures to libraries and supported a lively periodical press; just as Christian reformers had established the American Bible Society and the American Tract Society to spread "the Word," the freethinkers issued cheap editions of their own classics, especially works by Paine. American freethinkers universally revered Paine and made his birthday a grand occasion every year. These evenings traditionally opened with a dinner, followed by a major oration on Paine, and then rounds of toasts to him, to other freethought heroes, and to progressive ideals and causes such as "The People and popular sovereignty" and "Universal Education." A typical salute to Paine went, "[To] the memory of the immortal Thomas Paine, who with his dauntless mind and pen, lit up the brilliant sun of liberty, that kings, tyrants and priests will never be able to extinguish." Finally, in the larger locales the festivities would continue with a night of dancing.[29]

Freethinkers celebrated Paine as more than a champion of deism. His birthday orators would always start by addressing his fundamental role in the making of American freedom and the ensuing worldwide struggle for liberty. Refuting the "official" tale of 1776, which ignored Paine, they rendered a narrative of the Revolution that placed him at the heart of the story. They did so both to do him historical justice and to redeem the Revolution's grander meaning as a struggle for liberation, not simply from Britain but from all forms of tyranny, including the churchly variety.[30]

To some, Paine deserved more than verbal memorials. In 1837 (following New York's grandest Paine birthday celebration ever held, with three hundred attending the dinner and eight hundred the ball), Gilbert Vale, the editor of the leading freethought newspaper, the *Beacon*, announced plans to erect a monument to Paine in New Rochelle near the site of his cottage. John Frazee, a recognized sculptor, had volunteered his labor to the project, yet Vale still needed to raise $1,200 to accomplish it. Since the wealthier classes would have nothing to do with memorializing Paine, Vale secured the funds by soliciting donations from intellectuals, artisans, laborers, and small businessmen, many of them in the one-dollar range. At a ceremony on Thanksgiving Day 1839 he unveiled the monument. Of course, Vale knew well that words also mattered, and two years later he published a laudatory biography of Paine to counter Cheetham's.[31]

Whether clerics and conservatives believed their own claims or simply sought to legitimate their own endeavors and fund-raising, they accused freethinkers of "immorality and depravity" and vociferously warned that the spread of infidelity threatened to utterly undo American life. Some became so alarmed they called for a Christian political party and the "establishment of the constitutional primacy of Christianity." Once again preachers and tract writers targeted Paine. *The Spirit of the Pilgrims*, a monthly magazine founded by the Presbyterian minister and leader of New England revivalism Lyman Beecher, published "The Sketch of the Life of Thomas Paine," a truly vicious piece that repeated Cheetham's worst lies.[32]

The attacks on "infidelity" and Paine's memory expressed not only clerical and conservative nervousness about the nation's "spiritual and moral character" but also the apprehensions of the new northern financial, industrial, and professional bourgeoisie about the politics and aspirations of the laboring classes. Motivated by faith and fear, the former had endowed a "Benevolent Empire" of Christian missions, charities, and reform organizations, hoping in part to assuage, channel, and contain the rebelliousness of the latter. Though working people never inclined en masse toward religious skepticism, clergy and capitalists alike saw the movement as a threat. Workingmen constituted the majority of the freethought societies' members, and the societies regularly endorsed labor's demands. Even more critically, many of the leading freethinkers, such as Robert Dale Owen and Fanny Wright, were actively engaged in promoting, if not organizing, the workingmen's movement. And for it, too, Paine would serve as a primary source of ideas and inspiration.[33]

In Rochester, New York, and likely elsewhere, employers responded by insisting that their employees attend Sunday church services. But in Boston the elites went so far as to prosecute the local freethought leader, Abner Kneeland, for "blasphemy," which was still a crime in

Massachusetts. A former Universalist minister, the sixty-year-old Knee-land had settled in the city in 1831 and become "lecturer" to the First Society of Free Enquirers and founding publisher of the weekly *Boston Investigator*. Within a few years his congregation and readership had grown enormously, and Kneeland himself was speaking to siz-able audiences in towns all around New England. Nor did he limit himself to matters of reason and faith. From the start, he also es-poused the causes of labor and the equal rights of women.[34]

After trying to stamp out freethought from pulpit and press, Knee-land's enemies turned to the courts. In 1834—only weeks after the church was finally disestablished in Massachusetts and on the eve of Boston's first Paine birthday celebration (which would draw two hun-dred to dinner and three hundred to the ball that followed)—they se-cured an indictment against him for publishing articles that rejected biblical "truths" and the value of prayer. The whole thing was politically motivated. The judge at Kneeland's initial trial remarked to the jury that the *Boston Investigator* was read "by thousands of the poor and laboring classes of this community," and referring back to the English prosecu-tion of the publisher of *The Age of Reason*, he added that "the poor stand most in need of the consolations of religion, and the country has the deepest stake in their enjoying it . . . *because no man can be expected to be faithful to the authority of man, who revolts against the government of God*." A determined lot, Kneeland's persecutors would pursue him through several trials, during which time Kneeland himself continued to lecture and issue his newspaper, whose circulation grew ever larger. Fi-nally in 1838 the prosecution prevailed and Kneeland was sent to jail for sixty days. To some extent, his enemies had succeeded, for when he emerged he left Boston for good. But Kneeland did not recant. Accom-panied by his wife, he headed west to establish a freethought settlement in Iowa. And when he passed away in 1844, his burial chamber was adorned with portraits of Paine and other "infidels."[35]

Reacting to the advance of capitalism and industry, and realizing that the political parties of the day remained, at best, uninterested in their needs, northern workers—predominantly journeymen artisans (once again, Paine's own class of men)—began to organize and undertake collective action just after the middle of the 1820s. They formed trade unions, staged strikes and protests, set up labor presses, and created political parties of their own. But as much as material developments propelled them, they did not mobilize for narrow economic reasons or interests. Seeking time for family life, self-improvement, and civic participation, they demanded a reduction of the workday to ten hours. As well, they called for establishing free public schools (which looked toward ending child labor); ceasing the imprisonment of debtors; legislating protections for workers, such as guaranteeing their right to secure back wages from the estates of bankrupt or deceased employers; and terminating state-chartered monopolies, which fostered inequality and inhibited fair competition.[36]

With their American sensibilities heightened by the 1826 jubilee of national independence, artisans and laborers comprehended their mobilizations in patriotic terms. As they saw it, the revolutionary vision first articulated by Paine—in which prosperity progressed in tandem with democracy—stood seriously imperiled by the rise of an "aristocracy," a class that lacked titles, to be sure, but that was increasingly endowed with property, power, and privilege. Like the freethinkers, many of the workingmen's leaders were British émigrés who had no doubt about their movement's political lineage. At a dinner of the New York Committee of Mechanics and Working Men, the shoemaker Robert Walker recited the names of those whom they considered their political forebears: "But thanks! Immortal thanks! To the bold, daring and devoted spirits of a Jefferson, a Washington, a Franklin, an Adams, and a Paine, with the whole host of noble worthies, who placed in bold relief, and in practical operation, the 'Equal Rights of man, and his capability for self-government.'" In speeches and songs, workingmen celebrated Washington, Jefferson, and Paine.[37]

Derived from Jefferson and particularly Paine, the movement's most essential principles and perspectives—*democratic*-republicanism and an American "labor theory of value"—encouraged workingmen to conceive of themselves as the guarantors of freedom and the producers of society's wealth. In some ways the new labor movement recalled the Democratic-Republican societies of the 1790s, but workingmen activists articulated their campaigns against the ascendance of an American aristocracy much more emphatically in terms of class and class conflict. The editor of the *Mechanics' Free Press* exclaimed that America was dangerously dividing into "two distinct classes: the rich and the poor, the oppressor and the oppressed, those that live by their own labor and they that live by the labor of others." And Boston's "workie" leaders, A. H. Wood and Seth Luther, declared: "The work in which we are now engaged is neither more nor less than a contest between Money and Labor."[38]

The movement originated in Philadelphia in 1827, when hundreds of carpenters struck in pursuit of a ten-hour workday. Though the walkout failed, it inspired more than a dozen unions to band together in the Mechanics' Union of Trade Associations, out of which came the Philadelphia Working Men's Party. Soon artisans were organizing federations and parties in several dozen cities, even as the "Lowell mill girls" were organizing in Massachusetts.

While the new labor insurgency would last a decade, the workingmen's parties themselves would survive only a few years. Nonetheless both represented significant initiatives that had arisen from the ranks of the artisan classes, and attracted by the justice of their cause, a cohort of remarkable radical intellectuals and leaders emerged—American and immigrant, freethinker and Christian—including William Heighton, Thomas Skidmore, Robert Dale Owen, and George Henry Evans. Their theories and strategies varied considerably, causing serious rifts in some places. But in their respective ways they drew upon Paine's arguments and pushed workingmen's politics and political economy in original directions.

William Heighton played a fundamental role in organizing Philadelphia's workingmen's movement (both the labor federation and the party), and in 1828 he established its official newspaper, the *Mechanics' Free Press*. Born in England in 1800, he had come to America as a boy and, after the usual training, entered the shoemaking trade. Possibly advised by William Duane, the now senior, radical democratic editor of the *Aurora*, Heighton read Paine and various British economists, such as Robert Owen and David Ricardo, the latter of whom formally theorized the labor theory of value. Though Heighton would remain active in the Universalist Church, Paine's writings made him a rationalist and an antagonist of Christian revivalists. They also made him a democrat and helped him to imagine that working people could reduce the distance between America's ideals and its realities. The writings of the economists aided him in making critical sense of those realities.[39]

Heighton presented his own analysis and program in 1827 in *Address to the Members of the Trade Societies and to the Working Classes Generally*. Sounding almost like Karl Marx, he contended that working people were "the sole authors of . . . all the property or wealth . . . in existence." But the several nonproducing classes appropriated the products of their labor, "depriving" workers of "almost everything." The actual process of exploitation transpired through political and economic means. Controlling parties and governments, the nonproducing classes had licensed business and banking monopolies that favored members of their own classes. Making matters worse, "the system of competition" drove down wages and kept the producers themselves divided. Constituting the "majority of the nation," Heighton stated, workers needed to educate themselves about the causes of their impoverishment, unite across trade lines, and pursue democratic political action grounded in trade unionism and supported by labor periodicals.[40]

Thomas Skidmore played a comparable role in the New York movement, but he approached the plight of working people and the poor somewhat differently. Born in Vermont in 1790, Skidmore showed remarkable aptitudes as a child and at thirteen was appointed teacher in the local school. In the wake of the panic of 1819—after a youthful career as an itinerant teacher and, then, machinist in New Jersey— Skidmore, along with his wife, moved into New York, where he plied his skills and worked with John Quincy Adams's National Republicans. But in 1829 Skidmore became a radical when, in the midst of an economic downturn, employers tried to extend the workday beyond the ten hours that several New York trades had recently secured. Instrumental in organizing the mechanics' Committee of Fifty, out of which the New York Working Men's Party would emerge, he also succeeded in persuading the committee to endorse his call for "equal property to all adults."[41]

Like Heighton, Skidmore read Paine, Jefferson, and various English and American political economists; however, in contrast to Heighton, he concluded that the root cause of inequality and misery was not labor exploitation but the accumulation and transmission of property, which fundamentally divided society into rich and poor. Skidmore ardently believed in natural rights and democracy. And yet as much as he admired Jefferson and Paine for their insights and contributions, he criticized them for ignoring something most fundamental—the universal right to property. For as he argued, there can "in practice be no equal right to life, liberty and the pursuit of happiness if there is no equal right to property." Somewhere in the past the right to property had illegitimately and immorally turned into the power of the propertied, and he said it was now time to correct the tragedy.[42]

While serving on the Committee of Fifty, Skidmore published *The Rights of Man to Property!* Its title clearly indicated its connection to Paine—as did its publisher, Alexander Ming, Jr., whose father had been an old friend of Paine's—and its fuller title communicated its radical and original ambitions: *Being a Proposition to Make It Equal among the Adults of the Present Generation: and to Provide for Equal Transmission to Each Individual of Each Succeeding Generation, on Arriving at the Age of Maturity*. Paine had argued in *Agrarian Justice* that God had given the earth to humanity as a collective endowment; yet as much as he insisted that landowners were therefore obliged to pay a tax to the dispossessed, he had never called for the redistribution of property. Skidmore, seeking an egalitarian society in which there were "no lenders, no borrowers; no landlords, no tenants; no masters, no journeymen; no Wealth, no Want," would entertain nothing less. But like Paine, Skidmore was a democrat and in that spirit he called for a convention to rewrite New York's constitution.[43]

Skidmore's plan, and the responsiveness of the Committee of Fifty, frightened both conservative and moderate elements in the movement; among the leaders of the opposition to Skidmore was Robert Dale Owen. Apparently chastened by the New Harmony debacle, Dale Owen no longer subscribed to the radical political economy it represented. He now pressed for universal public education as the primary means to reform society—though his particular scheme, "state guardianship," showed just how utopian, if not authoritarian, he had become. Aided by Fanny Wright, he campaigned for a system in which children would be educated from two to sixteen years of age at state boarding schools, removed from the "corrupting environment" of their parents. The plan had admirers. But working people wanted public schools; they did not want to hand their children over to the government.

The Committee of Fifty ran its own "Working Men's" slate in the city elections of 1829, and though only one of their candidates won, they garnered a third of the votes cast and imagined greater things in the future. But Dale Owen and the moderates did not rejoice. Joining forces with the conservatives, they drove Skidmore and the radicals out of the party (initiating the left's tradition of self-destructive factionalism). Skidmore and his comrades tried to set up an alternative party but failed, and Skidmore himself died of an illness in 1832. Soon the conservatives drove out the moderates as well, and the party, after suffering defeat in the next election, expired. Folding up the Hall of Science, Robert Dale Owen returned to Indiana to pursue a career in politics and public service; Fanny Wright, after marrying in Europe, settled in Cincinnati, where she occasionally campaigned for the Democrats.

The workingmen's parties would rise and fall within just a few years, and their collapse was not due simply to factionalism. The appeal of Andrew Jackson's Democratic Party also hurt them. Jackson had begun to wage war against the monopoly of the government-chartered Bank of the United States, and concerned about the workingmen's "rebellion," the Democrats intensified their rhetoric about "the Democracy" or "the people" versus the "Aristocracy" and even incorporated some of the "workies'" demands into their own platform. Influenced in part by Paine's later writings, the workingmen's movement favored government action to support the equal rights and opportunities of working people. Still, it continued to share with the Democrats the essentially Jeffersonian and Painite ideal of limited government.[44]

Within the Jacksonian camp, workingmen activists organized a radical wing of the Democrats—the Equal Rights Party or "Locofocos"—and in this manner shaped the politics of northern state parties, especially New York's. And since many of the Locofoco leaders were freethinkers, Jackson and the Democrats soon found themselves accused of infidelity by their Whig opponents. (Whatever his reason, Jackson, it seems, privately admired Paine. Presumably informed of the plan for a Paine monument, he would remark in a letter that "Thomas Paine needs no monument made by hands; he has erected a monument in the hearts of all lovers of liberty.")[45]

The workingmen's movement survived the deaths of the working-men's parties, and in the mid-1830s many thousands of workers unionized, while labor federations in the northeastern cities formed the National Trades' Union. However, the Panic of 1837 devastated the economy and, with it, workers' capacities to organize. Still, the workies' ideals and aspirations did not die but persisted in the initia-tives of a generation of democratic intellectuals who would continue to draw upon Paine's arguments.

Movement veterans Orestes Brownson and George Henry Evans would try to keep workingmen's issues on the public agenda through the most difficult years. Born in 1803 to a poor Vermont family, Brown-son is often recalled for his lifelong religious quest, which led him from Presbyterianism through Universalism, freethought, Unitarianism, Transcendentalism, and finally in 1844 to Catholicism. Though he ulti-mately became a political conservative, Brownson, who trained as a printer, spent the early 1830s in New York alongside Robert Dale Owen and Fanny Wright, during which time he also apparently developed an appreciation for Paine. Then, declaring himself a Unitarian, Brownson moved to the Boston area, where he preached and issued the pro-Locofoco *Boston Quarterly Review*, in whose pages in 1840 he published "The Laboring Classes," which discussed the capital-labor relationship as a form of "slavery," censured churches and government, and pro-jected a class war between "the people and their masters."[46]

Born in England in 1805, George Henry Evans came to the United States as a boy and trained as a printer in upstate New York, during which time he read Paine and Jefferson and became a freethinker and a democrat. Moving to the city of New York in 1828, he allied himself with Robert Dale Owen and founded the *Working Man's Advocate*—in an early issue of which he published "The Working Men's Declaration of Independence," which he himself had drafted. The newspaper be-came the movement's leading periodical, and Evans one of the move-ment's central figures. Worn out by politics, however, he left the city in 1835 and settled on a farm in New Jersey. There he reflected on his experiences and the plight of working people—and also prepared a low-priced, two-volume edition of Paine's political writings, which im-portantly included *Agrarian Justice*. In 1840, refreshed and outfitted with a new program to address labor's needs, he returned to the fray.[47]

Launching a new newspaper, *The Radical*, Evans worked at putting together an American land reform movement and in 1844 he and his followers (former workies like John Commerford and agrarian utopians such as Lewis Masquerier) created the National Reform Association, whose slogan became "Vote Yourself a Farm." Advocating neither taxing nor dispossessing landowners, Evans's plan, while not as radical as those of either Paine or Skidmore, owed something to both of them. Specifically, Evans called for the distribution of public lands to those who would settle and farm them, a scheme he expected would benefit not only those workers who received holdings but also those who remained in the eastern cities, for it would doubtlessly reduce the labor supply and drive up wages. Passing away in 1856, Evans would never see his program enacted, yet his campaign laid the groundwork for the Homestead Act of 1862.[48]

The revival of Paine's memory also found its way into the teaching of American history. Some textbook authors, particularly theologians, continued to skip right over Paine; others acknowledged his role in the Revolution but noted that he had "debased himself as an infidel." Still others, such as the former New Hampshire Republican congressman Salma Hale, told forthrightly of how Paine was "universally read, and most highly admired" and of how the "effect of [*Common Sense*] in making converts, was astonishing, and probably without precedent in the annals of literature."[49]

Nonetheless most intellectuals, including many liberals of the day, would continue to publicly distance themselves from Paine even as they culled ideas and inspiration from him. The New England Transcendentalists, Ralph Waldo Emerson, Theodore Parker, and Henry David Thoreau, regularly tried to avoid direct association with Paine, but those critics who accused them of having become "infidels" or "Painites" were actually rather perceptive.[50]

Rebelling against Unitarianism, which still embraced scripture and miracles, the Transcendentalists expressed a more intense concern for spiritual questions than did the deists, whose own great "spirit" was Reason. They also differed on the question of God's "presence"—the deists saw God as having effectively stepped back from the Creation,

while the Transcendentalists perceived God as pervasively "imma-
nent" in and "transcendent" of it. But they shared the belief that the
"universe was created by a benevolent God whose handiwork is apparent in the perfect and harmonious operation of the laws of nature."[51]

Paine's own arguments seem to have shaped the Transcendentalists' professed antagonism toward a government that accepted slavery
and would pursue expansionist wars. Thoreau himself nodded to Jefferson and Paine in *Civil Disobedience*: "I heartily accept the motto,—
'That government is best which governs least'; and I should like to see
it acted up to more rapidly and systematically. Carried out, it finally
amounts to this, which I also believe,—'That government is best
which governs not all'; and when men are prepared for it, that will be
the kind of government they will have."[52]

Paine's words definitely heartened Emerson as he left Unitarianism
and rejected the hegemony of the New England Whig establishment.
In *Nature*, his very first book (published in 1836), Emerson repudiated
the Whigs' Burkean uses of the past to enjoin popular deference to tradition and the contemporary order of things. With Webster's 1825
Bunker Hill speech specifically in mind, Emerson alluded to and
quoted from Paine to suggest a different engagement with history:

> Our Age is retrospective. It builds the *sepulchers* of the fathers.
> It writes biographies, histories, and criticism. The foregoing
> generations beheld God and nature face to face; we, through
> their eyes. Why should we not have a poetry and philosophy of
> insight and not of tradition, and a religion by revelation to us,
> and not the history of theirs? . . . *The sun shines today also* . . .
> There are new lands, new men, new thoughts. Let us demand
> our own works and laws and worship.

In contrast to Webster, who had resurrected the Founders for the sake
of authority past and present, Emerson did so (as Lincoln would) to
persuade his fellow Americans that they too could act in revolutionary
ways. (Emerson would say of Webster that he "knew the patriots of '76
well, but would not have known the patriots of his own day if he had
met them in the street.") And though he did so in a less blatant manner than the freethinkers and workies, Emerson too made Paine the

spokesman for the founding generation. Moreover, just as *Common Sense* had led the way to July 4, *Nature* paved the way to "The American Scholar," Emerson's 1837 Phi Beta Kappa address at Harvard, his celebrated "Declaration of Intellectual Independence" from the "courtly muses of Europe." Finally, in 1844 Emerson would acknowledge Paine's encouragement: "Each man . . . is a tyrant in tendency, because he would impose his ideas on others. Jesus would absorb the race; but Tom Paine . . . helps humanity by resisting this exuberance of power."[53]

Another cohort of intellectuals—more politically engaged and less reticent about revealing their attachment to Paine—formed in New York around the *United States Magazine and Democratic Review* and its founding editor, John O'Sullivan. Known collectively as "Young America," those who contributed to the *Democratic Review* or moved in its circle, like those who participated in the contemporary European movements—Young Germany, Young Italy, Young Ireland, and others like them—were democrats and nationalists who wanted to break free from the bonds of the past.[54]

Connected to the New York Locofocos, the twenty-five-year-old Irish American O'Sullivan, an admirer of Paine, had great intentions for the *Democratic Review*. As he announced in the first issue in 1837, the magazine would advance "that high and holy *democratic principle* which was designed to be the fundamental element of the new social and political system created by the American experiment," insist upon limited government ("The best government is that which governs least"), *and* support reforms that favored freedom, equality, and opportunity.[55]

Yet O'Sullivan intended the *Democratic Review* to be more than a political periodical. Eager to contest the Whigs' "aristocratic" monopoly of American letters—represented by periodicals like the *North American Review* in Boston—O'Sullivan wanted to reconstruct knowledge. "All history has to be rewritten," he argued, "political science and the whole scope of all moral truth have to be considered and illustrated in the light of the democratic principle." Especially, he promised, the *Democratic Review* would seek to fashion an American literature, one that would reflect and enhance American democratic life.[56]

Ambitious and energetic, O'Sullivan lined up a talented roster of contributors. Novelists, poets, and essayists, they included Nathaniel Hawthorne, William Cullen Bryant, Edgar Allan Poe, George Bancroft, Orestes Brownson, James Russell Lowell, W. A. Jones, Walt Whitman, and (though he never actually published in the magazine, he was very much a part of its circle) Herman Melville. O'Sullivan also recruited the New York bibliophile Evert A. Duyckinck, another Paine admirer and the founding editor of the "Library of American Books," to serve as literary editor.[57]

In spite of the Panic of 1837, O'Sullivan and his associates exuded optimism about America's prospects, and in that vein Paine's arguments regularly resounded through the *Democratic Review*. In "The Great Nation of Futurity," O'Sullivan wrote of the "birth" of the nation as the "beginning of a new history," both for America and for the world. Observing that the American people originated from diverse nations, he contended that American nationality and patriotism were built not upon "soil or ancestry" but on the ideals of liberty and equality. And while granting that obstacles remained, he insisted that American working people would continue to improve agriculture and manufacturing and extend freedom, equality, and democracy. Sadly, Paine's hatred of slavery did not find its way into the magazine (probably for fear of antagonizing the slaveholders who constituted the Democratic Party's southern wing).[58]

In 1842 the editors of the *Democratic Review* openly registered their admiration for Paine by publishing W. A. Jones's "Political Pamphleteering." Though Jones would "have nothing to do" with Paine's religion, he had every kind of praise for Paine's political pen and proposed that Paine's "obscurity" may have been due not simply to his having written *The Age of Reason*, but also to the fact that he wrote "to and for . . . that 'many-headed monster,' the people." Noting that before Paine "the mass of laboring poor were without a representative," he averred that Paine was "the people's writer—expressing their views, as well as his own, but then better than any man could. Clear, plain, explicit, close, compact, he could be understood by all."[59]

Whig men of letters quickly responded. The editors of the *North American Review* published an adamantly hostile article on Paine that tore into his life and work. The unnamed author not only repeated the standard lies and rendered the predictable attack on *The Age of Reason*. He also dismissed the political value of *Common Sense*, adding that "judged by any originary standard of criticism it is beneath praise."[60]

Like Paine, the Young Americans saw the United States in exceptional but not necessarily exclusive terms. To them the nation stood in the vanguard of a global democratic struggle, endowed with the mission of assuring that struggle's progress and ultimate triumph. Yet they did not specify the means by which America was to fulfill its mission. Did it entail serving as an example, lending assistance, intervening directly, or something more? O'Sullivan himself was no "isolationist." In 1839 (likely influenced by Paine's *Letter to the Abbé Raynal*), he proposed a "Congress of Nations" to advance international peace and "republicanize the world." However, in line with the Democratic Party platform, his nationalism overwhelmed his internationalism, to the point where by 1845 he fully equated the United States with Democracy and reduced the progress of the latter to the interests of the former. Coining the term "Manifest Destiny," he still had in mind the extension of democracy but increasingly emphasized territorial expansion. And soon enough, jingoists were citing Manifest Destiny to justify not only the annexation of Texas and Oregon but also war against Mexico and military adventurism in Central America and the Caribbean.[61]

Manifest Destiny divided the Young Americans, and in the 1850s "Young America" would denote specifically those who supported aggressive expansion. (O'Sullivan himself followed a bizarre path that ultimately led him to sympathize with the Confederacy in the Civil War.) The group's original Painite vision lived on, however, in the labors of the nation's greatest democratic writers, Melville and Whitman. While they differed considerably, both believed in the nation's radical purpose and promised and strove to develop a literature worthy of them. And to both, Paine was democracy's first champion.[62]

In a patriotic spirit similar to Paine's, Melville declared: "Americans are the peculiar chosen people—the Israel of our time; we bear the ark of the liberties of the world." Indeed, Melville valued Paine's writings. Introducing his friend and comrade Jack Chase, a man he truly looked up to, he wrote in *White-Jacket*: "Though bowing to naval discipline afloat . . . ashore, he was a stickler for the Rights of Man, and the liberties of the world." A grandson of patriots, Melville also drew upon *Common Sense* ("Political republics should be the asylum for the persecuted of all nations") and shared Paine's appreciation of the American people's diversity and originality. "There is something in the contemplation of the mode in which America has been settled," he wrote in a very Painite vein, "that in a noble breast should forever extinguish the prejudices of national dislikes. Settled by the people of all nations, all nations may claim her for their own. You can not spill a drop of American blood without spilling the blood of the whole world."[63]

Though never a political activist, Melville was a radical democrat. Marking how "in all despotic governments . . . throne and altar . . . go hand-in-hand," he lauded America's separation of church and state and lamented that it did not extend to the nation's naval vessels. He esteemed the working classes, applauding "that democratic dignity" that was self-evidently "in the arm that wields a pick or drives a spike." And yet Melville was not naïve. He recognized the perils ahead and felt that his authorial responsibilities included speaking the truth to his fellow citizens. Whatever else he intended in *Moby-Dick*, he surely crafted the narrative of Ahab and the crew of the *Pequod* as a warning against the dangers of political demagoguery. And in later years, when he would grow increasingly anxious about America's future, he would more than once draw upon Paine's memory to admonish his fellow citizens about the corruption and decline of the democratic spirit.[64]

Artisan, teacher, journalist, and poet, Walt Whitman would often speak of Paine, almost boastfully so. He would tell how his father had met the great radical, how he himself had met Paine's old friend Colonel John Fellows, and—noting that he had delivered the Paine birthday oration in Philadelphia in 1877—how "determined" he always was to do all he could to "help set the memory of Paine right." But his affection for Paine involved more than a desire to redeem his memory.[65]

Sharing Paine's feelings for America, Whitman wrote: "The Americans of all nations at any time upon the earth have probably the fullest poetical nature. The United States themselves are essentially the greatest poem." And he shared Paine's confidence in the common people, who represented "the real heart of this mighty city [New

York]," and "under and behind all the bosh of the regular politicians," there burned in America's working class "the divine fire which more or less, during all the ages, has only waited a chance to leap forth and confound the calculations of tyrants, hunkers, and all their tribe."[66]

Interpreting, amplifying, and projecting himself beyond Paine, Whitman aspired to accomplish through poetry what Paine had accomplished through prose. Arguably, Whitman longed to be Paine. He wanted to articulate the American experience and make manifest the nation's still-unrealized democratic potential. He wanted to unify Americans to confront and transcend the crises of their own day, especially the deepening divisions of section and class, and he yearned for an organic connection with his fellow citizens. "The proof of a poet," he asserted, "is that his country absorbs him as affectionately as he has absorbed it."[67]

Melville and Whitman were not alone in their democratic affections and inclinations—or in their attachments to Paine—and arguably no author felt them more intensely than George Lippard of Philadelphia. A fascinating and energetic figure, Lippard wrote twenty-three books and hundreds of periodical pieces, produced several plays, lectured widely, founded a publishing house, edited his own weekly newspaper, and organized a fraternal order of workers, before dying of tuberculosis in 1854, at a mere thirty-two years of age. And though he would never attain the Olympian status of Melville and Whitman, he secured a greater following in his lifetime than either of them would in theirs.[68]

The most popular writer of the 1840s, Lippard was also surely the most radical, in word and deed. Inspired by ideals and figures from Christianity and American history, especially the Founding Fathers, he campaigned against capitalism as well as slavery and the oppression of women, helped to establish cooperative stores for working people, and in 1849 organized the Brotherhood of the Union, a secretive, revolutionary workers organization. Intended to "espouse the cause of all the masses, and battle . . . against corrupt Bankers . . . Land Monopolists . . . and all Monied Oppressors," the Brotherhood had more than twenty thousand members in 140 "circles" around the country within one year of its founding and would influence the later formation of the Knights of Labor. Lippard even conceived of literature in political terms: "LITERATURE merely considered as an ART is a despicable thing . . . A literature

which does not work practically, for the advancement of a social reform, or which is too dignified or too good to picture the wrongs of the
great mass of humanity, is just good for nothing at all." He himself became famous for two very distinct kinds of writing: sensationalist,
shockingly graphic, almost surreal works in which he "exposed" the
decadence, depravities, and depredations of Philadelphia's elites; and
romantic legends and patriotic historical tales—the former intended
to outrage, the latter to inspire.[69]

Born in 1822, Lippard was raised by two elderly aunts following the
death of his mother and a farm accident that incapacitated his father.
He grew up despising inequality and hypocrisy. Planning on a career as
a Methodist preacher, he enrolled at a New York college in 1837 but
quickly left, appalled by the selfish behavior of his ministerial teachers.
Hoping next for a career in the law, he returned to Philadelphia and
gained employment as a legal assistant. Disgusted by professional practices, he abandoned that plan as well. Further propelling his politics
and eventual writing, he lived among the city's laboring poor and came
to know personally the deprivations they suffered. He first made a living at a penny newspaper as a reporter and short fiction writer. Then, at
the *Citizen Soldier*, a weekly paper, he began penning historical "legends" from the Bible and the American Revolution, such as "Jesus the
Democrat" and "The Battle-Day at Brandywine." He also began to publish novels. Between the books and the stories, he garnered a growing
audience and income, both of which increased dramatically with the
publication in 1845 of *The Quaker City*, his most successful best-seller.
The work sold sixty thousand copies within twelve months and during
the next several years thirty thousand copies annually. But in a spirit
similar to Paine's, he applied his royalties to radical causes and as a consequence never became rich.[70]

Though a critic of churches and clerics, Lippard remained a devout
Christian. Still, in spite of his disagreements with *The Age of Reason*, he
worked to redeem not only Paine's political legacy but also his reputation. Speaking in Philadelphia in honor of Paine's 115th birthday,
Lippard, in his inimitable way, rendered the writing of *Common Sense*
as a tale that might yet show up in a Hollywood film: It's 1775. Washington, Adams, Rush, and Franklin are sitting around a table late in the
night. A "solitary lamp" lights the room. The men agonize about the

course of the war and what they are fighting for, but "shudder at that big word, that chokes their throats to speak—independence." Suddenly, an unexpected visitor is announced. A stranger to all save Franklin, Paine enters the room. The conversation continues, and the newcomer, sensing their anxieties, presents his vision of America as a free and republican nation, almost instantly turning their fears into hopes; after which, at their urging, he returns to his "garret" and, with "that unfailing quill in his hand," writes the words "that shall burn into the brains of kings like arrows winged with fire and pointed with vitriol." Recounting the rest of Paine's "heroic" life and labors, and decrying the unjust treatment accorded his memory, Lippard concluded by asking, "Who would not sooner be Thomas Paine there before the bar of Jesus, with all his virtues and errors about him, than one of the misguided bigots who refused his bones a grave?"[71]

Paine's first major political statement in America had been his call for the emancipation of the slaves, and his later arguments in *Rights of Man* ("Man has no property in man") were rightly understood as also demanding slavery's abolition. However—aside from the "Oration of Thomas Paine" (an anonymously written call for the end of slavery published in a Washington, D.C., newspaper in July 1819), the antislavery campaign that emerged in the United States in the 1820s and 1830s did not cite Paine as one of its forebears. Freethinkers and workies opposed slavery, but the men and women who constituted the early abolitionist movement were usually religious folk who could not abide Paine's "infidelity."[72]

Nevertheless, American abolitionism drew not only upon Christianity but also on the natural rights tradition, and even at the outset Paine's influence was evident. In Rochester, William C. Bloss—a remarkable man who advocated Christian evangelicalism, labor activism, and black emancipation—titled his abolitionist newspaper the *Rights of Man*. In New York, while white workers organized around the Committee of Fifty, the African American preacher and coeditor of *Freedom's Journal*, Samuel Cornish, was starting up the newspaper *The Rights of All*. In Boston, a free African American from North Carolina, David Walker, apparently moved by the Bible, the egalitarian spirit of the Declaration of Independence, *and* the revolutionary example of Paine's

Common Sense, issued his pamphlet, *An Appeal, in Four Articles, Together with a Preamble, to the Colored Citizens of the World, but in Particular, and Very Expressly to Those of the United States of America,* calling upon black slaves to rise up "against their white oppressors." And when William Lloyd Garrison launched his newspaper *The Liberator* in 1831 in Boston, he placed a version of Paine's words on its masthead: "Our Country Is the World—Our Countrymen Are Mankind."[73]

The antislavery movement first took shape as a drive to "repatriate" manumitted slaves to Africa, and the American Colonization Society established Monrovia (Liberia) in 1822 as a settlement for freed blacks. However, such schemes were attacked both by southerners (who opposed any kind of freedom for slaves) and by black and white northerners (who saw them as unjust and wrong-headed). Finally, after eleven years had passed, abolitionists organized nationally in favor of "immediate" emancipation by creating the small but aggressive American Anti-Slavery Society. Operating like a religious movement, the society recruited agents—usually zealous young men, often with ministerial training—to preach the cause and convert Americans to it. And they had no easy assignment. Coming in the wake of the 1831 Virginia slave rebellion led by Nat Turner, the society's formation and missionary activities engendered a powerful southern pro-slavery movement, as well as hostility and occasionally mob violence in the North, where people fearfully imagined masses of uneducated black workers flooding into their cities. Yet, convinced of the righteousness of their cause, abolitionist agents and lecturers passionately pursued their campaigns, and by the end of the decade membership in the society had reached nearly 250,000.[74]

The most commanding personality in the society, and the movement generally, was that of William Lloyd Garrison. Born in 1805 to a poor Massachusetts family, Garrison was raised, along with his siblings, solely by his Baptist mother, for his father had abandoned the family when he was only three. Given their meager resources, he left school early and apprenticed as a shoemaker, a cabinetmaker, and finally as a printer and newspaperman. Educating himself along the way, he fervently believed both in the grand idea of the Declaration of Independence, that "all men are created equal," and (after meeting the religious communitarian John Humphrey Noyes in 1837) in "salvation

from sin" through the pursuit of "perfectionism." Ever sensitive to oppression, Garrison started out as a "colonizationist" but quickly declared for "immediate" emancipation in 1829, when he moved to
Baltimore to work for an antislavery paper and witnessed the degrada-
tion of slavery firsthand. Returning to Boston soon thereafter, he
founded the *Liberator* (which depended heavily on the support of free
blacks in the North), worked to establish the New England and American Anti-Slavery Societies, and spent the 1830s endeavoring to impress his increasingly radical and absolutist positions on them.[75]

Garrison's fire and enthusiasm would energize the society, but also
divide it, as in 1839 when it split in two over the stance abolitionists
should take on the questions of electoral politics and the rights and
roles of women. Garrison and his followers, who would retain control,
conceived of the abolitionist cause in truly religious terms as a crusade
to be pursued through "moral suasion." They simply would not entertain political campaigns, because parties and elections presumed com-
promises on matters of principle. At the same time, because they
insisted on freedom for all, the Garrisonians strongly supported equal
rights for women, starting with their full participation in the society.
Garrison himself made a point of sitting with the American women
delegates at the World Anti-Slavery convention in London in 1840, after the convention directors prohibited them from joining in the business of the meeting on account of their sex. Garrison's opponents,
however, thought otherwise about both politics and women; withdrawing from the society, they set up the American and Foreign Anti-
Slavery Society and endorsed the new Liberty Party.[76]

Women were always a major force in the antislavery movement,
and the issue of their role in the society reverberated beyond the organization itself. Fearing that such involvements might corrupt "female character," orthodox New England clergy issued a pastoral letter
in 1837 expressing their anxiety. And in response the Garrisonian
Maria Weston Chapman, with a wink to Paine, composed a little poem
she titled "The Times That Try Men's Souls."[77]

In the course of the 1840s Garrison and his comrades, such as Lydia Maria Child, Parker Pillsbury, Henry Clarke Wright, and Wendell
Phillips, became ever more insurgent on matters of both religion and
politics. Exasperated by the churches' toleration of the "sin" of slavery,

they voiced increasingly anticlerical views. And rejecting the U.S. Constitution because it accepted slavery, the society in 1843 endorsed a position of "NO UNION WITH SLAVEHOLDERS!" that essentially called for northern secession from the Union to separate the Free states from the Slave.[78]

Paine would not have endorsed the breakup of the Union or, for that matter, an uncompromising stance on electoral politics. Nonetheless, as their radicalism intensified, he became an even more attractive figure to the Garrisonians. Garrison himself claimed he did not read Paine until 1845, but the words on the masthead of the *Liberator*, along with some of Garrison's own earlier remarks, indicate that he must have been familiar with at least some of Paine's political writings prior to that time. In any case, after 1845 he said that studying Paine had helped to further liberate him from the "thralldom of tradition and authority."[79]

Garrison never disavowed Christianity, but orthodox churchmen charged that he had started to "out-Paine Tom Paine," and with some perceptiveness, by the 1850s both the black abolitionist Frederick Douglass and a host of pro-slavery advocates were accusing the American Anti-Slavery Society of accommodating Painite infidels. A baker's daughter, Lydia Maria Child, who gained renown as a writer of children's works and a polemicist for abolition and women's issues, apparently admired Paine for his attacks on "aristocracy" and treated *The Age of Reason* with deep respect (as her personally constructed "Eclectic Bible," with excerpts from Paine, would later show). Also from an artisan background, Parker Pillsbury first trained for the Congregational ministry but in 1839, impressed by Garrison, enlisted as an abolitionist agent. More vehement than his mentor in opposing electoral politics and supporting "feminism," he would follow a more radical religious path as well, which, while serving as a freethought lecturer after the Civil War, included speaking on Paine's life and work. And Henry Clarke Wright pursued a similar course. Leaving the Congregational ministry for abolitionism and pacifism, he too would move in an anticlerical direction in the 1840s and 1850s and in 1870 deliver and distribute the speech "The Merits of Jesus Christ and the Merits of Thomas Paine."[80]

One of America's great nineteenth-century reformers and orators, Wendell Phillips would campaign for emancipation, racial equality, women's rights, and labor reform. However, in contrast to other Garrisonians, he laid siege to slavery and other tyrannies in the language of democratic-republicanism, not in that of the biblical prophets. Coming from a family of Boston Brahmins and Federalists, Phillips as a boy had revered both the Founding Fathers and various English figures, especially Edmund Burke, whom he considered a model "scholar and public leader." But as Phillips turned radical, he embraced Paine as well. He even took to copying Paine's words into his commonplace book, and in 1870 he would, recalling Paine's *Agrarian Justice*, propose a plan for a "graduated tax on real estate income."[81]

Many of the early and most prominent figures of the women's rights movement found inspiration in Paine, including Lucretia Mott, Elizabeth Cady Stanton, Ernestine Rose, and Susan B. Anthony. And though Paine never called for enfranchising women, even on that issue they would discover words of his to empower their efforts.[82]

All of the major first-generation activists of the movement came from antislavery backgrounds, and many began their careers in the abolitionist cause. In fact, the very idea for the movement originated in the meeting of Lucretia Mott and Elizabeth Cady Stanton at the 1840 World Antislavery Convention in London. Prohibited, unlike their husbands, from participating in the deliberations, the two women sat together in the gallery and quickly became friends. A Quaker minister who followed Elias Hicks in the faith and Garrison in the antislavery cause, the forty-seven-year-old Mott was not one to readily accept a marginal role, and the well-educated, newly married, twenty-five-year-old Stanton, though more secular in outlook, saw in Mott the kind of woman she wanted to become. Together they discussed convening a women's rights convention back in the United States, and before parting Mott encouraged her younger companion to read Wollstonecraft and Paine.[83]

Soon preoccupied by motherhood (she ultimately bore seven children), Stanton could not immediately pursue the planned meeting. But she did not abandon the idea, and in 1848, with the assistance of Mott and a few friends, she organized the now-celebrated Seneca Falls Convention. Conceivably influenced by *Common Sense*, Stanton herself drafted, and won approval for, the gathering's "Declaration of

Sentiments," which she modeled directly on the Declaration of Independence. Demanding political equality, it would become the manifesto of the women's suffrage movement.[84]

Stanton would turn to Paine at various times in the coming decades of struggle. A "militant anticleric," she responded to charges of "infidelity" in 1855 by reading *The Life and Writings of Thomas Paine*, along with works by Fanny Wright—and she would describe both Paine and Wright as "rational and beautiful writers." Later, following the Civil War, when Stanton herself would become an engaged freethinker, she not only befriended men like Robert Ingersoll and Moncure Conway, both of whom labored at redeeming Paine's memory, but also prepared *The Woman's Bible*, a controversial project reflecting Paine's critique of "revelation."[85]

Probably the most fascinating yet almost forgotten figure of the early women's movement—as well as its most ardent Painite—was the Polish Jewish immigrant Ernestine Rose. In the *History of Woman Suffrage*, edited by Stanton and Anthony, L. E. Barnard would write, "How much of the freedom they now enjoy, the women of America owe to this noble Polish woman, can not be estimated, for moral influences are too subtle for measurement." And Walt Whitman, who would set some of Rose's words to poetry, called her "big, rich, gifted, expansive—in body a poor sickly thing: a strong breath would blow her away—but with a head full of brains."[86]

Born Ernestine Louise Siismondi Potowski in 1810 to a rabbinical family, Rose showed her independence early. Afforded a good education, she turned away from Judaism because it failed to accord women equal status to men. Later she rejected her father's choice for her of a husband. And in 1827—following the death of her mother and the remarriage of her father—she left home on her own and headed west across Europe. Arriving in London in 1831, she set up a business producing household fragrances and joined in the Owenist cooperative and trade union movement, becoming friends with Robert Owen himself. Through the movement she also met William Rose, a silversmith, whom she married in 1836, and that same year the two of them emigrated to America.[87]

Settling in New York, William immediately found work, and Ernestine again made and marketed "cologne waters." Both also soon got involved in the freethought community, which included organizing the annual Paine festivities. Based on her remarks at those and related events, Ernestine, with William's support, rapidly rose to prominence as a public speaker. Paine was clearly her hero, and almost every year, right into the early 1860s, she would deliver a major address at his birthday celebrations (a few of which would draw well over six hundred people in the 1850s). In 1852 she said with great affection and purpose:

> There is no need to eulogize Thomas Paine. His life-long devotion to the cause of freedom; his undaunted, unshrinking advocacy of truth; his deep seated hatred to kingly and priestly despotism, are his best eulogies. He was the architect of his own monument . . . a monument that will last as long as the memory of man . . . But to honor the memory of Thomas Paine . . . We must endeavor to carry out what he so nobly began, for his principles were not for one age or nation, but for all.

Inspired both by Paine's life and writings and by the Declaration of Independence, Rose would passionately call upon Americans to live up to their professed ideals, and friend and foe alike recognized her as a feisty debater and tireless crusader. Opposing every form of oppression, she traveled the country in the 1840s appearing on freethought, Owenist, married women's property rights, and (alongside the likes of Garrison, Emerson, and Douglass) abolitionist platforms. After 1848 she also instinctively threw herself into the struggle for the vote, bringing her experiences as an immigrant Jew, freethinker, artisan, and socialist with her—aspects of which definitely perturbed some of her native-born Protestant comrades. Nevertheless, given her organizing and speaking skills, Rose would often be chosen to chair the agenda-setting "business committee" at national and state conventions, and even those whom she rattled—Stanton, most notably—would be influenced by her. And even more than Mott or Stanton, it may have been Rose, during an 1854 lecture tour of Baltimore, Washington, and Philadelphia, with Susan B. Anthony serving as her assistant, who cultivated Anthony's own appreciation of Paine.[88]

In sermons, publications, and town hall deliberations, attacks on Paine's memory continued right through the 1850s—no doubt further instigated by the Painite enthusiasms of radicals and reformers. At the University of North Carolina pro-slavery students burned Paine's works in bonfires along with those of Voltaire and Rousseau. And in Philadelphia the city council snubbed the offer of a portrait of Paine for Independence Hall.[89]

In these same years, however, Paine's memory also received increasingly favorable attention—and not just from the expected parties. Immigration played a part. The refugee flow from Germany and Central Europe in the wake of the aborted revolutions of 1848 rapidly augmented the number of men and women eager to honor and emulate Paine. Ever since 1776 German liberals and radicals had held him dear to their hearts, and those who came to America later continued to do so, perhaps even more than before. In Cincinnati, Milwaukee, Chicago, St. Louis, and the many smaller towns of Wisconsin, Minnesota, and the "Hill Country" of Texas where German American communities formed, '48ers created cultural and political societies whose activities included well-attended Paine birthday festivals, whose participants celebrated Paine as the greatest "American patriot, international revolutionary, and freethinker."[90]

Additionally, new editions of Paine's works appeared, and historians started to approach Paine's contributions in a more critical yet appreciative way. As early as 1840 the Methodist theologian Nathan Bangs felt compelled to distinguish between Paine's political and religious writings and to acknowledge the "eminent services he had rendered to his country during the war of revolution." But now, even as they too distinguished between the revolutionary Paine and the infidel Paine, both popular and scholarly writers—from Benjamin Lossing to Henry S. Randall—ever more strongly emphasized Paine's contributions to the making of American freedom. And when in 1860 the veteran Jacksonian Democrat George Bancroft published the volume of his grand *History of the United States* on the American Revolution, he devoted seven pages to Paine and *Common Sense*.[91]

Truly, diverse Americans were showing a fresh interest in Paine. Textile operatives in the Philadelphia area formed the Associated Working Women and Men, also known as the "Jubilee Association of the Daughters and Sons of Toil," a new kind of labor union, both Christian and radical, whose saints included Moses, Jesus, and Paine. In a different vein, the keynote speaker at the July 1859 dedication ceremony for the "First Free Bridge across the Connecticut River" recalled Paine the "stay maker, privateersman, exciseman, school-master, poet, politician, legislator and arch infidel" and described his bridge project "as one of the boldest experiments in engineering ever executed." That same month in Boston the elite *Atlantic Monthly* magazine published the first of three lengthy pieces on Paine's career. "The democratic movement of the last eighty years," the author wrote, "be it a 'finality,' or only a phase of progress towards a more perfect state, is the grand historical fact of modern times, and Paine's name is intimately connected with it." And in Virginia, while preparing for their assault on the federal arsenal at Harper's Ferry, the militant abolitionist John Brown and his men read *The Age of Reason* in their free time.[92]

With such developments apparently in mind, the Unitarian minister and abolitionist Moncure D. Conway (who would later publish the first major Paine biography) observed in his 1860 Paine birthday address in Cincinnati that "Thomas Paine's life up to 1809, when he died, is interesting; but Thomas Paine's life from that time to 1860 is more than interesting—it is thrilling!" And possessed of an even more fantastic notion of how Paine lived on, spiritualists—whose movement had grown rapidly since the late 1840s, especially among liberal and progressive-minded folk—had taken to "channeling" him more often than any other historical figure.[93]

Without doubt the extensive attention to Paine and his words owed tremendously to the struggles and redemptive efforts of radicals and reformers. But it also reflected something more. Facing deepening crises—the most perilous, a sectional fight that fully threatened to destroy the Republic—Americans were naturally seeking to connect anew with the very making of the nation. As Lincoln knew, and as increasing numbers of his fellow citizens were instinctively discovering, no one had articulated the American imperative—the exceptional purpose and promise of the United States—more effectively than Thomas Paine.

6

WHEN, IN COUNTRIES THAT
ARE CALLED CIVILIZED

As the United States approached its one hundredth birthday in 1876, Americans made plans to commemorate the Founding and celebrate the Republic. They would publish books, erect monuments, and hold dinners, assemblies, and parades. Congress would authorize the staging of an International Exhibition in Philadelphia to display America's accomplishments in the "Arts, Manufactures and Products of the Soil and Mine." Though only a decade had passed since the catastrophe of 1861–65 and depression currently gripped the economy, Americans had reason to celebrate. The country had grown tremendously since 1776. The Civil War had resolved the crisis of the House Divided absolutely in favor of the Union. The Homestead Act of 1862 promised fresh opportunities in the West. And recent scientific and technological advances heralded an age of material progress.

Yet those who organized the official Centennial intended their activities not only to recall the nation's past and highlight its achievements and prospects, but also to promote acceptance of the country's developing postwar order and bolster the standing and authority of its governing elites.

As Lincoln had implored, the Civil War had become a second American Revolution. It had led to the abolition of slavery and the extension of citizenship to the emancipated. Moreover, it had revived hopes, if not expectations, for other radical changes. Prominent liberal Unitarians and freethinkers, led by Octavius Brooks Frothingham, a follower of the late Theodore Parker, established the Free Religious Association in 1867 to cultivate a rational and egalitarian "religion of humanity" and, in response to renewed talk of a "Christian amendment" to the Constitution, to defend and advance the separation of church and state. Women's rights activists, outraged by the Fourteenth and Fifteenth Amendments' failure to enfranchise women, created two organizations in 1869, the American Woman Suffrage Association and the more radical (though nativist and racist) National Woman Suffrage Association, led by Elizabeth Cady Stanton and Susan B. Anthony. And still other middle-class radicals—"former abolitionists, communalists, spiritualists, feminists, and land reformers"—joined with immigrant German socialists in chapters of the International Workingmen's Association.[1]

Laboring people mobilized as well. Farmers, most aggressively in the Midwest, enlisted in the National Grange of the Patrons of Husbandry to propagate better agricultural practices, marketing cooperatives, and lobbying campaigns, while urban workers pursued new organizing drives, strikes, and political initiatives. Several major unions founded the National Labor Union in 1866 to foster producer and consumer cooperatives, secure an eight-hour workday, and eventually launch the National Labor Reform Party. Modeled after George Lippard's Brotherhood of the Union, the Noble and Holy Order of the Knights of Labor—which would become the largest American labor organization of the century—formed in Philadelphia in 1869 as a secret society under the leadership of Uriah Stephens, a skilled garment cutter. And in the coal-mining communities of eastern Pennsylvania, Irish American "Molly Maguires" responded to their bosses' tyranny with orchestrated acts of resistance and violence.[2]

As they did before the war, radicals and reformers grounded their aspirations and agencies in their understandings of America's revolutionary heritage, and many of them once again called specifically on the life and work of Thomas Paine. Religious liberals differed in their assessments of Paine and his *Age of Reason*, but almost all admired his democratic labors and in lectures and publications sought to overhaul his reputation and demonstrate the connection between rational faith and the nation's founding and purposes. Free Religionists in Boston opened the Thomas Paine Memorial Hall in 1875, and a San Francisco group called for a national subscription to underwrite a bust of Paine for Independence Hall in Philadelphia.[3]

Exasperated with both the Republican and the Democratic parties, the National Woman Suffrage Association endorsed the 1872 presidential campaign of Victoria Woodhull, the candidate of the new Equal Rights Party. A spiritualist, socialist, feminist, "free love" advocate, and coeditor of her own weekly, Woodhull contended that nothing in the Constitution actually prevented women from voting. Running for office, she would recount legend-maker George Lippard's fabricated story of a dramatic and pivotal encounter between Washington, Franklin, Adams, and the visionary Paine: "Rising from his seat when he had attentively listened to their doubts and queries, and, towering high above them, Mr. Paine answered them: 'We want independence, and I mean revolution.'"[4]

While Susan B. Anthony herself had serious reservations about the flamboyant Woodhull, she subscribed to Woodhull's argument about the franchise and somehow convinced her own local poll-keepers in upstate New York to allow her to vote. Prosecuted for doing so, Anthony strenuously defended her actions in a regional lecture tour, during which she too called on Paine to help make her case. Referring to him as a "Revolutionary patriot [and] authority on the principles upon which our government is founded," she quoted his words, "The right of voting for representatives is the primary right by which others are protected. To take away this right is to reduce a man to slavery." And spiritualists, who as a rule supported female suffrage, continued to convey Paine's voice from the afterworld, attesting not simply to the mediums' "powers"—Sarah Ramsdell communicated an entire volume of his words in rhyme!—but more realistically, to the growing interest in hearing directly from Paine.[5]

Though late nineteenth-century midwestern farmers did not cite Paine, they grappled with his writings at educational and social gatherings to "adjudicate what was worth while." No such adjudication was required for many a labor activist. The Pennsylvania iron-foundry worker William Sylvis, the driving figure in the National Labor Union—who would urge his "brothers" to extend their fight to include the abolition of "wage slavery"—read Paine after returning from army service in 1863, and his speeches and articles soon resonated with Painite arguments. Reflecting the influence of *Common Sense*, he drafted the manifesto of the National Labor Union in the fashion of the Declaration of Independence. And reciting the opening lines of the *Crisis*, he spoke of how the plight of workers, compelled to tramp from town to town in search of labor, "tries their *soles*."[6]

Immigrants, too, embraced Paine. Radical German American artisans, who had firmly supported the Union, continued to toast him at their annual Paine birthday galas. Coming to the United States in 1863, Marcus Thrane, who would be recognized as the founder of Norwegian social democracy, started two pro-labor periodicals in Chicago, on one of whose mastheads in 1869 he honored Paine with "My Fatherland is the World, and my Religion is to do Good." And remarkably, while still calling Paine an "infidel," Patrick Ford, the Catholic editor of the leading Irish American working-class newspaper, praised him as a champion of "political liberty."[7]

However, the Civil War also had encouraged the expectations and agencies of northern industrial and financial capitalists, many of whom had profited from the war effort and expected to reap even greater returns in the future. They too subscribed to a vision of radical change, but theirs entailed technological innovation, enterprise expansion, and capital accumulation, not the extension and deepening of freedom, equality, and democracy (at least not outside the Reconstruction South).

Reacting to the movements from below—and dreading the prospect of the Paris Commune of 1871 erupting in America—those who mounted the events and delivered the speeches of the official Centennial articulated a narrative of 1776 and the making of the United States that sanctioned the interests of the propertied and the powerful, a conservative tale that eviscerated America's revolutionary heritage and portrayed the nation's political purpose and promise as essentially realized. Naturally, they hearkened back to the Founders, but they did so carefully and selectively, rendering them as "statesmen . . . not revolutionaries" and continuing to deny Paine a place in the pantheon. Still, attending closely to the words and images, one could sense Paine's spirit haunting their proceedings.[8]

Boston's conservative city fathers invited the former Whig congressman Robert C. Winthrop—a man well known for his hostility to "mob violence"—to deliver the Independence Day oration. He would not disappoint. "Our Fathers," he intoned, "were no propagandists of republican institutions in the abstract." As he explained it, they were actually the "conservators of existing institutions," for they resisted the "radicalism" of "King and Parliament." The Revolution, he said, was "no wild breaking away from all authority," and lest anyone try to claim radical license from the events of 1776, he warned, "No incendiary torch can be rightfully kindled at our flame." Winthrop declared that above all else Americans should prize the "securing of Liberty," which "to-day," he assured his audience, "assumes its full proportions." And echoing Daniel Webster's words at the Bunker Hill Monument in 1825, he concluded by calling for the "renewal of that old spirit of subordination to Divine, as well as human, Laws."[9]

Drawing almost ten million people to its 250 pavilions, Philadelphia's Centennial Exhibition, as mandated, showed off American invention and industry, displaying everything from railway cars and agricultural equipment to Alexander Graham Bell's telephone, Thomas Edison's multimessage telegraph, and the massive 1,400-horsepower Corliss steam engine. Properly "domesticated [and] depoliticized," the Founders too made appearances, but even here—despite his own engineering work and identification with the city—Paine was not to be seen, and the members of Philadelphia's Select Council voted to reject the bust of him for Independence Hall.[10]

Paine, however, would not be forgotten in 1876. Free-Religion Unitarian ministers addressed his career and thought in their own Centennial sermons, and freethinkers from across the country—knowing that Christian denominations were to gather there—convened in Philadelphia on July 4 to "honor the memories of Jefferson, Franklin, Paine, and Ethan Allen." In San Francisco, when the organizers of its Centennial parade refused to have a painting of Paine carried along with those of the other "Fathers," James Lick, a formidable old infidel who lived along the procession's route, ran a line across the street from which he hung the portrait so everyone would have to "*march under*" Paine. But not only freethinkers remembered Paine. Columns by political liberals appeared in the popular magazines *Harper's* and *The Galaxy* lauding Paine and lamenting how "centennial writers" were failing to include him in the "immortal list" of Founders.[11]

Nevertheless, the interests and ambitions of industrial and financial capitalists would prevail. Stated bluntly, those who ran the Centennial would run the country and shape the nation according to their own radical vision. In the course of the late nineteenth century—known as the "Gilded Age," after the title of a novel by Mark Twain—they would subordinate the lives of laboring people to the demands of corporations, industry, and the market and transform the United States into the world's leading industrial nation, obtaining phenomenal wealth and power for themselves in the process.[12]

Yet as much as the new lords of industry and finance endeavored to control people, events, and developments—and they regularly succeeded in doing so—they could never fully discharge or suppress America's democratic impulse. As ever, Americans—both native-born and immigrant—arose in every decade to challenge the growing inequalities and exactions. Labor unionists, anarchists, populists, socialists, liberals, and progressives, along with freethinkers and feminists, would seek in their respective ways to reinvigorate America's revolutionary heritage and reassert the nation's democratic purpose and promise. In the face of original circumstances they would subscribe to new ideas and honor new figures. But many of them would also continue to find their most critical ideas and inspiration in Paine. And ironically, against the best efforts of the Centennial orators, the Gilded Age would witness a renaissance of interest in Paine and his work.

The Founders had envisioned the Republic's expansion and enrichment, but America's material progress in the late nineteenth century would have astounded them: "Iron replaced wood; steel replaced iron; and electricity and steam replaced horsepower." Trying to articulate the "movements" that transformed America between the Civil War and the First World War, some historians have penned lines that approach verse: "From agriculture to industry, from household and artisan to factory production, from water and animal power to fossil fuels, from economic independence to wage dependency, from the homeland of one's ancestors to a strange new land." In the end, however, the poetry of numbers proves most persuasive. While the patents issued in all of the decades before 1860 totaled 36,000, those in the next thirty years totaled 440,000. From 1860 to 1900 railway track miles increased from 30,000 to almost 200,000. The nation's population jumped from 31 million to more than 75 million (more than a quarter of whom lived west of the Mississippi); the number of farms increased from 2 million to 6 million; and the working class grew from 7 million to 18 million. Between 1865 and 1915, 25 million immigrants entered the country, changing the very face of America, as they came increasingly not from northern but from eastern and southern Europe, as well as from Asia and Mexico.[13]

Progress was the byword of the age, and the technological innovation, economic development, and capital accumulation that transpired so profoundly changed the nation that one might almost speak of inventors such as Thomas Alva Edison and Alexander Graham Bell and corporate empire-builders like Cornelius Vanderbilt, Jay Gould, Andrew Carnegie, John D. Rockefeller, and John Pierpont Morgan as a new generation of "Founders." And the Gilded Age they helped found did not get its name for nothing. While captains of industry and finance—in whose vanguard stood the robber barons—acquired incredible fortunes and lived like monarchs and aristocrats, and while the professional and salaried "white-collar" middle classes grew with the expansion of production and commercial operations, the vast majority of the laboring classes, both farmers and workers, those who actually produced America's wealth, suffered material insecurity and poverty.

Another set of numbers communicate a poetry more tragic than epic. By 1890 "the richest 1 percent of the population received the same total income as the bottom half of the population and owned more property than the remaining 99 percent." The Homestead Act enabled 375,000 settlers to secure 48 million acres, but railroad land companies were granted four times that amount. In the South, as merchants, bankers, and railroad bosses squeezed farmers' incomes, the percentage of holdings worked by tenants as opposed to owners increased from 30 percent in 1870 to 70 percent in 1900. Putting in ten hours a day, six days a week, workers steadily lost control of the results of their labors to new strata of managers and newly installed machines. Though real wages rose, and immigrants were apparently better off in America than where they had started out, 40 percent of workers and their families lived in poverty and a good percentage lived on the edge of it. Working-class life was not only hard, it was also precarious. Recessions and depressions in the 1870s, 1880s, and 1890s brought wage cuts and widespread unemployment. Every year hundreds of thousands of workers—men, women, and children—were killed or injured on the job.[14]

Racial oppression made the burdens of class all the more severe for blacks, especially in the South. With the end of Reconstruction southern whites steadily imposed a new regime of racial separation and oppression, whose brutal devices ranged from "Jim Crow" laws to lynch mobs. Severely reversing Lincoln's Second American Revolution, racism also affected white laboring folk, for it prevented farmers and workers from creating the kinds of social movements needed to effectively challenge regional and national power structures.

The concentration of wealth and power and the growth of large, hierarchical corporations fundamentally denied America's eighteenth-century republican ideal of small producers and independent citizens and the belief that political equality would engender economic equality. With its new extremes of rich and poor, it seemed the United States was coming to resemble Europe, the only difference being that whereas aristocrats ruled Europe, "plutocrats"—a far wealthier and more vigorous breed—ruled America. Tensions intensified; as one historian has put it, "Gilded Age America was a society dividing along class lines and spoiling for a fight."[15]

Abandoning the republican ideal (but not the Republican Party), the ascendant class adopted Social Darwinism, a theory of societal evolution formulated by the English philosopher Herbert Spencer and promoted in America by William Graham Sumner, a Yale professor in the new field of "social science." Professing no less of a commitment to political and, particularly, economic liberty than before, they came to understand society not as a compact among citizens but, in more animalistic terms, as a "struggle for existence" in which progress was driven by fierce competition and the "survival of the fittest." Anything that stood in the way of the "natural workings" of the market and the advance of industry—anything that would constrain them in the name of social justice, equality, or democracy—they construed as a threat, not merely to profits but more broadly to progress itself.[16]

Looking more to the future than to the past, Social Darwinism provided capitalists with a conservative ideology seemingly more in tune with the American spirit. However, while it might rationalize deepening class inequalities and intensifying exploitation and oppression to those who garnered wealth, power, and privilege in the process, it did not easily convince those who stood beneath them. And the former knew that. In pursuit of forever-renewed profit and to maintain the social order that made it possible, they resorted not merely to persuasion but also to manipulation, corruption, accommodation, and when necessary, coercion and force. With their fortunes they dominated party politics, Republican and Democratic bosses high and low, and exerted influence in every branch and level of government, especially the federal. Whatever their reservations, they deferred to the re-creation of the South's power structure and the fashioning of new systems of racial and class oppression. And when they murderously suppressed the Great Railway Strike of 1877, they clearly demonstrated their willingness to use force, including federal troops. Robber baron Jay Gould bragged, "I can hire half the working class to shoot the other half."

Of course, the propertied, powerful, and pious continued to anathematize Paine, though for differing reasons. To devout Christians, especially in the South, the "shrewd and blasphemous" author of *The Age of Reason* remained the chief infidel. In the Upper Cumberland of Tennessee, where in decades past Paine was avidly read as a champion of the common folk, Baptist and Presbyterian ministers vehemently denounced him in their sermons. But not only in the South did Paine's works still cause a stir. The directors of the Free Public Library in Hyde Park, Massachusetts—and presumably others elsewhere in New England and beyond in the 1870s—determined that they were too controversial to be included in their book collections. And yet clerical assaults on Paine's memory and legacy were losing their punch, both because orthodox Protestants themselves were becoming more anxious about the growth of the Catholic Church than about the enthusiastic but limited number of freethinkers and because moderates had begun to read the Bible in a more critical and historical fashion.[17]

Adulating Alexander Hamilton, the governing elites evinced their disdain for Paine by doing their utmost to publicly ignore him. But some of their ilk could not resist an opportunity to lash out. In his

1888 biography of Gouverneur Morris, Paine's foremost American adversary, the wealthy young Republican Theodore Roosevelt, a fervent admirer of both Hamilton and Morris and an antagonist of working-class politics and popular democracy, not only referred to Paine as an "Englishman"—apparently trying to absolve Morris for having abandoned Paine when the French imprisoned him in 1793—but all the more nastily as a "filthy little atheist."[18]

Prominent conservative scholars supported Roosevelt's assertions. John Bach McMaster, the first professor of American history at the University of Pennsylvania, wrote at length of Paine in his five-volume *History of the People of the United States of America*. But as much as McMaster acknowledged the importance of *Common Sense* and the *Crisis*, he repeated the old libels and portrayed Paine as a dirty and deceitful drunk. And whatever appreciation he felt for Paine's revolutionary pamphlets, he would leave any reference to them or their author out of his popular textbook for schools.[19]

Such attacks on Paine reflected real political animosities and class anxieties. The campaigns of radicals, reformers, and liberals and the struggles of labor had not ceased following the Centennial or the crushing of the national railway strike a year later. And Paine had not gone away either.

Hoping to suppress or at least contain dissent and popular struggles, the powers that be instinctively wished to erase or marginalize Paine's legacy. But the very forces unleashed in the Gilded Age—the progress of science, on the one hand, and the rise of plutocracy, on the other—would determine otherwise.[20]

Paine had argued that "natural philosophy" would enable humanity to better comprehend the Creation, and later freethinkers had always placed their "faith" in reason and scientific practice. Advances in science and technology now seemed to confirm those beliefs and expectations, leading freethinkers to heighten their efforts to "enlighten" their fellow citizens and upgrade Paine's standing in public memory. The fallen-away Unitarians and their comrades in the Free Religious Association cultivated their ideas and spread their message through "Radical clubs," a network of speakers, and their own national newspaper, *The*

Index, edited first by Francis Ellingwood Abbot, who had trained at Harvard for the ministry, and later by Benjamin F. Underwood, a self-educated freethought lecturer, both of whom were boosters of Paine's memory. Other freethought periodicals appeared as well, such as the continuing *Boston Investigator*, the Texas-based *Common Sense*, and the atheists' *Truth Seeker*, edited by D. M. Bennett, an Illinois seed merchant. Though Paine never gave up his belief in God, it didn't keep the atheists from claiming him as one of their heroes, and in later years they even took it upon themselves to publish sizable editions of his political and religious writings.[21]

While the freethought movement still perturbed the orthodox, it apparently represented something less of a threat to the powerful and propertied than it had in the past. Antebellum freethinkers characteristically had possessed strong attachments to or sympathies for the labor movement (many were themselves of the working class). But Gilded Age "infidels"—though they usually subscribed to progressive views, especially regarding women's rights—did not necessarily feel keen ties to or express great affection for working-class struggles. Notably, the ranks of the rationalists and worshippers of Paine's memory now included both Andrew Carnegie, the Scottish immigrant who had risen from "rags to riches," and Thomas Edison, the greatest of American inventors, neither of whom was renowned for solid democratic commitments or populist political sympathies (Carnegie's rhetoric and financial largesse to libraries aside). The Paine who excited Carnegie was the author of *The Age of Reason*, not *Rights of Man*, and in any case his reading of Paine did not stop Carnegie in 1892 from having his henchmen crack heads to destroy the union at his Homestead, Pennsylvania, steelworks. And Edison, who wrote of Paine that he was "one of the greatest of all Americans" ("Never have we had a sounder intelligence in this republic") praised Paine as an inventor and a libertarian, not as a democrat.[22]

The career of Robert Ingersoll clearly signaled the changing character and perception of religious liberalism. The most popular freethought lecturer, if not the most popular lecturer of the day, he was also a business lawyer and prominent Republican. Born in 1833 and raised in Illinois, the son of a liberal Congregational minister, Ingersoll was known as a most impressive public speaker even as a young man—and he was said to have given his first speech in 1856 at a church pic-

nic, speaking extemporaneously on, of all subjects, Thomas Paine. Admitted to the bar in 1854, Ingersoll entered politics as a Democrat. But he opposed slavery, and when the Civil War broke out, he personally organized a regiment of cavalry and, receiving a commission as a colonel in the Union army, served gallantly until captured in 1863 by Confederate forces in Tennessee.[23]

On his return to Illinois after the war, Ingersoll joined the Republicans and, working actively for the party, received a two-year appointment as the state's attorney general in 1867, at the end of which he ran unsuccessfully for governor. Eventually, however, he relocated with his family to New York, where he continued to practice the law, often representing major entrepreneurs, and cultivated his growing renown as a freethought orator. But it was not the big city that had turned him into a freethinker. In 1862 he had married Eva Parker, the daughter of religious rationalists, and once out of uniform Ingersoll himself delved into the classics of religious liberalism. Particularly impressed by the arguments of Paine and Voltaire, he soon began to profess first deist and then agnostic views openly, which, as much as it may have pleased his wife and in-laws, meant he could no longer hope to secure high elective office. And yet as famous, or infamous, as Ingersoll would become as an infidel, leading Republicans would still persistently call on him to speak at major party functions and to campaign for their candidates—attesting both to his own talents and rising popularity and to changing attitudes toward freethought.[24]

While differing from his infidel predecessors like Fanny Wright, Ingersoll was no less devoted to promoting freethought and Paine's memory. In tremendous demand as a speaker, he would appear all over the country, inspiring rationalists, angering Christians, and winning the admiration of diverse folk such as Walt Whitman, Andrew Carnegie, Mark Twain, and labor leader Eugene Debs. Ingersoll would exalt science and assail religion, insist on the separation of church and state, *and* acclaim freedom and the American Republic: "I love the Republic; I love it because I love liberty." He also would acknowledge the needs of labor: "This nation rests upon the shoulders of its workers and I want the laboring man to have enough to wear . . . enough to eat . . . I want him to feel that this is his country." But as much as he cared, he was no economic radical or socialist.[25]

Ingersoll delivered his first Paine birthday address in 1871 at the Hall of Free Thought in Fairbury, Illinois. And he would give the talk on many occasions in future years. In the most laudatory terms, he would say of Paine:

> He had more brains than books; more sense than education; more courage than politeness; more strength than polish. He had no veneration for old mistakes—no admiration for ancient lies. He loved the truth for truth's sake, and for man's sake. He saw oppression on every hand; injustice everywhere; hypocrisy at the altar; venality on the bench; tyranny on the throne; and with a splendid courage he espoused the causes of the weak against the strong—of the enslaved many against the titled few.[26]

Ingersoll made redeeming Paine's memory one of his primary causes, and he was prepared to stir up controversy in pursuit of it. In 1877 he offered to pay $1,000 in gold to any clergyman who could prove that Paine "died in terror because of religious opinions he had expressed." The wager created a furor, but Ingersoll rightly prevailed. And yet when he himself passed away in 1899—the last of the great infidels— some of his antagonists would spread the lie, as their counterparts had done after Paine's death, that he had recanted before expiring.[27]

Roiled by a changed America and the rapid rise of its plutocracy, many Americans, almost instinctively, reached back to Paine. Not every liberal or democratically inclined intellectual would turn to Paine's work, but certain critical figures did, among them the journalist Henry George, the scientist Lester Ward, and—the man who gave the Gilded Age its name—the novelist Mark Twain.

Born in 1839, George grew up in Philadelphia's Southwark district, a community composed in the late 1700s of revolutionary Painite artisans and, in the 1830s, of working-class Locofoco-Democrats. After apprenticing as a typesetter, George, while still in his teens, sailed around the world as a cabin boy on a merchant ship. Landing in San Francisco, he found work as a journeyman printer and eventually launched his own penny newspaper, for which he wrote editorials

questioning an economy in which the rich grew richer while the poor grew poorer. Though forced out of business in the Panic of 1873, he would not retreat. Menially employed, he spent his free time reading political economy and preparing to write a book that would address America's deepening inequalities and injustices.[28]

George's *Progress and Poverty: An Inquiry into the Cause of Industrial Depressions and of Increase of Want with Increase of Wealth* appeared in 1879. In it George contended that the fundamental cause of class strife and poverty was "inequality of land ownership," an inequality or, more precisely, a monopoly that enabled landowners to take advantage of capital and labor alike and had the effect of inducing class war between the latter two. But his analysis did not cause him to suggest outright land reform. Rather, he argued that government should severely tax landowners' profits. That single tax, he maintained, would not only liberate capitalists from the demands of the landed—allowing them to raise workers' wages and bring an end to class conflict and a whole range of associated social and moral ills—but would also generate so much revenue that the nation could abolish all other taxes.[29]

In spite of poor reviews, *Progress and Poverty* would become a best-seller and ignite a "single-tax movement" attracting both liberals and socialists. George himself would receive invitations to join the Knights of Labor and to run in 1886 for mayor of New York as labor's candidate. Though he did not cite Paine in the work, his plan to re-create American equality and democratic life descended directly from *Agrarian Justice* and clearly reflected Paine's spirit.[30]

Lester Ward would read Paine for both spiritual and political reasons. Born in 1841, Ward grew up in Iowa, the youngest of ten children. From his mother, the daughter of a minister, he learned to take ideas seriously, and from his father, a mechanic whose income barely sustained them, he acquired a strong work ethic and an egalitarian spirit. Though he later rejected his parents' Christianity, he would firmly hold on to their values.

In 1862, after a stint as a schoolteacher and a few terms at Susquehanna College in Pennsylvania, Ward, a passionate opponent of slavery, enlisted in the Union army, serving until wounded at the Battle of Chancellorsville in 1864. Married before going off to war, he immediately after his discharge sought work with the federal government and found employment in Washington at the Treasury Department (where he would stay until moving to the U.S. Geological Survey in 1881). Taking classes at the school that would become George Washington University, he completed both a master's degree in science and a law degree by 1872. At the same time he and his wife—skeptical of religion, committed to racial and gender equality, and worried about America's future—studied the writings of Paine and other radicals. And hoping to unify "Liberals, Skeptics, Secularists, Utilitarians, Socialists, Positivists, Spiritualists, Deists, Theists, Pantheists, Atheists, Freethinkers," they organized the National Liberal Reform League.[31]

Ward subscribed to Darwin's evolutionary theory, but possibly influenced by Paine, he utterly rejected Social Darwinism. He would insist that humanity could transcend laissez-faire economics and the "survival of the fittest" and consciously direct societal development by applying its collective intelligence. Seeing the concentration of wealth and power as the real threat to the progress of the Republic and its ideals, Ward further argued that government could be, and should be, democratically harnessed to defend and advance liberty and equality by publicly regulating business activity and publicly educating working people. Drawing on various sources for his alternative vision of social evolution, including the conservative French philosopher Auguste Comte, Ward granted a major role to "experts" in guiding the changes, particularly to social scientists. And yet Paine's democratic optimism and belief in the potential of laboring people would always remain at the heart of Ward's thinking. At a Paine birthday dinner in 1912, he would say:

> When men were in the political struggle, they imagined that when their political rights should be attained, the millennium would be here. But they found it was nothing of the kind. There was another great struggle to be gone through . . . a contest for the attainment of social and economic equality. It is the effort on the part of the fourth estate which used to be called the proletariat, the working classes, the mass of mankind, to secure social emancipation.

Ward's contemporary fame was limited. He would not even gain an academic position until Brown University appointed him to a professorship in 1906—the same year that the American Sociological Association elected him its first president. Decades later, however, he would be recognized as a prophet of twentieth-century liberalism and the "father of American sociology."[32]

Mark Twain first read Paine at about twenty years of age. Traveling east from Missouri in the mid-1850s, Twain wrote letters home from Philadelphia quoting the *Crisis* (at which time he may also have picked up *Common Sense* and *Rights of Man*), and not long afterward, while apprenticing as a pilot on a Mississippi River steamboat, he encountered another of Paine's works, which would lead to his becoming an avowed freethinker. "It took a brave man before the Civil War to confess he had read the *Age of Reason*," he would recall years later. "I read it first when I was a cub pilot, read it with fear and hesitation, but marveling at its fearlessness and wonderful power."[33]

Twain never wrote of Paine in his fiction, beyond referring to him in *Those Extraordinary Twins*, the tale of two physically conjoined brothers, one a Methodist, the other an infidel. Yet Twain genuinely admired Paine. Receiving a letter in 1908 inviting him to suggest names for a list of history's "One Hundred Greatest Men," defined as those who had had the "largest visible influence on the life and activities of the race," he nominated Alexander Graham Bell, Thomas Edison, and Thomas Paine. Moreover, Twain incorporated aspects of Paine's thought into his own work, most evidently in *A Connecticut Yankee in King Arthur's Court*, where he critically restated Paine's arguments against church, monarchy, and aristocracy in novel form. And when he had his protagonist Hank Morgan observe that "the master minds of all nations, in all ages, have sprung in affluent multitude from the mass of the nation, and from the mass of the nation only—not from its privileged classes," he was simply reaffirming Paine's assertion that "the greatest characters the world has known, have risen on the democratic floor. Aristocracy has not been able to keep a proportionate place with democracy."[34]

In the 1880s various historical writers also showed fresh interest in Paine, most notably Elihu Washburne, Moses Coit Tyler, and Moncure Conway. A sometime Radical Republican, Washburne published "Thomas Paine and the French Revolution" in *Scribner's Monthly* in 1880. Prepared while he was serving as President Grant's ambassador to France, Washburne's piece highlighted Paine's opposition to the execution of Louis XVI and Paine's own ensuing persecution at the hands of the Jacobins. A Cornell University professor, Tyler in 1884 presented a most appreciative address titled "The Influence of Thomas Paine on the Popular Resolution for Independence" at the first-ever meeting of the American Historical Association. While only excerpts of his talk would appear in print, the work he accomplished provided the basis for a lengthy and most favorable treatment of Paine in Tyler's two-volume classic, *The Literary History of the American Revolution*. And Moncure Conway, the Unitarian minister who had sermonized about Paine in Cincinnati in 1860, was in these later years pursuing the research for the first truly scholarly Paine biography, which when it came out in 1892 proved a powerful rejoinder to Cheetham's lies. Conway himself became a freethinker and committed himself to recovering the revolutionary's life and writings, which included serving as the first president of the Thomas Paine National Historical Association, organized in New York City in 1884.[35]

Still, the majority of scholars did not yet warm to Paine. The most popular historian of the time, John Fiske, though himself something of a freethinker, did not. A proponent of Social Darwinism, an advocate of "Anglo-Saxon traditions," and a xenophobic opponent of immigration, Fiske made very clear his disapproval of Paine's claims that "Europe, and not England, is the parent country of America" and that America was destined to serve as an "asylum for mankind."[36]

Radical working people, too, would continue to sustain Paine's memory and, even more, seek to reinvigorate his political legacy. Labor organizing boomed in the 1880s. Now headed by railway machinist Terence V. Powderly, the Knights of Labor abandoned secrecy and opened itself up to African Americans, women, and immigrants (though not Chinese). As a consequence its membership grew from 28,000 in 1880 to 100,000 in 1885 and—after triumphing in a confrontation with Jay Gould's Southwestern railroad—to more than 750,000 in 1886. With their own enrollments increasing, several national craft unions came together to create the Federation of Organized Trades and Labor Unions, which in 1886 became the American Federation of

Labor (AFL), with the immigrant English cigar-maker Samuel Gompers as its president. To the unions' political left, the Socialist Labor Party, led by Daniel DeLeon, an immigrant from the Dutch Caribbean, and the International Working People's Association, dominated by Johann Most, an immigrant Bavarian anarchist, gained recruits from New York to Chicago.[37]

The Knights of Labor viewed the wage system as antithetical to a republican polity and looked to the creation of a "cooperative commonwealth." Craft unions sought to protect the skills of their members and to garner them higher wages. And socialists and anarchists wanted to turn private corporations into state, public, or worker-owned enterprises. Organizational divisions would remain insurmountable, but following the lead of the Federation of Organized Trades and Labor Unions, the labor movement of the 1880s would roughly coalesce around the demand for "eight hours for work, eight hours for rest, and eight hours for what we will!"[38]

One might have expected artisans like Powderly and Gompers to admire Paine, but neither did, at least not publicly. Nevertheless, other figures such as Thomas Phillips, Joseph Labadie, and Albert Parsons definitely did. An English immigrant and Chartist veteran, Phillips had been active in Lippard's Brotherhood of the Union, the International Workingmen's Association, and the cordwainers' union, the Knights of St. Crispin, before joining the Knights of Labor. Organizing his fellow shoemakers into what would become the Knights' largest local, Phillips was appointed to the national "Committee of Progress," which had the task of formulating and propagating the Knights' positions. Phillips, however, did not get on well with Powderly, and in 1887 they split over Phillips's decision to run for mayor of Philadelphia, his public expressions of sympathy for the anarchists sentenced to die in the aftermath of Chicago's Haymarket tragedy, and his attachment to Paine, which included speaking at a Paine birthday gathering. Describing Powderly's leadership as "in the spirit of the Dark Ages," Phillips soon led the shoemakers out of the Knights and into the AFL.[39]

Born in 1850 and raised in the backwoods of Michigan, Joseph Labadie also circulated through the labor movement as a radical. After apprenticing in South Bend, Indiana, he had hit the road in 1867 to work as a "tramping" printer, along the way becoming a dedicated unionist and an organizer of the Kalamazoo Typographical Union. Finally, in 1872 he settled in Detroit, a city whose growing numbers of immigrant German and Bohemian workers included many a follower of the socialist ideas of Karl Marx and Ferdinand Lassalle. Drawn to a meeting of the Socialist Labor Party in 1877, Labadie quickly enlisted, persuaded that unions alone could not solve labor's problems. In that same year he started up *The Socialist*. But he soon gave up the newspaper to publish, with the party's support, a series of cheaply priced and accessible socialist tracts. An autodidact, Labadie spent what he could on works of literature, history, and political economy, and among his favorites were Paine's writings, which may well have prompted his own pamphleteering.[40]

While still with the Socialist Labor Party, Labadie joined the Knights of Labor and played a leading role in setting up its first chapter in Michigan. Then in the late 1880s he worked to found the state-level Michigan Federation of Labor. In these same years he moved away from socialism, *not* to the political center but to anarchism, believing that government was as oppressive as capital. As early as 1882 he would appear at labor-sponsored election rallies and—cheered on by his fellow workers—proclaim, "Tom Paine said that government, even in its best state, was an evil . . . organized to restrain our evil propensities."[41]

Albert Parsons's trajectory is even more fascinating. Born in Alabama but orphaned and raised in Texas by an older brother, at thirteen Parsons joined the Confederate army. Yet following the war, while working as a printer, he made a complete turnabout. Rejecting white supremacy absolutely, he launched a weekly newspaper that advocated equal rights for blacks. Now a Radical Republican, he held a series of Reconstruction jobs and campaigned for the party, during which time he also met Lucy Gathings, a young mulatto woman who would become his wife and devoted comrade.[42]

When the Democrats regained legislative control of Texas in 1873, Parsons returned to journalism. Feeling threatened by the new racist order, however, he and Lucy soon headed north to Chicago, a booming city of dynamic industries and diverse ethnic and immigrant communities. Admitted to the typographers' union, he again found work in the newspaper trade. But he did not reconnect with the Republicans. Reacting to Chicago's deepening class divisions—which were made all the deeper by the Panic of 1873—he joined the Socialist Labor Party's forerunner, the Working Men's Party, as well as the Knights of Labor. Already a war veteran, Parsons soon became a veteran of America's class struggles. When the Great Railway Strike spread across the country in July 1877, the Working Men's Party rallied thousands in support of the strikers. Parsons himself excoriated the railway company owners in a major speech that was quickly reported to his employers, who, in the midst of the strike's bloody suppression, sacked and blacklisted him.[43]

While Chicago's governing elites outfitted themselves for future battles, unionists and radicals continued to organize. Applying his energies to establishing the Chicago Trades and Labor Council, building the Socialist Labor Party, and campaigning for the eight-hour day, Parsons emerged as a leader of Chicago's labor movement. However, like many other radicals, he grew disillusioned with electoral politics. Leaving the party, he helped to found the "social-revolutionary" International Working People's Association, which brought together two currents of anarchist thought. The first, pushed by Johann Most, opposed unionism and reformism and held that workers should prepare themselves to violently overthrow capital and the state. The second, the "Chicago idea," propounded by Parsons and other midwesterners, also rejected the politics of the ballot box but insisted on the necessity of trade unions to secure immediate changes and to provide the foundations of a future good society. The manifesto drawn up at the 1881 founding convention accommodated both positions and, at Parsons's insistence, referred equally to European and American revolutionary traditions.[44]

Parsons had studied European socialist thought, but he had also read Paine and Jefferson and, however cynical he felt about America's Gilded Age politics, he continued to believe in America's revolutionary heritage and the nation's special purpose as Paine had portrayed it.

No group of working people in the 1880s revered Paine more than the anarchists, a movement of immigrant, predominantly German, and native-born Americans whose leaders regularly cited his words as proof that the Founders intended the United States to be a land of liberty and equality in the fullest sense. And those who would be arrested and tried for the deadly events in Chicago's Haymarket Square on May 4, 1886—Albert Parsons the most prominent among them—personally testified to Paine's importance to them and their cause.

In 1884 the Federation of Organized Trades and Labor Unions commenced a national campaign for the eight-hour day that, if necessary, was to culminate in a general strike on Saturday, May 1, 1886. And when that day came, 350,000 workers demonstrated nationwide. In Chicago, where 80,000 workers turned out, everything remained peaceful until police shot and killed several strikers at the McCormick Harvester Works on May 3. Responding to the deaths, the anarchists quickly organized a protest the next evening in the city's Haymarket Square. Drawing only a few thousand people, the gathering proceeded without incident. But just as folks started to head home, the police moved in, threatening force. Then, without warning, a bomb was thrown, killing one policeman, wounding several dozen more (some mortally), and causing the other officers to open fire, leaving at least one demonstrator dead and many more wounded.[45]

With the blessings of the city's elites and middle classes, Chicago's authorities rounded up known radicals and within weeks arranged for the trial of eight anarchists—Albert Parsons, August Spies, Adolph Fischer, George Engel, Louis Lingg, Michael Schwab, Samuel Fielden, and Oscar Neebe—whom they charged with "conspiracy to commit murder." Undeniably, the anarchist movement—by way of its violent rhetoric and militant street demonstrations—had cultivated a fearsome reputation. But Parsons and his seven comrades were innocent of the crime. (Several of them were not even present at the time the bomb was thrown.) The trial had far more to do with politics than with justice. In the words of the state's prosecuting attorney, Julius Grinnell, "These men have been selected, picked out by the grand jury and indicted because they were leaders. They are no more guilty than the thousands who follow them." Grinnell made clear that it was anarchism that was on trial: "Gentlemen of the jury: convict these men, make examples of them, hang them and save our institutions, our society." And the jury obliged, finding all eight guilty and providing the death penalty for all of them save Neebe.[46]

Before final sentencing, each of the eight addressed the court, speaking sincerely and at length of their beliefs and commitments. August Spies responded directly to Grinnell. An immigrant furniture upholsterer—who, like his native-born comrade Parsons, had immersed himself in the writings of Paine and Jefferson—Spies connected the anarchists' struggle to modern American and world history:

> "Anarchism is on trial!" foams Mr. Grinnell. If that is the case, your honor, very well; you may sentence me, for I am an Anarchist. I believe . . . with Paine, Jefferson, Emerson . . . and many other great thinkers of this century, that the state of castes and classes—the state where one class dominates over and lives upon the labor of another class, and calls this order— yes; I believe that this barbaric form of social organization, with its legalized plunder and murder, is doomed to die, and make room for a free society, voluntary association, or universal brotherhood.

Radicals and liberals mobilized to try to save the condemned men. Moderates equivocated. And some, like the Knights' Terence Powderly, turned their backs on them. In the end, Fielden and Schwab would escape death when Illinois governor Richard Oglesby commuted their sentences to life imprisonment. Lingg would take his own life the night before the scheduled execution. And on November 11, 1887, Parsons, Spies, Engel, and Fischer would hang.[47]

Haymarket ignited "red scares" and repressive tactics in cities around the nation. Theodore Roosevelt—who at this very time was writing of Paine as a "filthy little atheist"—expressed the ruling-class view when he noted in a letter from his Dakota ranch that "nothing would give [his cowboys] greater pleasure than a chance with their rifles at one of the mobs." And after the hanging Roosevelt and his ranch-hands burned effigies of the executed men.[48]

But not everyone saw things the way the future Rough Rider and president did. Already anxious about the widening of material inequality and the corruption of political life, Young American alumnus Herman Melville, who lived not far from Roosevelt back in New York, perceived the Haymarket affair as a portent of the demise of the nation's democratic spirit and attempted to warn his fellow citizens of their impending loss. In *Billy Budd*, a tale of class fear and injustice set in the 1790s (which would remain unfinished at his passing in 1891 and go undiscovered until the 1920s), Melville related the poignant story of a young, handsome, and much-admired British seaman. Impressed from the merchant vessel *Rights-of-Man* to serve on the warship *Bellipotent*, Billy would be wrongly accused by a petty officer of fomenting mutiny and, after striking and accidentally killing the man, would be executed by hanging, in good part to demonstrate to the crew the resolve of the King's authority. And lest anyone doubt the significance of the name of the ship from which Billy was taken—a ship on which he was beloved by crew and officers alike—Melville pointed out that its owner was "an admirer of Thomas Paine" and his book *Rights of Man* was a "rejoinder to Burke's arraignment of the French Revolution."[49]

Haymarket reinforced and even sparked the political commitments of some. The Russian Jewish immigrant Emma Goldman and the American-born Voltairine de Cleyre, the anarchist movement's foremost women activists, would often tell of how the deaths of the "martyrs" had spurred their actions. Moreover, they followed Parsons and Spies in believing that anarchism embodied America's best ideals and that they were heirs to a radical tradition going back to Paine and Jefferson. Goldman would exclaim to her working-class audiences: "If Jefferson and Paine . . . Wendell Phillips and John Brown were here to see your misery, they would be ashamed of their country." And de Cleyre would remind her listeners that 1776 was not just a war but also a revolution for "equal liberty" that needed renewal and extension. Starting out a militant freethinker, de Cleyre had become a militant leftist following the Haymarket tragedy and upon hearing attorney Clarence Darrow lecture on socialism at an 1887 Paine Memorial Convention. Moving ultimately to anarchism, she would chastise her fellow infidels for failing to properly appreciate Paine's "immense labors in the . . . struggle against the domination of man by man."[50]

Subjected to the power and demands of merchants, bankers, and railway companies, rural laboring folk, especially small farmers, both white and black, organized as well. Creating Farmers Alliances, they set up cooperatives, launched newspapers, held open-air rallies or "camps," and pressed politically for new systems of agricultural credit. Though Alliance leaders rarely referred directly to Paine (given farmers' religious attachments, especially in the South), they expressed classic Jeffersonian, Jacksonian, and Painite political views—"equal rights to all, and special privileges to none." In one crucial respect, however, they moved beyond their traditionally professed ideals. Increasingly they demanded government intervention in the economy and even government control and ownership of certain enterprises, particularly the railways.[51]

Through a dynamic system of lecturer-organizers, the Alliances recruited four million members in the South by the outset of the 1880s, and later in the decade enlistments took off in the Midwest as well. Due to inadequate management and the strength of the opposition, however, Alliance business enterprises foundered, and it became ever more apparent that farmers would have to challenge state and national power structures in a more united and more blatantly political fashion.[52]

An attempt in 1889 to nationally unify the several state Alliances would fail. But in 1892 the same energies gave birth to the People's Party, or Populists, who, in pursuit of democratic reforms and the creation of their own version of a "cooperative commonwealth," threatened to severely shake up American politics. As farmers became ever more politicized, Paine would emerge as a Populist "favorite." On the campaign trail Judge Thomas Nugent, the party's candidate for governor of Texas in 1892 and 1894—who, it was said, might well have won the next gubernatorial election had he not passed away in 1895—"studded his speeches" with quotes from philosophers and patriots, Paine prominently among them.[53]

In Kansas, where the Populists would eventually capture the governorship and five congressional seats and very briefly control the state legislature, Jeremiah Simpson, another admirer and student of Paine, as well as a follower of Henry George, first won election to Congress in 1890 as an independent Alliance candidate. Born in 1842, Simpson had gone to work in his teens as a sailor on the Great Lakes and during his time afloat—which was punctuated early on by service in the Union army—had devoured books such as Paine's and George's works

and developed radical democratic and freethinking views on government and religion. Marrying and starting a family, Simpson finally left
the lakes in 1878 and headed to Kansas, filled with plans of pursuing a
more settled life on the land. Confronting the same economic hard-
ships that plagued other Great Plains farmers, however, he entered
politics as a reform candidate. Called "unpatriotic," an "infidel," and
an "anarchist" by his enemies, Simpson, who was described as "Lincoln-
esque" in appearance and speech, parried their attacks with wit and hu-
mor, acquiring the nickname "Sockless Jerry," when he accused his
upper-class Republican opponent in 1890 of wearing "silk stockings."[54]

The Quaker-born Populist L. D. Lewelling, a Civil War veteran,
teacher, reformatory administrator, and editor, also would draw upon
Paine's lines but—like his namesake, the Methodist preacher Lorenzo
Dow—not necessarily mention their source. Elected governor of Kansas
in 1892, Lewelling spoke words in his inaugural address that dis-
tinctly echoed Paine's of a hundred years earlier: "If old men go to
the poor-house and young men to prison, something is wrong with the
economic system of government." Promising state protection of
the producer classes from the "ravages of combined wealth," the democratic and egalitarian Lewelling unfortunately would have to spend
most of his two-year term in heated combat with the Republicans
who, after a series of battles, would continue to dominate the state
legislature.[55]

In 1893 the United States entered its worst depression of the nineteenth century. Lasting almost five years, it wiped out banks and
businesses, ruined farmers, and pushed three million workers into
unemployment. At the same time, the decade also saw renewed labor
organizing, class struggle, and deadly violence between capitalists and
striking workers at places like Andrew Carnegie's Homestead steelworks and George Pullman's company town and railway car plant just
outside Chicago. In 1896 the People's Party, desperate to defeat the
Republicans, endorsed the Democrats' presidential candidate, the
young Nebraska congressman William Jennings Bryan. When the Republican William McKinley won the election, capitalists were relieved
and Populists devastated.

New movements, collectively known as "Progressivism," now arose to challenge the plutocratic order and try to reform capitalism. Often thought of as a singular force, probably as a consequence of the formation of the Progressive Party in 1912, Progressivism actually comprehended a variety of political currents and initiatives whose respective aspirations included "cleaning up" city and state governments, limiting and regulating the power of corporate "monopolies," improving the lives of the urban poor, prohibiting the sale of alcohol, and securing female suffrage. But in reaction to a social order sanctioned by the survival-of-the-fittest ideology, and worried about persistent class struggles in agriculture and industry, Progressives, for all their diversity of concerns, shared the view that America's problems required urgent and concerted public or, more precisely, state action. Characteristically educated white middle-class folk of Protestant upbringing, many stressed the values and practices of citizenship and pushed "direct democracy" schemes such as primary elections and referenda and recalls based on popular, as opposed to legislative, initiatives. However, their eagerness to counter the turbulence of Gilded Age life and the corruption of its politics also led many Progressives to emphasize "order, efficiency, and centralized management" and the "authority" of experts and scientists (not to mention, to accept the ongoing disenfranchisement of blacks in the South and immigrants in the North by way of poll taxes and literacy tests). As Herbert Croly, the founder of *The New Republic*, explained it, the Progressives sought "Jeffersonian ends" by way of "Hamiltonian means."[56]

By their own account, Paine's work influenced many a Progressive, including such figures as the attorney, editor, and advocate of labor and racial equality Louis Freeland Post, who would serve in Woodrow Wilson's administration and fight to protect aliens' civil liberties during the "Red Scare," and the muckraking journalist and political reformer George Creel, who would enter the Wilson administration to manage the wartime propaganda campaigns of the Committee for Public Information. While Progressive politicians and activists would not loudly promote Paine's memory (Theodore Roosevelt most definitely would not), Paine did achieve a new respectability in these years, due not simply to the publication of Conway's biography and Tyler's literary history but all the more to the Progressives' rhetoric of democratic citizenship.[57]

Reflecting a growing popular interest in the past, which included historical preservation projects and pilgrimages to historical sites, religious liberals—many of whom participated in Progressive campaigns—now advanced Paine's memory not only through their traditional lectures and Paine birthday dinners but also through the commemorative activities of the Thomas Paine National Historical Association. An exponent of the Arts and Crafts movement and the founder of the Roycroft community and press, Elbert Hubbard produced a handsome series of booklets titled *Little Journeys to Homes of Reformers*, including one on Paine, as well as *An American Bible* composed of extracts from the writings of the freethought "prophets," Franklin, Jefferson, Paine, Ingersoll, Emerson, Whitman, and Lincoln. He also published works such as *Lest We Forget*, a eulogy to Paine by the popular poet Ella Wheeler Wilcox, and *The Four Gospels* by lawyer and suffragist Marilla Ricker. Ricker's volume placed Thomas Paine and Robert Ingersoll alongside John Calvin and Jonathan Edwards and found the latter pair wanting by comparison.[58]

The new esteem accorded Paine did not go unnoted. In 1905 and again in 1909, the editors of the magazine *Current Literature* highlighted the fresh attention and revaluation. In their first piece they observed that the city of New Rochelle had accepted responsibility for the Paine monument erected there in 1839 and that Paine's bust had finally found a place in Philadelphia's Independence Hall. And in their second they cited the opening of a Paine museum in New Rochelle, the participation of clergymen in the 1909 assembly marking one hundred years since Paine's passing, and the publication of major new editions of Paine's works as evidence that "posterity will preserve the favorable, rather than the unfavorable, picture of Thomas Paine."[59]

To be sure, not everyone had had a change of heart. Presidents still did not speak openly of Paine. Orthodox religious folk—Protestant and Catholic—continued to recount the lies about Paine's deathbed agonies. And even among the Progressives there were those who remained hostile, like the pro–Teddy Roosevelt editors of *Outlook* magazine.[60]

Nevertheless, historians, literary scholars, political theorists, and philosophers were showing increasingly serious and ever more favorable interest in Paine. Ellery Sedgwick, who would go on to make a name for himself as the successful publisher and editor of *The Atlantic*

Monthly, authored a passionate treatment of Paine for the Beacon Biographies of Eminent Americans series. The president of Princeton University, Woodrow Wilson, a professor of government, political Democrat, and future president of the United States, wrote warmly of Paine's contribution to the cause of independence in his five-volume *A History of the American People*. And political scientist Charles Merriam of Columbia University, who would play a leading role in the Progressive Party, appreciatively portrayed Paine as an advocate of independence and radical democracy. Paine's star would rise even further when Progressive scholars such as the civil service reformer Sydney George Fisher and the younger Charles Beard began to "debunk" the traditional mythology of the nation's founding. Writing that "we owe Paine a great debt of gratitude for his services and *our people have always wished to think well of him*," Fisher essentially pointed a finger at the governing elites for their persistent efforts to suppress Paine's memory.[61]

Paine also secured a more prominent place in America's most official narrative, the history taught in schools. In fact, the author of the best-selling high school American history textbook, David Saville Muzzey—who, ironically, would come to hold the Gouverneur Morris Chair at Columbia University—was not only a Progressive and a free thinker but also a regularly featured speaker at Paine National Historical Association events, including the 1909 memorial celebration at New Rochelle, where he spoke of Paine as a great "prophet of democracy." In *An American History*, first published in 1911 and widely used in revised editions for the next fifty years, Muzzey wrote: "It is doubtful whether any printed work in all American history has had a greater influence than Paine's 'Common Sense.'" And in 1912 the Missouri Society of the Sons of the American Revolution made "The Political Writings of Thomas Paine and Their Influence on the Revolution" the theme of its annual state high-school essay contest.[62]

His new respectability made Paine no less anathema to conservatives and no less inspiring to radicals. In 1890 the two wings of the women's movement reunited in the National American Woman Suffrage Association, with Susan B. Anthony as its president. Although suffragists would now appeal to political expediency more often than to natural rights in their pursuit of the vote, many continued to employ Paine to afford a fundamental legitimacy to their demands. They cited the words Anthony had used—"The right of voting for representatives is the primary right by which others are protected"—but not those alone. Feminist writer Mary Putnam-Jacobi, America's leading woman physician, titled her 1894 book *"Common Sense" Applied to Women Suffrage* and opened with a discussion of Paine that highlighted lines like "The sun never shined on a cause of greater worth" and "The birthday of a new world is at hand."[63]

Further to the left, the Socialist Party formed in 1901. Incorporating elements of both the Socialist Labor Party and the People's Party, the new party found its greatest support among the Eastern European Jewish and German working classes of cities like New York, Chicago, and Milwaukee and the tenant farmers, small town artisans, and railroad, lumber, and mine workers of the Great Plains and Old Southwest. Contrary to the claims of the governing elites, Socialists garnered their ideas not simply from European sources but equally, if not more so, from the American radical tradition.

American socialists made a great deal of Paine and his work. Offering a "materialist" analysis of the American Revolution, the popular Socialist lecturer Arthur Morrow Lewis described the Founding Fathers as a "rather select circle of smugglers and land thieves" but celebrated Paine as a "man of thought [and] action" whose "ambition was not so much to enjoy the fruits of liberty as to toil for its achievement." Moreover, Socialists promoted Paine's memory not only among adults but also among the young. The *Young Socialist Magazine* regularly ran excerpts from the writings of radical intellectuals, and pieces by Paine featured significantly among them. And the *Little Socialist Magazine for Boys and Girls*, published by the party's Socialist Sunday schools, went even further. In a special series of articles, "History of Our Country for Boys and Girls," teacher Frederick Krafft portrayed Paine, not the "aristocratic Washington," as the "real father of our country." Other essayists, referring to Paine's revolutionary contributions both to the United States and to France and his outspoken opposition to slavery and the death penalty, presented Paine as an exemplary radical and humanist and a model for American children.[64]

Paine's life and labors mattered to Socialists of every background and in every corner of the country. They were presumably popular topics at the Rand School of Social Science, the party's adult education center in New York City. Providing classes to working people on a vast array of subjects ("U.S. history, economics, history of socialism, public speaking . . . labor organizing . . . poetry, composition and rhetoric, shorthand, science and music"), the school's teachers and lecturers included Paine admirers such as Charles Beard, David Saville Muzzey, and Lester Ward.[65]

Less formally, the teenaged Elizabeth Gurley Flynn, whom one journalist dubbed the "East Side Joan of Arc" for her passionate soapbox speeches, drew daily inspiration from Paine and the other radicals whose pictures adorned the walls of her Irish immigrant family's tiny apartment. Flynn herself was granted her very first indoor platform by the elderly former minister, lawyer, and then leader of New York's freethinking Unity Congregation, Hugh Owen Pentecost, a Paine devotee who had been born eighty years earlier at Robert Owen's New Harmony. Meanwhile, up in Harlem, Hubert Harrison, a working-class West Indian immigrant, read Paine as he made his own way from Christianity to freethought and went on to become the Socialist Party's most powerful voice in the African American community, as well as an editor of the "Lyrical Left's" magazine of politics and culture, the *Masses*. And at Columbia University the young student intellectual Randolph Bourne critically engaged Paine's *Rights of Man* in search of ideas for contemporary politics.[66]

Out in the Plains and the Old Southwest, Socialists enthusiastically recalled Paine's arguments at the massive summer "encampments" that they modeled after those of the Populists. Attracting tens of thousands of farming and working-class families, the new mass gatherings, like those before them, involved social, educational, and political activities, along with speaking appearances by beloved figures such as Eugene Debs, Mother Jones, Kate Richards O'Hare, and Oscar Ameringer, a German immigrant who had become a radical in America after reading Jefferson and Paine.[67]

In the Far West an equally diverse group of Socialists mined Paine's writings. In 1906 the Common Sense Publishing Company of Los Angeles issued (Miss) W. A. Corey's *Common Sense: A Reading of*

Thomas Paine's Famous Revolutionary Pamphlet, "Common Sense," in the Light of the Socialist Revolution. In 1908 the San Diego Baptist minister Reverend George Washington Woodbey, who was born a slave in the South in 1854 and would proudly state, "I stand on the declaration of Thomas Paine when he said 'The world is my country,'" urged the Socialist Party's national convention to oppose the exclusion of Asian immigrants from the United States. And in Portland, Oregon, in the 1910s, Charles Erskine Scott Wood, a veteran infantry officer, lawyer, and reformer, wrote a popular series of satirical stories for the *Masses* that placed Paine in dialogue with the likes of God, Satan, Voltaire, Mary Wollstonecraft, Robert Ingersoll, Mark Twain, and Lenin.[68]

Paine's life and writings afforded special inspiration and encouragement to many of the Socialist Party's most important figures, such as Julius Wayland and Eugene Debs. One biographer called Julius Wayland, the foremost newspaperman and "propagandist" of American socialism, a "reincarnate Thomas Paine," a distinction Wayland would have relished. Born in 1854 to a very poor Indiana family, Wayland left school early in his teens to work as an apprentice, then as a tramping printer, and somehow he saved enough money to buy his own newspaper in 1872. However, after successfully running the paper for ten years, with a Radical Republican editorial line, he relocated to Pueblo, Colorado, where, setting up the "One-Hoss Print Shop," he started a new newspaper and invested profitably in real estate. But money did not turn him into a conservative, for what he read trumped what he accumulated. Propelled by Laurence Gronlund's Marxian treatise *Cooperative Commonwealth*, Edward Bellamy's utopian novel *Looking Backward*, and the writings of the English cultural critic John Ruskin, Wayland moved toward socialism.[69]

Returning to Indiana in 1893, Wayland launched another newspaper, the *Coming Nation*, in which he endorsed both the People's and Socialist Labor Parties. And the following year he spent additional dollars creating Ruskin, a cooperative settlement in Tennessee. Though the community disappointed him and he soon sold off his interest in it, he did not abandon his commitment to socialism and radical publishing. Somewhere along the way he had encountered Paine, whose life and writings had critically reinforced his belief in the political potential of both the printed word and American working people. (Labor organizer and hero Mother Jones would recall in a letter to Wayland's son in 1918 how she and his late father would stay up deep into the night talking about Paine and their other favorite authors.) And in 1895 Wayland began to publish the *Appeal to Reason*, a new socialist weekly whose title was apparently inspired by Paine's words in the first *Crisis*: "I bring reason to your ears, and in language plain as A, B, C, hold up truth to your eyes."[70]

Issued from the small town of Girard, Kansas, the *Appeal* became American socialism's leading periodical. Recruited by an "army of salesmen and agitators," subscriptions grew steadily from 45,000 in 1896, to 100,000 in 1900, to 410,000 in 1910, to 760,000 in 1913. Connecting urban and rural radicals, the newspaper helped to mobilize hundreds of thousands of Americans to vote Socialist. Always a lively read, it published articles, reports, and editorials, excerpts from the speeches and writings of major radicals and socialists, a woman's column, and letters and poems from readers. Personally convinced that political literature could make a political difference, Wayland himself authored many pieces, including "The Literature of Discontent," a "syllabus" that included four works by Thomas Paine.[71]

Eugene Debs would run five times for president of the United States as the Socialists' candidate. He would never pose a grave threat to the major parties' candidates, but in 1912 he would garner almost one million votes and win the admiration of Americans well beyond the ranks of his own party. Born in 1855 in Terre Haute, Indiana, Debs was the son of French immigrants who, proud of their heritage, including its revolutionary and republican history, named their son after the novelists Eugène Sue and Victor Hugo. Their doing so apparently made an impression on Debs himself, for although he would drop out of high school after only one year, he never stopped reading and educating himself.[72]

Young Debs left school to work on the railway, first as a sign painter, then as a fireman. But after a friend was accidentally killed on the line, and at the urging of his own mother, he quit the railroad in 1874 and found a safer job in the city as a wholesale billing clerk. Still, remaining in touch with his former co-workers, he was accepted into and became a union activist of the Brotherhood of Locomotive

Firemen, which served primarily as a mutual benefit society for its members.

From the outset, Debs devoted his free time and money to self-improvement. He bought books and took night classes. History fascinated him, particularly the American and French Revolutions, and he came to feel a special affection for the radicals Patrick Henry and Thomas Paine. As Debs himself later would recall: "The revolutionary history of the United States and France stirred me deeply and its heroes and martyrs became my idols. Thomas Paine towered above them all. A thousand times since then I have found inspiration and strength in the thrilling words, 'These are the times that try men's souls.'" Debs also joined in founding the Occidental Literary Club, through which he and his friends brought speakers to Terre Haute such as Robert Ingersoll and Susan B. Anthony. Impressed by their talents, Debs successfully developed his own skills as an orator.[73]

Over the next twenty years Debs would work strenuously as a labor organizer, speaker, and editor and eventually won elections to become Terre Haute's city clerk in 1879 and one of its state legislators in 1885–88. While he originally fit right in to the Brotherhood of Locomotive Firemen—for in the 1870s he too held rather moderate views on the relations between management and labor—he eventually lost patience with the Railroad Brotherhoods' conservatism, as well as their incessant rivalries with the Knights and the AFL. And in 1893 he left to establish and serve as president of the American Railway Union (ARU), an "industrial union" that promised to unite *all* railway workers regardless of skill or status (though sadly, while women were accepted, a motion to include blacks failed).[74]

Successfully striking the Northern Railroad in 1894, the ARU became the fastest-growing union in the United States. However, just a few months later, in 1895, it faced a critical test when its members at George Pullman's railway car factories walked off the job. Believing they were unprepared for another major confrontation, Debs hoped to avoid a showdown, but union representatives voted to fight and 150,000 ARU railway workers across the country—plus 100,000 who did not belong to the ARU—initiated an embargo of all trains to which Pullman carriages were attached. In turn, the railroad companies quickly secured a court injunction against the ARU. When workers refused to give way, President Grover Cleveland sent in federal troops. The ensuing battles that summer in Chicago and elsewhere left dozens dead and larger numbers wounded. Debs, facing the prospect of further killings, eventually agreed to call off the action if union workers could have their jobs back. The companies balked and the strike ran out of steam. Utterly defeated, the ARU collapsed, its leaders were blacklisted, and Debs and other union officers spent six months behind bars.[75]

Reflecting on the power of capital, its tightening grip on government, and the dangers it posed to American life and ideals, Debs emerged from prison even more radical than when he had entered. He would continue to campaign for and feel confident about the political potential of working people. But he would now do so as a socialist, committed to replacing America's Gilded Age plutocratic order with a cooperative commonwealth. At the same time, he would continue to identify closely with the American radical tradition, for he understood socialism not as some foreign ideology but as the further articulation of America's historic struggle for freedom, equality, and democracy. Released from jail in November 1895, he told the crowd of one hundred thousand that greeted his arrival in Chicago, "Manifestly the spirit of '76 still survives. The fires of liberty and noble aspirations are not yet extinguished . . . To the unified hosts of American workingmen fate has committed the charge of rescuing American liberties from the grasp of the vandal horde that has placed them in peril, by seizing the ballot and wielding it to regain the priceless heritage." And on that evening and the innumerable evenings thereafter when he spoke, Debs evoked the legacy of his heroes, Thomas Paine, Patrick Henry, John Brown, Wendell Phillips, Abraham Lincoln, and the Haymarket martyrs.[76]

Paine's writings also shaped the thinking of the renowned attorney Clarence Darrow, who, though he never actually joined the Socialist Party, became closely identified with it on account of his political sympathies and his representation of Debs and other radicals of the labor movement. Born in Ohio in 1857, Darrow was the child of radical democrats and freethinkers who exposed him early in life to the works of Voltaire and Paine. Renowned to this day for his role as the defense counsel in the celebrated 1925 "Scopes 'Monkey' Trial," Darrow seems to have been destined to become the "attorney for the damned." But as much as young Clarence made his parents' political and religious commitments his own, he started his career as a government and corporate lawyer, and not until the Pullman strike case—when he defended Eugene Debs against criminal conspiracy charges—did he actually begin to apply his remarkable legal skills and talents to the cause of the underdog.[77]

Nevertheless, following his defense of Debs—whose six months in jail were, notably, not for criminal conspiracy but for contempt of court—Darrow went on to become labor's leading legal voice and America's foremost trial attorney. And on at least one critical occasion, he dared to invoke Paine's still-suspect name in court. Making his remarks to the jury in the 1898 Wisconsin criminal conspiracy trial of Thomas L. Kidd, the leader of the Oshkosh woodworkers' union, which had struck the—ironically named—Paine Lumber Company, Darrow looked over at the prosecutor F. W. Houghton and declared, "How Brother Houghton's mouth would have watered if he had been given a chance to convict Thomas Paine for daring to proclaim the rights of man!"[78]

Divisions among Socialists over America's entry into the First World War and the appropriate stance to take on the Soviet Revolution of 1917—along with the Wilson administration's repression of radicals during the war and "Red Scare" tactics in 1919–20—would cost the Socialist Party dearly and, while it would remain a political force for some years, the majority of American laboring people would continue to vote for Democrats or Republicans.

Undeniably, the radical and progressive campaigns of the Gilded Age failed to significantly transform the social order. Nevertheless, they made important, if not dramatic, contributions to the nation's development. Labor unions and agrarian organizations afforded dignity, comradeship, and solidarity to workers and farmers and helped to set limits to capitalist exploitation and oppression. Progressives exposed political corruption and social problems and reformed municipal, state, and federal government practices. Socialists, elected to city councils and mayoral offices, instituted an array of urban material improvements, including, most critically, public ownership of utility companies. And suffragists finally won women the right to vote in 1920 with the adoption of the Nineteenth Amendment to the Constitution.

Tragedy and irony would continue to mark American history, but when other peoples would resort, or fall, to authoritarian and totalitarian dictatorships in the turbulent and trying decades ahead, Americans would not. Variably inspired and encouraged by Paine, the movements of late nineteenth-century radicals, liberals, and laboring folk had served as America's prophetic memory. They had sustained the nation's democratic impulse, fundamentally enriched its democratic energies and resources, and helped to empower future democratic struggles. Lawyer and muckraking journalist Henry Demarest Lloyd, whose political activism encompassed Populism, Progressivism, and Socialism, articulated Paine's and their respective aspirations best when he said, "The price of liberty is something more than eternal vigilance. There must also be eternal advance. We can save the rights we have inherited from our fathers only by winning new ones to bequeath our children." And in the course of the twentieth century, new generations would once again call upon Paine as they too fought to realize America's exceptional purpose and promise, both at home *and* abroad.[79]

7

TYRANNY, LIKE HELL,

IS NOT EASILY CONQUERED

In the winter of 1941–42, Americans faced their gravest crisis since the Civil War. The Japanese assault on Pearl Harbor had propelled the United States into the Second World War, a global conflict against fascism in which the very survival of freedom, equality, and democracy were at stake. And things did not look good at all. Germany had conquered most of Europe, Japan had overrun East Asia, and on every front from the Atlantic to the Pacific the Axis powers were advancing and inflicting terrible losses on American and Allied forces. At home the reports of military disasters and setbacks triggered criticism of the government's handling of the war, rumors of invasion, and a sense of despair, if not defeat. Though he had spoken to the nation by radio in a "fireside chat" soon after securing a declaration of war from Congress, President Franklin Delano Roosevelt recognized he would have to talk to his fellow citizens once again—not only to clarify the military situation but also to reassure them of their strengths, mobilize their spirits and energies, and present them with a vision of a world worth fighting for.

Announcing that the president would deliver another fireside chat on Monday evening, February 23, at the close of the Washington Birthday weekend, the White House did not reveal any details beyond requesting that everyone have a map of the world at hand. Still, Americans anticipated something important. Stores quickly sold out their maps. Newspapers rushed their own into print. And when Monday night came, sixty-one million Americans—more than 80 percent of the possible audience—plus millions more around the world, tuned in to hear the broadcast.[1]

Roosevelt and his advisers understood that the president needed to firmly engage American collective memory and imagination. Rallying support for the New Deal, Roosevelt had regularly evoked historical images and personages, including heroes both Democratic and Republican, such as Thomas Jefferson and Abraham Lincoln, respectively. But on this occasion the president would reach even more deeply into America's revolutionary heritage, to the very crucible of war out of which the United States had emerged.[2]

Seated at a desk behind a bank of microphones in a first-floor White House room, Roosevelt opened by recalling George Washington and his Continental army. Pointing to the "formidable odds and recurring defeats" they had suffered, the president recounted how their conduct had served as a "model of moral stamina" to ensuing generations. Contrasting their bravery and fortitude to the behavior of America's Tories—those "selfish men, jealous men, fearful men" who preached defeatism and pressed for a negotiated peace—he observed that America's first soldiers had never given up because they "knew that no man's life or fortune was secure without freedom and free institutions." And returning to the present, with American isolationists in mind, he posited that the current "great struggle has taught us increasingly that freedom of person and security of property anywhere in the world depend upon the security of the rights and obligations of liberty and justice everywhere in the world."[3]

The present war, Roosevelt said, was a "new kind of war . . . not only in its methods and weapons but also in its geography." Referring to the maps he had asked Americans to have ready, he surveyed the far-flung battlefronts and communications and supply lines to show how the conflict was unavoidably a *global* struggle, involving "every continent, every island, every sea, every air lane in the world." While granting that Germany and Japan had the immediate advantage, and warning of further losses, the president defiantly added that despite the odds American soldiers and sailors were fighting valiantly and performing magnificently. And he promised that the United States and its allies would turn back the enemy, regain the ground lost, and ultimately prevail.[4]

The president spoke of the sacrifices Americans would have to make on the assembly lines and, even more heroically, at the front lines. And scoffing at Axis propaganda that portrayed them as "weak-lings" and "playboys" who were eager to "hire" others to fight for them, he exclaimed: "Let them tell that to General MacArthur and his men. Let them tell that to the sailors . . . Let them tell that to the boys in the Flying Fortresses. Let them tell that to the marines!"[5]

Just as fervently, the president reiterated America's commitment to pursue the war in partnership with its allies, the "United Nations," and insisted that doing so required the kind of "national unity that can know no limitation of race or creed or selfish politics." And apparently envisioning the extension of New Deal liberalism to the "whole world," he enunciated the principles they would seek to apply globally: "disar-mament of aggressors, self-determination of nations and peoples, and the four freedoms—freedom of speech, freedom of religion, freedom from want, and freedom from fear."[6]

Finally, after again acknowledging the awesome task Americans had before them, Roosevelt welded together past and present:

> "These are the times that try men's souls." Tom Paine wrote those words on a drumhead, by the light of a campfire. That was when Washington's little army of ragged, rugged men was retreating across New Jersey, having tasted naught but defeat. And General Washington ordered that these great words writ-ten by Tom Paine be read to the men of every regiment in the Continental Army, and this was the assurance given to the first American armed forces: "The summer soldier and the sunshine patriot will, in this crisis, shrink from the service of their coun-try; but he that stands it now, deserves the love and thanks of man and woman. Tyranny, like hell, is not easily conquered; yet we have this consolation with us, that the harder the sacrifice, the more glorious the triumph." So spoke Americans in the year 1776. So speak Americans today![7]

The New York Times called the address "one of the greatest of Roo-sevelt's career." Presidential speechwriter Judge Samuel I. Rosenman felt it had a "world-wide" impact and was "one of the most important and effective chats the President ever delivered." And from all around the country letters both supportive and critical flooded into the White House. They spoke of many things, but at least one, from Kansas, attended specifically to the president's closing lines. Writing that "words cannot express my gratitude for your high tribute to Thomas Paine," the letter's author happily contrasted it to the "libelous" treatment accorded Paine years earlier by another Roosevelt, the president's cousin Theodore.[8]

As the Kansan seemed to appreciate, FDR's "tribute" signified a remarkable change in Paine's "official" status. For the first time since Jefferson, a president of the United States had publicly uttered Paine's words and named their author. Moreover, Roosevelt had not merely quoted and cited Paine; using Paine's prose to declare the nation's commitment to defeat fascism and make freedom universal, the president had also identified Paine as the original and persistent voice of the American spirit.

To deliver the speech took courage, but not because it referred to Paine. Roosevelt surely understood how much Americans owed the old revolutionary. He probably believed Paine deserved better treatment than that traditionally granted by statesmen. And he likely grasped how Paine's arguments informed his own rhetoric and aspirations. However, he did not call Paine forth for Paine's own sake. The president knew what he had to accomplish that evening. He had to steel the nation for war and articulate the struggle as a campaign not simply to defend the country but also to realize its finest values and ideals. He could not afford to divide, confuse, or alienate his listeners. If he had suspected that referring to Paine would undermine his objectives, he no doubt would have avoided doing so. Yet far more than historians and even Paine's own biographers, Roosevelt perceived that Paine's revolutionary life and writings—in spite of the best efforts of the nation's political, economic, and cultural elites—had remained a powerful source of inspiration and encouragement to generations of Americans. He correctly figured that Paine and his words would remind Americans who they were and what they had to do.[9]

Between 1914 and 1945 Americans would fight two world wars and endure a devastating economic depression. At the same time, many would suffer their country's own persistent, sometimes intensifying, injustices, inequalities, and tyrannies. Yet Americans not only would avoid succumbing to the dictatorships and totalitarianisms that overwhelmed so many other nations. They also would accomplish great things. They would triumph over fascism and make the United States into the world's foremost power. And they would assert the ideals of the commonwealth over the imperatives of the market and enhance the authority of democratic government and the rights of labor against the power and privilege of capital. While some would see the hand of Providence at work, progress would require awesome struggle and sacrifice and entail many a tragic and ironic turn.

Responding to the crises and defending, advancing, or resisting the nation's democratic impulse, Americans high and low, left and right, would, as ever, reach back to the Founders for guidance and sanction. Liberals and radicals—not in every instance and all too often in conflict with the right and with each other—would continue to turn to Paine. Conservatives, still disdainful and fearful of his memory and legacy, would for the most part keep their distance from him.

Franklin Roosevelt was not actually the first twentieth-century president to quote Paine; nor was his presidency the first to recruit Paine to a war effort. Woodrow Wilson and his administration—in which FDR had served as assistant secretary of the navy—had engaged Paine during the First World War. While Wilson never acknowledged Paine by name, his articulation of "liberal" or "democratic internationalism" as the basis of American foreign policy and his formulation of the principles to govern postwar international relations bore Paine's imprint.

A Virginia Democrat, a serious Presbyterian, and a Princeton University scholar and president, Wilson seems an unlikely figure to have garnered ideas from Paine. Confronting the tumults of the 1890s, Wilson had identified the conservative Edmund Burke as his intellectual hero. And yet in his successful campaigns for the governorship of New Jersey in 1910 and the presidency in 1912, Wilson embraced Progressivism and expressed views both Jeffersonian and Painite.[10]

Four candidates—Republican incumbent William Howard Taft, Socialist Eugene Debs, National Progressive Theodore Roosevelt, and Democrat Woodrow Wilson—competed for the presidency in 1912.

However, the race really boiled down to a contest between the competing "Progressivisms" of former President Roosevelt and political newcomer Wilson, each of whom presented his own answer to the question of how to tame the corporate trusts that had formed during the Gilded Age. Whereas Roosevelt's Hamiltonian "New Nationalism" proposed accepting but regulating the trusts, Wilson's Jeffersonian "New Freedom" called for breaking them up in favor of restoring economic competition.[11]

The two principal contestants also espoused different perspectives on America's role in the world, which, though of seemingly lesser importance at the time, was hardly inconsequential considering the country's growing industrial and financial might and its status as a colonial power in the Caribbean and Pacific following the 1898 war with Spain. While Roosevelt had always emphasized America's capacity to assert its interests within the prevailing international balance of power, Wilson—as if he had just read *Common Sense*—had spoken of America as the bearer of mankind's hopes and the champion not of narrow national or imperial but of universal interests. In words reminiscent of Paine's, Wilson declared, "America is not distinguished so much by its wealth and material power as by the fact that it was born with an ideal, a purpose to serve mankind. And all mankind has sought her as a haven of equal justice."[12]

Though he had written appreciatively of Paine in *A History of the American People*, Wilson never actually referred to him in his presidential addresses; not even in 1914, when, using Paine's own words, he announced, "The United States must be neutral in fact as well as in name during these days that are to try men's souls." Nevertheless, Wilson's foreign affairs speeches increasingly resounded with Paine's arguments and ever more evidently so after he led the country into the war.[13]

Seeing little difference between the aims of the Central Powers, Germany, Austria-Hungary, and Ottoman Turkey, and those of the Allies, Britain, France, and Russia, Wilson—in the face of murderous German U-boat attacks on American ships, and in spite of his own sympathies for Britain—had tried both to keep the country out of the war and to get the belligerents to negotiate a "peace without victory." Yet in April 1917, no longer able to tolerate Germany's refusal to recognize America's rights as a neutral, he requested a declaration of war.

Appearing before Congress, he made clear his exasperation. But his message also revealed that he had fundamentally reconceived the significance of the conflict and what America's entry might mean both on the battlefield and, ultimately, at the peace table. He now viewed the war as an opportunity to fashion a new international order. Welcoming the February Revolution in Russia and decrying Germany's "Prussian autocracy," he pronounced America's objectives with missionary zeal and Painite spirit: "The world must be made safe for democracy. Its peace must be planted upon the tested foundations of political liberty. We have no selfish ends to serve. We desire no conquest, no dominion. We seek no indemnities for ourselves, no material compensation for the sacrifices we shall freely make. We are but one of the champions of the rights of mankind."[14]

Consciously or otherwise, Wilson made Paine's conception of America's world-historic role his own. Undeniably, Paine originally had warned America not to "dip her hands in the bloody work of Europe." However, in the early 1790s, as prospects for democratic revolution in Europe improved, he began to see things differently and then suggested that in favor of republicanism and peace—as well as to secure the independence of Spanish America and reduce the Atlantic powers' battle fleets—the United States ally itself with the projected new governments.[15]

Moreover, as Wilson developed his own vision of a democratic victory and peace—fully aware of anti-imperialist protests from the left—he seemed to draw ever more directly on Paine's work. As one of the president's supporters noted, Wilson's Fourteen Points—calling for open treaties, freedom of navigation, free trade, arms reduction, the end of European empires, the self-determination of peoples, and an international association of nations to replace the traditional balance of power with a system of collective security—revived ideas Paine first advanced in *Rights of Man*. Defending the American and French Revolutions and, again, envisioning similar struggles sweeping Europe, Paine pictured the new states creating a confederation to promote the republican cause and thereby bringing an end to the "intrigue of courts, by which the system of war is kept up." Paine wrote that "when all the governments of Europe shall be established on the representative system, nations will become acquainted, and the animosities and prejudices fomented by the intrigues and artifices of courts will cease."[16]

For reasons pragmatic, principled, and ancestral, Americans had little wish to fight in Europe. Even Progressives who cheered the Wilson administration's domestic initiatives expressed doubts about Wilson's war message. But encouraging a belief that victory over aristocratic autocracy in Europe would invigorate campaigns against corporate "autocracy" at home, the president's rhetoric soon won over the majority of Americans, most liberals, and against their own party's stance, quite a few Socialists.[17]

Still, sensitive to Americans' reservations and expecting antiwar resistance from isolationists, radicals, and the nation's German, Austrian, and Hungarian ethnic communities, the Wilson administration aggressively set about mobilizing not only men and matériel but also public opinion. Along with instituting a military draft and establishing agencies to coordinate industrial and agricultural production, the president set up the Committee on Public Information (CPI) and appointed George Creel, a well-known muckraking journalist and urban reformer, to direct it.

An admirer and, later, biographer of Paine, Creel apparently understood his commission in terms of Paine's role during the Revolution. "It was a fight for the *minds* of men, for the 'conquest of their convictions,'" Creel would write. "What we had to have was no mere surface unity, but a passionate belief in the justice of America's cause that should weld the people of the United States into one white-hot mass instinct with fraternity, devotion, courage, and deathless determination." Enlisting journalists, social scientists, historians, and artists to serve as pamphleteers, lecturers, and designers—among them many a leading liberal and socialist, such as Charles Merriam, Charles Beard, A. M. Simons, and Clarence Darrow—Creel pursued his assignment with impressive energy and enthusiasm. Under his direction the CPI issued 75 million booklets and leaflets, a comparably vast number of posters, reams of press releases, several motion pictures, and a host of "war-study curricula" for the nation's schools and colleges. It also signed up 75,000 volunteers, known as "four-minute men," to deliver short, pointed speeches on the progress and imperative of the war at movie theaters and other public venues.[18]

Whether promoting patriotism, stressing "Americanism" over "origins," depicting the enemy as monstrous, or selling Liberty Bonds, Creel and his colleagues repeatedly harnessed historical figures and symbols to their productions. Moreover—against the grain of a century of official practice, but acting on their own affections, as well as expectations of its popular appeal—they openly incorporated Paine's pen to their propaganda work. And soon Paine and his words were showing up on editorial pages, on public wall spaces, and in speeches at Independence Day and other patriotic celebrations. As the editors of *The New York Times* observed in a piece punctuated with quotes from *Common Sense* and the *Crisis*:

> There was a time—and it was not so long ago—when the name of Thomas Paine was anathema with many a good pious soul. Today, with the entrance of the United States into the war, the words and the teachings of this great writer of the days of the American Revolution are being brought vividly home to us through some of the literary propaganda of the Government on Liberty Loan posters and elsewhere.[19]

Unfortunately, while harvesting ideas and lines from Paine's writings, Wilson and his appointees ignored Paine's admonition, "He that would make his own liberty secure must guard even his enemy from oppression; for if he violates this duty he establishes a precedent that will reach to himself." Pursuing the war to make the world "safe for democracy," they would encourage fresh hopes, initiatives, and reforms, most critically the ratification in 1920 of the Nineteenth Amendment recognizing women's right to vote. However, they also would license authoritarian acts and foment a reactionary political climate that would outlast the war itself.[20]

For a start, the CPI's propaganda—pushing "one-hundred percent Americanism" and portraying Germans as beastly figures—not only engendered nationalism and a fearful hatred of the enemy; it also incited attacks upon German Americans and inflamed nativist passions that would lead Americans to practically renege on the country's long commitment to serve, in Paine's words, as "an asylum for mankind."[21]

Even more deliberately, Wilson himself made it clear that he would brook no dissent. On Flag Day in June 1917 he bluntly declared, "Woe be to the man or group of men that seeks to stand in our way." And the actions his administration took or tolerated in the name of national security went well beyond rallying the citizenry and defending against sabotage and subversion. Working with Congress, the Wilsonians approved passage in 1917 of the Espionage Act and, in 1918, an amended version known as the Sedition Act, the latter of which made it a crime—carrying a penalty of up to $10,000 or twenty years in prison or both—not only to "interfere with the operation or success of the military" but also to "utter, print, write, or publish any disloyal, profane, scurrilous, or abusive language about the form of government . . . the Constitution . . . the military or naval forces . . . the flag . . . or the uniform of the Army or Navy of the United States . . . [or] urge, incite or advocate any curtailment of production in this country."[22]

The Wilson administration also lined up allies to assist it in enforcing the two acts. It welcomed the cooperation of the American Protective League (APL), a newly formed vigilante-like organization, whose 250,000 members made it their job to report on the activities and attitudes of their fellow citizens. And it enthused capitalists by including anarchist groups, the Industrial Workers of the World (the IWW or "Wobblies"), and the Socialist party among its primary targets for surveillance and suppression. Notably, while the latter two opposed the war, neither moved to formally block conscription. However, in contrast to the far larger and more moderate American Federation of Labor (AFL), which supported the war, the IWW continued both to organize strikes and to try to create "One Big Union" of the working class, and the Socialists, to lambaste corporate plutocracy and its control of politics and the state.[23]

Aided by the APL, the Justice Department shut down radical periodicals and prosecuted speakers who challenged or criticized the war effort. Every group on the left underwent scrutiny and harassment. But some suffered in particular. Thousands of Wobblies and many a prominent Socialist, including the left's greatest champion, Eugene Debs, were arrested. And in those cases where the government did not act quickly or forcefully enough, businessmen colluded with local officials and groups like the APL to destroy radical labor, oftentimes using violence to do so.[24]

Yet as Debs, for one, would demonstrate, the Wilsonians had no lock on Paine's memory or legacy.

Debs himself was no pacifist. Like Wilson—though far more acknowledging of Paine's inspiration—he believed in America's world-historic purpose and promise and the imperative of extending democracy, if necessary by force of arms. Nevertheless, he opposed American involvement in the First World War, seeing the conflict as a struggle to enhance the power and profits of capital, not the lives of working people.[25]

Actually, for months Debs had remained a relatively marginal voice in the antiwar movement. However, outraged by the administration's jailing of dissidents, he undertook a speaking tour in June 1918, "determined either to open prison gates or to swing them shut behind myself." After two weeks in Illinois and Indiana, he headed to Canton, Ohio, to attend the Ohio Socialist Party convention. Arriving there on June 16, he stopped at the local county workhouse to see three Socialist leaders serving sentences for sedition and then went on to the convention.[26]

That afternoon—before a gathering of more than a thousand people (which included a U.S. attorney and his hired stenographers)—Debs proclaimed his antipathy both for "Prussian militarism" and for America's own political and social order. Noting the irony of its having become "extremely dangerous to exercise the constitutional right of free speech in a country fighting to make democracy safe in the world," he attacked the Wilson administration for suppressing Americans' liberties. Titling the nation's capitalists "Wall Street Junkers" (after the Prussian aristocracy), he chastised them for wrapping themselves in the flag while exploiting the American people. And referring to a Supreme Court decision striking down a child labor law, he accused the justices of allowing industrialists to "continue to grind the flesh and blood and bones of puny little children into profits." Finally, he beseeched American workers to struggle for industrial democracy. "It is our duty," he said, "to build the new nation and the free republic."[27]

As he had sought, Debs was indicted and arrested a fortnight later and tried in September on charges of obstructing enlistment and encouraging insubordination in the American military. Refusing to allow his lawyers to call any witnesses on his behalf, Debs requested and received permission to address the court himself, not so much to get himself acquitted as to advance a conception of patriotism critically different from that of the Wilsonians.

Taking the stand, Debs granted the "truth of all that has been testified to" and fully admitted to opposing the "present form of government" and the "present social system." Yet he stated he had "never advocated violence" and explicitly denied he was guilty of sedition. The trial, he contended, was not even really about him. "I am not on trial here," he declared. "There is an infinitely greater issue that is being tried . . . American institutions are on trial here before a court of American citizens. The future will tell."[28]

Making his case—that is, America's case—Debs imparted a narrative of the nation in which radicals served as the leading agents of America's political and moral progress, and in those terms he called George Washington, Samuel Adams, Patrick Henry, Benjamin Franklin, and his foremost hero, Thomas Paine, to appear alongside him. These "rebels of their day," Debs recounted, started out, like him, as minority voices, "but they had the moral courage to stand erect and defy all the storms of detraction." He next summoned abolitionists Elijah Lovejoy, William Lloyd Garrison, Thaddeus Stevens, and Wendell Phillips to join them, recalling that they too had been "regarded as public enemies" and yet Americans now taught their "children to revere their memories, while all of their detractors are in oblivion." And lastly, to show the unprecedented character of the government's actions, he pointed to Abraham Lincoln, Charles Sumner, and Daniel Webster and noted that as much as those eminent and now-honored men had opposed American wars and denounced presidents, they never suffered criminal indictment.[29]

Invoking America's finest radicals and submitting that Americans "are not yet free," Debs testified, "If I have criticized, if I have condemned, it is because I have believed myself justified in doing so under the laws of the land." Quoting the First Amendment, he reminded America that "the revolutionary fathers . . . understood that free speech, a free press, and the right of free assemblage by the people were fundamental principles of democratic government." And enjoining that if "Congress enacts any law that conflicts with this provision in the Constitution, that law is void," he warned, "If the Espionage Law finally stands, then the Constitution of the United States is dead."[30]

In the course of his remarks, which lasted almost two hours, Debs reaffirmed his love of America and its "symbol of freedom," the American flag. But he did not leave it at that. Those same feelings, he explained, compelled him to object "when that flag is prostituted to base ends . . . by those who, in the name of patriotism, would keep the people in subjection." And reciting Paine's words, "My country is the world. To do good is my religion," he declared his commitment to a "wider patriotism" and, like his hero, presented himself as a citizen of both the United States and the world.[31]

The jury found Debs guilty, and the judge sentenced him to ten years in prison. Nearly sixty-five years old, Debs would spend almost two years behind bars. But his address had "electrified Socialists throughout America." In 1920—while still incarcerated—he would again "run" for president and as in 1912, receive almost a million votes.[32]

Disappointing liberals and socialists who had rallied to Wilson's rhetoric (and confirming the worst expectations of those who had rejected it), the postwar years—the "Roaring Twenties"—would witness Republican presidencies, corporate aggrandizement, deepening class inequalities, persistent segregation and intensifying racism and anti-Semitism, restrictive immigration quotas, resurgent evangelicalism, Prohibition, and business, not liberal or democratic, internationalism.

While the left would not disappear, it would wither and further fragment into liberal Democrats, Progressives, Farmer-Laborites, Socialists, and—in the wake of the Bolshevik Revolution in Russia—Communists. Making matters worse, the labor movement would shrink rapidly, with union membership dropping from five million to three million between 1920 and 1929. Apparently bereft of a cause to fire their imaginations, many intellectuals would exercise their talents either as hucksters for American culture or as critics of it; the latter, such as journalist H. L. Mencken and writer William E. Woodward, turned the Progressive historians' "debunking" into a popular art form. The editors of *Survey* magazine would express leftists' shared discontents in a 1926 symposium that asked, "Where are the Pre-War Radicals?" Some others would do so by re-engaging Paine.[33]

Repression, disillusionment, and prosperity, as well as sectarianism, took their tolls on the left. War mobilization drew the nation's regions closer together, but it also intensified nativism and racism. (The fastest-growing movement in the early 1920s was probably the Ku Klux Klan.) Moreover, the suppression of dissent did not cease in 1918. Revolution in Russia, uprisings in Central Europe, and a postwar recession engendered a fear among America's political and economic elites that Communist revolution would soon erupt in the United States. And when a wave of strikes involving four million workers swept the country in 1919, the governing classes responded swiftly and forcefully with the first "Red Scare" of the century. States enacted new sedition laws, and in what historians have termed the "most massive violation of civil liberties in American history," the Justice Department under Attorney General A. Mitchell Palmer and his deputy J. Edgar Hoover raided homes and offices, rounded up thousands, and proceeded to arrange for the deportations of radical immigrants and aliens (among them anarchist Emma Goldman). Though only about five hundred people suffered expulsion—for Assistant Secretary of Labor Louis F. Post, an avid Paine admirer, bravely demanded that the government recognize the legal rights of the detained—the Scare's effects continued to reverberate through public life. And while capitalists themselves used every means to crush labor's militancy, organizations such as the American Legion formed to help combat the "Red Menace."[34]

Popular disenchantment with the Wilson administration further undermined Progressivism and the left. The postwar recession and Red Scare turned Americans against liberal reformism. And the costs of war and disappointments with the Versailles peace treaty turned them against liberal internationalism. The president got the rest of the world to subscribe to a League of Nations but failed to secure his own country's membership.[35]

Economic recovery, growth, and development also hampered the left. Industrial and agricultural production expanded rapidly, and per capita income rose in the 1920s. Yet with the greatest share of the new wealth and income generated going to making the capitalist rich richer and underwriting the expansion of the middle classes, life for most of the urban and rural laboring classes remained difficult. Class conflicts persisted and flared anew, but corporate carrots and sticks, promises of improvement, divisions on the left (exacerbated by Communist devotion to Soviet Russia's commands and Marxist-Leninist ideology), and the conservative unionism of the craft-based American Federation of Labor all served to effectively inhibit or deter industrial workers from organizing and protesting too loudly.

Though conservatism and corporate capitalism ruled—"The chief business of the American people is business," President Calvin Coolidge pontificated—Paine's public status actually improved. In spite of his "enlistment" in the war effort, Paine remained anathema to the religious orthodox. Concurring on little else, Southern Baptists and Catholics agreed that Paine was a despicable character whose arguments on God and the Bible were unforgivably subversive of Christian belief and society. Nevertheless the political elite, conservatives included, approached Paine differently. They still disdained him for his radicalism, but they now distinguished between his "patriotic" and his "other" labors.[36]

In 1923 the Greenwich Village Historical Society of New York decided to remember Paine by affixing a tablet to the exterior of the house in which he had passed away, and they invited President Warren Harding to participate in the memorial event. Stating, "There always will be many among us to differ keenly from some of the views of Thomas Paine," Harding saw fit to decline the invitation. But he added, "Surely there cannot be many to doubt the value and splendid sincerity of his patriotic service to the cause of liberty in his own country and elsewhere."[37]

Even more positively, and without qualification, General John J. "Blackjack" Pershing, who had commanded the American Expeditionary Force in Europe, spoke of Paine's influence at a 1924 Memorial Day ceremony dedicating a monument to America's "doughboys" at Camp Merritt in New Jersey. Reminding the gathered that Paine's "inspiring words . . . became an encouragement to Washington's troops as they met and defeated the enemy," Pershing declared that those same "sentiments filled the breasts of those who passed this spot to battle against tyranny beyond the seas."[38]

None less than the editors of *Better Homes and Gardens* felt up to honoring Paine in 1926, the sesquicentennial of American independence. As part of a series on "Homes of Famous Americans," they published a lengthy piece on him and his New Rochelle cottage that unreservedly stated, "We as a nation probably owe more to Thomas Paine than to any other human being."[39]

Paine's First World War "service" seemed to instigate other developments as well. A rejuvenated Thomas Paine National Historical Association again staged annual gatherings attended by a roster of prominent folk. Scholars reconsidered Paine's contributions both to independence and to American culture more broadly. And variously intended for devotees, college classrooms, and popular readers, new Paine biographies and anthologies were published.[40]

The notice afforded Paine expressed not simply Americans' belated desire to recognize his patriotism but also their instinctive yearnings to reinvigorate the democratic impulse he had done so much to instill in American experience. Describing Paine as the "Ragged Philosopher of his race" and "tribune of the people without self-interest," author and educator Carl Van Doren wrote in his introduction to the 1922 Modern Library selection of Paine's works that the famed pamphleteer "speaks to the common man in the common tongue" and that his writings remain the "textbook of radical thought." Introducing a later collection, poet Arthur Wallace Peach highlighted Paine's "fearlessness . . . idealism . . . and belief in the principle of democracy." And other liberal intellectuals, haunted by the conservatism, capitalism, and fundamentalism of the day, referred admiringly and longingly to Paine's libertarianism, egalitarianism, and deism. David Muzzey wistfully penned that Paine's "soul is marching on."[41]

In that spirit, many a liberal Democrat and Socialist continued to attend to Paine. Claiming a special attachment to him and believing that "the business of history is to arouse an intelligent discontent, to foster a fruitful radicalism," Vernon Parrington, a Progressive scholar from Kansas, rededicated himself to composing his magnum opus and classic-to-be, *Main Currents in American Thought*. Proudly registering that his English immigrant grandfather had been a "follower of Tom Paine," Parrington announced in 1918 that *"I become more radical with every year."* Voting for Debs in 1920 and the Socialist-endorsed Progressive Robert La Follette in 1924, he wrote *Main Currents* guided by sympathies "liberal rather than conservative, Jeffersonian rather than Federalistic."[42]

Commencing his narrative in the colonial period, Parrington articulated the history of American thought as a continuing argument between liberalism and conservatism that after 1790 became a "struggle between the spirit of the Declaration of Independence and the spirit of the Constitution, the one primarily concerned with the rights of man, the other . . . with the rights of property." Assigning Paine and Jefferson critical roles in the advancement of democracy, he explained that "Paine became the popular disseminator of the philosophy of republicanism and Jefferson, the practical statesman embodying it in political programs." And apparently confirming that others empathized with his anxiety about the triumph of conservatism and his aspirations to redeem liberalism, Parrington received the Pulitzer Prize in History in 1928.[43]

Believing that "democracy is the only thing in the world worth fighting for," University of Chicago historian William E. Dodd, who served as a foreign policy adviser to the Wilson administration after originally opposing American entry to the war, responded to the politics of the 1920s by touring the country with lectures on "Little Men of Great Influence" that included a major talk on Paine. And in a follow-up article Dodd broached the idea of a Paine monument in Washington, D.C.[44]

Socialists and labor union activists still regularly recited Paine's words and encouraged one another and their children to learn about the "heroic worker . . . and free-thinking leader of the American Revolution." *The Appeal to Reason* had ceased publication, but—now owned by the freethinking socialist Emanuel Haldeman-Julius, who said he "cut his eyeteeth" on Paine—the same presses that had printed the newspaper were producing an extraordinarily successful series of cheap three-and-a-half-by-five-inch pamphletlike texts for the laboring classes known as the Little Blue Books. And among its many best-selling titles were several by or about Paine.[45]

Reminiscent of the Haymarket martyrs, the immigrant Italian working-class anarchists Nicola Sacco and Bartolomeo Vanzetti were arrested during the Red Scare and in questionable proceedings convicted and sentenced to death for the murder of a factory paymaster in Braintree, Massachusetts. Refusing to give up hope, they read Paine, along with Jefferson, Lincoln, and Whitman, and petitioned for a new trial. However, their appeals failed, and—though they would receive posthumous pardons fifty years later—they were executed in the electric chair in 1927.[46]

Even debunkers occasionally turned to Paine. Recognized for their caustic commentary, debunkers acquired reputations as cynics for their eagerness to tread on the traditional, deflate the pompous, and belittle the naive, activities that entailed humorously skewering elites and masses alike and taking on figures as revered as the Founding Fathers. Yet as their treatments of Paine seem to show, the debunkers were not really cynics but, as one scholar has contended, dissenters and idealists who hid behind "comic masks." Even as they spoke of Paine in sarcastic and unflattering terms, they often did so with a certain affection and admiration, suggesting that they too yearned for a more democratic America and may have found encouragement in Paine's life and writings.[47]

In a work that incited a fair bit of public anger, William E. Woodward, who actually coined the word *debunk* in 1923, presented George Washington not as the saintly and brilliant general and statesman of legend but as a man with real failings. Less controversially, Woodward introduced Paine as an "intellectual desperado of the first rank." However, even as he mocked Paine, he revealed a respect for, if not envy of, his capacity to reach the people, and twenty years later Woodward would publish a most laudatory biography of Paine himself.[48]

Another debunker, a prolific and popular author of "psychography," Gamaliel Bradford approached Paine in the same way. Defining Paine as a "rebel" and "destructive" character, Bradford lumped the revolutionary in with those who "tear down and destroy," letting others "worry about building up again." Seemingly making clear his intent, he titled the original essay "Damaged Souls," reprinted it in a similarly titled volume, and situated it between chapters on Benedict Arnold and Aaron Burr. Yet Bradford must have intended something quite different, for in the course of the essay he repeatedly belied his own nasty assertions about Paine. Writing that Paine's words "burn everywhere with a large and splendid ardor for democratic ideals, for liberty, equality, and opportunity for everyone," Bradford observed that while others equivocated, Paine urged, "Be free, set up for yourselves, a great destiny is before you, show yourselves worthy of it"; and where others lacked vision, Paine "preached nationality, coordination, cooperation, that the people should feel that they were a people and should grow strong in that consciousness." Every American, Bradford would conclude, "ought to be grateful to him as one of the active Founders of the United States of America," for Paine "taught men to think." And finally, Bradford confessed, "I sometimes wish I had the courage and the character to be a rebel myself."[49]

The complacency of the 1920s would be undone, not by a resurgent left, but by the worst depression in American history. In 1929 the stock market crashed, and in the next three years banks, businesses, and factories closed; GNP fell 30 percent; cities went broke; unemployment soared to 25 percent (peaking in 1933 at fifteen million workers); median income dropped by 50 percent; 30 percent of farmers lost their homesteads; and the nation's birth rate declined by 15 percent to its lowest rate ever.[50]

Millions suffered, and Americans began to lose confidence both in themselves and in their nation's grand progressive story. James Truslow Adams articulated the anxiety in the epilogue to his 1931 book *The Epic of America*: "The American dream . . . has been a dream of being able to grow to fullest development . . . unhampered by the barriers which had slowly been erected in older civilizations, unrepressed by social orders which had developed for the benefit of classes rather than for simple human beings of any and every class . . . It has been a great epic and a great dream. *What, now, of the future?*"[51]

Seeking to answer that question, Americans not only looked around and ahead but also back to the very beginnings of the Republic, where once again many rediscovered Paine. Having made no reference to him in *The Epic of America*, Truslow Adams in his very next book, *The March of Democracy*, wrote enthusiastically of the "born revolutionist" and his work, noting specifically of *Common Sense* that "its sentences were to be the common-places in America for a century and to be recited by every schoolboy." More ironically, in 1931 the liberal Catholic magazine *Commonweal* published "The Revival of Thomas Paine," which essentially blessed Paine for having "shattered the foundations" not only of "imperial and monarchical institutions" but also of "Protestantism" and—however unintentionally—for having "helped to clear the way . . . for the triumphant return of the Catholic Church." Comparing him to Jefferson and Franklin on the subject of God and religion, it also presented Paine as the bravest and "sincerest" of the three.[52]

The attention Paine received in the 1930s would far surpass that of the previous decade. Four new biographies appeared, along with four new editions of his writings. Textbook coverage expanded, and extracts of his works became staples of anthologies of Americana. Study of Paine not only increased but also became more critically appreciative (indicating that sympathetic scholars could now treat him seriously).[53]

Moreover, as liberals, socialists, and communists sought to resurrect themselves and remake America, they would again eagerly seize hold of Paine and avidly cultivate his memory and legacy, from politics to the popular arts. Working in New York City in 1933, Mexican artist Diego Rivera painted "Portrait of America," a series of historical murals at the New Workers' School that prefigured later cultural work by the American left. Filling the panel on the Revolution with historical references, he placed Jefferson, Franklin, and Paine in the foreground with Jefferson looking to Franklin and Franklin pointing to a scroll held by Paine that read, "Rights of Man . . . My country is the world . . . to do good, my religion."[54]

Though the Depression soon instigated radical-led protests and demands for work and relief, they garnered repression as much as assistance, and the overwhelming majority of citizens, as anxious as they became, remained quiet. Americans, however, were far from apathetic, and in the 1932 presidential election they replaced Republican Herbert Hoover with Democrat Franklin Roosevelt. A New York patrician, Roosevelt was no radical and offered no comprehensive plan to rescue the American economy. Nevertheless he exuded confidence and seemed ready to use the powers of government to address the country's plight. And on taking office he would not simply use those powers but also dramatically extend them as he advanced the policies, programs, and projects known as the New Deal.

Actually, Roosevelt's presidency entailed two New Deals (both of which—the latter especially—the author of *Rights of Man* would have heartily approved). The first stressed economic recovery and relief through undertakings like the Emergency Banking Act, the Agricultural Adjustment Act, the National Industrial Recovery Act, the Tennessee Valley Authority, the Civilian Conservation Corps, and Federal Emergency Relief Administration. The second, commencing in 1935, emphasized social justice and reform through endeavors like the Social Security Act, the National Labor Relations Act (Wagner Act), the Works Progress Administration (which included the Federal Theater, Arts, Music, and Writers' Projects), the National Housing Act, and the Fair Labor Standards Act. Neither would bring an end to the Depression (unemployment never fell below 10 percent in the 1930s), but by recasting the democratic state as the regulator of the capitalist economy and guarantor of the basic welfare of the citizenry, they represented a revolution in government. Moreover, both served to renew Americans' hopes and energies, as the phenomenal revival and expansion of the labor movement attested. Encouraged by FDR's victories and empowered by New Deal legislation, labor—especially industrial unionism—experienced a dramatic rejuvenation, starting with a massive strike wave in 1934 and continuing through the next several years by way of the newly formed Congress of Industrial Organizations (CIO), concerted organizing drives, and major battles in the automobile, steel, and textile industries. And by the end of the decade union membership had grown from three to eight million.[55]

The New Deal as a whole never met universal approbation. But not just Republicans opposed it. Organizing the American Liberty League, businessmen and conservatives from both parties attacked FDR and his administration. Populist demagogues such as Louisiana politician Huey Long, with his "Share Our Wealth" platform, and "radio priest" Father Charles Coughlin, with his protofascist National Union for Social Justice, first backed and then turned against the president. Left politicians, intellectuals, and activists within and without the Democratic camp variously scorned, criticized, and cheered the president while pressing him to move more deliberately against corporate capital and in support of progressive causes. Yet out of the fray Roosevelt would build a new Democratic governing coalition that, along with the traditional white southern Democrats, would include northern industrial workers, immigrant and second-generation ethnic Catholics and Jews, and African Americans. Though burdened by segregationists, this coalition would serve as the basis for a liberal politics that would shape American public life for almost forty years.[56]

The struggles of the 1930s entailed fights not only over political economy and public policy but also over history. Attempting a revolution in government, Roosevelt and the New Dealers asserted the posthumous support of the Founding Fathers, particularly that of Jefferson (for whom, as a fellow patrician Democrat, FDR felt a special affinity). Incensing the likes of the Liberty Leaguers—who hotly disputed the idea that Jefferson would have endorsed expanding the state's powers at the expense of property rights—the president and his colleagues pressed their claims by quoting Jefferson in their speeches, creating the Jefferson Memorial, helping to refurbish Monticello, placing Jefferson's image on the nickel and the three-cent stamp, and—hinting at Paine's influence as well—referring to obstructionist businessmen as "economic royalists."[57]

Roosevelt was hardly alone in taking recourse to hisory. Hoping to recharge America's democratic impulse, most leftists also looked to the nation's past. Rejecting the debunkers' practices, Marxist writer and editor V. F. Calverton contended that "the great problem confronting and challenging us today . . . is not that of debunking our past but of revaluating it." Eschewing the practices of the Communists as well, he further argued that "the radical thought which has been promulgated here has been of alien extraction, totally out of line with the development of the American revolutionary tradition." And proudly recalling Paine, Jefferson, and others, he insisted that "we must learn not to scoff at our revolutionary past but to build upon it and advance it."[58]

While liberals and radicals alike made a great deal of Jefferson and ended up elevating him for the first time to the Founders' most elite ranks, those who stood to Roosevelt's left made just as much, if not more, of Paine (and in this instance faced no competition from the right in doing so). Paine offered no immediate solution to the crisis and catastrophe of industrial capitalism, but 1930s leftists found his attack on power and privilege, his faith in working people, and his vision of America inspiring. Calverton would write, "To few men does the birth of democracy owe as much as to Thomas Paine. Paine infused it with the spirit of revolutionary idealism; those who came after him robbed it of that glow and turned it into the pawn of privilege." And Paine's career encouraged many to imagine that they too could make a revolutionary difference.[59]

Exasperated by politicians' failures to rescue the country from the Depression, and convinced that Roosevelt offered no real alternative, Alfred Bingham, a young socialist from a prominent New England family, started up the magazine *Common Sense* in late 1932. "What is needed in the United States," he wrote, "is a native American radicalism, a radicalism free from affiliation with any of the existing organized groups." And recruiting contributors like the philosophers John Dewey and Reinhold Niebuhr, labor radical A. J. Muste, historian Charles Beard, and writers V. F. Calverton, John Dos Passos, James Rorty, Lewis Mumford, and Upton Sinclair, Bingham and his co-editor Selden Rodman strove to foment a "Second American Revolution."[60]

Titling the magazine *Common Sense* was more than symbolic. Announcing their commitment to the "American ideals of liberty, democracy, and equality of opportunity" and their opposition to capitalism, Bingham and Rodman called both for immediate state action to address the Depression and for a "constitutional convention to adapt the principles of the American Revolution to modern needs." Bingham himself envisioned the magazine serving as the voice of a new party uniting the middle and laboring classes in a movement to construct a rationally organized, democratically controlled economy based on "production-for-use." He had traveled to Russia and, though impressed by its economic development, found its authoritarianism deeply disturbing. Also, he had read Marx and, while influenced by his theory of class conflict, concluded that Marx had overestimated the industrial working class's capacity to transform society and underestimated the middle classes' potential. Rejecting the Soviet model and Marxist politics, Bingham tried to create a socialist alternative to both capitalism and communism based on the technocratic and egalitarian ideas of Edward Bellamy and the radical democratic ideals of Paine.[61]

Competing with *The New Republic* and *The Nation, Common Sense* became, as historian Arthur Schlesinger, Jr., would later put it, "the most lively and interesting forum of radical discussion in the country." Aligned with John Dewey's League for Independent Political Action, it supported the growth of Farmer-Laborite parties like that in Minnesota led by then-governor Floyd Olson, and it welcomed the formation of similar political initiatives such as Upton Sinclair's EPIC (End Poverty in California). Yet *Common Sense* never became the popular force its editors hoped it would, and in 1936, fearing the rise of an American fascist movement, Bingham endorsed Roosevelt and repositioned the magazine on the left wing of the Democratic Party.[62]

Though at the outset of the 1930s the Communist Party of the United States (CPUSA) had shown little interest in America's revolutionary heritage, it too would lay claim to Paine. The party took its orders from the Soviet Union, which in the early years of the Depression meant obstinately insisting on the imminence of working-class revolution and foolishly denouncing other leftists as "social fascists." However, as the real threat of European fascism grew, Soviet thinking shifted dramatically and in 1935, ostensibly for the purpose of defending democracy but more obviously to secure friends for Stalin's Russia against Hitler's Germany, Moscow directed Communist parties around the world to drop their revolutionary rhetoric and establish "Popular Fronts" with other progressive groups. In favor of antifascist unity, the CPUSA reached out to the Socialists and Farmer-Laborites, and by 1937 it was backing FDR and energetically espousing support for the New Deal.[63]

The Popular Front had a significant impact on the left and on American culture more broadly. While CPUSA membership never totaled more than about 85,000, Communists represented a force far greater than their numbers implied. Often the most committed and effective organizers, they brought great verve and skill to labor campaigns and strikes, and given their own party's antiracist stance, they positively advanced the CIO's policy of developing multiethnic and multiracial unions.[64]

The CPUSA also professed a new patriotism that it defined in a radical yet rather exclusive fashion. Party general secretary Earl Browder declared that "the revolutionary tradition is the heart of Americanism" and that *Communism is the Americanism of the twentieth century.*" As historians have made clear, Browder himself was no "Jeffersonian Democrat." But imbued by his Kansas parents with Populist ideas, including Paine's, he clearly relished the line "Communism is Twentieth-Century Americanism." And however Janus-faced Communist leaders may have been, the great majority of party members—the greatest number of them the children of immigrants (and many of those from Eastern European Jewish families)—loved their country and enthusiastically adopted the slogan as their own.[65]

Communists soon took to identifying themselves as the political heirs of the Founding Fathers and Abraham Lincoln, and they always included Paine in that illustrious company. Urging his comrades to push the "people's movement" toward a more "complete conception of national unity," Browder would say, "In doing this we will continue . . . that democratic work begun by Washington, Jefferson, and Paine, and continued by Lincoln."[66]

Communists adored Paine the immigrant working-class intellectual and boosted him far and wide. On July 4, 1935, the CPUSA newspaper, the *Daily Worker*, published both the Declaration of Independence and excerpts from Paine's writings. Communists put Paine forward not just in the North but also as far south as Alabama, where the party took shape as a "black working-class organization." Opening a bookshop in downtown Birmingham, members adorned its windows with sketches of Jefferson, Franklin, and Paine. And in an anthology of Paine's writings published by the national party in 1937—presumably to honor the bicentennial of his birth—writer James Allen lionized Paine as a "foremost fighter for world democracy," the "chief propagandist and agitator of the revolution," a "Deist," and a radical who, seeing "beyond the limits of the bourgeois revolution," criticized the "accumulation of property" and envisioned a "system of social insurance."[67]

Advancing the New Deal, the Popular Front, and the CIO involved not only political and industrial actions but also efforts on the "cultural front." And here too leftists enlisted and promoted Paine. Pursuing the "laboring of American culture"—the process by which the labor movement more firmly and favorably embedded itself in public life and, in tandem with the New Deal, infused the nation with liberal and social-democratic understandings—progressive artists and intellectuals deployed Paine in some of the most brilliant and popular works of the day, such as the show *Pins and Needles*, the cantata "Ballad for Americans," and the novel *The Grapes of Wrath*.[68]

Sponsored by the garment workers' union, *Pins and Needles* opened in November 1937 and became one of the most successful musicals in Broadway history. Written by Harold Rome and staged by union members, its many wonderful tunes included "Status Quo," which presented Paine "writing books with might and main" and responding to Tory demands that he stop with the catchy:

> When you got to go, you got to go
> You can't stand still on freedom's track
> If you don't go forward, you go back
> You can't giddyup by saying Whoa
> And sitting on your status quo.

Similarly, in *Ballad for Americans*, a rousing, twelve-minute-long, operatic telling of American history, Communist composer Earl Robinson and lyricist John LaTouche spotlighted Paine as one among the generations of American "nobodies" who had the faith and courage to fight for liberty. Performed by the illustrious African American artist Paul Robeson and the American People's Chorus on the CBS radio network in November 1939, *Ballad* so excited Americans even the Republicans wanted it sung at their national convention in 1940. And in *The Grapes of Wrath*, his moving tale of the "Okie exodus" to the fields of California, John Steinbeck evoked Paine when speaking of the social revolution to come. After beautifully suggesting how working-class mutualism might lead to socialism, Steinbeck wrote, "If you who own the things people must have could understand this, you might preserve yourself. If you could separate causes from results, if you could know that Paine, Marx, Jefferson, Lenin, were results, not causes, you might survive. But that you cannot know. For the quality of owning freezes you forever into 'I,' and cuts you off forever from the 'we.'"[69]

Paine seemed to show up everywhere. His two-hundredth birthday in 1937 was marked by gatherings in several cities and by the publication of new biographies, anthologies, essays, and reviews. The Ohio School of the Air broadcast a radio show on him. The sculptor of Mount Rushmore, Gutzon Borglum, produced an American-commissioned Paine statue to be erected in Paris (the unveiling of which many a notable—including Helen Keller, a great Paine admirer—planned to attend). And in 1938 even former president Hoover spoke well of him publicly while visiting Philadelphia.[70]

The escalating attention accorded Paine involved a desire not simply to memorialize but also to reconnect with his radical democratic spirit in the face of persistent troubles at home and the perilous spread of tyranny abroad. In *The New York Times Magazine*, R. L. Duffus titled Paine the "Firebrand of Our Revolution" and observed that were he still alive he surely would have joined the International Brigades and composed a new *Crisis* to defend Republican Spain against Franco and the Falangists. In the *Charlotte News*, W. J. Cash dubbed Paine the "Real Father" of the United States and maintained that his enemies hated him not for *The Age of Reason* but for *Rights of Man*. And in *Scholastic*, a leading magazine for high school students, Israel Solemnick anointed him a "crusader for liberty" and "one of the most vigorous, courageous, and advanced thinkers of the eighteenth century." Even the editors of the Protestant *Christian Century* praised Paine as a "humanitarian," and those at the liberal Unitarian *Unity* devoted an entire issue to discussing his "heroic" contributions to political and religious freedom.[71]

Moreover, public interest in Paine did not subside in the wake of the bicentennial. With the increasing likelihood of another war—and its outbreak in 1939—Americans wondered anxiously about what their nation's exceptional purpose and promise demanded. And they naturally looked to Paine, the revolutionary patriot who had "dreamed America" and of "a world freed of the shackles of tyranny."[72]

Writers of every sort engaged Paine all the more frequently and all the more urgently. Hating fascism, but disgusted with the Communist Party and Soviet intrigues, John Dos Passos, the celebrated author of the *U.S.A.* trilogy, dug deeply in search of America's democratic roots. Preparing *The Ground We Stand Upon*, a volume on the early history of American self-government, he found himself so enthralled by Paine's radical arguments and "extraordinary courage and steadfastness" that he penned two essays on him for the magazine *Common Sense* and soon after edited *The Living Thoughts of Tom Paine*. Similarly motivated, the producers of the popular radio series *Cavalcade of America* presented the show *Thomas Paine*, and the Dramatists Play Service issued Ridgely Torrence's *Common Sense*, a script for schools relating Paine's role in the making of an independent and democratic United States. And even as federal appeals court judge Jerome Frank cited Paine in a legal opinion regarding free speech, stating that, "Such men as Thomas Paine, John Milton, and Thomas Jefferson were not fighting for the right to peddle commercial advertising," the Mark Cross Pen company filled the window of its New York store on Fifth Avenue with patriotic quotes, positioning Paine's "These are the times . . ." strikingly among them.[73]

Even before Roosevelt delivered his Washington's birthday fireside chat, his administration christened one of the "ugly duckling" Liberty ships that would convey men and matériel overseas the *Tom Paine*. Yet FDR's speech publicly linked Paine all the more closely to the war effort, and in the months and years that followed many and diverse Americans would use Paine's life and words to express their commitment not only to defeating fascism but also to securing and advancing democracy.[74]

Only weeks after the president spoke, *Invitation to Learning*, a radio series on the "Great Books of Western Civilization," dedicated a program to contrasting Burke and Paine on liberty. Reaching even more listeners, *Cavalcade of America* broadcast *In This Crisis*, a new play about Paine starring the renowned actor Claude Rains. In this

production, an agitated but distraught Paine is confronted by a mysterious "Stranger" who encourages him to compose the revolutionary
lines that would determine America's immediate fate and forever give
hope and confidence to the people when they most desperately
needed it. Responding to Paine's demand that he identify himself, the
Stranger replies: "I, Mr. Paine, am the first and last citizen of a country
known as the United States of America—a country that is yet a dream—
that may, or may not become reality, depending greatly upon you today.
I am not one man, I am a nation." And *The World We Are Fighting For*,
a 1943 radio series, had Jefferson, Lincoln, Paine, and John Paul Jones
sailing "Old Ironsides," the frigate USS *Constitution*, into war against a
German battleship.[75]

Not everyone bestowed affection on Paine. Participating in the
Great Books radio series, conservative cultural historian Jacques Barzun
made his disdain for Paine and his ideas quite clear. Even more critically, Philadelphia's Fairmount Park Commission refused to approve
the placement of a Paine statue on park grounds because Paine's "religious views" might make doing so "objectionable."[76]

Yet such animus was rare. Facing total war, the majority of Americans openly embraced Paine. Another biography and several new anthologies appeared, along with numerous articles treating Paine's ideas
on themes from natural rights to religion and human progress to international relations. And however much their subjects varied, all emphasized Paine's fundamental contributions to *democratic* life and thought.
Voicing the views of many, University of Chicago philosopher T. V.
Smith called Paine the "flaming symbol of human hope . . . the harbin-
ger in darkness of our democratic way."[77]

The wartime studies also provided a few surprises. With Paine's
constitutional and commercial arguments in mind, University of Wisconsin literary scholar Harry Hayden Clark introduced a valuable edition of Paine's writings with the observation that his "ideas were . . .
not without considerable elements of conservatism." Lecturing on
Paine, the Methodist bishop Francis John McConnell criticized his
handling of the Bible yet clearly distinguished his deism from atheism
and cogently argued that those of Paine's contemporaries who despised him did so not because of his "infidelity" but because he "hated
privilege," which they correctly perceived as threatening their status
and ambitions. And considering Paine's *Letter to the Abbé Raynal*, Dar-

rell Abel, a South Dakota State College history professor, appreciatively emphasized Paine's "internationalist" thought.[78]

In a far more popular vein, Communist writer Howard Fast in 1943
published *Citizen Tom Paine*, a fictional account of Paine's career that
became a national best-seller. Although he portrayed Paine as homely,
unkempt, and a "mighty drinker," Fast brilliantly and admiringly captured Paine's working-class sensibilities, love of America, and visionary
pursuit of global liberation. Relating Paine's deepening understanding
of America's world-historic possibilities, he wrote, "It was the inevitability of America that stirred him most; here was a new breed of men, not
of blood nor class, nor birth, but of a promise pure and simple; and the
promise when summed up, when whittled down, when made positive
and negative, shorn of all the great frame of mountains, rivers, and val-
leys, was freedom, and no more and no less than that."[79]

Throughout the country Americans grabbed hold of Paine and his
words to recall the nation's birth and meaning and to proclaim their
fighting spirit and determination. In Hollywood director and actor Orson Welles recorded an album of dramatic readings for distribution,
which, along with speeches by Jefferson, Lincoln, Wilson, and FDR,
included Paine's first *Crisis*. In New York, composer Burrill Phillips
penned the classical overture *Tom Paine*, and Earl Robinson and Lewis
Allan (Abel Meeropol) wrote "The House I Live In," a patriotic ballad
filled with democratic and multiethnic images that referred specifically
to Lincoln, Jefferson, and Paine that Paul Robeson, Josh White, and
Frank Sinatra would each in turn make popular. And in the predominantly Catholic, blue-collar city of Green Bay, Wisconsin, the
Altrusa Women's Club invited the well-known speaker Mrs. Kathryn
Turney Garten to lecture on Fast's *Citizen Tom Paine* because of its
"timeliness," and about a thousand people turned out to hear her. Introducing a new selection of Paine's writings, Fast himself explained the
great passion for Paine: "It is the nature of democratic nations, in times
of crisis, to seek out of their past men who fought tyranny bravely and
forthrightly. It gives us a sense of continuing tradition, a link not only
with the past but with the still unborn future, and thereby we take our
places in the timeless march of men of good will."[80]

"Yanks" carried Paine with them overseas, not only via the ship
named after him and by tucking Fast's novel into their duffel bags, but

also in their hearts and minds. Stationed near Paine's birthplace in England, airmen of the 388th Bomber Group presented to the town of Thetford a commemorative plaque whose words included "THOMAS PAINE, 1737–1809 . . . From his talented pen came the voice for the democratic aspirations of the American Republic . . . [and] this simple son of England lives on through the ideals & principles of the democratic world for which we fight today." Captain Marvin Hilton of Los Angeles even took him into combat over Hitler's Germany by dubbing his B-17 Flying Fortress the *Tom Paine* and painting "Tyranny, Like Hell, is not easily Conquered" on its fuselage.[81]

Finally, as victory came into sight, Americans accorded Paine long-overdue official recognitions. Rectifying the vengeful act of 139 years before, in which Tory locals denied him the right to vote on the purported grounds that he had given up his American nationality during the French Revolution, the municipal leaders of New Rochelle formally "restored" his citizenship on July 4, 1945. And that same year the governing board of the Hall of Fame for Great Americans elected Paine (along with Susan B. Anthony) to its roster of national heroes, an honor that entailed placing a large bust of Paine alongside those of Washington, Franklin, and Jefferson in the institution's magnificent pantheon on the Bronx campus of New York University and inscribing on the wall beneath Paine's sculpted image, "Those who expect to reap the blessings of freedom, must, like men, undergo the fatigue of supporting it."[82]

Reaffirming the nation's exceptional purpose and promise through Paine's life and words, Americans had rightly made Paine an iconic figure of patriotism and the struggle for freedom, equality, and democracy. Yet even at the moment of the country's greatest triumph since the Revolution, some would draw back from his memory and legacy. The majority of conservatives would continue to abhor him and his radical vision and arguments, and others would turn away as well. America's democratic impulse would survive, but for more reasons than Americans might have realized, the times that tried men's souls were far from over.

8

WE HAVE IT IN OUR POWER

When Ronald Reagan accepted the Republican presidential nomination in 1980, he might easily have resorted to saying "These are the times that try men's souls." Once again the United States faced a daunting, and apparently worsening, national crisis. In the wake of the struggles, reforms, and blows of the 1960s—the civil rights revolution; the Great Society and the War on Poverty; the assassinations of John Kennedy, Martin Luther King, and Robert Kennedy; the war in Southeast Asia, antiwar mobilizations, ghetto riots, feminist resurgence, and workplace insurgencies—Americans were then subjected to an equally, if not more, unsettling wave of developments, including defeat in Vietnam; Watergate and the resignation of President Richard Nixon; fuel shortages, economic recession, industrial decline, fiscal problems; Americans held hostage in their own embassy in Iran; and Soviet advances in Africa and Asia.

Everyone seemed to agree that America was in "deep and serious trouble." Pollsters revealed a people distrustful of its foremost institutions—"business, labor, medicine, organized religion, and the media"—and increasingly pessimistic about the future. Prominent politicians and corporate executives openly worried about a "crisis of governance." Intellectuals right and left wrote of the "twilight of authority," the "twilight of capitalism," and the possibility that the United States was not only "exhausted" but also "declining." Even President Jimmy Carter, in his quickly dubbed "malaise" speech, warned of a "crisis of confidence" so severe that it threatened to "destroy the social and political fabric." He urged Americans to lower their expectations, conserve energy, and "say something good about our country."[1]

Though no less concerned than Carter, Reagan comprehended America's predicament differently. "While [Americans] talk about . . . inflation, energy, etc.," he noted in a letter to a supporter, "they hunger for a spiritual revival to feel once again as they felt years ago about this nation of ours." And perceiving the unique opportunity that circumstances afforded, he began to recite—even before the Republican National Convention—not the famous line from the *Crisis* but another, more radical one from *Common Sense*. As he related in that same letter, "I have been using a quote . . . from Tom Paine back in the dark days of the Revolutionary War when it didn't seem possible this nation could come into being. He told his fellow Americans, 'We have it in our power to begin the world over again.' I have tried to suggest that might be the destiny for our party." Reagan did not discount the nation's difficulties. Yet whereas Carter and others spoke as if America suffered some fundamental flaw for which the American people themselves were to blame, he would argue that the fault lay neither in the country nor in its citizenry but in those whom they had chosen to represent them.[2]

Reagan probably did not know that for two hundred years conservatives had sought to suppress or limit Paine's presence in public life. Nor is it likely he knew that just sixteen years earlier, his right-wing Republican comrade Barry Goldwater had avoided mentioning Paine's name in his own acceptance speech even as he drew directly on Paine's words— "Moderation in temper is always a virtue; but moderation in principle, is a species of vice"—to famously pronounce *"Extremism in defense of liberty is no vice. Moderation in the pursuit of justice is no virtue."*[3]

Reagan's own experience, however, would have taught him the significance of associating with Paine. Before moving right in the 1950s, Reagan had been a fervent Democrat and the energetic president of a Hollywood union, the Screen Actors Guild. An ardent supporter of Franklin Roosevelt, whom he continued to admire throughout his life, Reagan had undoubtedly heard FDR's 1942 fireside chat mustering Paine to declare America's commitment to defeat fascism and realize the Four Freedoms. An avid reader of popular history, especially of the founding era, Reagan had probably picked up Howard Fast's bestseller,

Citizen Tom Paine. And if he had not already done so in 1965 as the narrator of *Freedom's Finest Hour*, a recorded history of the Revolution, he likely had reacquainted himself with Paine during the Bicentennial in his unsuccessful but not unpromising bid for the 1976 Republican presidential nomination.[4]

As Paine had once admitted, "It is from our enemies that we often gain excellent maxims," and to the chagrin of friends and foes, Reagan often incorporated into his addresses references to and lines from revered liberals. Yet in Reagan's case it involved more than mere poaching, for even as he shifted rightward, he continued to subscribe to the same story of American greatness that he had in the 1930s and 1940s. He changed the details along the way, but not the grand narrative. As biographer Lou Cannon would show, Reagan's speeches as a conservative clearly echoed those he gave as a liberal; it was simply that "big government had replaced big business as the enemy."[5]

Reagan probably felt a particular affinity for Paine. Like Paine, he had come from a relatively poor background, risen by his own efforts, and achieved extraordinary things. Like Paine—though according God a more interventionist role—he truly believed Providence had granted America exceptional purpose and promise. And like Paine, he grasped that no political movement could succeed in the United States that did not project "progressive" understandings of the nation's prospects and possibilities. Moreover, he apparently recognized, as had FDR— perhaps because of him—that Paine was a popular symbol of patriotism and democracy, and he likely imagined that, just as the revolutionary's name and words had moved him, so too would they move the electorate. Indeed, Reagan so relished Paine's proposition that he used it repeatedly, not only during the campaign but also as president, including in his famous "evil empire" speech to, of all groups, the National Association of Evangelicals.[6]

Of course, quoting Paine did not make Reagan a "Painite." Attacking "liberal elites," "big government," "high taxes," and "riotous radicals," Reagan entered politics in the 1960s as a conservative Republican and won two elections to California's governorship. Reiterating his assaults and mobilizing the diverse hostilities and anxieties engendered by the battles and traumas of the 1960s and 1970s, he eventually secured the party's presidential nomination by fashioning a new political coalition—

a New Right—encompassing not only traditional Republicans and capitalists big and small, but also former southern Democrats, evangelicals, social issue conservatives, and neoconservative intellectuals. And as president he would pursue policies at home that clearly favored private interests over the public good and the welfare of the wealthy over that of working people and the poor, and policies abroad that—while they supposedly paved the way for the Soviet Union's collapse—involved defending South Africa's apartheid regime, underwriting terrorism (and illegally diverting funds from a covert arms-for-hostages deal with Iran to the Nicaraguan contras), and embracing murderous authoritarian governments in Latin America.

Arriving at the convention podium to deliver his presidential nomination acceptance speech, Reagan knew that, more than to the Republican faithful, he had to speak to the many Americans who, still representing the majority of voters, identified themselves as Democrats. Especially, he needed to reach out to working people, including the longtime base of the now-fragmented liberal coalition: labor unionists. He had to convince them that, in contrast to the incumbent Carter, he remained truly confident and optimistic about the nation's future and about them. With that in mind, he would appropriate from the left two of their very own champions, Thomas Paine and Franklin Roosevelt, figures who had never lost confidence or failed to express optimism regarding America and its people:

> This evening marks the last step, save one, of a campaign that has taken Nancy and me from one end of this great nation to the other . . . There are no words to express the extraordinary strength and character of this breed of people we call Americans . . . Everywhere, we've met thousands of Democrats, Independents, and Republicans from all economic conditions, walks of life, bound together in that community of shared values of family, work, neighborhood, peace, and freedom. They are concerned, yes; they're not frightened. They're disturbed, but not dismayed. They are the kind of men and women Tom Paine had in mind when he wrote, during the darkest days of the American Revolution, "We have it in our power to begin the world over again" . . . Nearly 150 years after Tom Paine wrote

those words, an American President told the generation of the Great Depression that it had a "rendezvous with destiny." I believe this generation also has a rendezvous with destiny.[7]

For the first time a leading politician had openly called upon Paine—not to mention FDR—to bolster conservatism and the Republican Party. Arguably, only a onetime man of the left could have done so. But arguably as well, he could only have done so because so much of the left had apparently lost contact with Paine.

In 1943 Yale political scientist Howard Penniman wrote, "These may be 'the times that try men's souls,' as President Roosevelt recently told the nation, but they may also be the times when free and courageous men may push forward toward the better society of which Thomas Paine dreamed when he pleaded with the colonists for unity in the cause of freedom." And when the country emerged from the Second World War more prosperous and powerful than ever, Americans had good reason to expect just such strivings.[8]

In addition to deploying twelve million troops, the government had instituted planning mechanisms that had halted the Depression, organized the nation as the "Arsenal of Democracy," and redistributed income down to the working class. Though still divided between the AFL and the CIO, the labor movement had grown from nine to fifteen million members, and CIO officials had established a "political action committee" and floated ideas of securing workers a greater voice in industry. And while segregation continued in the South and in the U.S. military, African Americans had mobilized and compelled the Roosevelt administration to ban racial discrimination in defense industries and set up a Fair Employment Practices Commission. Moreover, whereas the Depression had revealed the bankruptcy of laissez-faire capitalism, the fight against Nazism had discredited racialist ideologies.[9]

Eminent figures also promised progress. Vice President Henry Wallace—who had praised Paine as a "hell-raiser"—spoke of the war as inaugurating the "century of the common man." Harvard University president James B. Conant called for a new generation of "American radicals" committed to "equality," "truly universal educational opportunity," "jobs and full employment," and "human rights" over "property rights." And in January 1944 Roosevelt himself proposed an "economic bill of rights" to guarantee good jobs, food, clothing, housing, schooling, health care, education, and recreation.[10]

At war's end liberals worked with Roosevelt's successor, Harry Truman, in trying to translate FDR's envisioned second bill of rights into legislation; unions unleashed a massive national strike wave and a major southern organizing drive; and African American groups renewed demands for racial justice and equality. And yet within just a few years, thoughts of social, industrial, and radical democracy would come to be considered utopian, if not *un*-American.

Business executives, Republicans, and southern Democrats had their own ambitions for postwar America. In provisioning the war effort, captains of industry had accumulated not only profits but also a great deal of goodwill, and even before the conclusion of hostilities they had started up public relations and lobbying campaigns to promote capitalism and push politics to the right. Taking advantage of the difficulties of reconverting to a peacetime economy, Republicans, backed both by Wall Street and by Main Street, won both Houses of Congress in 1946. And with southern blacks still disenfranchised, the Dixiecrats remained firmly in control below the Mason-Dixon line. In favor of "free enterprise," "management's right to manage," and "states' rights," capitalists and conservatives pushed ahead with their plans to roll back and limit the powers of the federal government and labor.[11]

Compounding the left's troubles, the postwar world was splitting anew into a United States–led liberal-capitalist West and a Soviet-dominated Communist East, and the ensuing "cold war" was chilling not only international affairs but also American politics and public life. In 1947 Truman responded to Soviet expansionism by declaring the commitment of the United States to contain Communism and support freedom globally, and he fended off Republican accusations that Democrats were "soft on Communism" by instituting "loyalty" checks of government and defense-industry employees. These actions abetted right-wing interests as they ignited a new "Red Scare" and further divided liberals and radicals, with Henry Wallace and other leftists withdrawing from the Democratic Party in 1948 to launch the ill-fated Progressive Party.

Exploiting the fears engendered by the cold war, congressional conservatives soon pursued their own investigations into "un-American activities," going after not just the already-dwindling number of American Communists but also the left as a whole. Ruining lives and careers, the repressive activities and assaults on civil liberties that we have come to call McCarthyism—the red-baiting, blacklists, firings, hearings, prosecutions, jailings, censorship, and equation of dissent with disloyalty—would serve to curb liberals, marginalize radicals, corral labor, constrict public debate, and suffocate progressive possibilities. As early as 1950 historian Henry May would lament, in words reminiscent of the 1920s, that "radicalism in America is scattered, demoralized, and numerically insignificant. Almost never in this country's history have there been so few bold and vigorous critics of the social order."[12]

Moreover, while the "Truman Doctrine" led the United States to aid in Western Europe's reconstruction and to organize the North Atlantic Treaty Organization (NATO), postwar American foreign policy had a dark and tragic side as well. Persuaded that every populist insurgency and nationalist government portended a Soviet advance, Americans all too often allowed their leaders not only to abandon the nation's commitment to decolonization and "self-determination" but also to act imperially, as in Iran in 1953, in Guatemala in 1954, and disastrously so in Vietnam.[13]

Concurrently, the United States was entering upon an unprecedented economic expansion that—driven to some extent by defense expenditures—would last for twenty-five years. Though inequality and poverty would persist, a 250 percent increase in the gross national product between 1945 and 1960 would afford higher living standards for almost all Americans and a dramatic enlargement of the "middle classes," who would also secure for themselves a greater share of the nation's total wealth. Together these developments would lead the nation's elites and their intellectual allies to assert that the country had overcome capitalism's most critical contradictions.

Instead of beholding the enhancement of democracy, however, Americans witnessed the formation of a new governing consensus. Subscribed to by both Democrats and Republicans, it involved the "affirmation" of capitalism, the "expectation" that an expanding economy would supply the financial wherewithal to resolve social conflicts, the "assumption" that America would halt Communism's spread, and the "belief" that the United States represented the vanguard of human history. Often called liberal but very much corporate-dominated, this new consensus depended on the articulation of a "social compact" in which: government was to provide a modest welfare system and regulate the "mixed economy" through fiscal policies intended to sustain or, when necessary, stimulate growth and maintain full employment; corporations were to control investment and production but accept worker representation and collective bargaining; and unions were to negotiate wages and benefits but defer to management's authority in and over the enterprise.[14]

United in 1955 as the AFL-CIO, labor remained the backbone of the Democratic Party and continued to nominally support liberalism and civil rights, even as it ceased to act as a progressive movement of the working class. Purged of "reds" and debilitated by the restrictive 1947 Taft-Hartley Act, unions, representing a quarter of the workforce, fought to keep wages high but emphasized private over public welfare, became ever more bureaucratic, and operated to guarantee productivity and circumscribe workers' rebellious instincts.[15]

Even liberal academic thought reflected the conservative climate. Wrongly presuming that both Fascism and Communism ("totalitarianism") had originated as populist movements of the laboring classes, and believing that McCarthyism portended just such possibilities, a cohort of important scholars—many of whom had started out as Marxists—abandoned their youthful "idealism" and "illusions" and signed on to a more "realistic" politics of the "vital center," as Arthur Schlesinger, Jr., labeled it. Expressing their new understandings and sensibilities in their writings, "consensus historians" such as Richard Hofstadter, Louis Hartz, and Daniel Boorstin challenged the presiding historiographical paradigm in which conflict propelled the advance of democracy, and social scientists like Seymour Martin Lipset and Daniel Bell portrayed the United States as having all but transcended history, for in their own respective words, the country was resolving the "fundamental political problems of the industrial revolution" and witnessing "the end of ideology." As Cornell government professor Clinton Rossiter observed in 1954, "We Americans are now passing through a period of political and cultural conservatism quite without precedent in all our history."[16]

In 1949 Paine biographer Hildegarde Hawthorne happily noted that "Paine has at last outlived the calumnies. The Federalists are dust, blown away. Both Jefferson and Paine were strong for the common man, for real liberty, equality and justice for all men. They stand higher than ever in the love and admiration of us common citizens of the United States." While Hawthorne correctly sized up American esteem for the two revolutionaries, she failed to see that Paine at least remained not only a critical but also a contested figure. There were those, mostly on the right, who still disdained him and, empowered by the antiradicalism of the day, anxiously sought to limit his remembrance. Others, especially among the liberal elites, conscious of his popular appeal, endeavored to sunder his patriotism from his radicalism and harness the former in support of the developing postwar consensus. And yet there were still others who—against the grain of the times—insisted on the intimacy, if not identity, of Paine's patriotism and radicalism and continued to turn to him as they tried to revitalize America's democratic impulse.[17]

Given his association with the left, Paine's name inevitably came up in the course of the "red hunts" of the late 1940s and 1950s, most notably so in the McCarthyite pursuit of the popular writer and Communist Howard Fast, the author of *Citizen Tom Paine*. "Commanded to appear" in 1946 before the House Committee on Un-American Activities (HUAC) regarding his work with the Joint Anti-Fascist Rescue Committee, a Spanish Civil War relief effort, Fast was charged with "contempt of Congress" for refusing to "name the names" of its contributors. But not everyone agreed with the proceedings. New York Democrat Emanuel Celler called Paine himself to the House floor to denounce the charges:

> Why if Tom Paine or Tom Jefferson . . . were alive today, they would, I believe, run afoul of this Un-American Activities Committee. The radicalism of these patriots would not . . . sit well upon the stomachs of some of the members of this committee . . . Many years ago Tom Paine, whose pen proved mightier than the sword during the American Revolution, said: "Prejudice like a spider makes everywhere its home, and lives where there seems nothing to live on."

Representative Celler, however, spoke for the minority that day, and Fast went on to suffer indictment, conviction, and a three-month imprisonment in 1950.[18]

Fast's literary works also came under attack. In 1947 the New York City Board of Education announced that it was withdrawing *Citizen Tom Paine* from all public school libraries—*not*, the Board's spokesman dubiously claimed, because the author was a Communist but because the novel contained too much "vulgarity." Belying the suggestion that this decision was motivated by colorful language, in 1949 FBI director J. Edgar Hoover sent agents to the nation's major libraries bearing instructions that all of Fast's titles be removed and destroyed. Meanwhile, federal loyalty reviews were asking questions such as "Do you read Howard Fast? Tom Paine? Upton Sinclair?" Even Truman's special counsel, Clark Clifford, was compelled to explain why he had distributed fifty copies of *Citizen Tom Paine* as gifts.[19]

Released from jail, Fast found himself blacklisted by publishers and still subject to harassment. The Permanent Subcommittee on Investigations of the Senate Committee on Government Operations, chaired by the Wisconsin Republican Senator Joseph McCarthy himself, called Fast to appear at hearings in 1953 concerning the State Department. McCarthy and his colleagues, however, were not really after Fast. In their sights was the State Department, for allowing Voice of America Radio (for which Fast had worked during World War II) to broadcast excerpts of his writings and for continuing to make available books such as *Citizen Tom Paine* in its overseas libraries. And the committee apparently prevailed. The State Department prohibited Voice of America from using Fast's words and—against the American Library Association's efforts to defend the "Freedom to Read"—culled additional volumes from its libraries, including not only Fast's novels but also Fast's edition of Paine's *Selected Works*.[20]

Paine's name also came up when HUAC called Earl Robinson, the composer of *Ballad for Americans* and *The House I Live In*, to testify. Asked to cite one "poem" he had written encouraging schoolchildren to "support the Constitution," Robinson recited the latter tune's lyrics, "What is America to me? A name, a man, the flag I see, a certain word, democracy . . . The words of old Abe Lincoln, of Jefferson and Paine."[21]

At times Paine himself became the target. In 1954 a memorial association offered to erect a statue of him in Providence, Rhode Island, if the city agreed to provide a site in one of its parks. The group believed Providence a most fitting location for such a monument since Roger Williams had founded Rhode Island in 1636 as a haven of religious freedom. But Mayor Walter "Scratchy Ass" Reynolds, a figure in the local Democratic machine, rejected the deal. Failing to note if he was acting under pressure from the Catholic Church, businessmen, McCarthyites, or all of the above—for presumably he did not recall Paine's futile efforts in 1782 to persuade Rhode Islanders to accept new taxes to finance the Revolution—Reynolds stated simply that "it's out of the question because Paine was and remains so controversial a character."[22]

Further registering the enervation of liberal thought and energy, even historians of the "consensus school" took aim at Paine. Arrogantly and ignorantly referring to him as a mere "popularizer," Harvard's Perry Miller stated in a 1946 review of Paine's writings for *The Nation* that "to appreciate Paine today requires an exercise of the historical imagination, from which one comes away impressed on the one hand with his integrity and courage and on the other with the limitations of his mind and the fatiguing insistence of his optimism." Exhibiting a similar set of biases, Smith College faculty member Cecelia Kenyon in 1951 published "Where Paine Went Wrong" in the *American Political Science Review*. Failing to comprehend Paine's originality regarding democracy, constitutional thought, and federalism, not to mention their appeal to working people, Kenyon foolishly asserted that Paine's "theory of democratic politics was defective because it was immature" and belittlingly referred to Paine as the "Peter Pan of the Age of Reason." And maintaining that American history was anything but revolutionary, University of Chicago professor Daniel Boorstin in 1953 (the same year he would appear before HUAC to name names from his student days as a Communist) perversely contended in *The Genius of American Politics* that the "greatest defender of the Revolution—in fact, the greatest political theorist of the American Revolution" was not Paine but the "great theorist of British conservatism—Edmund Burke."[23]

Oddly enough, some conservatives spoke well of Paine, or at least one aspect of his thinking. Standing to the right of the liberal-corporate consensus, farther to the right than the Republican mainstream, was the so-called Old Right. Marginalized by their past attachments to isolationism and in some cases anti-Semitism, and divided into traditionalists and libertarians, these ideological conservatives and intellectual reactionaries—dubbed "the Remnant" by Albert J. Nock, one of their prewar prophets—were neither inactive nor inert. Joined by ex-Marxists like the former editor of *The Masses* Max Eastman, they became staunch anti-communists and McCarthyites. While traditionalists like Russell Kirk worshiped Burke and desperately sought a connection to the American Founders by grabbing hold of John Adams and John Quincy Adams, libertarians such as Frank Chodorov and Murray Rothbard celebrated Adam Smith and latched on to Jefferson and Paine, citing lines from the latter like "Society in every state is a blessing, but government, even in its best state, is but a necessary evil." Of course, inducting Paine into their fraternity meant that libertarians had to excise him of not only his social democratic but also his radical democratic arguments, for as much as they valued liberty, they, like their traditionalist comrades, viewed "the people" suspiciously and had little interest in expanding democracy. All of this would soon become moot, however, when in 1955 William F. Buckley, Jr., brought Burkeans and Smithians together under the umbrella of his new "fusion" magazine, the *National Review*. This proto–New Right would banish Paine from its pantheon for more than a generation (though diehard antistatists, like those who established the Libertarian Party in 1971 and the Cato Institute in 1977, continued to claim Paine).[24]

Even with all the abuse, Paine remained an iconic figure. An impressive monument to him went up in Morristown, New Jersey; the Hall of Fame of Great Americans proceeded with his formal installation; and most academic and popular writers smartly attended to the power of his pen. Historian Eric F. Goldman listed *Common Sense* first in his highly touted roster of ten "Books That Changed America"; *Saturday Review* editor Norman Cousins accorded Paine a full appreciative chapter in his *"In God We Trust": The Religious Beliefs and Ideas of the American Founding Fathers*; and other scholars discussed his "humanitarianism," his zeal for freedom, and—while making sure to state that he was no "extremist"—his contributions both to the "American Idea of Mission" and to the modern welfare system.[25]

Aware of American affections, the elites, Democrats especially, soon recalled Paine to national service. President Truman quoted him at the dedication of the Chapel of the Chaplains in Philadelphia; the U.S. Army enlisted him to its recruiting efforts; and magazines published lengthy excerpts from the *Crisis* when American forces experienced setbacks in Korea. But just as subsuming the left and labor to the liberal-corporate consensus entailed divesting them of their more radical elements, so too did incorporating Paine into the official narrative, as illustrated by his representation on the Freedom Train, the grandest public-history undertaking of the postwar years.[26]

An exhibition on rail of many of America's most esteemed documents, the Freedom Train was proposed in 1946 by the Justice Department, in the words of Attorney General Tom C. Clark, "as a means of aiding the country in its internal war against subversive elements and as an effort to improve citizenship by reawakening in our people their profound faith in the American historical heritage." To assuage Republican concerns that it would boost the Democrats, however, the Truman administration handed it off to a group of enthusiastic media, financial, and industrial executives who, operating as the American Heritage Foundation, secured the needed capital, gathered a phenomenal selection of 133 documents and artifacts (including Jefferson's draft of the Declaration of Independence, the Bill of Rights, the Emancipation Proclamation, and Lincoln's handwritten copy of the Gettysburg Address), and laid out the story of American freedom as a triumphal tale.[27]

Trimmed in red, white, and blue and pulled by the *Spirit of 1776*, the Freedom Train set off with great fanfare from Philadelphia in September 1947 on a sixteen-month journey, stopping along the way at 322 towns and cities. African Americans protested that southern state laws invalidated the message being conveyed, leading the foundation to order the train to bypass cities whose officials insisted on enforcing segregated visits; and radicals and pacifists denounced the whole thing as a cold war propaganda vehicle, instigating (further) FBI surveillance of them. But while not everyone shared in the excitement, 3.5 million people toured the train—all of whom were urged to recite a Freedom Pledge and sign a Freedom Scroll—and many millions more participated in related activities.[28]

Declaring the Freedom Train a "war-time" campaign to "re-sell Americanism to Americans," the foundation's corporate directors disclosed what that meant not only through what they chose to exhibit but also through what they chose to exclude. They refused to display "controversial" items, including such pivotal primary documents of labor history and the New Deal as the Wagner Act and Roosevelt's speech enunciating the Four Freedoms.[29]

Remarkably, the Freedom Train featured three of Paine's writings: a first edition of *Common Sense*, a copy of the original *Crisis*, and a letter of 1790 to Benjamin Rush from Paris. However, Paine's inclusion was evidently intended not to cultivate critical reflection but to serve as a posthumous endorsement of the nation's new global, cold war stance. The curators positioned *Common Sense* to highlight "The Cause of America is in a great Measure the Cause of all Mankind," the *Crisis* to emphasize "These are the times that try men's souls," and the letter to underscore "I wish most anxiously to see my much-loved America—it is the Country from whence all reformations must originally spring."[30]

Still, there remained notable liberals and radicals who would defer neither to the country's "mood" nor to the censorship and rending of Paine's life and labors. Eschewing Communism yet scorning Mc-Carthyism, they saw Paine and his work as fundamental to the making of American democracy and to the possibility of renewing it.

A passionate advocate of the New Deal and progressive causes— who did not shrink from decrying the upper classes' backing of Mc-Carthyism—southern writer and journalist Gerald Johnson stalwartly defended free speech and regularly cited the Founders, Paine centrally among them when he did so. Opening *This American People* with "*Democracy* is a dangerous form of government. The United States is a democracy . . . [And] one quality essential to genuine Americanism [is a] willingness to assume a risk," Johnson pointed to the exemplary courage and drive of "John and Samuel Adams, Tom Paine, Benjamin Franklin, Thomas Jefferson, Patrick Henry and the rest." And in a volume of biographical portraits titled *The Lunatic Fringe*, Johnson asked where the nation would have been without its rebels and situated Paine at the very forefront of the lot.[31]

Columbia University professor Henry Steele Commager creatively integrated Paine into his work. Following the example of his intellectual mentor, William E. Dodd (who had publicly lectured on Paine to challenge the conservatism of the 1920s), Commager believed he had a duty to speak out on critical issues, especially when civil liberties were at stake. And wanting, as he would say, "to live with Jefferson, not Hamilton, or with Tom Paine, not Edmund Burke," Commager felt particularly inclined to stand with democratic dissenters versus the powerful. Thus he too strenuously opposed McCarthy and his ilk and occasionally resurrected Paine to fight them, most pointedly so in reaction to the Providence mayor's rebuff of the Paine monument. In "Tom Paine Talks Back to Providence," Commager "subpoenaed" Paine to testify to a committee regarding his credentials as a "loyal" American. Cleverly, Commager had the chair of the inquiry grilling Paine on his citizenship record, internationalism, radicalism, association with other radicals (the Founding Fathers), social democratic ideas, and religious beliefs, with Paine answering in words from his own patriotic and revolutionary writings. Deliberately, Commager had Paine close with "but *these* are the times that try men's *souls*."[32]

Saul Alinsky stressed power over reason in his approach to politics, but—developing "in your face" tactics like dumping garbage on a slumlord's own front steps to protest his refusal to attend to his properties—Alinsky relished Paine's originality, brashness, and dedication. Starting out as a criminology graduate student, Alinsky gave up academe for activism while working in Chicago's poor "Back of the Yards" section in the late 1930s. Winning the support of the Catholic Church (even though he himself was Jewish), aligning with a CIO union's organizing drive among packinghouse workers, and mobilizing residents, he directed a community-organizing campaign that involved empowering those who lived there to act as "citizens," not "the needy." And raising funds from sympathetic rich folk, he established the Industrial Areas Foundation with the goal of reproducing the project elsewhere.

Yet as Alinsky made clear in his manifesto, *Reveille for Radicals* (which became a *New York Times* best-seller), he really aspired to do more than initiate a series of disparate urban programs. He wanted to forge a new populist movement. Using Paine's defiant words from the first *Crisis*, he proclaimed: "Let them call me rebel and welcome, I feel no concern from it; but I should suffer the misery of devils, were I to make a whore of my soul." As the epigraph to his book, and paying tribute to Paine himself in the text, he argued that "the history of America is the story of America's Radicals. It is a saga of revolution, battle, words on paper setting hearts on fire, ferment and turmoil; it is the story of every rallying cry of the American people. It is the story of the American Revolution, of the public schools, of the battle for free land, of emancipation, of the unceasing struggle for the ever increasing liberation of mankind." And he called upon present-day Americans to create "people's organizations" through which they might transform the nation in a way alternative to both capitalism and communism.[33]

A. J. Muste likely encountered Paine many times. Born in 1885 to Dutch working-class parents who moved to America when he was a child, Muste trained for the ministry, but after losing his first pulpit because of his opposition to America's entry into the First World War, he discovered his calling in activism. A labor educator in the 1920s, he organized Unemployed Leagues in the early Depression and established the American Workers Party in 1933, at which time he also became a part of the intellectual circle around Alfred Bingham's *Common Sense*. Appointed head of the Fellowship of Reconciliation in 1940, he devoted his energies during the war to defending the rights of conscientious objectors and campaigning for racial integration, the latter of which involved him in the formation of the Congress of Racial Equality (CORE). And even after retiring in 1953, he continued to protest injustice and (to use President Eisenhower's own term) the "military-industrial complex," which led him in 1956 to cofound *Liberation*, a magazine whose first editorial named the biblical prophets, the American revolutionaries Jefferson and Paine, the European and American socialist and labor movements, and past and present practitioners of "non-violence" as the "root traditions" to be drawn upon for a new "independent radicalism."[34]

An East Texan who apparently absorbed the region's populist spirit, C. Wright Mills more than admired Paine—he wanted to be Paine. Determined to redeem the scholarly tradition of Karl Marx and Max Weber, in which sociologists made sense of the world not by counting heads or fashioning grand theories but by attending to history, social structure, and biography, Mills as a young Columbia University professor produced critical studies of labor, the middle classes, and the governing class. Yet angry that the highest strata of the corporate, bureaucratic, and military orders, which together constituted the "power elite," were monopolizing control of national life and turning American citizens into a "mass of cheerful robots," he felt compelled to do more than advance the "sociological imagination."[35]

Even during the war, the ever-maverick Mills had spoken of contesting the centralization of power and decision-making: "I am learning American history in order to quote it at the sons-of-bitches who run American big business. When I get thru they'll think American history was one big farmer-labor rally. Which in large part it damn well was." And in the late 1940s he had suggested that intellectuals and the labor movement join together in a new party to reenergize democracy and press for workers' control of industry. But coming to see unions as organs of social control, not change, he began to recommend that intellectuals act independently, applying their knowledge and skills to educating citizens, cultivating publics, and challenging the power elite. The problem, as he repeatedly observed, was that "between the intellectual and his potential public stand technical, economic, and social structures which are owned and operated by others. The world of pamphleteering offered to a Tom Paine a direct channel to readers that the world of mass circulations supported by advertising cannot usually afford to provide one who does not say already popular things." Nevertheless, recognizing the possibilities provided by paperback books, Mills provocatively and rather successfully took to writing what he would call his "pamphlets"—*The Causes of World War Three* and *Listen, Yankee: The Revolution in Cuba* (the latter of which brought him to the attention of the FBI)—before his untimely death in 1962, when he was not yet forty-five years old.[36]

While cold war politics and prosperity contained or dispersed the nation's democratic energies for several years, they did not discharge them. The very language of the consensus reminded Americans of their historically prized ideals and afforded ground on which courageous citizens might stand in dissent. Moreover, invigorated by *Brown v. Board of Education* (the 1954 Supreme Court decision finding racial segregation in the schools unconstitutional), black Americans continued to campaign for equal rights; workers regularly demonstrated their insurgent potential in strike actions; and though they were not to realize their grandest aspirations, Alinsky, Muste, Mills, and others like them helped to keep alive America's democratic impulse and to convey Paine's radical memory and legacy to a "New Left." And just as the "power elite" was proclaiming, as ruling classes are universally wont to do, that the United

States represented not only the vanguard but also the culmination of world history, diverse Americans started shaking off the torpor of the 1950s and reminding everyone that American history was far from over.

Inspired especially by the civil rights movement, students, women, and workers would also soon confront the inequalities and injustices that continued to oppress them and to contradict the nation's exceptional purpose and promise. Their efforts would encounter determined opposition and unexpected impediments. They would strain, and contribute to the fracturing of, both FDR's Democratic coalition and the liberal-corporate consensus. They would fail to create a new alliance of the left. And they would find themselves incapable of deterring the rise of the New Right in the 1970s. Nevertheless, they would accomplish great things. Dismantling racial and sexual apartheid, instigating a resuscitation and expansion of New Deal liberalism, and provoking a reconsideration of the nation's military and foreign policies, they would extend and deepen freedom, equality, and democracy.

Staking out their respective claims to the nation and its meaning as they articulated their positions on those causes and struggles, Americans right and left once again reached back to the Founders. Admittedly, not every liberal and radical was to link arms with Paine. In spite of his pioneering public opposition to slavery, civil rights leaders, many of whom were Protestant ministers, did not. But, from presidents to protesters, many others did—though ultimately perhaps not tightly enough.

Marked by the nightmares of the Cuban missile crisis, the murders of civil rights activists, and the assassination of President Kennedy, the first half of the 1960s were nonetheless years of exceptional hope and optimism and exhilarating democratic advances. A war hero, the first Catholic president, and still only in his early forties when he took office in 1961, Kennedy, a Massachusetts Democrat, while no populist or radical, had spoken of a "New Frontier" and heralded progressive developments. And though he was to accomplish little, he raised expectations and spurred action. Hearing his inaugural line, "Ask not what your country can do for you; ask what you can do for your country," young people in particular responded—some by enlisting in the military or the new Peace Corps, others by joining what would come to be called "the Movement" and challenging the liberal-corporate consensus that Kennedy himself represented.

Even before the 1960 elections, black collegians had reinvigorated the fight against Jim Crow by sitting in at "whites-only" southern lunch counters and forming the Student Nonviolent Coordinating Committee (SNCC) to continue and extend the struggle. Enduring racial abuse and assault at every turn, they would work alongside folks from CORE and the Southern Christian Leadership Conference (though not always smoothly) and with them secured national sympathy and support when northern whites witnessed with their own eyes via television white policemen and gangs attacking peacefully protesting black men, women, and children, most brutally in the streets of Birmingham in the spring of 1963. And joining with liberals, progressive student organizations, unions, and religious groups, they brought the struggle to Washington, D.C., in August 1963 by way of a 250,000-strong multiracial March for Jobs and Freedom, at which Martin Luther King, Jr., delivered his moving "I Have a Dream" speech on the steps of the Lincoln Memorial.

Stirred by the cause of racial justice and equality, hundreds of young northern whites—mostly the children of left-leaning parents, many of them "red diaper babies" (the kids of Communists or former Communists)—went south to serve in campaigns like the 1961 Freedom Rides and the 1964 Mississippi voter registration drive known as "Freedom Summer." And upon their return home, they played fundamental roles in the ongoing formation of the New Left, including the development of Students for a Democratic Society (SDS).

Starting in 1960 with a small network of groups scattered around a few major northeastern universities, SDS would grow into a national movement that in 1968 reached 350 chapters with 100,000 members. Though best remembered for mobilizing student opposition to the Vietnam War, it always set out far broader concerns and aspirations. Drafted by Michigan student Tom Hayden, who had worked with SNCC, SDS's original 1962 manifesto, the Port Huron Statement, drew directly upon C. Wright Mills's arguments to express a generation's anxieties and yearnings. Criticizing America for its hypocritical denial of freedom and equality, toleration of poverty, pursuit of an irrational cold war, deference to the military-industrial complex, disregard of third-world peoples, and acceptance of the ideological claim that "there simply are no alternatives," the statement urged liberals, socialists, labor unionists, civil rights activists, pacifists, and students to jointly revitalize the left, revise the nation's public and foreign policies, and reconstruct society with the values and practices of hope, love, reason, solidarity, and "participatory democracy." And in 1963 SDS demonstrated its own commitment to social change by launching the Economic Research and Action Project (ERAP), which sent 125 of its members into several northern cities to organize poor black and white neighborhoods.[37]

Both civil rights and New Left activists were skeptical of, if not antagonistic to, "Big Labor" for its submission to the political and industrial status quo and its toleration of the racial discrimination still practiced by several major craft unions. Yet the AFL-CIO remained committed to liberalism, and sharing the same enemies, many of its leading member unions gave valuable assistance to the new movements. While from the very outset SNCC and other civil rights groups received moral and material support from labor, SDS itself originated as the youth wing of the labor-socialist League for Industrial Democracy and ERAP was actually made possible by a grant from the United Auto Workers. Indeed, however much the goal of forming a broad left coalition in the 1960s might seem chimerical to us today, the alliance of forces that pulled together for the 1963 March for Jobs and Freedom attested to that very possibility.[38]

Garnering popular sympathy and the backing of the New Left and labor, the civil rights movement initiated nothing less than a "second American Revolution." It pushed Kennedy's successor Lyndon Johnson not only to secure passage of the historic 1964 Civil Rights and 1965 Voting Rights Acts (even though he knew that in doing so he was probably handing the South over to the Republicans for years to come), but also to call upon his fellow citizens "to make good on the promise of America" by fighting a "War on Poverty and creating a Great Society." A brilliant politician and former New Dealer who had risen from humble beginnings in Texas to become "master of the Senate" and eventually president, Johnson himself firmly believed government could improve the lives of working people and the poor, and his administration proceeded to pursue a truly astonishing array of reforms and programs that included Medicare, Medicaid, Head Start, federal aid to education, job training, consumer and environmental protection, cabinet-level departments for housing and transportation, the national endowments for the arts and the humanities, freedom of information laws, and the Immigration Act of 1965 (which replaced ethnic quotas with a system favoring applicants with family ties or with skills that would enhance the country's development). Poverty persisted, but the administration-led war against it definitely reduced the number of those afflicted by it.

Paralleling the Great Society, a liberal if not "activist" Supreme Court under Chief Justice Earl Warren issued a series of historic decisions advancing civil rights and liberties such as *Engel v. Vitale* (1962), banning school prayer, and *Miranda v. Arizona* (1966), protecting the rights of the accused. Even after Warren's retirement the Court continued to push the law in a liberal direction with decisions like *Roe v. Wade* (1973) guaranteeing a woman's right to terminate a pregnancy.[39]

Reflecting—if not in some cases anticipating—the resurgence of the nation's democratic impulse, Americans evinced mounting interest in Thomas Paine in the early 1960s. Publishers released new editions of his writings; popular authors prepared new biographies for young and old; and working "from the bottom up" and against the grain of the consensus school, a new generation of historians began to look afresh at how Paine helped to turn rebellious colonists into revolutionary citizens.

Paine's career once again became music to American ears. The hit labor revue of the late 1930s, *Pins and Needles*, was revived on Broadway in 1962, with a young performer named Barbra Streisand singing the Paine-featured tune "Status Quo." And that very same year the University of Michigan Broadcast Service commissioned Philip Bezanson to compose *Homage to Great Americans,* whose four movements treated Theodore Roosevelt, Abraham Lincoln, Thomas Paine, and George Washington, respectively. Moreover, boards of education in Illinois and New Jersey broke truly new ground by building elementary schools named after Paine.[40]

Back in the White House the Democrats too showed a new enthusiasm for Paine. Eager to publicly reaffirm America's commitment to halting the spread of Communism in the wake of the Cuban Revolution and the erection of the Berlin Wall, Kennedy quoted Paine to Latin American and African diplomats and German trade union delegates, among others. And the same president who in solidarity with the people of Berlin would declare "*Ich bin ein Berliner*" seemed to particularly enjoy recounting the tale of how Paine responded to Franklin's "Where freedom lives, there is my home," with "Where freedom is not, there is my home."

It might even have seemed that Paine himself had returned, for despite the power of television, "pamphlets" were playing a critical role in fomenting political action. Michael Harrington's *The Other America* helped lift poverty onto the public agenda. Rachel Carson's *Silent Spring* propagated fresh concern for the environment. Betty Friedan's *The Feminine Mystique* rekindled the cause of women's liberation. And Ralph Nader's *Unsafe at Any Speed* put consumer rights into gear.[41]

Many of the New Leftists who organized SDS carried Paine with them into and through the decade. Activists like Mickey Flacks, Bob Ross, and Steve Max apparently encountered the revolutionary as youngsters. Attending Communist summer camps as a child, Flacks learned "by heart" to sing *Ballad for Americans*. Entering the University of Michigan at seventeen, Ross, a Jewish kid from New York whose parents were veterans of the Popular Front and union politics, had already come to "revere" Paine after reading *Citizen Tom Paine*, for Paine's life and writings seemed to Ross not only to demonstrate the revolutionary democratic roots of the United States but also to point to the making of socialism. And Max, who had thrown himself into community and labor organizing as a high school student and become a leader of the New York City Tom Paine Club and editor of its newsletter *Common Sense* (which would serve SDS as a press outlet in the mid-1960s), likely inherited his affection for Paine from his father, an ex-Communist and former managing editor of *The Daily Worker*.[42]

Not all of the young "Painites" grew up as red-diaper babies, however. Todd Gitlin, who would become SDS president in 1963, also discovered Paine as a boy, but his parents were liberals, not Marxists. Essentially confirming McCarthy's fears about Fast's book, Gitlin would later recall, "I read through Tom Paine's collected works, which my father had bought in the Thirties, and Howard Fast's Popular Front novel, *Citizen Tom Paine*, a library find; I was moved to tears by the fate of the great pamphleteer eventually spurned by the Americans for whom he harbored such hopes, and whose ashes were scattered, 'for the world was his village.'"[43]

SDS members of the early 1960s proudly conceived of themselves as renewing America's revolutionary heritage, with Paine standing at the heart of it. Gitlin would recount of a November 1965 antiwar rally: "Carl Oglesby [then president of SDS] stole the show . . . by treating the war as the product of an imperial history . . . But Oglesby, the son of an Akron rubber worker, also self-consciously invoked 'our dead revolutionaries' Jefferson and Paine against Lyndon Johnson and [national security adviser] McGeorge Bundy. He romantically summoned up a once-democratic America against the 'colossus of . . . our American corporate system.'"[44]

Even many years later, SDS veterans would have recourse to Paine when recollecting their early activist days and what they were about. In his own memoir, Tom Hayden would write, "The goal of the sixties was, in a sense, the completion of the vision of the early revolutionaries and the abolitionists, for Tom Paine and Frederick Douglass wanted even more than the Bill of Rights or Emancipation Proclamation. True Democrats, they wanted the fulfillment of the American promise." And yet as much as the young New Leftists were inspired and encouraged by Paine, because of either his association with the Old Left or his incorporation to the nation's official narrative—or possibly due to their own eagerness to celebrate figures who would more readily connect them to their brethren in the civil rights movement—they did not collectively promote his memory, which as Gitlin observed many years later was "probably unfortunate . . . for things might have gone differently if we had all taken his principles to heart."[45]

The years 1964–65 represented the high point of liberal, social, and radical democratic hopes and possibilities, for soon the energies and dynamics of the day would become entangled in the violent confrontations, ugly divisions, and crazy distractions spawned by the pursuit of an imperial war, the persistence of racial injustices, and the flowering of an American "counterculture." Movements arose for women's liberation, gay liberation, the rights of welfare recipients, the rights of Latino and Native American peoples, and the protection of consumers and the environment. Workers newly asserted themselves against the demands of capital. And advances were made in all of these areas, extending from Supreme Court decisions regarding "equal pay for equal work" and a "woman's right to choose" to the establishment of the Consumer Products Safety Commission, the Environmental Protection Agency (EPA), the Occupational Safety and Health Administration (OSHA), and affirmative action. But the chance of fashioning a broad, multiracial, and populist left out of those diverse forces, one capable of securing, reforming, and redirecting the Democratic Party, would swiftly recede. The left would splinter, not only into several liberal and radical camps but also along the lines of class, race, and gender, and FDR's New Deal coalition would fall apart. In the process, the fragments would lose touch both with each other and with Paine.

Even as Johnson was reviving American liberalism, he was committing the nation to war. He sent hundreds of thousands of young Americans to Vietnam—and 58,000 of them would die there before the United States withdrew in 1973. He spent huge sums of money on the conflict that he might have invested in the War on Poverty. And paving Nixon's path to the White House, he undermined his own administration and the Great Society by driving millions of Americans to oppose both the war and his presidency.

At the same time, civil rights campaigns were giving way to race riots and a new black militancy. Pressing not only for southern desegregation but also for public action against the North's own apartheid-like social order, African American groups met growing and, sometimes, virulent resistance from whites who perceived demands for equal access to employment, education, and housing as threats to their own jobs, schools, and communities. And with rising expectations turning into agonizing frustrations, ghettos from Watts to Bedford-Stuyvesant exploded in deadly rage, and America witnessed the sudden ascent of black leaders like Stokely Carmichael of SNCC and Bobby Seale, Huey Newton, and Eldridge Cleaver of the newly organized Black Panther Party. Inspired by the respective ideologies of Black Muslim separatist Malcolm X and African and Caribbean anticolonial struggles, the Panthers preached "self-defense" and "Black Power" rather than nonviolence and integration.

These years also saw the development of an "alternative culture" among young people that, while overlapping with the New Left, particularly in opposition to the war, differed from it in important ways. The early SDS had called on citizens to mobilize politically. Counterculture prophets and "hippies" tended to reject political action in favor of personal and cultural change that all too often reduced to "doing your own thing." Undeniably, the latter shaped the continuing development of the

New Left, as in 1968 when radicals Abbie Hoffman and Jerry Rubin—both of whom professed affection for Paine—announced the birth of the Youth International Party or "Yippies" and added carnivalesque comedy and street theater to the repertoire of protest. Yet however much the counterculture's playfulness and pursuit of "sex, drugs, and rock and roll" helped to erode the puritanical codes of the 1950s, they did little to advance the left's politics, and soon enough capital found ways to make hedonism profitable.[46]

Meanwhile, interest in Paine grew. More biographies and anthologies were published, the U.S. Post Office issued a stamp bearing his image, and as in the 1930s, his career again inspired artists. New York's La Mama Experimental Theater Club staged Paul Foster's critically acclaimed play *Tom Paine*; folk musician Bob Dylan—who had received the National Emergency Civil Liberties Committee's Tom Paine Award in 1963 for his contributions to the civil rights cause—released an album that included "As I Went Out One Morning," in which Paine liberates the singer from the grip of a seductive creature; and Benjamin Levin wrote *To Spit Against the Wind*, a fictionalized account of Paine's life that went into a popular paperback edition.[47]

Asserting his posthumous endorsement of their respective positions, politicians also engaged Paine. While Johnson used lines like "These are the times . . ." to verbally buttress his administration's foreign policies, his fellow Democrat, South Dakota senator George McGovern (who would carry the party's presidential standard against Nixon in 1972), cited Paine, one of his personal heroes, to question the nation's actions abroad. Quoting from the *Crisis* ("'Tis surprising to see how rapidly a panic will sometimes run through a country"), McGovern warned Americans against becoming "neo-imperialists" who, driven either by "hysteria" or by a belief in their own "omnipotence," seek to "unilaterally" impose their will upon the world.[48]

However, while student activists still called on Paine, they increasingly looked abroad for inspiration. Betrayed by Johnson (who had run against Goldwater in 1964 as the peace candidate), the more radical cadres of the now-booming SDS and associated smaller parties and sects turned not only against the administration but also, it seemed, against America itself. Taking their cues from the black militants, they rhetorically and symbolically identified themselves with third-world revolutionaries. They chanted "Ho, Ho, Ho Chi Minh / The NLF is gonna win," mouthed the "teachings" of Mao, Che, and Lenin, and flew Vietcong flags alongside the star-spangled banner, making them appear decidedly anti-American to their fellow citizens and isolating them all the more from them, even as the latter themselves were turning against the war.[49]

Tragically for the left and the nation, all of this unfolded just as millions of industrial, agricultural, service, and government workers were commencing the biggest strike wave since 1946. Continuing well into the 1970s, and often having as much to do with questions of workplace power and authority as with issues of wages and benefits, the job actions would become so intense that they would instigate the Department of Health, Education, and Welfare to create a "Work in America" task force. And to the chagrin of capital, the resulting report would recommend instituting "living wages," redesigning jobs, and creating worker-participation schemes.[50]

Even as they grew more class conscious, however, white workers became ever more critical and suspicious not only of African Americans but also of middle-class liberals and New Leftists. As they did, they grew all the more susceptible to the reactionary and "law and order" appeals of figures like former Alabama governor and segregationist George Wallace and the old Republican red-baiter Nixon. Alarmed by ghetto riots and black power rhetoric, even as they watched welfare rolls growing, crime rates rising, and the rights of the accused expanding, white working people perceived liberal politicians as more concerned about the needs of minorities and the poor than those of "law-abiding" and "tax-paying" citizens. Concerned about family members and friends in the military, they were, while no more pro-war than any other class of Americans, outraged by student protestors who, privileged with draft deferments, spouted anti-Americanism and unfurled the enemy's flag at antiwar demonstrations. And committed to making an "honest living" and providing for their families, they were disgusted by the counterculture's disparagement of traditional morality and rejection of the values of self-discipline and hard work.

In 1968 Johnson decided not to seek reelection, both King and Robert Kennedy were assassinated, and the Democratic National Convention in Chicago was disrupted by street battles between police and protestors that incited venomous exchanges on the convention floor. And after Nixon won the presidency, what remained of FDR's coalition finally collapsed when the AFL-CIO withheld its support from the party's 1972 presidential nominee, the antiwar candidate George McGovern.

Liberal Democrats were not the only ones in a state of confusion; the New Left was as well. Factionalism tore SDS apart in 1969, sending the "Weathermen" group heading off on their own disastrous path of "armed struggle." Still, opposition to the war continued to grow, and when Nixon announced the invasion of Cambodia in May 1970, a national student strike shut down American higher education, in the course of which National Guardsmen killed four students at Ohio's Kent State University and state police killed two black students at Mississippi's Jackson State College.

While neither the war nor America's involvement in it came to an end, Nixon proceeded with the "Vietnamization" of the conflict and a reduction of American troops. And as casualties declined, the antiwar struggle itself retreated. But opposition to the war had already spread to the ranks of the military itself. Opening off-base antiwar coffeehouses, publishing their own newspapers and periodicals (one of which was titled *Common Sense*), and refusing combat duty (which in some instances included "fragging" their own officers), thousands of servicemen stood against the war in the late 1960s. As the total number of American troops in Vietnam decreased, their resistance to the conflict intensified. Moreover, back in America ex-GIs mobilized to the point of organizing their own antiwar groups, the most significant among them being Vietnam Veterans Against the War (VVAW).

The founders of VVAW, like so many of their fellow antiwar soldiers and veterans, sought an immediate halt to America's involvement in the war. But as their statement of principles indicated, they saw themselves as more than antiwar activists: "We believe in the United States of America, its Constitution and laws. We believe in freedom to speak, to think, to change our mind, and to dissent. We believe in democracy . . . We support our buddies in Vietnam. We want them home now. We want an end to the war now. We believe that this is the highest form of patriotism."[51]

For several years VVAW, a multiracial organization, marched side by side with "civilian" groups. But with Americans still dying in combat, its leaders, increasingly anxious about the enervation of the anti-war movement, decided to stage their own events, including the Winter Soldier Investigation and Dewey Canyon III. Held in Detroit in early 1971—following the exposure of the My Lai Massacre—the Winter Soldier Investigation involved dozens of veterans giving testimony on the violence and atrocities they had witnessed and perpetrated in Vietnam. Signifying that they had served the country in uniform and were doing so now by speaking the truth, the organizers derived the hearing's title from Paine's first *Crisis*: "The summer soldier and the sunshine patriot will in this crisis shrink from the service of his country, but he that stands it now deserves the love and thanks of man and woman." And as one of the VVAW leaders, former Army Lieutenant Bill Crandell, explained in his opening statement, "Like the winter soldiers of 1776 who stayed after they had served their time, we veterans . . . know that America is in grave danger. What threatens our country is not Redcoats or even Reds; it is our crimes that are destroying national unity by separating those of our countrymen who deplore these acts from those of our countrymen who refuse to examine what is being done in America's name."[52]

Calling themselves "winter soldiers," the veterans were also sending a message to the powers that be and their fellow antiwar protestors that they were redeeming America's own revolutionary heritage and reaffirming the nation's radical purpose and promise. As Crandell would later note, "The identification with Paine's pamphlet marked the beginning of VVAW's self-awareness that ours was a revolutionary role, and it noted our embracing of the American tradition of revolution rather than aping Lenin's, Mao's or Castro's ways."[53]

Dewey Canyon III, titled after the code name for two secret American incursions into Laos, entailed five days of rallies and lobbying efforts in Washington, D.C., in April 1971, during which eight hundred veterans threw their medals and ribbons onto the steps of the Capitol Building. This "incursion into the land of Congress" also saw one of their leaders, former Navy Lieutenant John Kerry, appear before the Senate Foreign Relations Committee and offer remarks that would remain both inspiring and controversial more than a generation later. Invoking Paine's name and memory and citing the testimonies given by the new "winter soldiers," Kerry (who would later pursue a long career in the Senate representing Massachusetts and in 2004 run unsuccessfully as the Democratic candidate for president) denounced the war as immoral, ill conceived, and destructive and indicted both those who had initiated it and those who now insisted on continuing it. Yet he did more than attack. He avowed that he and his fellow veterans hoped not merely to "search out and destroy the last vestige of this barbaric war" but also to "conquer the hate and fear that have driven this country these last ten years and more, so when thirty years from now our brothers go down the street without a leg, without an arm, or a face, and small boys ask why, we will be able to say 'Vietnam' and not mean a desert, not a filthy obscene memory, but mean instead the place where America finally turned and where soldiers like us helped in the turning."[54]

Still reeling from the 1960s, Americans experienced shocks and setbacks in the 1970s that would lead them to worry once again not only about the nation's immediate prospects and possibilities but also about its historic purpose and promise. Like the previous decade, the new one would witness rebellions, but the most dramatic of these would now come from above, not below. The governing elites, led by the corporate class, would react to the troubles of the day by abandoning the postwar consensus and trying to squelch America's democratic energies, if not reverse some of the nation's recent progressive advances. As ever, the ensuing struggles would have antagonists reaching for the Founders, and predictably, while elements of the left would seek out Paine in particular, and the political elite would adopt facets of him, conservatives, aside from the libertarians, would still openly scorn him. And yet something unexpected would happen as well. Seeking to realign American politics by constructing a new, popular conservative coalition from the fallout from the 1960s, Reagan would hijack Paine and attach the revolutionary to the cause of the right.

During 1973–74 the nation suffered an Arab oil embargo, defeat in Vietnam, and the first-ever resignation of a president (after the vice president, Spiro Agnew, had already stepped down in disgrace). Coming in the wake of the turbulence of the late 1960s and quickly following one upon the other, these events, plus revelations of corporate corruption and government misdeeds at home and abroad, seriously undermined American confidence and self-esteem. Yet worse was unfolding. The phenomenal economic expansion that had financed the postwar social compact and higher living standards for almost everyone was coming to a close in the recession of 1973–75. No mere downturn, the slump registered a major transformation in the global organization of capital and division of labor, as the United States faced intensifying industrial competition from Germany, Japan, and other countries (made all the worse by capital's failure to invest in modernizing American manufacturing). And Americans in the next few years would undergo an unprecedented mix of rising unemployment and accelerating inflation ("stagflation"), along with shattering fiscal crunches, widening inequality, and a devastating process of deindustrialization, as companies turned the Northeast and Midwest into the "Rust Belt" by moving operations overseas to escape organized labor, government regulation, and taxes.

Distressed by events that seemed beyond their control, Americans became ever more suspicious of the nation's leaders and institutions and ever more doubtful and anxious about what lay ahead. Looking for new ideas and direction, they found neither. The left remained in disarray. Nixon's downfall merely enabled the Democrats to avoid addressing the breakup of their traditional alliance. And while union, feminist, civil rights, and environmental activists fought on, they offered no collective vision and remained mutually antagonistic in the face of the competing pressures of job losses, affirmative action, and ecological protection. Meanwhile, Republicans scrambled to survive Nixon's ignominious departure, and though the forces that would constitute the New Right were beginning to assert themselves, they had yet to coalesce.

Radical possibilities existed. Yet reactionary ones were to prevail. Fearing that capitalism was under siege and that business was losing the battle for American hearts and minds, corporate executives mobilized to pursue class war and subdue the nation's democratic aspirations. Needing to silence hostile voices, deflate popular demands, and deter additional reforms and impositions, they joined together in organizations like the Conference Board, the Business Roundtable, and the Trilateral Commission. And endeavoring to reshape public policy, transform public opinion, and quash opposition, they intensified their lobbying efforts, invested in political action committees, endowed pro-business think tanks like the American Enterprise Institute and Heritage Foundation, sponsored new public relations and advocacy campaigns, and undertook not only to defeat but also to bust labor unions.[55]

Making no secret of their views, the corporate folk admitted their anxieties, identified their enemies, and revealed their aims. In 1975 the Trilateral Commission—which included prominent members of the political elite, both Republican and Democratic, along with similar figures from Western Europe and Japan—released a report on the "governability" of the Western nations titled *The Crisis of Democracy*. Observing that "the 1960s witnessed a dramatic renewal of the democratic spirit in America," Harvard professor Samuel P. Huntington contended that the heightened activism of public interest groups, minorities, women, students, and "value-oriented intellectuals," together with the "marked expansion of white-collar unionism," had produced a "democratic distemper." And postulating that a "democratic political system usually requires some measure of apathy and noninvolvement on the part of some individuals and groups," he warned that "some of the problems of governance in the United States today stem from *an excess of democracy*."[56]

In response to the crises, and with the bicentennial year 1976 fast approaching, Americans naturally turned back to the Founders—some for solace, others for political and commercial advantage, and still others, as almost never before, to chastise and denigrate them as imperialists, racists, and sexists. The official Bicentennial itself would clearly and sometimes crudely reflect the political and economic elites' interests and ambitions. In 1966, looking ahead, President Johnson established the American Revolutionary Bicentennial Commission (ARBC) and gave it the task of planning ways to honor the Revolution's significance for America and the world. Due to costs of the war, however, the commission received little funding and made little headway. And yet poor funding and inertia turned out to be only part of its problem. In 1972 journalists revealed that Nixon had loaded the commission with Republican appointees, fully expecting them to boost his presidency. A minor scandal compared to Watergate, it nonetheless compelled the ARBC's termination and the creation of a more pluralistic American Revolution Bicentennial Administration (ARBA).

It was not only Nixon who sought to exploit the Bicentennial. With ARBA and its associated state commissions and local groups desperately seeking dollars to pay for the thousands of activities projected, corporate executives—who were themselves anxiously looking to improve the image of business—eagerly signed up their companies as sponsors in order to identify them with the celebration of America's past, present, and future. And ARBA further commercialized the whole affair by licensing Bicentennial products and memorabilia of every imaginable sort, from statuettes to toilet seats (so much of which, ironically enough, was often manufactured overseas).

Less crassly, though perhaps more insidiously, the governing elites also saw the anniversary of independence as an opportunity to address popular dissent by promoting patriotism, loyalty, and the status quo. ARBA and its affiliated committees arranged a vast array of national and local commemorative activities—including historical reenactments, concerts and recitals, parades and fireworks, tall ship "sail-bys" and airplane "fly-overs," and religious services and naturalization ceremonies. However, like the directors of the Centennial, those of the Bicentennial would render the Revolution an event to be celebrated and revered, not emulated. In January 1976 ARBA director John Warner, a former secretary of the navy, promised that the events would "honor the great men who forged and then steered a nation so strong and so flexible that one revolution had proved enough." As Richard B. Morris, the president of the American Historical Association, critically noted, "The two words most muted during the two hundredth year of American independence, have been 'people' and 'revolution.'" And yet as much as the organizers and underwriters of the Bicentennial, like their predecessors a hundred years earlier, would downplay the revolutionary character of 1776, they would not follow suit in their handling of Paine.[57]

Talk of revolution may have been muted, but talk of Paine definitely was not. New and reprinted biographies, anthologies, and articles continued to appear, along with children's books and plays and a growing number of graduate theses and dissertations. Citing Paine and his words, the U.S. Postal Service issued an eight-cent stamp in 1973 saluting the printers and pamphleteers whose presses and pens spread the idea of independence. In "A Prophet Honored," *Time* magazine gave Paine a full page of attention in a special bicentennial issue. Composer Henry Leland Clarke turned the words of the *Crisis* into musical lyrics for bicentennial performance. And in January 1977 Paine himself would make his television debut (opposite Teddy Roosevelt, Queen

Cleopatra, and Thomas Aquinas) on the premiere episode of *Meeting of Minds*, a series produced by the multitalented Steve Allen that placed great historical figures in conversation with one another.[58]

Conservatives, however, remained as ready as ever to denigrate Paine. Speaking of "The American Revolution as a Successful Revolution," Irving Kristol, the recognized godfather of neoconservatism, would say, "To perceive the true purposes of the American Revolution, it is wise to ignore some of the more grandiloquent declamations of the moment— Tom Paine, an English radical who never really understood America, is especially worth ignoring." And in the *National Review*, Aram Bakshian wrote of Paine as if instructed by James Cheetham himself.[59]

But the political elite's own needs led to a different approach to Paine. Recognizing his status and appeal, and following pre-existing cold war practice, centrist politicians coopted Paine the patriot in support of the existing order. Studiously avoided by officialdom in 1876, he was now introduced at the most formal of occasions. Becoming the first president of his party to openly quote Paine while in office, Republican Gerald Ford would cite him in his January 1976 State of the Union message to Congress.

The only president never to have been elected to national office (for he was appointed vice president on Agnew's resignation and elevated to the presidency when Nixon himself resigned), Ford opened his "Bicentennial" State of the Union address with references to the "stirring deeds of 1776" and the progress of the nation through "eight generations." Yet he did so not only to take pride in America. Speaking of failure at home and defeat abroad, and of the economic and fiscal problems that now threatened, he also did so to reassure the citizenry that they could "win" over the crises of the day. Laying hold of Paine, he said: "History and experience tell us that moral progress cannot come in comfortable and complacent times, but out of trial and out of confusion. Tom Paine aroused the troubled Americans of 1776 to stand up to the times that try men's souls because the harder the conflict, the more glorious the triumph." And then a few moments later he added, "To paraphrase Tom Paine, 1975 was not a year for summer soldiers and sunshine patriots. It was a year of fears and alarms and of dire forecasts—most of which never happened and won't happen." Strangely, in light of his use of Paine, Ford did not so much rally Americans to fight the good fight as urge them—in line with the wishes of the corporate class—to lower their aspirations and expectations. Contending that they had taken on too much, he preached "realism," "balance," and "self-discipline."[60]

The governing elites' approach to the Bicentennial and their renditions of the Revolution and Paine did not go unanswered. In 1971 a group of New Leftists, headed by Jeremy Rifkin, who had worked on projects with the VVAW and may well have been inspired by its patriotism, launched the People's Bicentennial Commission (PBC) with the proclaimed goal of honoring America's revolutionary past not simply by toasting it but also by reasserting it. Opposing the exploitation of the "Buy-centennial," they stated that while "modern-day tories will attempt to present themselves and the institutions they control—the corporations, the White House—as the true heirs and defenders of the struggle waged by the first American revolutionaries . . . we will be celebrating radical heroes like Jefferson, Paine, and [Samuel] Adams, and radical events like the Boston Tea Party."[61]

In the spirit of Paine, to whose life and labors they continually referred, PBC activists set out to highlight the radical and popular character of the Revolution and to propagate an understanding and appreciation of that struggle that would lead Americans to reject the status quo and "reclaim the democratic ideals upon which this nation was founded." Just as Americans had needed to fight monarchy and aristocracy in 1776, so too did present-day Americans, but now the enemy was "economic royalty . . . and the aristocracy of giant corporations." And hoping to tap into the spreading anticorporate sentiment and assemble progressive forces from labor to religion in a single movement, they called not for reform but for a new American Revolution and the making of a "democratic economy." Most immediately, they set themselves the task of raising the consciousness of their fellow citizens to their great revolutionary heritage and legacy.[62]

Garnering the support of several major organizations, most notably the National Council of Churches, the PBC succeeded in generating significant enthusiasm for its efforts, as well as critical media attention. In addition to publishing a magazine, *Common Sense*, and books like *How to Commit Revolution American Style*, *Common Sense II*, and *Voices of the American Revolution* (the latter two, plus others, in mass-market paperback editions), it produced newspaper columns, television programs, and radio spots, distributed syllabi, pamphlets, and posters

to schools, libraries, and community groups, and staged "guerrilla theater" performances, demonstrations, and "media-oriented" stunts.[63]

PBC activities drew furious reactions from groups like the Daughters of the American Revolution and the American Legion. They also
incited Senator James O. Eastland, a Mississippi Dixiecrat and white
supremacist, to convene the Senate Judiciary Committee's "Subcommittee to Investigate the Administration of the Internal Security Act
and Other Internal Security Laws" and to issue a report, *The Attempt
to Steal the Bicentennial*, portraying the PBC as Communist-inspired
and intent upon "overthrowing our free society."[64]

While the PBC did a good job of upsetting the right, turned out
thousands of people for its demonstrations, and served as the conscience of the Bicentennial, it failed to engender the movement its
founders envisioned. For all of its imaginative labors and rambunctiousness, it could not overcome the left's divisions, transcend the "identity
politics" of minority and feminist activists, or dispel popular suspicions
of the New Left. And when it called for two hundred thousand citizens
to declare "Independence from Big Business" by rallying in Washington, D.C., on July 4, 1976, only twenty thousand showed up.

The Bicentennial also witnessed a renewed contest in academe to
define America's Revolutionary heritage. Reading the past from the
vantage point of the elites and favoring the traditional "Founders," historians such as Bernard Bailyn and David Freeman Hawke treated
Paine, at best, in an ambivalent fashion. Referring to *Common Sense*
as "one of the most brilliant pamphlets ever written in the English language," Harvard professor Bailyn, the dean of Revolutionary studies,
wrote that "not only does [the pamphlet] voice some of the deepest aspirations of the American people on the eve of the Revolution, but it
also evokes, with superb vigor and with perfect intonation, longings
and aspirations that have remained part of American culture to this
day." Yet—apparently haunted by the campus turmoil of the 1960s and
possessed of lingering anxieties about radicals—Bailyn proceeded to
call Paine himself "an ignoramus, both in ideas and the practice of politics," and while utterly ignoring questions of class to contend that
Paine's arguments were "rejected by the Revolutionary generation."
And Hawke, who actually published a new Paine biography in 1974,
treated Paine so snidely it led other scholars to ask why he had "ever

bothered to write" about him at all. However, radical historians such as Alfred Young, Jesse Lemisch, Gary Nash, and Eric Foner brought fresh questions and sensibilities to bear on the past to reveal not only the laboring classes' crucial role in the Revolution but also Paine's in capturing their deepest thoughts and highest aspirations and imbuing the new nation with radical democratic meaning and significance.[65]

If the media were to be believed, the Bicentennial had bound up the nation's wounds, unified the citizenry, and stabilized the ship of state. Yet such talk reflected mostly wishful thinking, for though Americans celebrated, they did so ambivalently. Moreover, ensuing events would make Americans ever more worried about the direction and future of the nation. In the elections of 1976 the moderate Democrat Carter, a member of the Trilateral Commission, defeated the moderate Republican Ford. But anxiety would intensify when inflation resurged, the Soviets increased their activity in Asia and Africa, and a revolution in Iran brought gasoline lines back to filling stations and saw the U.S. Embassy occupied and the mission to free the American hostages fail disastrously.

The nation's democratic impulse and aspiration survived, but increasingly the right, not the left, would mobilize it. While liberals and radicals failed to offer a progressive alternative to the recurring crises, conservatives gathered force. Funded by corporate interests, libertarians and traditionalists alike pursued grassroots campaigns among increasingly anxious and angry white middle-class and working-class people, and soon populist-style "taxpayers' revolts" and "evangelical revivals" joined the rebellion of the economic elite in rending the already frayed governing consensus. They too might have remained divided and weak, if not at odds with one another. But they did not, for a former FDR Democrat would gather them together and strengthen their appeal. And he would do so not simply by articulating their fears and ambitions but also by speaking to their persistent belief in America's exceptional purpose and promise and reminding them and their fellow citizens that they had it in their power "to begin the world over again."

9

IT IS YET TOO SOON TO WRITE
THE HISTORY OF THE REVOLUTION

Americans—their contradictions, their energies, and their possibilities—turned Thomas Paine into a radical, a patriot, and a writer, and Paine, convinced that America could be "as happy as she pleases" and that their cause was "the cause of all mankind," turned Americans into revolutionaries. Through prose such as "The sun never shined on a cause of greater worth," "We have it in our power to begin the world over again," and "These are the times that try men's souls," he not only moved them to declare their independence and create a republic; he also imbued the nation they were founding with democratic impulse and aspiration and exceptional—indeed, world-historic—purpose and promise. And for 230 years Americans have drawn ideas, inspiration, and encouragement from Paine and his work.

Fearing their example and influence, the powers that be repeatedly have tried to suppress, obscure, or denigrate Paine and his contributions. Yet repeatedly they have failed. Instinctively Americans have turned to Paine at times of war and peril to remind themselves of who they are and what they need to do. And in every generation there were those—rebels, reformers, and critics, native-born and immigrant—who actively redeemed his life and labors and, energized by them, served as the prophetic memory of his American vision.

Heartened and animated by Paine, we have pressed for the rights of workingmen; insisted upon freedom of conscience and the separation of church and state; demanded the abolition of slavery; campaigned for the equality of women; confronted the power of property and wealth; opposed the tyrannies of fascism and communism; and challenged our own government's authorities and policies, domestic and foreign. We have suffered defeats, committed mistakes, and endured tragedy and irony. But we have achieved great victories, and far more often than not, as Paine himself fully expected, we have in the process transformed the nation and the world for the better.

Now, after two centuries, it seems we have all become Painites. Today references to Paine abound in public debate and culture; in contrast to the past, not only the left but also the right claims him as one of their own. Still, appearances and rhetoric can deceive, for if we all truly revered Paine, then for a start we surely would have built the promised monument to him on the Mall in the nation's capital. We would have placed his statue where it belongs, near the images of and memorials to George Washington, Thomas Jefferson, Abraham Lincoln, Franklin Roosevelt, and the veterans of the Second World War, as well as those of Vietnam—whose lives and acts he so powerfully informed and motivated. And we would have engraved Paine's words in marble to remind us of how it all began and to keep us from forgetting that "much yet remains to be done."[1]

But the truth is that not all of us are Painites. For all of their citations of Paine and his lines, conservatives do not—and truly cannot—embrace him and his arguments. Bolstered by capital, firmly in command of the Republican Party, and politically ascendant for a generation, they have initiated and instituted policies and programs that fundamentally contradict Paine's own vision and commitments. They have subordinated the Republic—the *res publica*, the commonwealth, the public good—to the marketplace and private advantage. They have furthered the interests of corporations and the rich over those of working people, their families, unions, and communities and overseen a concentration of wealth and power that, recalling the Gilded Age, has corrupted and enervated American democratic life and politics. And they have carried on culture wars that have divided the nation and undermined the wall separating church and state. Moreover, they have pursued domestic and foreign policies that have made the nation both less free and less secure politically, economically, environmentally, and militarily. Even as they have spoken of advancing freedom and empowering citizens, they have sought to discharge or at least constrain America's democratic impulse and aspiration. In fact, while poaching lines from Paine, they and their favorite intellectuals have disclosed their real ambitions and affections by once again declaring the "end of history" and promoting the lives of Founders like John Adams and Alexander Hamilton, who in decided contrast to Paine scorned democracy and feared "the people."

Still, conservatives do, in their fashion, end up fostering interest in Paine. It's not just that, aware of his iconic status, they insist on quoting him. It's also that their very own policies and programs, by effectively denying and threatening America's great purpose and promise, propel us, as in crises past, back to the Revolution and the Founders, where once again we encounter Paine's arguments and recognize them as our own. Arguably, the heightened popular interest in Paine we have witnessed these past several years reflects anxieties and longings generated not simply by the grave challenges we face but by the triumph of right-wing politics, as well.

And yet those of us who might make the strongest historical claim on Paine have yet to properly reappropriate his memory and legacy. Continuing to cite Paine, we on the left have not made his vision and commitments once again our own. In contrast both to the majority of our fellow citizens and to generations of our political predecessors, liberals and radicals no longer proclaim a firm belief in the nation's exceptional purpose and promise, the prospects and possibilities of democratic change, and ordinary citizens' capacities to act as citizens not subjects. We have lost the political courage and conviction that once motivated our efforts.

Electrified by America and its people, and the originality of thought and action unleashed by the Revolution, Paine argued that the United States would afford an "asylum for mankind," provide a model to the world, and support the global advance of republican democracy. But apparently still bogged down in the late 1960s, many on the left have eschewed notions of American exceptionalism and patriotism and allowed politicians and pundits of the right to monopolize and define them. Presuming that such ideas and practices can serve only to justify the status quo or worse, and ignoring how, historically, progressives have articulated them to advocate the defense *and* extension and deepening of freedom, equality, and democracy, many of us have failed to recognize their critical value as weapons against injustice and oppression.

Moreover, whereas Paine declared that Americans had it in their power to "begin the world over again," liberals and radicals seem to have all but abandoned the belief that democratic transformation remains both imperative and possible. While we reject the right's end-of-history declarations, we do not actually counter them with fresh ideas and initiatives—ideas and initiatives that would stir the American imagination and offer real hope of addressing the threats to our freedom and security, the causes of our deepening inequalities, and the forces undermining our public life and solidarities by enhancing the authority of democratic government and the power of citizens against the authority of the market and the power of corporations. We must rediscover and reinvigorate the optimism, energy, and imagination that led Paine to declare, "We are a people upon experiments" and "From what we now see, nothing of reform on the political world ought to be held improbable. It is an age of revolutions, in which everything may be looked for."[2]

And while Paine had every confidence in working people and wrote to engage them in the Revolution and nation-building, we, for all our rhetoric, have remained alienated from, if not skeptical of, our fellow citizens. Asking labor unions to underwrite their campaigns and appealing to working people for their votes, Democrats—the party of the people—hesitate to actually mobilize them to fight for democratic political and social change. Taking office in January 1993, eager to signal a new, progressive direction in public life after twelve years of Republican administrations, William Jefferson Clinton—who would also speak of Paine at various times in his two terms—made every effort to identify himself with the revolutionary author of the Declaration of Independence, Thomas Jefferson. En route from Arkansas to the capital to take the oath of office, Clinton retraced Jefferson's inaugural trek from Monticello to Washington and filled his inaugural address with Jeffersonian references. But the way Clinton presented the Founder and third president, however stirring it may have sounded, revealed an elitist dread of popular democratic energies and a desire to keep "the people" at some distance from power. Calling on Americans to "be bold, embrace change, and share the sacrifices needed for the nation to progress," he stated that "Thomas Jefferson believed that to preserve the very foundations of our nation, we would need dramatic change from time to time." Yet as Clinton surely knew, Jefferson did not say that we needed merely *change* to sustain the Republic. What Jefferson said was, "I hold that a little *rebellion* now and then is a good thing, and as necessary in the political world as storms in the physical."[3]

Nevertheless, the struggle to expand American freedom, equality, and democracy will continue, for as Paine proudly observed of his fellow citizens after they turned out the Federalists in 1800, "There is too much common sense and independence in America to be long the dupe of any faction, foreign or domestic." Indeed, we have good reason not only to hope but also to act, for Americans' persistent and growing interest in and affection for Paine and his words signify that our generation too still feels the democratic impulse and aspiration that he inscribed in American experience. Responding to those yearnings, we may well prove—as Paine himself wrote in reaction to misrepresentations of the events of 1776—that "it is yet too soon to write the history of the Revolution."[4]

NOTES

For Thomas Paine's works the author has made use of Philip Foner, ed., *The Complete Writings of Thomas Paine* (New York: The Citadel Press, 1945), published in two volumes. Citations of Paine's writings and words refer to that edition, indicated by the abbreviation *CW*.

INTRODUCTION

1. Ronald Reagan, "Acceptance Speech to the 1980 National Republican Convention," reprinted in *Ronald Reagan Talks to America* (Old Greenwich, Conn.: Devin Adair, 1983), pp. 63–78.
2. Paine, *Common Sense*, in *CW*, p. 1:17.
3. Dixon Wecter, "Hero in Reverse," *Virginia Quarterly Review* 18, no. 2 (Spring 1942), p. 243; Gordon Wood, "Disturbing the Peace," *New York Review of Books*, June 8, 1995, p. 20.
4. J.G.A. Pocock, *Virtue, Commerce and History: Essays on Political Thought and History, Chiefly in the Eighteenth Century* (New York: Cambridge University Press, 1985), p. 276.
5. Chris Matthews, *Now, Let Me Tell You What I Really Think* (New York: Free Press, 2001), p. 207; Jack Hitt, "Common Sense: 'Tis time to Part," in Robert Wilson and Stanley Marcus, eds., *American Greats* (New York: Public Affairs, 1999), pp. 2–3; and Jon Katz, *Virtuous Reality* (New York: Random House, 1997), pp. 112, 124.
6. See George H. W. Bush, "Address to the Nation Announcing Allied Military Action in the Persian Gulf" (January 16, 1991), in *Public Papers of the President of the United States 1991* (Washington, D.C.: Government Printing Office, 1992), p. 116.
7. Rachel Jones (Knight-Ridder Newspapers), "Activists Try to Free Statue Marking Female Suffrage," *Arizona Republic*, July 21, 1995, p. A1; Aaron Beck, "Did Those Phrases of Clinton's Address Sound a Bit Familiar?" *Columbus Dispatch*, February 1, 1998, p. 3H.

8. Gordon Wood, "The Greatest Generation," *New York Review of Books*, March 29, 2001, p. 17; and Francis Jennings, *The Creation of America* (New York: Cambridge University Press, 2000), p. 197.

9. Steven H. Jaffe, *Who Were the Founding Fathers: Two Hundred Years of Reinventing American History* (New York: Henry Holt, 1996), p. 7.

10. The Post-Modernity Project (James Davison Hunter), *The State of Disunion: 1996 Survey of American Political Culture* (Charlottesville, Va.: In Media Res Foundation, 1996).

11. John Dos Passos, *The Ground We Stand On* (New York: Harcourt, Brace, 1941), p. 3.

12. Neil Postman, *Building a Bridge to the Eighteenth Century: How the Past Can Improve the Future* (New York: Alfred A. Knopf, 1999), p. 17.

13. Regarding Cobbett and Paine's remains, see Leo A. Bressler, "Peter Porcupine and the Bones of Thomas Paine," *Pennsylvania Magazine of History and Biography* 82 (April 1958), pp. 176–85.

14. William J. Bennett, ed., *Our Sacred Honor: Words of Advice from the Founders in Stories, Letters, Poems and Speeches* (New York: Simon and Schuster, 1997), p. 18.

1. A FREEBORN BRITON

1. James Otis, *The Rights of the British Colonies Asserted and Proved* (1764), in Merrill Jensen, ed., *Tracts of the American Revolution, 1763–1776* (Indianapolis: Bobbs-Merrill, 1977), pp. 21, 24, 36; and Francis Hopkinson (1766) quoted in Liah Greenfeld, *Nationalism: Five Roads to Modernity* (Cambridge, Mass.: Harvard University Press, 1992), p. 410.

2. Joseph Warren quoted in Elaine K. Ginsberg, "The Patriot Pamphleteers," in Everett Emerson, ed., *American Literature: The Revolutionary Years, 1764–1789* (Madison: University of Wisconsin Press, 1977), p. 22; Thomas Jefferson letter (November 29, 1775), in Henry Steele Commager and Richard B. Morris, eds., *The Spirit of 'Seventy-Six: The Story of the American Revolution as Told by Recipients* (New York: Da Capo, 1975), p. 283; and Page Smith, *A New Age Now Begins* (New York: McGraw-Hill, 1976), p. 682.

3. Connecticut letter (to *Pennsylvania Evening Post*, February 13, 1776) quoted in Eric Foner, *Tom Paine and Revolutionary America* (New York: Oxford University Press, 1976), p. 79; Maryland letter (to *Pennsylvania Evening Post*) quoted in W. E. Woodward, *Tom Paine: America's Godfather 1737–1809* (New York: E.P. Dutton, 1946), p. 80; and New York letter (to *Constitutional Gazette*, February 27, 1776) in Frank Moore, *Diary of the American Revolution from Newspapers and Original Documents* (New York: Charles Scribner, 1858), pp. 209; Josiah Bartlett quoted in Pauline Maier, *American Scripture: The Making of the Declaration of Independence* (New York: Alfred A. Knopf, 1997), p. 32; and George Washington quoted in Commager and Morris, *Spirit of 'Seventy-Six*, p. 283.

4. Rhode Island letter (to *Newport Mercury*, April 8, 1776) quoted in John Keane, *Tom Paine, A Political Life* (Boston: Little, Brown, 1995), p. 112; and Abigail Adams letters (April 14 and March 2, 1776), in *Adams Family Correspondence*,

vol. 1, *December 1761–May 1776*, ed. L.H. Butterfield (New York: Atheneum, 1965), pp. 380, 352.

5. Horatio Gates letter (January 22, 1776) quoted in Keane, *Tom Paine*, p. 111.

6. Paine's family name was variably spelled Payne, Pain, and Paine. Apparently he opted for Paine on coming to America.

7. E. P. Thompson, *The Making of the English Working Class*, rev. ed. (London: Penguin, 1980), p. 86.

8. Thomas Paine, *The Age of Reason*, in *CW*, p. 1:497.

9. Roy Porter, *English Society in the Eighteenth Century* (London: Penguin, 1990), p. 8; and Paine, *Rights of Man: Part 2*, in *CW*, p. 1:405.

10. Paine, *Common Sense*, in *CW*, p. 1:33; Alyce Barry, "Thomas Paine, Privateersman," *Pennsylvania Magazine of History and Biography*, vol. 101, no. 4, 1977, pp. 451–61; and Keane, *Tom Paine*, pp. 31–35.

11. Roy Porter, *The Creation of the Modern World: The Untold Story of the British Enlightenment* (New York: W.W. Norton, 2000), pp. 46, 6–11.

12. Caroline Robbins, *The Eighteenth-Century Commonwealthman: Studies in the Transmission, Development, and Circumstance of English Liberal Thought from the Restoration of Charles II until the War with the Thirteen Colonies* (Cambridge, Mass.: Harvard University Press, 1961); and John Dunn, *The Political Thought of John Locke* (Cambridge, Eng.: Cambridge University Press, 1969).

13. David Wilson, *Paine and Cobbett: The Transatlantic Connection* (Kingston, Ont.: McGill-Queen's University Press, 1988), pp. 20–29; and Porter, *Creation of the Modern World*, p. 54.

14. Keane, *Tom Paine*, pp. 45–49; and Thompson, *The Making of the English Working Class*, pp. 45–58, 385–440.

15. For many years it was believed that Paine was the author of "An Occasional Letter on the Female Sex," which, published in the *Pennsylvania Magazine* in 1775, argued for women's liberation. But it is now assumed otherwise. See Frank Smith, "The Authorship of 'An Occasional Letter on the Female Sex,'" *American Literature* 2 (November 1930), pp. 277–80. But as Philip Foner notes in his editorial preface to the essay, Paine was the editor who published the piece and "some of the language of the essay is his" (*CW*, p. 2:34).

16. Keane, *Tom Paine*, pp. 52–62.

17. George Rudé, *Wilkes and Liberty* (London: Lawrence and Wishart, 1983).

18. Thomas Clio Rickman, *The Life of Thomas Paine* (1819; reprinted, New York: Peter Eckler, 1892), p. 35; Keane, *Tom Paine*, pp. 66–71; and Jack Fruchtman, Jr., *Thomas Paine: Apostle of Freedom* (New York: Four Walls Eight Windows, 1994), pp. 31–34.

19. Paine, *The Case of the Officers of Excise* (1772), in *CW*, pp. 2:3–15.

20. Franklin letter is in David Hawke, *Paine* (New York: Norton, 1974), p. 20; Franklin's relations with Paine are discussed in H. W. Brands, *The First American: The Life and Times of Benjamin Franklin* (New York: Doubleday, 2000), pp. 508–10.

21. Benjamin Franklin (1760) quoted in Winthrop S. Hudson, *Nationalism and Religion in America: Concepts of American Identity and Mission* (New York: Harper and Row, 1970), p. xix.

22. Gordon Wood, *The Radicalism of the American Revolution* (New York: Alfred A. Knopf, 1992), pp. 27, 53.

23. Statements by George Washington and John Adams quoted in ibid., p. 27; that by Gouverneur Morris quoted in Roy Rosenzweig et al., eds., American Social History Project, *Who Built America?* (New York: Worth, 2000), p. 1:227.

24. Wilson, *Paine and Cobbett*, pp. 41–42; and Carl Becker, *The History of Political Parties in the Province of New York, 1765–1776* (Madison: University of Wisconsin Press, 1909), p. 5.

25. James T. Austin, *The Life of Elbridge Gerry with Contemporary Letters* (Boston: Wells and Lilly, 1828), p. 78.

26. Paine recounts his voyage to and settling in at Philadelphia in a letter to Franklin (March 4, 1775), in *CW*, pp. 2:1130–32.

27. Richard Alan Ryerson, *The Revolution Is Now Begun: The Radical Committees of Philadelphia, 1765–1776* (Philadelphia: University of Pennsylvania Press, 1978), p. 185; Foner, *Revolutionary America*, pp. 63–66; and Ron Schultz, *The Republic of Labor: Philadelphia Artisans and the Politics of Class, 1720–1830* (New York: Oxford University Press, 1993), pp. 1–37.

28. Paine (as "The Editor"), "The Magazine in America," *Pennsylvania Magazine*, January 24, 1775, in *CW*, pp. 2:1110–11; and A. Owen Aldridge, *Thomas Paine's American Ideology* (Newark: University of Delaware Press, 1984), pp. 29–30.

29. Paine (as "Justice and Humanity"), "African Slavery in America," *Pennsylvania Journal and the Weekly Advertiser*, March 8, 1775, in *CW*, pp. 2:15–19.

30. Paine, "American Crisis #7," November 21, 1778, in *CW*, pp. 1:143–44. The battles also left 273 British dead or wounded. On "April 19, 1775," see William H. Hallahan, *The Day the Revolution Began* (New York: William Morrow, 2000).

31. Paine (as "Vox Populi"), "Reflections on Titles," *Pennsylvania Magazine*, May 1775, in *CW*, p. 2:33; and Paine (as "A Lover of Peace"), "Thoughts on Defensive War," *Pennsylvania Magazine*, July 1775, in *CW*, p. 2:53.

32. Paine, "Liberty Tree," *Pennsylvania Evening Post*, September 16, 1775, in *CW*, pp. 2:1091–92.

33. Paine (as "Humanus"), "A Serious Thought," *Pennsylvania Journal*, October 18, 1775, in *CW*, p. 2:20.

2. AN AMERICAN REVOLUTIONARY

1. Paine, "Letter to Henry Laurens" (1778), in *CW*, pp. 2:1142–43.

2. Paine, *The Age of Reason* (1794), in *CW*, p. 1:496; and *Rights of Man: Part 2* (1792), in *CW*, p. 1:406.

3. Paine, "To the Citizens of the United States, Letter VIII" (1805), in *CW*, p. 2:957.

4. For John Adams's assertion that Paine had said nothing new, see *Diary and Autobiography of John Adams*, ed. L. H. Butterfield (Cambridge, Mass.: Harvard University Press, 1962), p. 3:333.

5. Paine, "To Robert Morris, Esq.," in *CW*, p. 2:1207; Paine, *Letter to the Abbé Raynal*, in *CW*, p. 2:219; and Samuel Williams, *The Natural and Civil History of Vermont* (Walpole, N.H., 1794), pp. 372–73.

6. David Freeman Hawke, *Benjamin Rush, Revolutionary Gadfly* (Indianapolis: Bobbs-Merrill, 1971), pp. 82–119.

7. Benjamin Rush, "Travels Through Life," in *The Autobiography of Benjamin Rush* ed. George W. Corner (Westport, Conn.: Greenwood Press, 1970), p. 114.

8. Benjamin Rush to James Cheetham (July 17, 1809), in *Letters of Benjamin Rush*, vol. 1, *1761–1792*, ed. L. H. Butterfield, (Princeton, N.J.: Princeton University Press, 1951), p. 1008; and Paine, *Common Sense* in *CW*, p. 1:36.

9. Paine, *The American Crisis I* (hereafter *Crisis*), in *CW*, p. 1:56. Robert A. Ferguson, "The Commonalities of *Common Sense*," *William and Mary Quarterly*, vol. 57, no. 3, July 2000, pp. 465–504.

10. Rush to Cheetham, p. 1008. Paine issued the "third edition" in response to a battle with his original publisher, Robert Bell. Bell denied making a profit on the work and proceeded to issue an unauthorized second edition, compelling Paine to produce the "third edition," which would become the standard text (and is the text of *Common Sense* hereafter referred to). It contained an appendix, in which Paine included an "Epistle to the Quakers," attacking those elements of the Society of Friends who he believed had formally aligned themselves with the Tories (in *CW*, pp. 2:55–60).

11. Paine, *Common Sense*, in *CW*, pp. 1:4–5

12. Ibid., pp. 1:5–6. Paine discussed "simple democracy" in *Rights of Man: Part 2*, in *CW*, p. 1:371.

13. Ibid.

14. Ibid., pp. 1:6–9.

15. Ibid., pp. 1:10–12.

16. Ibid., p. 1:13.

17. Ibid., pp. 1:14–16.

18. Ibid., pp. 1:17–19.

19. Ibid., p. 1:19.

20. Ibid., pp. 1:20–21, but also see pp. 1:27, 39.

21. Ibid., p. 1:21.

22. Ibid., p. 1:23.

23. Ibid., pp. 1:28–29.

24. Paine, *Rights of Man: Part 2*, in *CW*, pp. 1:369, 371; *Dissertations on Government; the Affairs of the Bank; and Paper Money* (1786), in *CW*, pp. 2:372–73.

25. *Common Sense*, in *CW*, pp. 1:29–30.

26. Ibid., p. 1:37.

27. Ibid., p. 1:29.

28. Ibid., pp. 1:31–36.

29. Ibid., pp. 1:29–30, 36–39.

30. Paine's only reference to African Americans was that the British had "stirred up the Indians and the Negroes to destroy us; the cruelty hath a double guilt, it is dealing brutally by us, and treacherously by them" (Paine, *Common Sense*, in *CW*, pp. 1:4–5). But in 1780 Paine helped to write the preamble to legislation in Pennsylvania leading to the abolition of slavery in that state, the first law of its kind in the country. And though he never publicly called for a slave rebellion, he did privately contemplate such an initiative: "I despair of seeing an abolition of the infernal

traffic in Negroes . . . I wish that a few well instructed could be sent among their brethren in bondage; for until they are enabled to take their own part, nothing will be done" ("To Anonymous," March 16, 1789, in *CW*, p. 2:1286).

31. Paine, *Common Sense*, in *CW* pp. 1:30–31, 3, 45.

32. See *Letters of Delegates to Congress, 1774–1789*, vol. 3, *January 1–May 15, 1776*, ed. Paul H. Smith (Washington, D.C.: Library of Congress, 1978). Paine later claimed to have "timed" the pamphlet to coincide with the arrival of the King's speech. See letter to Henry Laurens (January 14, 1779), in *CW*, p. 2:1162.

33. E. Stanly Godbold, Jr., and Robert H. Woody, *Christopher Gadsden and the American Revolution* (Knoxville: University of Tennessee Press, 1982), pp. 147–51.

34. Deacon Palmer to John Adams quoted in Page Smith, *A People's History of the American Revolution*, vol. 1., *A New Age Now Begins* (New York: McGraw-Hill, 1976), p. 683; Joseph Tiedemann, *Reluctant Revolutionaries: New York City and the Road to Independence, 1763–1776* (Ithaca, N.Y.: Cornell University Press, 1992), p. 246; John Penn's note referred to in a letter of John Adams to James Warren, in *Letters of Delegates to Congress, 1774–1789*, p. 3:558; and Edmund Randolph, *History of Virginia*, ed. Arthur H. Shaffer (Charlottesville: University Press of Virginia, 1970), pp. 233–34.

35. "An American" [Charles Inglis], *The True Interest of America Impartially Stated in Certain Strictures on a Pamphlet Intitled Common Sense* (1776), excerpts reprinted in L.F.S. Upton, ed., *Revolutionary Versus Loyalist* (Waltham, Mass: Blaisdell, 1968), pp. 70–83; and "Candidus" [James Chalmers], *Plain Truth* (1776), reprinted in Merrill Jensen, ed., *Tracts of the American Revolution* (Indianapolis: Bobbs-Merrill, 1967), pp. 447–88.

36. Elias Boudinot, "Thoughts on the Present State of Affairs" (June 11, 1776), quoted in Larry Gerlach, *Prologue to Independence: New Jersey in the Coming of the Revolution* (New Brunswick, N.J.: Rutgers University Press, 1976), p. 485; Landon Carter, "Diary of Landon Carter," *William and Mary Quarterly* 16, nos. 3 and 4 (January and April 1908), pp. 149, 152, 264; and "Cato" [William Smith], in Peter Force, ed., *American Archives* 5, ser. 4 (Washington, D.C., 1837–53), pp. 125–27, 188–90, 443–46, 514–17, 542–46, 839–43, 850–53, 1049–51.

37. John Adams to Abigail Adams (March 19, 1776), in *Adams Family Correspondence*, vol. 1, *December 1761–May 1776*, ed. L. H. Butterfield (New York: Atheneum, 1965), p. 363; *Autobiography of John Adams*, in *Diary and Autobiography of John Adams*, ed. Butterfield et al., p. 3:333; and John Adams to Thomas Jefferson, in *The Adams-Jefferson Letters*, ed. Lester J. Cappon, (Chapel Hill: University of North Carolina Press, 1959), p. 542.

38. Abigail Adams to John Adams (March 31, 1776), in *Adams Family Correspondence*, ed. Butterfield et al., p. 1:369; and John Adams to Abigail Adams (April 14, 1776), in ibid., p. 1:382.

39. John Adams, *Thoughts on Government* (1776), in *The Selected Writings of John and John Quincy Adams*, ed. Adrienne Koch and William Peden (New York: Alfred A. Knopf, 1946), pp. 50–57. Adams feared aristocrats, as much as working people, but later in life he would entertain the prospect of an American hereditary monarchy and aristocracy.

40. Anonymous (Paine), *Four Letters on Interesting Subjects* (1776), in *Common Sense and Other Writings*, ed. Gordon S. Wood (New York: Modern Library, 2003), pp. 57–80; and A. Owen Aldridge, *Thomas Paine's American Ideology* (Newark: University of Delaware Press, 1984), pp. 119-39.

41. In early 1777 Paine served as secretary to a delegation negotiating an alliance with several tribes of the Iroquois. Though they successfully reached an agreement, Congress later rejected it, claiming the Indians had pretended to negotiate on behalf of the whole Iroquois Confederacy while most of the Iroquois had already aligned with the British. Though the American revolutionaries did find Indian allies, they regularly described the native peoples as "savages." But Paine, admiring their dignity, reason, and intelligence, as well as their love of liberty and spirit of resistance, called them his "brothers." See John Keane, *Tom Paine, A Political Life* (Boston: Little, Brown, 1995), pp. 147–50.

42. John Ferling, *Setting the World Ablaze: Washington, Adams, Jefferson, and the American Revolution* (New York: Oxford University Press, 2000), p. xvii; Edward Countryman, *A People in Revolution: The American Revolution and Political Society in New York, 1760–1790* (New York: W.W. Norton, 1989), p. 163; Tiedemann, *Reluctant Revolutionaries*, p. 246; and Richard Walsh, *Charleston's Sons of Liberty: A Study of the Artisans* (Columbia: University of South Carolina Press, 1959), p. 122.

43. Correspondent to *Pennsylvania Packet* (February 12, 1776) quoted in Eric Foner, *Tom Paine and Revolutionary America* (New York: Oxford University Press, 1976), p. 79; James Warren to John Adams, quoted in Smith, *People's History of the American Revolution*, p. 684; and letter of Edward Burd (March 15, 1776) quoted in David Hawke, *In the Midst of a Revolution* (Philadelphia: University of Pennsylvania Press, 1961), pp. 91–92.

44. Woody Holton, *Forced Founders: Indians, Debtors, Slaves, and the Making of the American Revolution in Virginia* (Chapel Hill: University of North Carolina Press, 1999), pp. 191–97.

45. Ibid., pp. 197–99.

46. Paine (in April 3, 10, 24, and May 8), "The Forester's Letters," in *CW*, pp. 2:60–87.

47. Robert Livingston, quoted in Alfred A. Young, *The Democratic Republicans of New York: The Origins, 1763–1797* (Chapel Hill: Unversity of North Carolina Press, 1967), p. 15.

48. Christopher Grasso, *A Speaking Aristocracy: Transforming Public Discourse in Eighteenth Century Connecticut* (Chapel Hill: University of North Carolina Press, 1999), p 424

49. George Washington to Lund Washington (December 17, 1776), in *The American Revolution: Writings from the War of Independence* (New York: Library of America, 2001), p. 236.

50. Paine, *The American Crisis I*, in *CW*, p. 1:50.

51. Richard Ketchum, *The Winter Soldiers: The Battles for Trenton and Princeton* (New York: Doubleday, 1973) and David Hackett Fischer, *Washington's Crossing* (New York: Oxford University Press, 2004).

52. Paine, *Crisis I*, in *CW*, pp. 1:50–57.

53. Paine wrote thirteen regular *Crisis* papers, plus three special installments.
54. *Crisis I*, p. 1:56; *Crisis II*, pp. 1:59, 62, 66, 71; *Crisis III*, p. 1:77; *Crisis VII*, p.1:155.
55. *Crisis II*, pp. 1:68, 71; *Crisis V*, pp. 1:105–29.
56. *Crisis IV*, pp. 1:102; *Crisis V*, p. 1:123; *Crisis III*, p. 1:83.
57. Paine, *Public Good* (1780), in *CW*, pp. 2:303–33.
58. *Crisis X*; Paine, "Six Letters to Rhode Island" (1782–83), in *CW*, pp. 2:333–66.
59. Paine, "A Serious Address to the People of Pennsylvania on the Present Situation of Their Affairs" (1778), in *CW*, p. 2:281.
60. Ibid., pp. 2:277–302.
61. Ibid., pp. 2:284–85.
62. Ibid., pp. 2:284–89. Paine at this time would have excluded from the franchise only those men "in voluntary [and temporary] servitude," specifically, those holding "offices or employments in or under the state . . . to which there are profits annexed" and "servants in families, because their interest is in their master" (p. 2:287).
63. Paine, *Crisis XIII*, in *CW*, p. 1:230.
64. Ibid., pp. 1:232, 234.
65. Ibid., pp. 1:233–34, 231.

3. A CITIZEN OF THE WORLD
1. Thomas Paine, *Letter to the Abbé Raynal* (1782), in *CW*, p. 2:243.
2. Ibid., pp. 2:215, 220; and Paine, *The American Crisis II*, in *CW*, p. 1:58. In *Crisis XIII* he hinted at foreign ventures (p. 1:235). Guillaume Raynal's *Révolution d'Amérique* appeared in an English translation in 1781.
3. *Letter to Raynal*, pp. 2:240–43, 256.
4. Jeremiah Greenman, *Diary of a Common Soldier in the American Revolution, 1775–1783*, ed. Robert C. Bray and Paul E. Bushnell (DeKalb: Northern Illinois University Press, 1978), p. 266.
5. Sara Bache quoted in David Hawke, *Paine* (New York: W.W. Norton, 1974), p. 114.
6. Gouverneur Morris quoted on aristocracy in Alan Taylor, *William Cooper's Town: Power and Persuasion on the Frontier of the Early American Republic* (New York: Alfred A. Knopf, 1995), p. 156. On Morris and Paine during the Deane controversy, see Jack Fruchtman, Jr., *Thomas Paine, Apostle of Freedom* (New York: Four Walls Eight Windows, 1994), pp. 110–120; and John Keane, *Tom Paine, A Political Life* (London: Bloomsbury, 1995), pp. 170–80.
7. Paine, "To a Committee of the Continental Congress," in *CW*, pp. 2:1226–42.
8. Paine, *Dissertations on Government; The Affairs of the Bank; and Paper Money*, plus a selection of letters, in *CW*, pp. 2:367–438.
9. Paine was also eager to see his now-elderly parents. Sadly, when he finally got to Thetford, he discovered his father had passed away. But his mother, now ninety, told him how she fasted every July 4th in his honor, and before leaving, he arranged for her to receive a regular allowance from his income.

10. Paine, *Prospects on the Rubicon* (1787), in *CW*, pp. 2:621–51.
11. W.H.G. Armytage, "Thomas Paine and the Walkers: An Early Episode in Anglo-American Cooperation," *Pennsylvania History* 18, no. 1 (January 1951), pp. 16–30.
12. Paine to George Washington (October 16, 1789), in *Thomas Paine: Collected Writings*, ed. Eric Foner (New York: Library of America, 1995), p. 370.
13. Edmund Burke, *Reflections on the Revolution in France* (1790), ed. Conor Cruise O'Brien (Harmondsworth: Penguin, 1968), p. 173. On Burke, see Conor Cruise O'Brien, *The Great Melody: A Thematic Biography of Edmund Burke* (Chicago: University of Chicago Press, 1992).
14. Paine, *Rights of Man, Parts 1 and 2* (1791, 1792), in *CW*, pp. 1:242–458.
15. Ibid., p. 1:260.
16. Ibid., pp. 2:251–52, 266–67, 273–75.
17. Ibid., p. 2:368.
18. Paine to Anonymous [Benjamin Rush] (March 16, 1789), in *CW*, p. 2:1286; and Paine, *Rights of Man, Part 1*, in *CW*, pp. 1:292–93.
19. Paine, *Rights of Man, Part 1*, pp. 1:299–300, 326.
20. Ibid., p. 1:344.
21. Ibid., p. 1:291.
22. Francis Oldys (George Chalmers), *The Life of Thomas Pain, Author of the "Rights of Man," with a Defence of His Writings* (London, 1791).
23. *Rights of Man, Part 2*, p. 1:348.
24. Ibid., pp. 1:353–56, 414.
25. Ibid., pp. 1:359, 404–405.
26. Ibid., p. 1:360.
27. Ibid., pp. 1:431–38, 446.
28. Ibid., p. 1:400.
29. Ibid.
30. Ibid., pp. 1:447–51.
31. Ibid., pp. 1:344, 449–52.
32. E.P. Thompson, *The Making of the English Working Class* (London: Victor Gollancz, 1963), pp. 103, 121. The reception of *Rights of Man* in the United States will be treated in Chapter 4.
33. Paine, *Letter Addressed to the Addressers on the Late Proclamation* (1792), in *CW*, p. 2:511 (my italics).
34. Thompson, *English Working Class*, pp. 34, 200–202.
35. Paine had a major hand in writing the accompanying "Declaration of Rights," but the committee's complete draft was ultimately rejected in early 1793—in good part because Condorcet, who led the committee, had written up the eighty-five-page document as if it were a scholarly dissertation, not a constitution. For Paine's piece, see "Plan of a Declaration," in *CW*, pp. 2:558–60.
36. Paine, "Reasons for Preserving the Life of Louis Capet," in *CW*, p. 2:555; and for Paine's final desperate effort to save the king's life, see "Shall Louis XVI be Respited?" pp. 2:555–58. In the former, Paine referred to himself as a "citizen of the world" (p. 2:552).

37. Paine to Thomas Jefferson (April 20, 1793), in *CW*, pp. 2:1330–32.
38. Paine, *Age of Reason, Part 1* (1794), in *CW*, p. 1:465. In *Thomas Paine and the Religion of Nature* (Baltimore: Johns Hopkins University Press, 1993), Fruchtman argues that Paine was really more a pantheist than a deist.
39. Ibid., p. 1:464.
40. Paine, "To John Inskeep, Mayor of the City of Philadelphia" (February 1806), in *CW*, p. 2:1480.
41. Paine, *Age of Reason, Part 1*, p. 1:464.
42. Ibid., pp. 1:467–69, 477, 486.
43. Some years later, Paine also explained his writing of what became *Age of Reason* in a letter to Samuel Adams (January 1, 1803), in *CW*, pp. 2:1434–38.
44. Ibid., pp. 2:465, 482, 500, 487, 490.
45. Richard Watson, *An Apology for the Bible, in a series of letters addressed to Thomas Paine, author of The Age of Reason* (1796).
46. The reception and effects of *The Age of Reason* in America will be treated in Chapter 4.
47. Simon Schama, *Citizens: A Chronicle of the Revolution* (New York: Alfred A. Knopf, 1989), pp. 746–847.
48. Harry Ammon, *James Monroe: The Quest for National Identity* (New York: McGraw-Hill, 1971), pp. 136ff.
49. Thomas Paine, *Dissertation on First Principles of Government* (1795), in *CW*, pp. 2:578–79.
50. Paine, *Agrarian Justice* (1797), in *CW*, p. 1:620.
51. Ibid., p. 1:609, 617.
52. Ibid., pp. 1:609, 612–13, 620.
53. Ibid., p. 1:612.
54. Ibid., pp. 1:610–11, 621.
55. Paine, *Letter to George Washington* (1796), in *CW*, pp. 2:689–723.
56. Ibid., pp. 2:692, 695, 723.
57. Paine, "Letter VII" of "To the Citizens of the United States" (April 21, 1803), in *CW*, pp. 2:939–48.

4. THE AGE OF PAINE

1. Thomas Jefferson to Thomas Paine (March 18, 1801), in *The Writings of Thomas Jefferson*, vol. 3, *1801–1806*, ed. Paul Leicester Ford (New York: G.P. Putnam's Sons, 1897), pp. 18–19.
2. Editorials in the *Gazette of the United States* (July 21, 1801), *The Mercury and New-England Palladium* (1801?), and *Port Folio* (July 18, 1801), quoted in Jerry W. Knudson, "The Rage Around Tom Paine," *New-York Historical Society Quarterly* 53, no. 1 (January 1969), pp. 40–41.
3. Jefferson to Francis Eppes (January 19, 1821), Jefferson to James Madison (September 6, 1789), and Jefferson, "First Inaugural Address (1801)," in *Thomas Jefferson, Writings*, ed. Merrill Peterson (New York: Library of America, 1984), pp. 1451, 959, 495, 493. Also see Judith N. Shklar, "The Boundaries of Democracy"

(undated essay), in Judith N. Shklar, *Redeeming American Political Thought*, eds. Stanley Hoffman and Dennis F. Thompson (Chicago: University of Chicago Press), pp. 127–45.

4. Jefferson to Jonathan B. Smith (April 26, 1791), in *The Papers of Thomas Jefferson*, vol. 20, *1 April to 4 August 1791*, ed. Julian P. Boyd (Princeton, N.J.: Princeton University Press, 1982), p. 290. Though Jefferson did not name Adams in his note, he had him in mind and the publication of the note—which Jefferson insisted he never intended—inevitably caused problems between them. Adams never publicly responded, but essays severely criticizing Paine's and Jefferson's views appeared under the nom de plume "Publicola," which, while presumed to have been Adams, was actually his son John Quincy Adams.

5. Jefferson to Paine (July 29, 1791), in *Papers of Jefferson*, ed. Boyd, p. 20:308. On the postmaster's position, see Stanley Elkins and Eric McKitrick, *The Age of Federalism: The Early American Republic, 1788–1800* (New York: Oxford University Press, 1993), p. 240.

6. Jefferson to Paine (June 19, 1792), in *Papers of Jefferson*, ed. Boyd, p. 20:312.

7. Jefferson to Paine (March 18, 1801), in *Writings of Jefferson*, ed. Ford, p. 3:19.

8. Jefferson to Judge Spencer Roane (September 6, 1801), in *Jefferson, Writings*, ed. Peterson, p. 1425; and John Adams to Benjamin Waterhouse (October 29, 1805), in *The Selected Writings of John* and *John Quincy Adams*, ed. Adrienne Koch and William Peden (New York: Alfred A. Knopf, 1946), p. 148.

9. Paine, "Letter II" of "To the Citizens of the United States" (November 22, 1802), in *CW*, p. 2:913.

10. Robert J. Taylor has contended that the farmers of western Massachusetts "learned" their radicalism from Paine's *Common Sense*. See *Western Massachusetts in the Revolution* (Providence, R.I.: Brown University Press, 1954), p. 175.

11. Hamilton's initiatives included restructuring the debt and issuing new interest-bearing bonds (benefiting the speculators who had bought up the certificates issued by the Congress during the Revolution); having the federal government assume state debts (benefiting those states that still had them); and establishing a national bank to create a sounder and better-regulated financial order. Carrying out these initiatives required imposing an excise tax on distilled liquor and   to also stimulate domestic industries—a tariff on manufactured imports (both of which would raise the cost of living of farmers). See Elkins and McKitrick, *Age of Federalism*, pp. 92–123, 258–63.

12. See James Madison, Alexander Hamilton, and John Jay, *The Federalist Papers* (1788), ed. Isaac Kramnick (New York: Penguin, 1987).

13. See Jefferson's *Notes on the State of Virginia* (1782) and his letter to John Adams (October 28, 1813) in *Jefferson, Writings*, ed. Peterson, pp. 290–91 and 1304–10; as well as Henry F. May, *The Enlightenment in America* (New York: Oxford University Press, 1976), pp. 287–88; James Roger Sharp, *American Politics in the Early Republic: The New Nation in Crisis* (New Haven, Conn.: Yale University Press, 1993), pp. 66–70.

14. Gordon Wood, *The Radicalism of the American Revolution* (New York: Alfred A. Knopf, 1992), p. 281; and Alan Taylor, *William Cooper's Town: Power and Persuasion*

on the Frontier of the Early American Republic (New York: Alfred A. Knopf, 1995), p. 257.

15. Michael Merrill and Sean Wilentz, eds., *The Key of Liberty: The Life and Democratic Writings of William Manning, "A Laborer," 1747–1814* (Cambridge, Mass.: Harvard University Press, 1993), p. 7; and Taylor, *William Cooper's Town*, p. 257.

16. Joyce Appleby, *Capitalism and a New Social Order: The Republican Vision of the 1790s* (New York: New York University, 1984), p. 4. While Appleby acknowledged Paine, she made relatively little of his contributions to "Jeffersonian" Republicanism. I am not the first to recognize historians' neglect of Paine's influence in the 1790s. See, for example, Seth Cotlar, "In Paine's Absence: The Trans-Atlantic Dynamics of American Popular Political Thought, 1789–1804," Ph.D. diss., Northwestern University, December 2000 (forthcoming from University of Virginia Press).

17. On Jefferson's and Paine's respective visions, see Eric Foner, *Tom Paine and Revolutionary America* (New York: Oxford University Press, 1976), pp. 98–106.

18. Alfred F. Young, "*Common Sense* and the *Rights of Man* in America," in K. Gavroglu, J. Stachel, and M. Wartofsky, eds., *Science, Mind and Art* (Boston: Kluwer Academic, 1995), pp. 423–24.

19. Thomas Greenleaf (July 27, 1791), quoted in Alfred F. Young, *The Democratic Republicans of New York: The Origins, 1763–1797* (Chapel Hill: University of North Carolina Press, 1967), p. 207; Thomas Paine, *The Writings of Thomas Paine* (Albany: Charles R. & George Webster, 1792); Richard Beale Davis, *Intellectual Life in Jefferson's Virginia, 1790–1830* (Chapel Hill: University of North Carolina Press, 1964), pp. 78ff; E. Merton Coulter, "Early Frontier Democracy in the First Kentucky Constitution," *Political Science Quarterly* 39, no. 4 (December 1924), pp. 665, 671; Niels Henry Sonne, *Liberal Kentucky, 1780–1828* (New York: Columbia University Press, 1939), p. 26; and Harriett Simpson Arnow, *Flowering of the Cumberland* (Lincoln: University of Nebraska Press, 1996), p. 164.

20. Noah Webster quoted in Russell Blaine Nye, *The Cultural Life of the New Nation, 1776–1830* (New York: Harper and Row, 1960).

21. Huntley Dupre, "The Kentucky Gazette Reports the French Revolution," *Mississippi Valley Historical Review* 26, no. 2 (September 1939), pp. 163–80; Coulter, "Early Frontier Democracy," pp. 671–72; and Sonne, *Liberal Kentucky*, p. 26.

22. Jeffrey L. Pasley, *"The Tyranny of Printers": Newspaper Politics in the Early American Republic* (Charlottesville: University Press of Virginia, 2001); and Donald H. Stewart, *The Opposition Press of the Federalist Period* (Albany: State University of New York Press, 1969).

23. Pasley, *"Tyranny of Printers,"* pp. 48–78. Fenno started his newspaper in New York, where the government was first situated, but moved it to Philadelphia when that city became the federal capital. Bache's newspaper was first titled the *General Advertiser* but later was renamed and became known as *Aurora*, on which see Richard Rosenfeld, *American Aurora: A Democratic-Republican Returns* (New York: St. Martin's Press, 1997).

24. Philip Freneau, "On Mr. Paine's Rights of Man" (1791), in Giles Gunn, ed., *Early American Writing* (New York: Penguin, 1994), pp. 562–63. When Freneau later started up a new periodical, *Time-Piece*, he again regularly featured Paine's work.

25. "Mirabeau" in *Aurora* (December 7, 1792), quoted in Pasley, *"Tyranny of Printers,"* p. 85, letter to *National Gazette* (May 1, 1793), quoted in Sharp, *American Politics in the Early Republic*, p. 67; *Newark Gazette* (March 19, 1794), quoted in Philip Foner, ed., *The Democratic-Republican Societies, 1790–1800: A Documentary Sourcebook of Constitutions, Declarations, Addresses, Resolutions, and Toasts* (Westport, Conn.: Greenwood Press, 1976), p. 5.

26. On Abraham Bishop, see Wood, *Radicalism of the American Revolution*, pp. 271–76; David Waldstreicher and Stephen Grossbart, "Abraham Bishop's Vocation," *Journal of the Early Republic* 18, no. 4 (1998), pp. 617–57; and Tim Matthewson, "Abraham Bishop, 'The Rights of Black Men,' and the American Reaction to the Haitian Revolution," *Journal of Negro History* 67, no. 2 (Summer 1982), pp. 148–54.

27. On Jedidiah Peck, see Taylor, *William Cooper's Town*, pp. 241–49, 257, 267–91; Young, *Democratic Republicans of New York*, pp. 508ff; and James Morton Smith, *Freedom's Fetters: The Alien and Sedition Laws and American Civil Liberties* (Ithaca, N.Y.: Cornell University Press, 1956), pp. 390–98.

28. On William Manning, see Merrill and Wilentz, *Key of Liberty*; for specific references to Paine, see pp. 56–57.

29. Aleine Austin, *Matthew Lyon: "New Man" of the Democratic Revolution, 1749–1822* (University Park: Pennsylvania State University Press), pp. 77–81.

30. Ibid.

31. Michael Durey, "Thomas Paine's Apostles: Radical Emigrés and the Triumph of Jeffersonian Republicanism," *William and Mary Quarterly* 44, no. 4 (October 1987), p. 686. Also see Michael Durey, *Transatlantic Radicals and the Early American Republic* (Lawrence: University Press of Kansas, 1997), pp. 176ff; and David Wilson, *United Irishmen, United States: Immigrant Radicals in the Early Republic* (Ithaca, N.Y.: Cornell University Press, 1998), pp. 36ff.

32. David Waldstreicher, *In the Midst of Perpetual Fetes: The Making of American Nationalism, 1776–1820* (Chapel Hill: University of North Carolina Press, 1997), pp. 156–58; Michelle Gillespie, *Free Labor in an Unfree World: White Artisans in Slaveholding Georgia, 1789–1860* (Athens: University of Georgia Press, 2000), pp. 45, 55; and Young, *"Common Sense* and *Rights of Man,"* pp. 425–26.

33. In Kingston, Jamaica, one runaway slave proudly and defiantly identified himself as "John Paine." See Douglas R. Egerton, *Gabriel's Rebellion: The Virginia Slave Conspiracies of 1800 and 1802* (Chapel Hill: University of North Carolina Press, 1993), p. 47. For Paine's remark, see his letter to anonymous (Benjamin Rush?) (March 16, 1789), in *CW*, p. 2:1286.

34. Eugene Perry Link, *Democratic-Republican Societies, 1790–1800* (New York: Columbia University Press, 1942); and Foner, ed., *Democratic-Republican Societies*. For a complete list of the societies, see Link, pp. 12–15.

35. Link, *Democratic-Republican*, pp. 6, 71–99; and Foner, *Democratic-Republican*, pp. 6–9, 13.

36. Foner, *Democratic-Republican*, p. 25; Link, *Democratic-Republican*, p. 109; and Cotlar, "In Paine's Absence," p. 64.

37. Link, *Democratic-Republican*, p. 104.

38. Nathan O. Hatch, *The Democratization of American Christianity* (New Haven, Conn.: Yale University Press, 1989).

39. Anson Phelps Stokes and Leo Pfeffer, *Church and State in the United States*, rev. ed. (New York: Harper and Row, 1964), esp. pp. 48–63, 65–71; and William Lee Miller, *The First Liberty: Religion and the American Republic* (New York: Alfred A. Knopf, 1986). On postrevolutionary American Protestantism, see Mark Noll, *America's God: From Jonathan Edwards to Abraham Lincoln* (New York: Oxford University Press, 2002), and for figures on denominational growth, see pp. 161–66.

40. John Leland, *The Rights of Conscience Inalienable* (1791) and "Oration" (1802), in *The Writings of John Leland, Including Some Events in His Life* (New York, 1845), pp. 179–91, 259.

41. Charles Frances Kilgore, *The James O'Kelly Schism in the Methodist Episcopal Church* (Mexico City: Casa Unida de Publicaciones, 1963); Hatch, *Democratization of American Christianity*, p. 70; and Dee Andrews, *The Methodists and Revolutionary America, 1760–1800: The Shaping of an Evangelical Culture* (Princeton, N.J.: Princeton University Press, 2000), pp. 202–5.

42. Hatch, *Democratization*, pp. 9–11.

43. Ibid., pp. 36–40, 130–33; and Charles Coleman Sellers, *Lorenzo Dow: The Bearer of the Word* (New York: Minton, Balch, 1928).

44. Thomas P. Slaughter, *The Whiskey Rebellion: Frontier Epilogue to the American Revolution* (New York: Oxford University Press, 1986).

45. Ibid., p. 194. Oddly enough, the so-called Vendeites had risen up in 1793 *against* France's revolutionary government.

46. For a critical discussion of the Federalist-clerical alliance, see Gary Nash, "The American Clergy and the French Revolution," *William and Mary Quarterly* 22, no. 3 (July 1965), pp. 392–412.

47. May, *The Enlightenment in America*, pp. 116–49; Miller, *First Liberty*, pp. 236–37; and Norman Cousins, *"In God We Trust": The Religious Beliefs and Ideas of the Founding Fathers* (New York: Harper and Brothers, 1958).

48. David Ludlum, *Social Ferment in Vermont, 1791–1850* (New York: Columbia University Press, 1939), p. 29.

49. G. Adolf Koch, *Republican Religion: The American Revolution and the Cult of Reason* (New York: Henry Holt, 1933); Herbert M. Morais, *Deism in Eighteenth Century America* (New York: Columbia University Press, 1934); Kerry Walters, ed., *The American Deists: Voices of Reason and Dissent in the Early Republic* (Lawrence: University Press of Kansas, 1992); and Roderick S. French, "Elihu Palmer, Radical Deist, Radical Republican: A Reconsideration of American Free Thought," in *Studies in Eighteenth-Century Culture*, ed. Roseann Runte (Madison: University of Wisconsin Press, 1979), pp. 8:87–108.

50. Lyman Beecher, *Autobiography, Correspondence, etc.*, ed. Charles Beecher (New York: Harper and Brothers, 1864), p. 43; and Colin Wells, *The Devil and Doctor Dwight: Satire and Theology in the Early American Republic* (Chapel Hill: University of North Carolina Press, 2003).

51. Samuel Eliot Morison, *Three Centuries of Harvard, 1636–1936* (Cambridge, Mass.: Harvard University Press, 1965), p. 185; Princetonian Joseph Scott

quoted in Varnum Lansing Collins, *President Witherspoon, A Biography* (Princeton, N.J.: Princeton University Press, 1925), p. 199; John Allen Krout and Dixon Ryan Fox, *The Completion of Independence, 1790–1830* (New York: Macmillan, 1944), pp. 270–71; May, *Enlightenment in America*, pp. 246–47; and Kemp P. Battle, *History of the University of North Carolina, 1789–1868* (Raleigh: Edwards and Broughton, 1907), pp. 66–158.

52. Sonne, *Liberal Kentucky*, pp. 33–45.

53. James H. Smylie, "Clerical Perspectives on Deism: Paine's *The Age of Reason* in Virginia," *Eighteenth-Century Studies* 6, no. 2 (Winter 1972–73), pp. 203–20.

54. Cotlar, "In Paine's Absence," pp. 131, 158–173; Rosenfeld, *American Aurora*, pp. 44–45; Pasley, *"Tyranny of Printers,"* pp. 94–102; and Banning, *Jeffersonian Persuasion*, pp. 238–45. For *Agrarian Justice*, see *CW*, pp. 1:605–23; and for *Letter to George Washington*, see *CW*, pp. 2:691–723.

55. William Cobbett, "Life of Thomas Paine" (1796), quoted in Richard Gimbel, *The Resurgence of Thomas Paine with the Catalogue of an Exhibition, Thomas Paine Fights for Freedom in the Three Worlds* (Worcester, Mass.: American Antiquarian Society, 1961), p. 108; William Cobbett, *Peter Porcupine in America: Pamphlets on Republicanism and Revolution*, ed. David A. Wilson (Ithaca, N.Y.: Cornell University Press, 1994), pp. 219–23; and on the physical attacks on Bache, see Pasley, *"Tyranny of Printers,"* pp. 96–102.

56. Thomas Robbins quoted in Charles Roy Keller, *The Second Great Awakening in Connecticut* (New Haven, Conn.: Yale University Press 1942), p. 1; and Wells, *Devil and Doctor Dwight*, p. 9.

57. Jedidiah Morse, *A Sermon . . .* (May 9, 1798), quoted in Koch, *Republican Religion*, pp. 251–54; also Nash, "American Clergy and French Revolution," pp. 392–93.

58. Mariam Touba, "Tom Paine's Plan for Revolutionizing America," *Journalism History* 20, nos. 3–4 (Autumn–Winter 1994), pp. 116–25.

59. For a full treatment, along with the texts of the acts, see Smith, *Freedom's Fetters*.

60. Ibid., pp. 188–204 (Bache), 221–46 (Lyon), 257–70 (Brown), 277–306 (Duane), and 390–98 (Peck). For a sample of Brown's words, see David Brown, "Seditious Writings" (October 1, 14, and 22, 1798), in Irving Mark and Eugene L. Schwaab, eds., *The Faith of Our Fathers: An Anthology Expressing the Aspirations of the American Common Man, 1790–1860* (New York: Alfred A. Knopf, 1952), pp. 44–47.

61. Quoted in Christopher Grasso, *A Speaking Aristocracy: Transforming Public Discourse in Eighteenth-Century Connecticut* (Chapel Hill: University of North Carolina Press, 1999), p. 467

62. See Paine, "To the French Inhabitants of Louisiana," and various letters to Jefferson, in *CW*, pp. 2:963–68, 1441ff., 1465ff.

63. Paine, "Letter I" of "To the Citizens of the United States" (November 15, 1802), in *CW*, pp. 2:910–11.

64. Thomas D. Scoble, Jr., *Thomas Paine's Citizenship Record* (New Rochelle, N.Y.: Thomas Paine National Historical Association, 1946).

65. Madame de Bonneville, quoted in Alfred Owen Aldridge, *Man of Reason: The Life of Thomas Paine* (New York: J. B. Lippincott, 1959), p. 316.

5. FREEDOM MUST HAVE ALL OR NONE

1. Garry Wills, *Lincoln at Gettysburg: The Words That Remade America* (New York: Simon and Schuster, 1992).

2. James M. McPherson, *Abraham Lincoln and the Second American Revolution* (New York: Oxford University Press, 1990).

3. Daniel Webster, "The Bunker Hill Monument" (1825), excerpted and examined by Eduardo Caleva, *Emerson and the Climates of History* (Stanford, Calif.: Stanford University Press, 1997), pp. 106–8.

4. I have borrowed the term "militant democracy" from Alice Felt Tyler, *Freedom's Ferment* (Minneapolis: University of Minnesota Press, 1944), p. 1.

5. William Herndon and Jesse Weik, *Herndon's Life of Lincoln*, ed. Paul M. Angle (New York: Albert and Charles Boni, 1930), pp. 355–56; and Douglas L. Wilson, *Honor's Voice: The Transformation of Abraham Lincoln* (New York: Alfred A. Knopf, 1998), pp. 77–83.

6. Roy Basler, "Lincoln's Development as a Writer," in *Abraham Lincoln: His Speeches and Writings*, ed. Roy Basler (Cleveland: World, 1946), pp. 5–6. On Lincoln reading *Common Sense*, see Douglas L. Wilson and Rodney O. Davis, *Herndon's Informants: Letters, Interviews, and Statements about Abraham Lincoln* (Urbana: University of Illinois Press, 1998), pp. 172, 210.

7. In *Lincoln Speeches and Writings*, ed. Basler, see Lincoln's "A House Divided" (1858), p. 372, and "Annual Message to Congress" (1862), p. 688. Undeniably, Lincoln's "last, best hope of earth" repeated Jefferson's "world's best hope." But as indicated in Chapter 4, Jefferson clearly derived that conception of America from Paine.

8. Ibid., Lincoln's "Speech at Edwardsville" (1858), p. 473; "The Perpetuation of Our Political Institutions" (1838), pp. 76–85; "First Inaugural Address" (1861), pp. 579–88; "Address to the Senate of New Jersey" (1861), pp. 574–75; "Address in Independence" (1861), pp. 577–78; and "Gettysburg Address" (1863), p. 734.

9. Ibid., "Fragment: On Slavery" (1858), p. 427; Paine, "A Serious Address to the People of Pennsylvania on the Present Situation of their Affairs" (1778), in *CW*, p. 2:284.

10. Charles Sellers, *The Market Revolution: Jacksonian America, 1815–1846* (New York: Oxford University Press, 1991); and Daniel Feller, *The Jacksonian Promise, 1815–1840* (Baltimore: John Hopkins University Press, 1995).

11. Alexis de Tocqueville, *Democracy in America*, trans. and ed. Harvey C. Mansfield and Delba Winthrop (1835–40; reprinted, Chicago: University of Chicago Press, 2000).

12. James Cheetham, *The Life of Thomas Paine* (1809; reprinted, Delmar, N.Y.: Scholar's Facsimiles, 1989). For examples of conservatives' uses of Paine, see Martin E. Marty, *The Infidel: Freethought and American Religion* (Cleveland: World, 1961); Shirley Samuels, *Romances of the Republic: Women, the Family, and Violence in the Literature of the Early American Nation* (New York: Oxford University Press, 1996), pp. 23–29; author unknown, *Some Account of Thomas Paine in His Last Sickness* (New York, 1820); Forbes Winslow, *The Anatomy of Suicide* (London: Renshaw, 1840), pp. 87–89; Jonathan Plummer, *The Dreadful Earth-*

quake and the Fatal Spotted Fever, a broadside (Newburyport, Mass.: 1840); and John Neal, *American Writers: A Series of Contributions to Blackwood's Magazine* (1824–25), ed. Fred Lewis Pattee (Durham, N.C.: Duke University Press, 1937), pp. 170–71.

13. Charles A. Johnson, "Camp Meeting Hymnody," *American Quarterly* 4, no. 2 (1952), p. 123; Lorenzo Dow, *Analects Upon the Rights of Man* (1812), in *History of Cosmopolite or the Four Volumes of Lorenzo Dow's Journal* (Wheeling, W.Va.: Joshua Martin, 1849), pp. 419–70; Nathan O. Hatch, *The Democratization of American Christianity* (New Haven, Conn.: Yale University Press, 1989); Paul R. Conkin, *American Originals: Homemade Varieties of Christianity* (Chapel Hill: University of North Carolina Press, 1997), pp. 1–53; Michael G. Kenny, *The Perfect Law of Liberty: Elias Smith and the Providential History of America* (Washington, D.C.: Smithsonian Institution Press, 1994), pp. 163–64; Michael Garrett West, *Barton Warren Stone: Early American Advocate of Christian Unity* (Nashville, Tenn.: Disciples of Christ Historical Society, 1954), pp. 22, 93; Robert Frederick West, *Alexander Campbell and Natural Religion* (New Haven, Conn.: Yale University Press, 1948); [Paine,] "Of Monarchy and Hereditary Succession," *Herald of Gospel Liberty* 5, no. 19 (May 14, 1813), pp. 489–91; Niels Henry Sonne, *Liberal Kentucky, 1780–1828* (New York: Columbia University Press, 1939), pp. 117, 131; and Dee E. Andrews, *The Methodists and Revolutionary America, 1760–1800: The Shaping of an Evangelical Culture* (Princeton, N.J.: Princeton University Press, 2000), p. 230.

14. Edwin G. Burrows and Mike Wallace, *Gotham: A History of New York City to 1898* (New York: Oxford University Press, 1999), p. 497.

15. Anne Marie Taylor, *Young Charles Sumner and the Legacy of the American Enlightenment, 1811–1851* (Amherst: University of Massachusetts Press, 2001), pp. 11–15, 336–38; Gay Wilson Allen, *The Solitary Singer: A Critical Biography of Walt Whitman* (New York: Macmillan, 1955), pp. 7–8; and David S. Reynolds, *Walt Whitman's America: A Cultural Biography* (New York: Alfred A. Knopf, 1995), pp. 21–29.

16. Leo A. Bressler, "Peter Porcupine and the Bones of Thomas Paine," *Pennsylvania Magazine of History and Biography* 82, no. 2 (April 1958), pp. 176–85. Cobbett's plans failed for lack of funds, and Paine's bones were lost along the way.

17. On reaction to Cobbett's theft, see Mary Rhodes, "Three Episodes in the Posthumous Reputation of Thomas Paine as Reflected in American Newspapers, 1819–1820," M.A. thesis, University of Virginia, 1970, pp. 51–59.

18. J.F.C. Harrison, *Quest for the New Moral World: Robert Owen and the Owenites in Britain and America* (New York: Charles Scribner's Sons, 1969); and Donald E. Pitzer, "The New Moral World of Robert Owen and New Harmony," in Donald E. Pitzer, ed., *America's Communal Utopias* (Chapel Hill: University of North Carolina Press, 1997), pp. 88–134.

19. Robert Owen's speeches to Congress and "Declaration of Mental Independence" are collected in Oakley C. Johnson, ed., *Robert Owen in the United States* (New York: Humanities Press, 1970).

20. Pitzer, "New Moral World of Owen."

21. *Debate on the Evidences of Christianity Containing an Examination of the "Social System" between Robert Owen and Alexander Campbell* (Bethany, Va., 1829). On Campbell and the debate, see West, *Campbell and Natural Religion*; Frances Trollope, *Domestic Manners of the Americans* (1832), ed. Donald Smalley (New York: Alfred A. Knopf, 1949), pp. 145–53; and Rich Cherok, "A Comparison of Millennial Rhetoric: Alexander Campbell's Christian Millennialism and Robert Owen's Secular Millennialism," *Journal of Millennial Studies* 2, no. 2 (Winter 2000) (http://www.mille.org/publications/winter2000/cherok.PDF).

22. Mark A. Lause, "The 'Unwashed Infidelity': Thomas Paine and Early New York City Labor History," *Labor History* 27, no. 3 (Summer 1986), p. 403; Sean Wilentz, *Chants Democratic: New York City and the Rise of the American Working Class, 1780–1850* (New York: Oxford University Press, 1984), pp. 153–57; Thomas Paine, *The Theological Works of Thomas Paine* (New York: Baldwin, 1821); *The Political Writings of Thomas Paine* (Charlestown, Mass: G. Davidson, 1824); and *The Political Writings of Thomas Paine* (Springfield, Mass: Peter Reynolds, 1826).

23. Anthony F. Wallace, *Rockdale: The Growth of an American Village in the Early Industrial Revolution* (New York: Alfred A. Knopf, 1978), pp. 339–40; and Annie Laurie Gaylor, ed., *Women Without Superstitions* (Madison, Wis.: Freedom From Religion Foundation, 1997), pp. 23–26.

24. Celia Morris Eckhardt, *Fanny Wright: Rebel in America* (Cambridge, Mass.: Harvard University Press, 1984).

25. On Lafayette's return to America, see Andrew Burstein, *America's Jubilee: A Generation Remembers the Revolution After Fifty Years of Independence* (New York: Alfred A. Knopf, 2001), pp. 8–33.

26. Ibid., pp. 108–67. On Robert Dale Owen, see Richard William Leopold, *Robert Dale Owen, A Biography* (Cambridge, Mass.: Harvard University Press, 1940).

27. Lori D. Ginzberg, "'The Hearts of Your Readers Will Shudder': Fanny Wright, Infidelity, and American Freethought," *American Quarterly* 46, no. 2, (January 1994), pp. 195–226. For examples of Wright's speeches, see *A Course of Popular Lectures* (New York, 1829), in Joseph L. Blau, ed., *Social Theories of Jacksonian Democracy: Representative Writings of the Period, 1825–1850* (New York: Liberal Arts Press, 1954), pp. 282–88; and Frances Wright, "The Meaning of Patriotism in America" (July 4, 1828), in Diane Ravitch, *The American Reader* (New York: HarperCollins, 2000), pp. 90–93.

28. Albert Post, *Popular Freethought in America, 1825–1850* (New York: Columbia University Press, 1943), pp. 75–121, and Wilentz, *Chants Democratic*, p. 154.

29. Post, *Popular Freethought*, pp. 34–74, 122–28.

30. For examples of Paine birthday celebration orations, see N. C. Rhodes, *An Oration Delivered Before the Society of Moral Philanthropists* (Providence, R.I., 1833); Edward Thompson, *Oration on the Anniversary of the Birth Day of Thomas Paine to The Society of Free Enquirers* (Philadelphia, 1834); Samuel Underhill, *Oration* (Cleveland, Oh., 1836); and *An Address on the Centennial Anniversary of the Birth of Thomas Paine* (Cleveland, Oh., 1837); Joseph W. Pomroy, *An Oration on the Anniversary of the Birth Day of Thomas Paine* (Philadelphia, 1838); and M. R.

Miller, *An Address on the Life and Revolutionary Services of Thomas Paine* (Cincinnati, Oh., 1842).

31. Frederick Voss, "Honoring a Scorned Hero: America's Monument to Thomas Paine," *New York History* 68, no. 2 (April 1987), pp. 132–50; Gilbert Vale, *The Life of Thomas Paine* (New York, 1841).

32. Arthur M. Schlesinger, Jr., *The Age of Jackson* (Boston: Little, Brown, 1945), pp. 350–52; Wallace, *Rockdale*, pp. 435–36; and "Sketch of the Life of Thomas Paine," *Spirit of the Pilgrims*, June 1831, pp. 338–43.

33. Clifford S. Griffin, "Religious Benevolence as Social Control, 1815–1860" (1957), reprinted in David Brion Davis, ed., *Ante-Bellum Reform* (New York: Harper and Row, 1967), pp. 81–96.

34. Paul E. Johnson, *A Shopkeeper's Millennium: Society and Revivals in Rochester, New York, 1815–1837* (New York: Hill and Wang, 1978), pp. 119–21; and Roderick S. French, "Liberation from Man and God in Boston: Abner Kneeland's Free-Thought Campaign, 1830–1839," *American Quarterly* 32, no. 2 (Summer 1980), pp. 202–21.

35. The judge's statement is quoted in Schlesinger, *Age of Jackson*, p. 359. On Kneeland's departure to Iowa, see Post, *Popular Freethought in America*, p. 107.

36. Ronald G. Walters, *American Reformers, 1815–1860*, rev. ed. (New York: Hill and Wang, 1997), pp. 188–89.

37. Robert Walker, "Address at the Working Men's Dinner" (1830), in Irving L. Mark and Eugene L. Schwaab, eds., *The Faith of Our Fathers: An Anthology Expressing the Aspirations of the American Common Man, 1790–1860* (New York: Alfred A. Knopf, 1952), p. 56; and Philip S. Foner, *American Labor Songs of the Nineteenth Century* (Urbana: University of Illinois Press, 1975), pp. 16–45.

38. Amy Bridges, "Becoming American: The Working Classes in the United States Before the Civil War," in Ira Katznelson and Aristide Zolberg, eds., *Working-Class Formation: Nineteenth-Century Patterns in Western Europe and the United States* (Princeton, N.J.: Princeton University Press, 1986), pp. 163–64; *Mechanics Free Press* (1830), quoted in Franklin Rosemont, "Workingmen's Parties," in Paul Buhle and Alan Dawley, eds., *Working for Democracy: American Workers from the Revolution to the Present* (Urbana: University of Illinois Press, 1985), p. 13; and A. H. Wood and Seth Luther, *Ten-Hour Circular* (Boston, 1835), in Mark and Schwaab, eds., *Faith of Our Fathers*, p. 342.

39. Ronald Schultz, *The Republic of Labor: Philadelphia Artisans and the Politics of Class, 1720–1830* (New York: Oxford University Press, 1993), pp. 220–33; David Harris, *Socialist Origins in the United States: American Forerunners of Marx, 1817–1832* (Assen, Netherlands: Van Gorcum, 1966), pp. 82–90; Philip S. Foner, *William Heighton: Pioneer Labor Leader of Jacksonian Philadelphia—With Selections from Heighton's Writings and Speeches* (New York: International Publishers, 1991); Bruce Laurie, *Working People of Philadelphia, 1800–1850* (Philadelphia: Temple University Press, 1980), pp. 75–79; and Bruce Laurie, *Artisans into Workers: Labor in Nineteenth-Century America* (New York: Hill and Wang, 1989), pp. 66–72.

40. Quoted words from Heighton's "Address to the Members of the Trade Societies and to the Working Classes Generally" (1827) are drawn from Schultz, *Republic of Labor*, pp. 222–23.

41. Burrows and Wallace, *Gotham*, p. 519. On Skidmore, see Harris, *Socialist Origins*, pp. 91–139; and Amos Gilbert, *The Life of Thomas Skidmore* (1834), ed. Mark A. Lause (Chicago: Charles H. Kerr, 1984). On Skidmore and the New York workingmen's movement, see Walter Hugins, *Jacksonian Democracy and the Working Class: A Study of the New York Workingmen's Movement, 1829–1837* (Stanford, Calif.: Stanford University Press, 1960); Wilentz, *Chants Democratic*, pp. 176–216.

42. Harris, *Socialist Origins*, p. 98.

43. Thomas Skidmore, *The Rights of Man to Property!* (New York, 1829); Lause, "'Unwashed Infidelity,'" p. 405; and for the Skidmore quote, Burrows and Wallace, *Gotham*, p. 518.

44. Feller, *Jacksonian Promise*, pp. 162–77.

45. Andrew Jackson quoted in Dixon Wecter, "Hero in Reverse," *Virginia Quarterly Review* 18, no. 2 (Spring 1942), p. 253. The Locofocos acquired their name from a meeting at which their opponents tried to cut off the lights, but the gathered folk responded by lighting the room with friction matches known as "locofocos."

46. Orestes A. Brownson, "The Laboring Classes" (*Boston Quarterly Review*, July 1840), edited version in Perry Miller, ed., *The Transcendentalists: An Anthology* (Cambridge, Mass.: Harvard University Press, 1950), pp. 436–46. For Brownson's references to Paine in the 1830s, see Patrick W. Carey, *The Early Works of Orestes A. Brownson* (Milwaukee, Wis.: Marquette University Press, 2000), pp. 1:269, 276; 2:64; 3:76, 351.

47. "The Working Men's Declaration of Independence" (1829), in Philip S. Foner, ed., *We, the Other People: Alternative Declarations of Independence by Labor Groups, Farmers, Woman's Rights Advocates, Socialists, and Blacks, 1829–1975* (Urbana: University of Illinois Press, 1976), pp. 47–50; and *The Political Writings of Thomas Paine*, ed. George H. Evans (Granville, N.J., 1839). On Evans, see Jeffrey J. Pilz, *The Life, Work and Times of George Henry Evans, Newspaperman, Activist and Reformer (1829–1849)* (Lewiston, N.Y.: Edwin Mellen Press, 2001).

48. The full title of Evans's periodical was *The Radical, in continuation of the Working Man's Advocate*. Evans would publish Lewis Masquerier's "Declaration of Independence of the Producing from the Non-Producing Class" on September 28, 1844 (see Foner, *We, the Other People*, pp. 64–70), and Masquerier would eventually issue his own Paine-inspired land reform scheme, *Sociology: Or, The Reconstruction of Society, Government, and Property* (New York, 1877).

49. Noah Webster, *History of the United States* (New Haven, Conn.: Durrie and Peck, 1832), p. 240; and Salma Hale, *History of the United States* (New York: Collins and Hannay, 1827).

50. Gay Wilson Allen, *Waldo Emerson, A Biography* (New York: Viking, 1981), pp. 320–21; C. E. Schorer, "Emerson and the Wisconsin Lyceum," *American Literature* 24, no. 4, (January 1953), pp. 464–65; and Dean Grodzins, *American Heretic: Theodore Parker and Transcendentalism* (Chapel Hill: University of North Carolina Press, 2002), pp. 250–53, 302–3.

51. On the influences of deism on Transcendentalism, see Arnold Smithline, *Natural Religion in American Literature* (New Haven, Conn.: College and University

Press, 1966). In *Thomas Paine and the Religion of Nature* (Baltimore: Johns Hopkins University Press, 1993), Jack Fruchtman, Jr., has contended that Paine's deism was actually pantheistic, which would have made his arguments all the more appealing to the Transcendentalists.

52. Henry David Thoreau, "Civil Disobedience" (1849), in *Walden and Civil Disobedience* (New York: Penguin, 1986), p. 385.

53. Ralph Waldo Emerson, *Nature* (1836), "The American Scholar" (1837), and "Nominalist and Realist" (1844), in *The Essential Writings of Ralph Waldo Emerson*, ed. Brooks Atkinson (New York: Modern Library, 2000), respectively, pp. 3, 37, 397. Emerson's use of "sepulchers" (my italics in the quotation) drew directly from Paine's *Rights of Man* (see *CW*, p. 1:386), and "The sun shines . . ." (again, my italics) from *Common Sense*. I owe these insights on Emerson to Eduardo Cadava, *Emerson and the Climates of History* (Stanford, Calif.: Stanford University Press, 1997), pp. 106–39. Emerson's quip about Webster is quoted in Melinda Lawson, *Patriot Fires: Forging a New American Nationalism in the Civil War North* (Lawrence: University Press of Kansas, 2002), p. 139.

54. Edward Widmer, *Young America: The Flowering of Democracy in New York City* (New York: Oxford University Press, 1999); Thomas Bender, *New York Intellect: A History of Intellectual Life in New York City, from 1750 to the Beginnings of Our Own Time* (New York: Alfred A. Knopf, 1987), pp. 140–56; and John Stafford, *The Literary Criticism of "Young America": A Study in the Relationship of Politics and Literature, 1837–1850* (Berkeley: University of California Press, 1952).

55. "Introduction," *United States Magazine and Democratic Review* 1, no. 1 (October 1837), pp. 1–15, reprinted in Blau, *Social Theories of Jacksonian Democracy*, pp. 21–37.

56. Ibid.

57. Widmer, *Young America*, pp. 64–93, 103–111. With his brother George, Evert A. Duyckinck also coedited the two-volume *Cyclopedia of American Literature* (New York, 1855–56), which contained a lengthy entry on and excerpts from Paine.

58. (John O'Sullivan), "The Great Nation of Futurity," *United States Magazine and Democratic Review* 6, no. 23 (November 1839), pp. 426–30.

59. (W. A. Jones), "Political Pamphleteering," *United States Magazine and Democratic Review* 11, no. 52 (October 1842), pp. 384–85.

60. "The Life and Character of Thomas Paine," *North American Review* 57 (1843), pp. 1–57.

61. (John O'Sullivan), "Peace and War," *United States Magazine and Democratic Review* 5, no. 15 (March 1839), pp. 288–309; and Widmer, *Young America*, pp. 55–62. Also see Norman Graebner, ed., *Manifest Destiny* (Indianapolis: Bobbs-Merrill, 1968), which includes O'Sullivan's key pieces on the subject.

62. Bender, *New York Intellect*, pp. 151–56.

63. Herman Melville, *White-Jacket* (1850; New York: Modern Library, 2002), p. 151, 150; Widmer, *Young America*, p. 113; and Herman Melville, *Redburn* (1849; New York: Modern Library, 2002), p. 194.

64. Melville, *White-Jacket*, pp. 156–57; and Herman Melville, *Moby-Dick* (1851; New York: Modern Library, 2000), pp. 166.

65. Horace Traubel, ed., *With Walt Whitman in Camden (1888–1889)* (New York: Rowman and Littlefield, 1961), pp. 1:79; 2:135, 205–6; 3:139–140, 191–92; and Walt Whitman, "In Memory of Thomas Paine" (1877), in Walt Whitman, *Poetry and Prose*, ed. Justin Kaplan (New York: Library of America, 1996), pp. 821–23.

66. Walt Whitman, "Leaves of Grass" (1855), in Whitman, *Poetry and Prose*, pp. 5, 26, 50; and Whitman on the common people (1852) quoted in David S. Reynolds, *Walt Whitman's America*, p. 135.

67. Whitman, "Leaves of Grass," p. 26

68. Robert Butterfield, "George Lippard and His Secret Brotherhood," *Pennsylvania Magazine of History and Biography* 74, no. 3 (July 1955), pp. 285–86.

69. Quoted lines are from ibid., pp. 286, 290.

70. David S. Reynolds, *George Lippard* (Boston: Twayne, 1982), pp. 1–26; David S. Reynolds, ed., *George Lippard, Prophet of Protest: Writings of an American Radical, 1822–1854* (New York: Peter Lang, 1986); and George Lippard, *The Quaker City; or, The Monks of Mink Hall* (1845), ed. David S. Reynolds (Amherst: University of Massachusetts Press, 1995).

71. George Lippard, *Thomas Paine, Author-Soldier of the American Revolution* (1852; reprinted Philadelphia, 1894), pp. 3–5, 13.

72. Thomas Paine, "African Slavery in America" (1775), in *CW*, pp. 2:15–19; and *Rights of Man, Part 1* (1791), in *CW*, p. 1:251. On the "Oration of Thomas Paine" (1819), see Rhodes, "Three Episodes in the Posthumous Reputation of Thomas Paine," pp. 94–97, 104–7. Also see David Brion Davis, *The Problem of Slavery in the Age of Revolution, 1770–1823*, rev. ed. (New York: Oxford University Press, 1999), pp. 101, 268–69, 279–86, 327; and Paul Goodman, *Of One Blood: Abolitionism and the Origins of Racial Equality* (Berkeley: University of California Press, 1998), pp. 161–72.

73. Burrows and Wallace, *Gotham*, pp. 548–51; Jama Lazerow, *Religion and the Working Class in Antebellum America* (Washington, D.C.: Smithsonian Institution Press, 1995), pp. 123–24; Elizabeth McHenry, *Forgotten Readers: Recovering the Lost History of African American Literary Societies* (Durham, N.C.: Duke University Press, 2002), pp. 25–27; David Walker, *An Appeal, in Four Articles, Together with a Preamble, to the Colored Citizens of the World, but in Particular, and Very Expressly to Those of the United States of America* (1829; reprinted, New York: Hill and Wang, 1965); and William E. Cain, ed., *William Lloyd Garrison and the Fight Against Slavery: Selections from "The Liberator"* (Boston: Bedford, 1995), pp. 4–5. For Paine's own words, see *Rights of Man, Part 2* (1792), in *CW*, p. 1:414.

74. Goodman, *Of One Blood*, pp. 23–35, 133–34; Bruce Levine, *Half Slave and Half Free: The Roots of the Civil War* (New York: Hill and Wang, 1992), pp. 145–60; and Walters, *American Reformers*, pp. 77–102.

75. Henry Mayer, *All on Fire: William Lloyd Garrison and the Abolition of Slavery* (New York: St. Martin's Press, 1998), pp. 3–188, 224–26.

76. Ibid., pp. 280–99.

77. For Maria Weston Chapman's "The Times That Try Men's Souls," see Elizabeth Cady Stanton, Susan B. Anthony, and Matilda Joslyn Gage, eds., *History of Woman Suffrage*, vol. 1, *1848–1861* (Rochester, N.Y.: Charles Mann, 1889), pp. 81–83.

78. William Lloyd Garrison, "The American Union" (January 10, 1845), in Cain, ed., *Garrison and the Fight Against Slavery*, pp. 112–15.
79. John L. Thomas, *The Liberator: William Lloyd Garrison* (Boston: Little, Brown, 1963), pp. 352–53; Aileen Kraditor, *Means and Ends in American Abolitionism: Garrison and His Critics on Strategy and Tactics, 1834–1850* (New York: Pantheon, 1969), pp. 92–93; and Staughton Lynd, *Intellectual Origins of American Radicalism* (New York: Pantheon, 1968), pp. 134–35.
80. Mayer, *All on Fire*, pp. 342, 377; A. Woodward, *A Review of Uncle Tom's Cabin or, An Essay on Slavery* (Cincinnati, Oh.: Applegate, 1853), pp. 100–101; Rev. Fred Ross, *Slavery, Ordained of God* (Philadelphia: J.B. Lippincott, 1857), pp. 5–7, 144; Carolyn Karcher, *The First Woman of the Republic: A Cultural Biography of Lydia Maria Child* (Durham, N.C.: Duke University Press, 1994), pp. xiv, 68, 595–96; Stacey M. Robertson, *Parker Pillsbury: Radical Abolitionist, Male Feminist* (Ithaca, N.Y.: Cornell University Press, 2000); Parker Pillsbury, "French Revolution, Voltaire, and Thomas Paine" (1881, from the Pillsbury Papers at Colby Sawyer College, kindly provided to me by Stacey Robertson); and Henry C. Wright, *The Merits of Jesus Christ and the Merits of Thomas Paine* (Boston, 1869).
81. James Brewer Stewart, *Wendell Phillips, Liberty's Hero* (Baton Rouge: Louisiana State University Press, 1986), pp. 26–35, 64–72, 194–95, 300.
82. On Paine and the question of the liberation of women, see Fruchtman, *Paine and the Religion of Nature*, pp. 64–65.
83. Kathryn Kish Sklar, *Women's Rights Emerges within the Antislavery Movement, 1830–1870: A Brief History with Documents* (Boston: Bedford, 2000), pp. 47–55.
84. Ellen Carol DuBois, *Feminism and Suffrage: The Emergence of an Independent Women's Movement in America, 1848–1869*, rev. ed. (Ithaca, N.Y.: Cornell University Press, 1999), pp. 15–52. For the text of the Declaration of Sentiments, see Foner, ed., *We, the Other People*, pp. 77–83.
85. Ellen Carol DuBois, *Women's Suffrage and Women's Rights* (New York: New York University Press, 1998), p. 161; Elizabeth Cady Stanton, *Letters, Diary and Reminiscences*, ed. Theodore Stanton and Harriot Stanton Blanch (New York: Harper and Bros., 1922), pp. 2:60–61; Elizabeth Cady Stanton, *The Woman's Bible* (New York: European Publishing, 1895); and Kathi Kern, *Mrs. Stanton's Bible* (Ithaca, N.Y.: Cornell University Press, 2000).
86. Stanton, Anthony, and Gage, eds., *History of Woman Suffrage*, p. 1:100; Reynolds, *Walt Whitman's America*, p. 220; and Sherry Ceniza, *Walt Whitman and 19th-Century Reformers* (Tuscaloosa: University of Alabama Press, 1998), pp. 140–80.
87. Yuri Suhl, *Ernestine L. Rose: Women's Rights Pioneer* (New York: Biblio Press, 1990), pp. 3–39; and Carol A. Kolmerten, *The American Life of Ernestine L. Rose* (Syracuse, N.Y.: Syracuse University Press, 1999), pp. 1–20.
88. Kolmerten, *American Life*, pp. 86–87, 133–34, 140–56. For a wonderful collection of Rose's addresses, see Keri A. Bodensteiner, "The Rhetoric of Ernestine L. Rose, with Collected Speeches and Writings," Ph.D. diss., University of Kansas, 2000.
89. Eugene D. Genovese, *The Southern Front* (Columbia: University of Missouri Press, 1995), pp. 94–96; and Dixon Wecter, "Hero in Reverse," *Virginia Quarterly Review* 18, no. 2 (Spring 1942), p. 253.

90. Carl Wittke, *Refugees of Revolution: The German-American Forty-Eighters in America* (Philadelphia: University of Pennsylvania Press, 1952); Mark O. Kistler, "German-American Liberalism and Thomas Paine," *American Quarterly* 14, no. 1 (Spring 1962), pp. 81–91; Sister M. Hedwigis Overmoehle, "The Anti-Clerical Activities of the Forty-Eighters in Wisconsin, 1848–1860," Ph.D. diss., St. Louis University, 1941; Berenice Cooper, "*Die Freie Gemeinde*: Freethinkers on the Frontier," *Minnesota History* 41, no. 2 (Summer 1968), pp. 53–60; and Edwin E. Scharf, "'Freethinkers' of the Early Texas Hill Country," *Freethought Today*, April 1998 (http://www.ffrf.org/fttoday/april98/scharf.html).

91. *The Works of Thomas Paine, A Hero of the American Revolution, with an Account of His Life* (Philadelphia: Moss, 1854); Nathan Bangs, *A History of the Methodist Episcopal Church*, vol. 2, *1793–1816* (New York: Mason and Lane, 1840), p. 21; Benjamin Lossing, *Pictorial Field Book of the Revolution*, 2 vols. (New York: Harper Brothers, 1855), pp. 2:68–69; Henry S. Randall, *The Life of Thomas Jefferson*, 3 vols. (New York: Derby and Jackson, 1858), pp. 1:136–38; and George Bancroft, *History of the United States* (Boston: Little, Brown, 1860), pp. 8:236–43. Also see Calvin Blanchard, *The Life of Thomas Paine* (New York, 1860); and Joseph N. Moreau, comp., *Testimonials to the Merits of Thomas Paine* (Burlington, N.J.: F.L. Taylor, 1861).

92. Wallace, *Rockdale*, pp. 454–55; Lazerow, *Religion and the Working Class*, pp. 219–21; E. D. Sanborn, *An Address in Commemoration of the Completion of the First Free Bridge! Across the Connecticut River* (Hanover, N.H.: B.D. Howe, 1859); Frederick Shelton (?), "Thomas Paine's Second Appearance in the United States," "Thomas Paine's First Appearance in America," "Thomas Paine in England and in France," *Atlantic Monthly* 4, nos. 21, 25, 26 (July, November, December 1859), pp. 1–17, 565–75, 690–709; Stephen B. Oates, *To Purge This Land with Blood; A Biography of John Brown* (New York: Harper and Row, 1970), p. 280; and *The Magnificent Activist: The Writings of Thomas Wentworth Higginson*, ed. Howard N. Meyer (New York: Da Capo Press, 2000). Though seemingly distant and unrelated, the last two events were essentially linked through the person of the Boston Unitarian minister and radical Thomas Wentworth Higginson, a major literary contributor to the *Atlantic Monthly* and one of the "Secret Six" who bankrolled Brown's disastrous raid.

93. M. D. Conway, *Thomas Paine: A Celebration* (Cincinnati, Oh.: Dial, 1860); Ann Braude, *Radical Spirits: Spiritualism and Women's Rights in Nineteenth-Century America* (Boston: Beacon Press, 1989); R. Laurence Moore, *In Search of White Crows: Spiritualism, Parapsychology, and American Culture* (New York: Oxford University Press, 1977), pp. 19–21; and for the premier example of a spiritualist's channeling of Paine, see Rev. C. Hammond (medium), *Light from the Spirit World: The Pilgrimage of Thomas Paine and Others to the Seventh Circle in the Spirit World* (New York: Partridge and Brittan, 1852).

6. WHEN, IN COUNTRIES THAT ARE CALLED CIVILIZED

1. Sidney Warren, *American Freethought, 1860–1914* (New York: Columbia University Press, 1943), pp. 96–116; Stow Persons, *Free Religion: An American Faith*

(New Haven, Conn.: Yale University Press, 1947); J. Wade Carruthers, *Octavius Brooks Frothingham* (University: University of Alabama Press, 1977); Philip Hamburger, *Separation of Church and State* (Cambridge, Mass.: Harvard University Press, 2002), pp. 289–95; Sara M. Evans, *Born for Liberty: A History of Women in America* (New York: Free Press, 1989), pp. 119–24; and Timothy Messer-Kruse, *The Yankee International: Marxism and the American Reform Tradition, 1846–1876* (Chapel Hill: University of North Carolina Press, 1998), p. 1.

2. Dennis Nordin, *Rich Harvest: A History of the Grange, 1867–1900* (Oxford: University Press of Mississippi, 1974); David Montgomery, *Beyond Equality: Labor and the Radical Republicans, 1862–1872* (1967; reprinted Urbana: University of Illinois Press, 1981); Priscilla Murolo and A. B. Chitty, *From the Folks Who Brought You the Weekend: A Short Illustrated History of Labor in the United States* (New York: New Press, 2001), pp. 97–109; Leon Fink, *The Knights of Labor and American Politics* (Urbana: University of Illinois Press, 1983); and Kevin Kenny, *Making Sense of the Molly Maguires* (New York: Oxford University Press, 1998).

3. Warren, *American Freethought*, pp. 22–23; and Whitfield J. Bell, Jr., *The Bust of Thomas Paine* (Philadelphia: American Philosophical Society, 1974), pp. 8–10.

4. Victoria Woodhull, "New Doctrine of States Rights" (1872), in *The Victoria Woodhull Reader*, ed. Madeline B. Stern (Weston, Mass.: M & S Press, 1974), p. 3.

5. Susan B. Anthony, "Women Already Voters" (1871) and "Is it a Crime for a U.S. Citizen to Vote?" (1873), in *The Selected Papers of Elizabeth Cady Stanton and Susan B. Anthony*, vol. 2, *Against an Aristocracy of Sex, 1866 to 1873*, ed. Ann D. Gordon (New Brunswick, N.J.: Rutgers University Press, 2000), pp. 458, 573: Thomas Paine, *Dissertation on First Principles of Government* (1795), in *CW*, p. 2:579; and Sarah A. Ramsdell (medium), *Paine's Age of Thought* (San Francisco: Bancroft, 1872).

6. Larzer Ziff, *The American 1890s* (New York: Viking, 1966), p. 76; Jonathan Grossman, *William Sylvis, Pioneer of American Labor* (New York: Columbia University Press, 1945), p. 182; and William H. Sylvis, "Speech Delivered at Birmingham, Penn., September 1868," "Platform of Principles of the National Labor Union" (1868), "Co-Operation" (1868?), in *The Life, Speeches, Labors, and Essays of William H. Sylvis*, ed. James C. Sylvis (Philadelphia: Claxton, Remsen, and Haffelfinger, 1872), pp. 223–25, 284–92, 387.

7. Mark O. Kistler, "German-American Liberalism and Thomas Paine," *American Quarterly* 14, no. 1 (Spring 1962), p. 88; Arlow W. Anderson, *The Norwegian Americans* (Boston: Twayne Publishers, 1975), p. 89; and Eric Foner, *Politics and Ideology in the Age of the Civil War* (New York: Oxford University Press, 1980), p. 158.

8. Michael Kammen, *A Season of Youth: The American Revolution and the Historical Imagination* (Ithaca, N.Y.: Cornell University Press, 1978), pp. 61–64.

9. Robert C. Winthrop, *Oration on the Centennial Anniversary of the Declaration of Independence* (Boston: Press of John Wilson and Son, 1876), pp. 21, 45–47, 52–54.

10. Gary B. Nash, *First City: Philadelphia and the Forging of Historical Memory* (Philadelphia: University of Pennsylvania Press, 2002), p. 277.

11. John W. Chadwick, *Thomas Paine—A Lecture* (New York: Chas. M. Green, 1876); Martin K. Schermerhorn, *Centennial Lecture on Thomas Paine* (Buffalo, N.Y.: Baker, Jones, 1876); Warren, *American Freethought*, p. 162; George E. Macdonald, *Fifty Years of Freethought* (New York: Truth Seeker Co., 1929), p. 1:511; (George William Curtis), "Editor's Easy Chair," *Harper's New Monthly Magazine*, April 1876, pp. 769–70; and Marcus Casey, "A Plea for a Patriot," *Galaxy*, May 1876, pp. 593–601.

12. Mark Twain and Charles Dudley Warner, *The Gilded Age, A Tale of Today* (1873; reprinted, New York: Penguin, 2001).

13. Sean Dennis Cashman, *America in the Gilded Age* (New York: New York University Press, 1993), pp. 3–4, 10; Nelson Lichtenstein et al., American Social History Project, *Who Built America?* (New York: Worth, 2000), p. 2:31; and Alan Brinkley, *The Unfinished Nation* (New York: Alfred A. Knopf, 1993), p. 463.

14. Eric Foner, *The Story of American Freedom* (New York: W.W. Norton, 1998), p. 117.

15. Lichtenstein et al., *Who Built America?*, p. 2:75.

16. The classic work on the subject remains Richard Hofstadter, *Social Darwinism in America* (1944; reprinted, Boston: Beacon Press, 1992). For William Graham Sumner's arguments, see his *What Social Classes Owe to Each Other* (New York: Harper and Bros., 1883); and *Social Darwinism: Selected Essays of William Graham Sumner*, ed. Stow Persons (Englewood Cliffs, N.J.: Prentice-Hall, 1963).

17. Rev. William F. Warren, "American Infidelity: Its Factors and Phases," in Rev. Philip Schaff and Rev. S. Irenaeus Prime, eds., *History, Essays, Orations, and Other Documents of the Sixth General Conference of the Evangelical Alliance* (New York: Harper and Brothers, 1874), pp. 249–53; Jeannette Keith, *Country People in the New South: Tennessee's Upper Cumberland* (Chapel Hill: University of North Carolina Press, 1995), p. 215; and Robert H. Abzug, *Passionate Liberator: Theodore Dwight Weld and the Dilemma of Reform* (New York: Oxford University Press, 1980), pp. 290–91.

18. Theodore Roosevelt, *Gouverneur Morris* (Boston: Houghton Mifflin, 1888), pp. 288–89; and Stephen F. Knott, *Alexander Hamilton and the Persistence of Myth* (Lawrence: University Press of Kansas, 2002), pp. 77–79, 87–90.

19. John Bach McMaster, *A History of the People of the United States of America, From the Revolution to the Civil War* (New York: D. Appleton, 1883), pp. 1:150–151ff; and *A School History of the United States* (New York: American Book Company, 1897).

20. Warren, *American Freethought*, p. 113.

21. Clarence F. Gohdes, *The Periodicals of Transcendentalism* (Durham, N.C.: Duke University Press, 1931), pp. 229–41; Persons, *Free Religion*, pp. 85–91; Warren, *American Freethought*, pp. 27,184–205. Also see D. M. Bennett, "140th Anniversary of Thomas Paine's Birthday" (1877), reprinted in *Truth Seeker* 120, no. 1 (1993); and *The Great Works of Thomas Paine: Complete Political and Theological* (New York: Truth Seeker, 1900).

22. Thomas A. Edison, introduction to *The Life and Works of Thomas Paine*, ed. William M. Van der Weyde (New Rochelle, N.Y.: Thomas Paine National Histori-

cal Association, 1925), pp. 1:vii–ix. Also see Joseph Frazier Wall, *Andrew Carnegie* (New York: Oxford University Press, 1970), pp. 541–45, 806–7, 942–45; and Neil Baldwin, *Edison: Inventing the Century* (Chicago: University of Chicago Press), pp. 25–26.

23. *The Letters of Robert G. Ingersoll*, ed. Eva Ingersoll Wakefield (New York: Philosophical Library, 1951), p. 93.

24. Orvin Larson, *American Infidel: Robert G. Ingersoll* (New York: Citadel Press, 1962), pp. 52–53, 76–80, 101–6.

25. Ibid., pp. 210–13, 230, 235–42, 277–78; and Robert G. Ingersoll, "Human Rights," "Free Speech and an Honest Ballot," in *Colonel Robert G. Ingersoll's 44 Complete Lectures* (Chicago: M.A. Donohue, 1924), pp. 115, 294.

26. Ingersoll, "Life and Deeds of Thomas Paine," in ibid., p. 211.

27. "Ingersoll's Vindication of Thomas Paine," in ibid., pp. 148–72. Also see J.B. McClure, ed., *Mistakes of Ingersoll on Thomas Paine as Shown by E. P. Goodwin [et al.]* (Chicago: Rhodes and McClure, 1880).

28. John L. Thomas, *Alternative America: Henry George, Edward Bellamy, Henry Demarest Lloyd and the Adversary Tradition* (Cambridge, Mass.: Harvard University Press, 1983), pp. 7–17, 58–71.

29. Henry George, *Progress and Poverty: An Inquiry into the Cause of Industrial Depressions and of Increase of Want with Increase of Wealth* (1879; reprinted, New York: Robert Schalkenbach Foundation, 1979).

30. Thomas, *Alternative America*, pp. 175–202; J. Morrison Davidson, *Concerning Four Precursors of Henry George and the Single Tax* (1899; reprinted, Port Washington, N.Y.: Kennikat Press, 1971), pp. 47–56; and Lillian Symes and Travers Clement, *Rebel America: The Story of Social Revolt in the United States* (1934; reprinted, Boston: Beacon Press, 1972), p. 183.

31. Gillis Harp, *Positivist Republic: Auguste Comte and the Reconstruction of American Liberalism, 1865–1920* (University Park: Pennsylvania State University Press, 1995), pp. 108–23.

32. Lester Ward at Paine birthday dinner (1912), quoted in Samuel Chugerman, *Lester F. Ward: The American Aristotle* (Durham, N.C.: Duke University Press, 1939); Henry Steele Commager, *The American Mind* (New Haven, Conn.: Yale University Press, 1950), p. 215; and Hofstadter, *Social Darwinism*, pp. 67–84.

33. Minnie M. Brashear, *Mark Twain, Son of Missouri* (Chapel Hill, N.C.: University of North Carolina Press, 1934), pp. 162–65, 244–48.

34. Mark Twain, *A Connecticut Yankee in King Arthur's Court* (1889; reprinted, New York: Penguin Books, 1971), p. 230; and Paine, *Rights of Man, Part 1*, p. 1:289. Twain's 1908 correspondence referred to in *The Selected Letters of Mark Twain*, ed. Charles Neider (New York: Harper and Row, 1982), p. 310. And also see Mark Twain, *Pudd'nhead Wilson and Those Extraordinary Twins* (1894; reprinted, New York: Penguin Books, 1969), pp. 240–41.

35. E. B. Washburne, "Thomas Paine and the French Revolution," *Scribner's Monthly* 20, no. 5 (September 1880), pp. 771–86. For a summary and excerpts of Moses Coit Tyler's "The Influence of Thomas Paine on the Popular Resolution of American Independence," see *Papers of the American Historical Association* (New York:

G.P. Putnam's Sons, 1886), pp. 35–36; Moses Coit Tyler, *The Literary History of the American Revolution, 1763–1783* (1897; reprinted, New York: Burt Franklin, 1970); and Moncure Daniel Conway, *The Life of Thomas Paine* (New York: G.P. Putnam's Sons, 1892). Also see Moncure Daniel Conway, *Autobiography of Moncure Daniel Conway* (Boston: Houghton Mifflin, 1904), pp. 1:268–69, 304–5.

36. John Fiske, *The American Revolution* (Boston: Houghton Mifflin, 1891), pp. 1:204–5; and Kammen, *Season of Youth*, pp. 62, 64.

37. Murolo and Chitty, *From the Folks Who Brought You the Weekend*, pp. 121–27.

38. I. G. Blanchard, "Eight Hours" (1886), reprinted in Lichtenstein et al., *Who Built America?*, p. 2:99.

39. Messer-Kruse, *Yankee International*, pp. 234–35; Montgomery, *Beyond Equality*, pp. 221–22; and Clifton K. Yearley, Jr., *Britons in American Labor: A History of the Influence of the United Kingdom Immigrants on American Labor, 1820–1914* (Baltimore: John Hopkins Press, 1957), pp. 198–216, 224–28, 261–64, 276–79.

40. Carlotta R. Anderson, *All-American Anarchist: Joseph A. Labadie* (Detroit: Wayne State University Press, 1998), pp. 27, 36, 47–49, 57–63.

41. Ibid., pp. 85, 159–71.

42. Paul Avrich, *The Haymarket Tragedy* (Princeton, N.J.: Princeton University Press, 1984), pp. 3–14.

43. Ibid., pp. 15, 26–38.

44. Ibid., p. 74.

45. Ibid.

46. Julius Grinnell quoted in Donald I. Miller, *City of the Century: The Epic of Chicago and the Making of America* (New York: Simon and Schuster, 1996), p. 477. Oscar Neebe was sentenced to fifteen years in prison.

47. August Spies, "Address of August Spies," in *The Accused, The Accusers: The Famous Speeches of the Eight Chicago Anarchists in Court* (Chicago: Socialistic Publishing Society, 1886), p. 6. Also see Philip Foner, *The Autobiographies of the Haymarket Martyrs* (New York: Humanities Press, 1969). The five executed would be buried at the Waldheim Cemetery in Forest Park, Illinois. In 1892 Governor John Altgeld would pardon Fielden, Schwab, and Neebe.

48. Eric Rauchway, *Murdering McKinley: The Making of Theodore Roosevelt's America* (New York: Hill and Wang, 2003), p. 99; and Avrich, *Haymarket Tragedy*, p. 401.

49. Herman Melville, *Billy Budd, Sailor* (1924; reprinted, New York: Penguin, 1995), p. 13; Robert K. Wallace, "Billy Budd and the Haymarket Hangings," *American Literature* 47, no. 1 (March 1975), pp. 108–13; and Ray Browne, *Melville's Drive to Humanism* (Lafayette, Ind.: Purdue University Studies, 1971), pp. 370–94. In *American Sympathy: Men, Friendship, and Literature in the New Nation* (New Haven, Conn.: Yale University Press, 2001), pp. 269–70, Caleb Crain has hinted that the title of Melville's *Billy Budd* may owe something to Paine by directing attention to the last page of *Rights of Man*, where Paine wrote of plucking a twig from an English tree in February: "By chance [I] might observe, that a *single bud* on that twig had begun to swell. I should reason very unnaturally, or rather not reason at all, to suppose *this* was the *only* bud in England which had this appearance . . . What pace the political summer may keep with the natural, no human foresight can determine."

50. Emma Goldman, "Excerpt from Trial Transcript: The People vs. Emma Goldman" (1893), in Candace Falk et al., eds., *Emma Goldman: A Documentary History of the American Years*, vol. 1: *Made for America, 1890–1901* (Berkeley: University of California Press, 2003), p. 174; and Voltairine de Cleyre, "Anarchism and American Traditions" and "Thomas Paine," in *Selected Works of Voltairine de Cleyre*, ed. Alexander Berkman (New York: Mother Earth, 1914), pp. 119, 277. Also see Paul Avrich, *An American Anarchist: The Life of Voltairine de Cleyre* (Princeton, N.J.: Princeton University Press, 1978), pp. 39–49.

51. Norman Pollack, ed., *The Populist Mind* (Indianapolis: Bobbs-Merrill, 1967), p. xlii.

52. Theodore R. Mitchell, *Political Education in the Southern Farmers' Alliance, 1887–1900* (Madison: University of Wisconsin Press, 1987).

53. Lawrence Goodwyn, *Democratic Promise: The Populist Moment in America* (New York: Oxford University Press, 1976), p. 329; Mrs. Catherine Nugent, *Life Work of Thomas L. Nugent* (Stephenville, Tex.: Laird and Lee, 1896), pp. 15–16; and Thomas Nugent, Speech (1892?), in Pollack, ed., *Populist Mind*, p. 298.

54. William E. Connelley, *A Standard History of Kansas and Kansans* (Chicago: Lewis, 1918), pp. 2:1151–52; Goodwyn, *Democratic Promise*, pp. 198–99; and O. Gene Clanton, *Kansas Populism: Ideas and Men* (Lawrence: University Press of Kansas, 1969), pp. 82–87.

55. L. D. Lewelling, "A Dream of the Future" (January 9, 1893), in Pollack, ed., *Populist Mind*, p. 53.

56. Herbert Croly, *The Promise of American Life* (1914), quoted in Foner, *Story of American Freedom*, p. 153. Also see Michael McGerr, *A Fierce Discontent: The Rise and Fall of the Progressive Movement in America, 1870–1920* (New York: Free Press, 2003).

57. On Louis Freeland Post, see Dominic Candeloro, "Louis F. Post and the Red Scare of 1920," *Prologue* 11, no. 1 (Spring 1979), pp. 41–55; and on George Creel, see his autobiography, *Rebel at Large* (New York: G.P. Putnam's Sons, 1947).

58. Elbert Hubbard, *Thomas Paine—Little Journeys to Homes of Reformers* (East Aurora, N.Y.: Roycrofters Press, 1907); Alice Hubbard, ed., *An American Bible* (East Aurora, N.Y.: Roycrofters Press, 1911); and Marilla M. Ricker, *The Four Gospels* (East Aurora, N.Y.: Roycrofters Press, 1911).

59. "A Rehabilitation of Thomas Paine," *Current Literature* 39 (1905), pp. 521–22; and "Conflicting Estimates of Thomas Paine," *Current Literature*, 47, (1909), pp. 535–36. The new editions of Paine's works included *The Writings of Thomas Paine*, ed. Moncure D. Conway (New York: G.P. Putnam's Sons, 1894–96); and *The Life and Writings of Thomas Paine*, ed. Daniel Edwin Wheeler (New York: V. Parke, 1908).

60. Anonymous, "Influence of Paine on American Thought: His Sad End," *American Catholic Quarterly Review* 39 (1914), pp. 347–48; and "Thomas Paine," *Outlook* 94 (February 12 and March 19, 1910), pp. 334–35, 608.

61. Ellery Sedgwick, *Thomas Paine* (Boston: Small, Maynard, and Company, 1899); Woodrow Wilson, *A History of the American People* (New York: Harper and Bros.,

1902), pp. 3:91–92; C. E. Merriam, "Thomas Paine's Political Theories," *Political Science Quarterly* 14, no. 3 (September 1899), p. 402; Sydney George Fisher, *The Struggle for American Independence* (Philadelphia: J.B. Lippincott, 1908), p. 442 (italics added); and Charles Beard, *An Economic Interpretation of the Constitution of the United States* (New York: Macmillan, 1913).

62. David Saville Muzzey, speech at *Memorial Celebration of the One Hundredth Anniversary of the Death of Thomas Paine* (1909) pp. 10–14; David Saville Muzzey, *An American History* (Boston: Ginn, 1911), p. 132; Missouri Society, *Prize Medal Essay Contest by the High School Scholars, 1912: The Political Writings of Thomas Paine and Their Influence on the Revolution* (New York: Thomas Paine National Historical Association, 1912).

63. Isabella Beecher Hooker, *The Constitutional Rights of the Women of the United States—An Address Before the International Council of Women in Washington, D.C., March 30, 1888* (Hartford, Conn.: Hartford Press, 1900), p. 86; and Mary Putnam-Jacobi, *"Common Sense" Applied to Women Suffrage* (New York: G.P. Putnam's Sons, 1894), pp. 2–4.

64. Arthur M. Lewis, "The American Revolution and Thomas Paine," in *Vital Problems in Social Evolution* (Chicago: Charles H. Kerr, 1917), pp. 93, 99, 109; Kenneth Teitelbaum, *"Schooling for Good Rebels": Socialist Education for Children in the United States, 1900–1920* (Philadelphia: Temple University Press, 1993), pp. 155–57; Frederick Krafft, "History of Our Country for Boys and Girls," *Little Socialist Magazine for Boys and Girls* 3, nos. 2–10 (February–October 1910, esp. April–June), p. 5 in each issue; "Two Birthdays," *Little Socialist Magazine for Boys and Girls* 3, no. 2 (February 1910), p. 8; and F. Powers, "Reign of Terror," *Little Socialist Magazine for Boys and Girls* 3, no. 6 (June 1910), p. 6.

65. Teitelbaum, "Schooling for Good Rebels"; and Rachel Cutler Schwartz, "The Rand School of Social Science, 1906–1924," Ph.D. diss., State University of New York at Buffalo, 1984.

66. Elizabeth Gurley Flynn, *The Rebel Girl, An Autobiography: My First Life (1906–1926)* (New York: International Publishers, 1955), pp. 61–65; Oakley C. Johnson, *Robert Owen in the United States* (New York: Humanities Press, 1970), pp. 4–5; Hugh O. Pentecost, "Thomas Paine," in *Some Typical Reformers and Reforms* (New York: Twentieth Century, 1891), pp. 1–10; Jeffrey B. Perry, ed., *A Hubert Harrison Reader* (Middletown, Conn.: Wesleyan University Press, 2001); and Randolph Bourne, "The Doctrine of the Rights of Man as Formulated by Thomas Paine" (1912), in Randolph Bourne, *The Radical Will: Selected Writings, 1911–1918* (New York: Urizen Books, 1977), pp. 233–47.

67. James R. Green, *Grass Roots Socialism: Radical Movements in the Southwest, 1895–1943* (Baton Rouge: Louisiana State University Press, 1978). Also see Bernard J. Brommel, *Eugene V. Debs: Spokesman for Labor and Socialism* (Chicago: Charles H. Kerr, 1978), pp. 92–93; and Oscar Ameringer, *If You Don't Weaken: An Autobiography* (New York: Henry Holt, 1940), pp. 68–70.

68. W. A. Corey, *Common Sense: A Reading of Thomas Paine's Famous Revolutionary Pamphlet, "Common Sense," in the Light of the Socialist Revolution* (Los Angeles: Common Sense Publishing Company, 1906); George Washington Woodbey, speech

to the National Convention of the Socialist Party (1908), quoted in Philip S. Foner, "Reverend George Washington Woodbey: Early Twentieth Century California Black Socialist," *Journal of Negro History* 61, no. 2 (April 1976), p. 149; Edward Bingham and Tim Barnes, *Wood Works: The Life and Writings of Charles Erskine Scott Wood* (Corvallis: Oregon State University Press, 1997); and Charles Erskine Scott Wood, *Heavenly Discourse* (New York: Vanguard Press, 1927).

69. Howard H. Quint, "Julius Wayland, Pioneer Socialist Propagandist," *Mississippi Valley Historical Review* 35, no. 4 (March 1949), p. 585.

70. Mother Jones, "To Walter Wayland" (November 15, 1918), in *Mother Jones Speaks: Collected Writings and Speeches*, ed. Philip S. Foner (New York: Monad Press, 1983), p. 621; and Paine, *Crisis I*, in *CW*, p. 1:56.

71. Elliott Shore, *Talkin' Socialism: J. A. Wayland and the Radical Press* (Lawrence: University Press of Kansas, 1988), pp. 104–14, and John Graham, *"Yours for the Revolution": The Appeal to Reason, 1895–1922* (Lincoln: University of Nebraska Press, 1990), pp. xi, 6–7; and "Literature of Discontent," *Appeal to Reason*, June 2, 1900.

72. Ray Ginger, *The Bending Cross: A Biography of Eugene Victor Debs* (New Brunswick, N.J.: Rutgers University Press, 1949), pp. 6–11; and Nick Salvatore, *Eugene Debs, Citizen and Socialist* (Urbana: University of Illinois Press, 1982), pp. 9–11.

73. Eugene Debs, "The Secret of Efficient Expression" (1918), in *Labor and Freedom: The Voice and Pen of Eugene Debs*, ed. Phil Wagner (St. Louis, 1916), pp. 15–22; and Ginger, *Bending Cross*, pp. 25–28.

74. Ginger, *Bending Cross*, pp. 90–93; Salvatore, *Eugene Debs*, pp. 115–26.

75. Ginger, *Bending Cross*: pp. 108–67; Salvatore, *Eugene Debs*, pp. 114–146.

76. *Writings and Speeches of Eugene V. Debs*, ed. Arthur M. Schlesinger (New York: Hermitage Press, 1948), pp. 6, 11; Ginger, *Bending Cross*, pp. 187–202; and Salvatore, *Eugene Debs*, pp. 149–55.

77. Arthur Weinberg, ed., *Attorney for the Damned* (New York: Simon and Schuster, 1957); and Arthur Weinberg and Lila Weinberg, *Clarence Darrow, A Sentimental Rebel* (New York: G.P. Putnam's Sons, 1980), pp. 16–21.

78. Weinberg, ed., *Attorney for the Damned*, pp. 77–79; and Weinberg and Weinberg, *Clarence Darrow*, pp. 280–83.

79. Henry Demarest Lloyd, "The Divinity of Humanity" (1894), in Pollack, ed., *Populist Mind*, p. 69.

7. TYRANNY, LIKE HELL, IS NOT EASILY CONQUERED

1. Samuel I. Rosenman, *Working with Roosevelt* (New York: Harper and Brothers, 1952), pp. 3–8, 329–33; Doris Kearns Goodwin, *No Ordinary Time—Franklin and Eleanor Roosevelt: The Home Front in World War II* (New York: Simon and Schuster, 1994), pp. 316–20; and Kenneth S. Davis, *FDR: The War President, 1940–1943* (New York: Random House, 2000), pp. 433–35.

2. Rosenman, *Working*, pp. 3–8; George Mowrey, "The Uses of History by Recent Presidents," *Journal of American History* 53, no. 1 (June 1966), pp. 8–10; and Merrill D. Peterson, *The Jefferson Image in the American Mind* (Charlottesville:

University of Virginia Press, 1998), pp. 355–63; and Merrill D. Peterson, *Lincoln in American Memory* (New York: Oxford University Press, 1994), pp. 318–22.

3. Franklin Delano Roosevelt "Fighting Defeatism" (February 23, 1942), in *FDR's Fireside Chats*, ed. Russell D. Buhite and David W. Levy (Norman: University of Oklahoma Press, 1992), p. 208.

4. Ibid., pp. 209–16.

5. Ibid., p. 216.

6. Ibid., pp. 216–17.

7. Ibid., pp. 217–18.

8. *New York Times* editorial note quoted in Davis, *FDR*, p. 435; Rosenman, *Working*, p. 333, and quoted in Davis, *FDR*, p. 435; and H.G. Hayes, letter to the president (March 2, 1942), in Lawrence W. Levine and Cornelia R. Levine, *The People and the President: America's Conversation with FDR* (Boston: Beacon Press, 2002), pp. 428–29.

9. Actually, FDR had used Paine and his words before. In a press conference on April 25, 1941, the president had cast the isolationists and Nazi sympathizers of the America First Committee—most notably, the popular hero and aviator Charles Lindbergh, who had accepted medals from Hitler—as "summer soldiers" and "sunshine patriots" by referring reporters to the opening lines of Paine's first *Crisis*. See Davis, *FDR*, pp. 170–72.

10. For Wilson on Edmund Burke, see "You Must Lead Your Own Generation, Not the Next" (1893?), in *The Political Thought of Woodrow Wilson*, ed. E. David Cronin (Indianapolis: Bobbs-Merrill, 1965), pp. 20–27; and John Mulder, *Woodrow Wilson: The Years of Preparation* (Princeton, N.J.: Princeton University Press, 1978), pp. 125–30.

11. Arthur S. Link, *Woodrow Wilson and the Progressive Era, 1910–1917* (New York: Harper and Brothers, 1954); and James Chace, *1912: Wilson, Roosevelt, Taft & Debs—The Election Changes the Country* (New York: Simon and Schuster, 2004).

12. Woodrow Wilson, speech at New Jersey Democratic Convention, September 17, 1910, and campaign address of September 23, 1912, quoted in H. W. Brands, *Woodrow Wilson* (New York: Times Books, 2003), p. 18.

13. Woodrow Wilson, "Be Neutral in Fact as Well as in Name . . ." (August 19, 1914), in *Political Thought of Wilson*, ed. Cronin, p. 303. For Wilson's historical remarks on Paine, see his *A History of the American People* (New York: Harper and Brothers, 1902), pp. 3:91–92.

14. Woodrow Wilson, "The Right Is More Precious Than Peace . . ." (April 2, 1917), in *Political Thought of Wilson*, ed. Cronin, pp. 344–46. Also see Robert W. Tucker, "A Benediction on the Past: Woodrow Wilson's War Address," *World Policy Journal* 17, no. 2 (Summer 2000), pp. 73–99.

15. Thomas Paine, *Crisis III*, in *CW*, p. 1:82, and *Rights of Man, Part 2* (1792), in *CW*, p. 1:448.

16. R. C. Roper, "Citizen of the World" and "Thomas Paine First to Urge League of Nations," *Public* 22 (March 15 and May 10, 1919, respectively); Woodrow Wilson, "The Fourteen Points," in *Political Thought of Wilson*, ed. Cronin, pp. 438–45; and Paine, *Rights of Man, Part 1* (1791) and *Rights of Man, Part 2* (1792), in *CW*, pp. 1:344, 448–49.

17. Michael McGerr, *A Fierce Discontent: The Rise and Fall of the Progressive Movement in America, 1870–1920* (New York: Free Press, 2003), pp. 279–313; and Alan Dawley, *Changing the World: American Progressives in War and Revolution* (Princeton, N.J.: Princeton University Press, 2003).

18. George Creel, *How We Advertised America* (New York: Harper and Brothers, 1920), pp. 3, 5. Also see George Creel, *Tom Paine—Liberty Bell* (New York: Sears, 1932); *Rebel at Large* (New York: G.P. Putnam's Sons, 1947); and David M. Kennedy, *Over Here: The First World War and American Society* (New York: Oxford University Press, 1980), pp. 53-78.

19. Editorial, *New York Times Book Review*, June 9, 1918, p. 270. Also see Editors, "Chronicle and Comment," *Bookman* 47 (1918), 432–34; and Stephen Vaughn, *Holding Fast the Inner Lines: Democracy, Nationalism, and the Committee on Public Information* (Chapel Hill: University of North Carolina Press, 1980), pp. 286–87.

20. Paine, *Dissertation on First Principles of Government* (1795), in *CW*, p. 2:588.

21. John Higham, *Strangers in the Land: Patterns of American Nativism, 1860–1925* (New York: Athenuem, 1973), pp. 194–263.

22. Wilson quoted in Meirion Harries and Susie Harries, *The Last Days of Innocence: America at War, 1917–1918* (New York: Vintage Books, 1997), p. 308; "Espionage Act (as Amended—40 Stat. 555, 1918)," in Nicholas N. Kittrie and Eldon D. Wheelock, Jr., eds., *The Tree of Liberty*, vol. 1, *Colonial Era to World War II* (Baltimore: John Hopkins University Press, 1998), p. 299.

23. On the American Protective League, see Joan M. Jensen, *The Price of Vigilance* (Chicago: Rand McNally, 1968).

24. Ibid., pp. 56–81, 225–28; and Sidney Lens, *Radicalism in America* (New York: Thomas Crowell, 1969), pp. 245–56.

25. Jonathan M. Hansen, *The Lost Promise of Patriotism: Debating American Identity, 1890–1920* (Chicago: University of Chicago Press, 2003), pp. 96–98, 149–56.

26. Ray Ginger, *The Bending Cross: A Biography of Eugene Victor Debs* (New Brunswick, N.J.: Rutgers University Press, 1949), pp. 354–59.

27. Eugene Debs, "The Canton, Ohio Speech" (June 16, 1918), in *Writings and Speeches of Eugene V. Debs*, ed. Arthur M. Schlesinger, Jr. (New York: Hermitage Press, 1948), pp. 417–33.

28. Eugene Debs, "Address to the Jury" (September 12, 1918), recounted in David Karsner, *Debs; His Authorized Life and Letters* (New York: Boni and Liveright, 1919), pp. 43–44.

29. Ibid., pp. 27–34.

30. Ibid., pp. 35–36.

31. Ibid., p. 32.

32. Nick Salvatore, *Eugene V. Debs: Citizen and Socialist* (Urbana: University of Illinois Press, 1982), p. 296. While Wilson ignored Debs's plight, Republican President Warren Harding pardoned Debs soon after taking office in 1921.

33. "Where are the Pre-War Radicals?" *Survey* 55 (February 1, 1926).

34. Gary Nash et al., *The American People* (New York: Longman, 1998), p. 800; Dominic Candeloro, "Louis F. Post and the Red Scare of 1920," *Prologue* 11, no. 1 (Spring 1979), pp. 40–55; and Robert K. Murray, *Red Scare: A Study in National Hysteria, 1919–1920* (Minneapolis: University of Minnesota Press, 1955). Louis

Post not only had to fight for the rights of immigrants and aliens; he also had to fight efforts by congressional Republicans to impeach him.

35. Harries and Harries, *Last Days of Innocence*, pp. 403–61; Dawley, *Changing the World*, pp. 259–94; and Kennedy, *Over Here*, pp. 359-62.

36. Lewis L. Gould, *Grand Old Party: A History of the Republicans* (New York: Random House, 2003), pp. 241–42; James T. Gillis, "Tom Paine," *Catholic World* 121 (April 1925), pp. 48–58; and John T. Christian, *A History of the Baptists* (Nashville, Tenn.: Sunday School Board of the Southern Baptist Convention,1926), pp. 348–49.

37. George E. MacDonald, *Fifty Years of Freethought* (New York: Truth Seeker, 1931), pp. 576–78; and Albert Ulmann, *New Yorkers, From Stuyvesant to Roosevelt* (New York: Chaucer Head Books, 1928), p. 76.

38. General John Pershing, "Speech at Camp Merritt Memorial Monument Dedication" (May 30, 1924), as reported in *Bergen Evening Record*, May 31, 1924 (http://www.cresskillboro.com/pershing.htm).

39. Chesla C. Sherlock, "Home of Thomas Paine," *Better Homes and Gardens*, March 1926, p. 75.

40. F. J. Gould, *Thomas Paine* (Boston: Small, Maynard, 1925); William M. Van der Weyde, *The Life and Works of Thomas Paine*, 10 vols. (New Rochelle, N.Y.: Thomas Paine National Historical Association, 1925); Mary Agnes Best, *Thomas Paine, Prophet and Martyr of Democracy* (New York: Harcourt, Brace, 1927); *Selections from the Writings of Thomas Paine*, ed. Carl Van Doren (New York: Modern Library, 1922); *Selections from the Works of Thomas Paine*, ed. Arthur Wallace Peach (New York: Harcourt, Brace, 1928); and John W. Gunn, *Life of Thomas Paine* (Girard, Kan.: Haldeman-Julius, 1924).

41. *Writings of Paine*, ed. Van Doren, pp. vii–viii; *Works of Paine*, ed. Peach, pp. x, xlvii; and David S. Muzzey, "Thomas Paine and American Independence," *American Review* 4 (1926), p. 288. Also see Lewis Mumford, "The Origins of the American Mind" (1926), in his *Interpretations and Forecasts, 1922–1972* (New York: Harcourt, Brace, Jovanovich, 1973), pp. 13–15; and Gilbert Seldes, "The Old Disbeliever," *New Republic* 52 (September 21, 1927), pp. 124–25.

42. H. Lark Hall, *V.L. Parrington: Through the Avenue of Art* (Kent, Oh.: Kent State University Press, 1994), pp. 197, 198, 201, 207; and Vernon Louis Parrington, *Main Currents in American Thought: An Interpretation of American Literature from the Beginnings to 1920*, 3 vols. (New York: Harcourt, Brace, 1930), p. 1:i.

43. Ibid., p. 327, p. 3:285.

44. Robert Dallek, *Democrat and Diplomat: The Life of William E. Dodd* (New York: Oxford University Press, 1968), pp. 82, 154–56. For Dodd on Paine in print, see William E. Dodd, "Tom Paine" (1930), reprinted in Lawrence E. Spivak and Charles Angoff, eds., *The American Mercury Reader* (Philadelphia: Blackiston, 1944), pp. 55–62.

45. Grace Poole and Solon De Leon, *What Shall I Read? A Book List for Boys and Girls* (New York: Workmen's Circle, 1929), pp. 129, 182; Sue Haldeman-Julius, "Profile," in Albert Mordell, ed., *The World of Haldeman-Julius* (New York: Twayne, 1960), p. 9; and E. Haldeman-Julius, *The First Hundred Million* (New York: Simon and Schuster, 1928), pp. 85–86, 91, 115. Also see McAlister Cole-

man, *Pioneers of Freedom* (New York: Vanguard Press, 1929), pp. 1–14; H. H. Broach and M. H. Hedges, *Speech and Scrap Book for Speakers* (Minneapolis: Speakers Service Bureau, 1924), pp. 246, 256, 268, 300; and Eric Schocket, "Proletarian Paperbacks: The Little Blue Books and Working-Class Culture," *College Literature* 29, no. 4 (Fall 2002), pp. 67–77. And among the Little Blue Books (Girard, Kan.: Haldeman-Julius Publications), see H. M. Tichenor, *Voices from the Past* (1921), Robert Ingersoll, *Vindication of Thomas Paine* (1923), John W. Gunn, *Life of Thomas Paine* (1924), Joseph McCabe, *Thomas Paine's Revolt Against the Bible* (1927), and James Vincent Nash, *Great Fighters for Freedom* (1928).

46. After indicating a desire to read Paine and Jefferson, Sacco and Vanzetti received a copy of Hubbard's *American Bible* (East Aurora, N.Y.: Roycrofters, 1911), which contained writings by Paine and several other American radicals. See *The Letters of Sacco and Vanzetti*, ed. Marion Denman Frankfurter and Gardner Jackson (New York: Penguin Books, 1997), pp. 83, 323; and Fred Somkin, "How Vanzetti Said Goodbye," *Journal of American History* 68, no. 2 (September 1981), pp. 298–312.

47. Edward A. Martin, *H. L. Mencken and the Debunkers* (Athens: University of Georgia Press, 1984), p. 29.

48. W. E. Woodward, *George Washington, the Image and the Man* (New York: Boni and Liveright, 1926), pp. 281–82; and W. E. Woodward, *Tom Paine: America's Godfather, 1783–1809* (New York: E. P. Dutton, 1946). Woodward coined *debunk* in his 1923 novel *Bunk*. See Martin, *Mencken*, pp. 8–9.

49. Gamaliel Bradford, "Damaged Souls," *Harper's Magazine* (1923), reprinted in Gamaliel Bradford, *Damaged Souls* (Boston: Houghton Mifflin, 1923), pp. 53, 57, 84. In the privacy of his own journals, Bradford wrote while preparing the Paine piece: "The man [Paine] is a writer . . . Why he is a real writer, a master of style . . . who can write like that today?" quoted in Jay B. Hubbell, ed., *American Life in Literature* (New York: Harper and Brothers, 1936), p. 116.

50. Statistics found in Alan Brinkley, *The Unfinished Nation: A Concise History of the American People* (New York: McGraw-Hill, 2004), pp. 650–57.

51. James Truslow Adams, *The Epic of America* (Boston: Little, Brown, 1931), p. 317 (italics added).

52. James Truslow Adams, *The March of Democracy* (New York: Charles Scribner's Sons, 1932), p. 120; and Elizabeth S. Kite, "The Revival of Thomas Paine," *Commonweal* 14 (May 27, 1931), pp. 93–94.

53. For the new biographies and editions of Paine's writings, see Creel, *Tom Paine*; Hesketh Pearson, *Tom Paine, Friend of Mankind* (New York: Harper and Brothers, 1937); S. M. Berthold, *Thomas Paine, America's First Liberal* (Boston: Meador, 1938); Frank Smith, *Thomas Paine, Liberator* (New York: Frederick A. Stokes, 1938); Thomas Paine National Historical Association, *The Works of Thomas Paine*, 6 vols. (New York: W. H. Wise, 1934); *Selections from the Writings of Thomas Paine*, ed. Sherman Mittell (Washington: National Home Library Foundation, 1935); *Thomas Paine: Selections from His Writings*, ed. James S. Allen (New York: International Publishers, 1937); and *The Living Thoughts of Tom Paine*, ed. John Dos Passos (New York: Longman, Green, 1940).

54. Diego Rivera, *Portrait of America* (New York: Covici, Friede, 1934), pp. 81–232.

55. Robert S. McElvaine, *The Great Depression: America, 1929–1941* (New York: Random House, 1993), pp. 224–49, 287–305; and David M. Kennedy, *Freedom from Fear: The American People in Depression and War, 1929–1945* (New York: Oxford University Press, 1999), pp. 288–322.

56. George Wolfskill, *The Revolt of the Conservatives: A History of the American Liberty League, 1934–1940* (Boston: Houghton Mifflin, 1962); Alan Brinkley, *Voices of Protest: Huey Long, Father Coughlin, and the Great Depression* (New York: Alfred A. Knopf, 1982); McElvaine, *Great Depression*, pp. 225–49; and Kennedy, *Freedom from Fear*, pp. 214–48.

57. Peterson, *Jefferson Image*, pp. 355–76; Dixon Wecter, *The Hero in America* (New York: Charles Scribner's Sons, 1941), pp. 175–80; John Taliaferro, *Great White Fathers: The Story of the Obsessive Quest to Create Mount Rushmore* (New York: Public Affairs, 2002), pp. 249–91; and Stephen F. Knott, *Alexander Hamilton and the Persistence of Myth* (Lawrence: University Press of Kansas, 2002), pp. 113–40.

58. V. F. Calverton, "The American Revolutionary Tradition," *Scribner's Magazine* 95 (May 1934), pp. 352–57.

59. V. F. Calverton, "Thomas Paine: God-Intoxicated Revolutionary," *Scribner's Magazine*, 95, no. 1 (January 1934), p. 22.

60. Alfred Bingham, quoted in Donald I. Miller, *The New American Radicalism: Alfred M. Bingham and the Non-Marxian Insurgency in the New Deal Era* (Port Washington, N.Y.: Kennikat Press, 1979), p. 11.

61. Platform and Editorial, *Common Sense* 1 (December 5, 1932), pp. 2–3; and Miller, *New American Radicalism*, pp. 23–30, 39–42, 50–112. Also see Alfred M. Bingham, *Insurgent America: Revolt of the Middle Classes* (New York: Harper and Brothers, 1935).

62. Miller, *New American Radicalism*, pp. 112–62; and Arthur M. Schlesinger, Jr., *The Politics of Upheaval* (Boston: Houghton Mifflin, 1960), pp. 147–61.

63. Fraser M. Ottanelli, *The Communist Party of the United States: From the Depression to World War II* (New Brunswick, N.J.: Rutgers University Press, 1991), pp. 17–80. It should be noted that American Communists showed at least some interest in Paine as early as 1920. See Theodore Draper, *The Roots of American Communism* (New York: Viking, 1957), p. 205.

64. Ottanelli, *Communist Party*, pp. 37–43, 137–57.

65. Earl Browder, "Who Are the Americans?" (1935), in Earl Browder, *What Is Communism?* (New York: Workers Library Publishers, 1936), pp. 19–21; Maurice Isserman, *If I Had a Hammer . . . : The Death of the Old Left and the Birth of the New Left* (New York: Basic Books, 1987), p. 11; Maurice Isserman, *Which Side Were You On?: The American Communist Party During the Second World War* (Middletown, Conn.: Wesleyan University Press, 1982), pp. 9–11; Ottanelli, *Communist Party*, pp. 122–23; and James G. Ryan, *Earl Browder: The Failure of American Communism* (Tuscaloosa: University of Alabama Press, 1997), pp. 4–8.

66. Earl Browder, "The American Tradition" (1937), in Earl Browder, *The People's Front* (New York: International Publishers, 1938), pp. 166–67.

67. Robin D. G. Kelley, *Hammer and Hoe: Alabama Communists During the Great Depression* (Chapel Hill: University of North Carolina Press, 1990), pp. xii, 122,

132–33; and James S. Allen, introduction to *Thomas Paine: Selections from His Writings* (New York: International Publishers, 1937), pp. 7–24.

68. Michael Denning, *The Cultural Front: The Laboring of American Culture in the Twentieth Century* (London: Verso, 1996), pp. xvi–xviii.

69. Ibid., pp. 115–59, 259–82, 295–309. For "Status Quo," see Harold Rome's *Pins and Needles*, featuring Barbra Streisand, 25th anniversary edition (New York: Columbia Records, 1962). For "Ballad for Americans," see Paul Robeson, *The Original Recording of "Ballad for Americans" and Great Songs of Faith, Love and Patriotism* (Santa Monica, Calif.: Vanguard Records, 1989). And for John Steinbeck's words, see *The Grapes of Wrath* (1939; reprinted, New York: Penguin Books, 1972), pp. 152–53.

70. Herbert B. Nichols, ed., *Thomas Paine Bicentennial Celebrations, 1737–1937* (New Rochelle, N.Y.: Thomas Paine National Historical Association, 1937); Meredith Page, *Prophet Without Honor*, a radio script broadcast on April 22, 1937 (Columbus: Ohio School of the Air—Radio Workshop of the Ohio State University, 1937); *Helen Keller's Journal, 1936–1937* (London: Michael Joseph, 1938), pp. 109–10; and Herbert Hoover, "On Benjamin Franklin" (May 21, 1938), in *Addresses Upon the Road, 1933–1938* (New York: Charles Scribner's Sons, 1938), p. 366.

71. R. L. Duffus, "The Firebrand of Our Revolution," *New York Times Magazine*, January 24, 1937, pp. 10, 21; W. J. Cash, "Justice to Thomas Paine," *Charlotte News*, February 21, 1937 (http://users.aol.com/WJCASH1/Charlotte.News.Articles/Paine. htm); Israel Solemnick, "Thomas Paine, Who Changed Men's Minds," *Scholastic*, January 30, 1937, pp. 8–9; Editors, "Tom Paine, Patriot and Heretic," *Christian Century* 54 (January 27, 1937), p. 102; and *Unity* 118, no. 10 (January 18, 1937).

72. Kent Pellett, "He Dreamed America," *Common Ground* 3 (1942), pp. 97–98.

73. John Dos Passos, "Tom Paine's 'Common Sense,'" and "Tom Paine's 'Rights of Man,'" in *Common Sense* 8, nos. 9–10 (September–October 1939), pp. 3–6 and 12–15, respectively; *Living Thoughts of Paine*, ed. Dos Passos, p. 12; *Thomas Paine*, episode 185 of *Cavalcade of America*, broadcast April 30, 1940, transcript in Frank Monaghan, *Du Pont Presents the Cavalcade of America* (1940); Ridgely Torrence, *Common Sense—Play in One Act* (New York: Dramatists Play Service, 1941); Dissent of Judge Jerome Frank in *Christensen v. Valentine* (2nd Circuit 1941), quoted in Wayne McIntosh and Cynthia Cates, "Advancing Speech Rights of Corporations: The Changing First Amendment," paper delivered at the annual conference of the American Politics Group, University of Essex, January 3, 2002, p. 8; and Amanda Vaill, *Everybody Was So Young: Gerald and Sara Murphy—A Lost Generation Love Story* (Boston: Houghton Mifflin, 1998), pp. 309–10. A veritable flood of writings on Paine appeared, including Wallace P. Rusterholz, *American Heretics and Saints* (Boston: Manthorne and Burack, 1938), pp. 107–44; Allan Seager, *They Worked for a Better World* (New York: Macmillan, 1939), pp. 34–55; William F. Russell, *The New "Common Sense"* (New York: Macmillan, 1941); and Struthers Burt, "Thomas Paine," in Henry Morgenthau, Jr. (Secretary of the Treasury), ed., *They Were Giants in the Land: Twenty-eight Historic Americans as Seen by Twenty-eight Contemporary Americans* (New York: Farrar and Rinehart, 1942), pp. 104–13.

74. L. A. Sawyer and W. H. Mitchell, *The Liberty Ships: The History of the "Emergency" Type Cargo Ships Constructed in the United States During World War II* (Cambridge, Md.: Cornell Maritime Press, 1970), p. 62. The *Tom Paine* was launched in October 1941 and delivered to the U.S. Army Transport Service in March 1942. It was finally scrapped in 1960.

75. Mark Van Doren, ed., *The New Invitation to Learning* (New York: Columbia Broadcasting System and Random House, 1942), pp. 368–83; Robert Loring Richards, *In This Crisis* (New York: E.I. du Pont de Nemours, 1942), p. 16; and Jerome Lawrence et al., *The World We Are Fighting For*, Script 15 (Los Angeles: Bullock's, 1943).

76. Van Doren, ed., *New Invitation*, pp. 376–80; Woodward, *Tom Paine*, p. 18; and *New York Times*, June 12, 1942, p. 19.

77. T. V. Smith, "Thomas Paine: Voice of Democratic Revolution," in Charner M. Perry, *The Philosophy of American Democracy* (Chicago: University of Chicago Press, 1943), pp. 1–27. For the biography, see Woodward, *Tom Paine*, and for the anthologies, see *Basic Writings of Thomas Paine*, ed. Richard Huett (New York: Willey Book Company, 1942); *Thomas Paine: Representative Selections, with Introduction, Bibliography, and Notes*, ed. Harry Hayden Clark (New York: American Book Company, 1944); *Selected Writings of Thomas Paine*, ed. Richard Emery Roberts (New York: Everybody's Vacation Publication Company, 1945); *The Selected Work of Tom Paine and Citizen Tom Paine*, ed. Howard Fast (New York: Modern Library, 1943, 1945); and *The Complete Writings of Thomas Paine*, ed. Philip S. Foner (New York: Citadel Press, 1945).

78. *Thomas Paine*, ed. Clark, p. xi; Francis John McConnell, "Thomas Paine," in *Evangelicals, Revolutions and Idealists: Six English Contributors to American Thought and Action* (New York: Whitmore and Sons, 1942), pp. 101–31; and Darrell Abel, "The Significance of the *Letter to the Abbé Raynal* in the Progress of Thomas Paine's Thought," *Pennsylvania Magazine of History and Biography* 66, no. 2 (April 1942), pp. 176–90.

79. Howard Fast, *Citizen Tom Paine* (1943; reprinted, New York: Grove Press, 1983).

80. Orson Welles, "Thomas Paine: Tyranny Is Not Easily Conquered" (originally recorded in November 1944 for Decca Records), on *Dramatic Readings* (Pavillion Records, 2001); Burrill Phillips, *Tom Paine—Overture for Orchestra* (New York: Hargail Music Press, 1946); Earl Robinson with Eric A. Gordon, *Ballad of an American: The Autobiography of Earl Robinson* (Lanham, Md.: Scarecrow Press, 1998), pp. 151–57 (for Robeson's performance of "The House I Live In," see Robeson, *The Original Recording of "Ballad for Americans,"* and for Sinatra's— which left out the line about Lincoln, Jefferson, and Paine—see the short Oscar-winning film of 1945, *The House I Live In*, directed by Mervyn LeRoy and produced by RKO Radio Pictures); "Mrs. Garten Comes Here on April 24," *Green Bay Press-Gazette*, April 11, 1944, p. 8; Howard Fast, "Author's Foreword," in *Selected Work* and *Citizen Paine*, ed. Fast, p. 343.

81. "Plaque to Thomas Paine Is Unveiled in Britain," *New York Times*, October 22, 1943, p. 4; William Rose Benêt, "The Phoenix Nest," *Saturday Review of Literature*, November 23, 1946, p. 48; J. Frank Dobie, *A Texan in England* (Boston: Little, Brown, 1945), pp. 84–85; and Edward J. Huntzinger, *The 388th at War* (San Angelo, Texas: Newsfoto Yearbooks, 1979).

82. "Paine, Barred from Voting 139 Years Ago, Has Citizenship 'Restored' by New Rochelle," *New York Times*, July 5, 1945, p. 4; Thomas D. Scoble, Jr., *Thomas Paine's Citizenship Record* (New Rochelle: N.Y.: Thomas Paine National Historical Association, 1946); and Theodore Morello, ed., *The Hall of Fame for Great Americans at New York University* (New York: New York University Press, 1962), p. 37. The actual placement of Paine's and Anthony's busts occurred in 1952. See the program for "Unveiling of the Busts and Tablets for Susan B. Anthony and Thomas Paine," Hall of Fame, New York University, May 18, 1952.

8. WE HAVE IT IN OUR POWER

1. William G. Mayer, *The Changing American Mind: How and Why American Public Opinion Changed Between 1960 and 1988* (Ann Arbor: University of Michigan Press, 1992), esp. pp. 98–110; Michael Crozier, Samuel Huntington, and Joji Watanuki, *The Crisis of Democracy: Report on the Governability of Democracies to the Trilateral Commission* (New York: New York University Press, 1975), p. 113; Robert Nisbet, *Twilight of Authority* (New York: Oxford University Press, 1975); Michael Harrington, *The Twilight of Capitalism* (New York: Simon and Schuster, 1976); Peter N. Carroll, *It Seemed Like Nothing Happened: America in the 1970s* (New York: Holt, Rinehart and Winston, 1982), pp. 207–33; and Stephen F. Hayward, *The Age of Reagan: The Fall of the Old Liberal Order, 1964–1980* (Roseville, Calif.: Forum, 2001), pp. 535–608, which includes a lengthy extract from President Carter's "malaise" speech of July 15, 1979.

2. Ronald Reagan to Otis Carney (November 1979), in Kiron Skinner, Annelise Anderson, and Martin Anderson, eds., *Reagan: A Life in Letters* (New York: Free Press, 2003), p. 259; and Ronald Reagan, "We Need a Rebirth in Leadership" (Presidential Nomination Acceptance Address, July 17, 1980), in *A Time for Choosing: The Speeches of Ronald Reagan* (Chicago: Regnery Gateway, 1983), p. 220.

3. Barry Goldwater, "Acceptance Speech at the Republican National Convention," in Goldwater's *Where I Stand* (New York: McGraw-Hill, 1964), p. 16. The speech was co-written by the renowned Lincoln scholar Harry V. Jaffa, a conservative who actually admired Paine. In phone conversations in May 2001 and July 2003, Jaffa acknowledged that he derived Goldwater's famous lines from Paine. But he also noted that he had found Paine's words in *Bartlett's Familiar Quotations*, which, instead of citing *Letter Addressed to the Addressers on the Late Proclamation* (in *CW*, p. 2:511), mistakenly cites *Rights of Man* as the source.

4. On Reagan's reading preferences, see Dinesh D'Souza, *Ronald Reagan: How an Ordinary Man Became an Extraordinary Leader* (New York: Free Press, 1997), pp. 74–75. And for Reagan's narration of the American Revolution, see *Freedom's Finest Hour—Adapted from the Academy Award Winning Documentary Film* (MCA Records, 1967, 1981).

5. Lou Cannon, *Governor Reagan: His Rise to Power* (New York: Public Affairs, 2003), p. 123.

6. Ronald Reagan, "Remarks at the Annual Convention of the National Association of Evangelicals" (March 8, 1983), in *Public Papers of the Presidents of the United*

States: Ronald Reagan, 1983 (Washington, D.C.: Government Printing Office, 1984), pp. 364–65.

7. Reagan, "Rebirth in Leadership," pp. 232–33.

8. Howard Penniman, "Thomas Paine—Democrat," *American Political Science Review* 37, no. 2 (April 1943), p. 244.

9. Alan Brinkley, *The End of Reform: New Deal Liberalism in Recession and War* (New York: Alfred A. Knopf, 1995), pp. 201–65.

10. Henry A. Wallace, "The Power of Books" (1937), in Wallace, *Democracy Reborn* (New York: Reynal and Hitchcock, 1944), p. 131; and "The Price of Free World Victory" (1942), in Wallace, *The Century of the Common Man* (New York: Reynal and Hitchcock, 1943), pp. 14–23; James B. Conant, "Wanted: American Radicals," *Atlantic Monthly*, May 1943, pp. 41–45; and Franklin Delano Roosevelt, "Economic Bill of Rights," January 11, 1944, in *FDR's Fireside Chats*, ed. Russell O. Buhite and David W. Levy (Norman: University of Oklahoma Press, 1992), p. 292. Also see Cass Sunstein, *The Second Bill of Rights: FDR's Unfinished Revolution and Why We Need It More Than Ever* (New York: Basic Books, 2004).

11. Elizabeth A. Fones-Wolf, *Selling Free Enterprise: The Business Assault on Labor and Liberalism, 1945–60* (Urbana: University of Illinois Press, 1994), p. 35; Alan Brinkley, "Legacies of World War II" (1995), in Brinkley, *Liberalism and Its Discontents* (Cambridge, Mass.: Harvard University Press, 1998), pp. 94–110; and Nelson Lichtenstein, *State of the Union: A Century of American Labor* (Princeton, N.J.: Princeton University Press, 2002), pp. 114–22.

12. Ellen Schrecker, *Many Are the Crimes: McCarthyism in America* (Boston: Little, Brown, 1998), p. x; and Henry F. May, "The End of American Radicalism," *American Quarterly* 2, no. 4 (Winter 1950), p. 291.

13. Tony Smith, *America's Mission: The United States and the Worldwide Struggle for Democracy in the Twentieth Century* (Princeton, N.J.: Princeton University Press, 1994).

14. Jerome L. Himmelstein, *To the Right: The Transformation of American Conservatism* (Berkeley: University of California Press, 1990), pp. 23–25; and Godfrey Hodgson, *America in Our Time* (New York: Random House, 1976), pp. 76ff.

15. Lichtenstein, *State of the Union*, pp. 98–140.

16. Clinton Rossiter, "The Shaping of the American Tradition," *William and Mary Quarterly* 11, no. 4 (October 1954), p. 519. Also see Arthur M. Schlesinger, Jr., *The Vital Center* (1949; reprinted, New Brunswick, N.J.: Transaction, 1998); Richard Hofstadter, *The Age of Reform: From Bryan to FDR* (New York: Alfred A. Knopf, 1955); Louis Hartz, *The Liberal Tradition in America* (New York: Harcourt, Brace and World, 1955); Daniel Boorstin, *The Genius of American Politics* (Chicago: University of Chicago Press, 1953); Seymour Martin Lipset, *Political Man* (New York: Doubleday, 1960), p. 442; and Daniel Bell, *The End of Ideology* (1960; reprinted, Harvard University Press, 2000).

17. Hildegarde Hawthorne, *Thomas Paine, His Country Was the World* (New York: Longmans, Green, 1949), p. vi.

18. Emanuel Celler, remarks in *Congressional Record*, House of Representatives, April, 16, 1946, p. 3763.

19. Louise Robbins, *Censorship and the American Library* (Westport, Conn.: Green-wood Press, 1996), pp. 23–24, 75–76; Robert Justin Goldstein, *Political Repression in Modern America from 1870 to 1976* (Urbana: University of Illinois Press, 2001), p. 303; and Howard Fast, *Being Red—A Memoir* (New York: Dell, 1990), pp. 135–36, 202–3.

20. Frances Stonor Saunders, *The Cultural Cold War: The CIA and the World of Arts and Letters* (New York: New Press, 1999), pp. 193–94.

21. Earl Robinson Testimony (April 11, 1957), in Eric Bentley, ed., *Thirty Years of Treason: Excerpts from Hearings before the House Committee on Un-American Activities, 1938–1968* (New York: Nation Books, 2002), p. 844.

22. "Thomas Paine Is Still Too Controversial, So Providence Doesn't Want Statue of Him," *New York Times*, September 23, 1955, p. A27.

23. Perry Miller, "Thomas Paine, Rationalist," *Nation*, February 23, 1946, p. 232; Cecelia Kenyon, "Where Paine Went Wrong," *American Political Science Review* 45, no. 1 (December 1951), pp. 1095–96, and Boorstin, *Genius of American Politics*, pp. 73, 80–81. And for Boorstin's testimony to the HUAC, see Bentley, ed., *Thirty Years of Treason*, pp. 601–12.

24. George H. Nash, *The Conservative Intellectual Movement in America Since 1945* (New York: Basic Books, 1979).

25. Eric F. Goldman, "Books That Changed America," *Saturday Review of Literature*, July 4, 1953, pp. 7–9, 37–38; Norman Cousins, *"In God We Trust": The Religious Beliefs and Ideas of the American Founding Fathers* (New York: Harper and Brothers, 1958), 389–443; and *Thomas Paine: Common Sense and Other Political Writings*, ed. Nelson F. Adkins (Indianapolis: Bobbs-Merrill, 1953).

26. Harry Truman, "Address in Philadelphia at the Dedication of the Chapel of the Four Chaplains," in *Public Papers of the Presidents of the United States: Harry S. Truman, 1951* (Washington, D.C.: Government Printing Office, 1965), p. 30; "Thomas Paine" in the radio series *So Proudly We Hail*, produced by the U.S. Army (broadcast on December 28, 1952); Thomas Paine, "Say Not That Thousands Are Gone," *New Republic*, December 25, 1950, pp. 13–16; and Editorial, "The Price Is Not Too Great," *Collier's*, January 27, 1951, p. 78.

27. Attorney General Tom C. Clark quoted in Michael Kammen, *Mystic Chords of Memory: The Transformation of Tradition in American Culture* (New York: Alfred A. Knopf, 1991), p. 574.

28. Ibid., pp. 572–81, and Eric Foner, *The Story of American Freedom* (New York: W. W. Norton, 1998), pp. 249–52.

29. American Heritage Foundation quoted in Kammen, *Mystic Chords*, p. 576; Foner, *Story of Freedom*, pp. 249–50.

30. Frank Monaghan, *Heritage of Freedom: The History and Significance of the Basic Documents of American Liberty—An Official Book of the Freedom Train* (Princeton, N.J.: Princeton University Press, 1948), pp. 25–28, 94–95.

31. Gerald Johnson, *This American People* (New York: Harper and Brothers, 1951), pp. ix, 7, and *The Lunatic Fringe* (Philadelphia: J. B. Lippincott, 1957), p. 21.

32. Henry Steele Commager quoted in Neil Jumonville, *Henry Steele Commager: Midcentury Liberalism and the History of the Present* (Chapel Hill: University of

North Carolina Press, 1999), p. 37 (and on Dodd's influence on Commager, see pp. 10–13); Henry Steele Commager, "Tom Paine Talks Back to Providence," *Saturday Review*, December 24, 1955, pp. 5–7, 32.

33. Sanford D. Hewitt, *Let Them Call Me Rebel: Saul Alinsky—His Life and Legacy* (New York: Alfred A. Knopf, 1989), pp. 163–85; and Saul Alinsky, *Reveille for Radicals* (Chicago: University of Chicago Press, 1946), pp. 3, 208.

34. Editors, "Tract for the Times," *Liberation* 1, (March 1956), pp. 3–4; and Jo Ann O. Robinson, *Abraham Went Out: A Biography of A.J. Muste* (Philadelphia: Temple University Press, 1981).

35. C. Wright Mills, *The New Men of Power: America's Labor Leaders* (New York: Harcourt, Brace, 1948); *White Collar: The American Middle Classes* (New York: Oxford University Press, 1951); *The Power Elite* (New York: Oxford University Press, 1956); and *The Sociological Imagination* (New York: Oxford University Press, 1959).

36. C. Wright Mills (early 1940s) quoted in Jim Miller, "Democracy and the Intellectual: C. Wright Mills Reconsidered," *Salmagundi*, nos. 70–71 (1986), p. 86; Mills, "The Social Role of the Intellectual" (1944), reprinted in *Power, Politics, and People: The Collected Essays of C. Wright Mills*, ed. Irving Louis Horowitz (New York: Ballantine Books, 1963), p. 296; Mills, *The Causes of World War Three* (New York: Simon and Schuster, 1958); and Mills, *Listen, Yankee: The Revolution in Cuba* (New York: Ballantine Books, 1960).

37. The SDS Port Huron Statement is reprinted as an appendix in James Miller, *Democracy Is in the Streets: From Port Huron to the Siege of Chicago* (New York: Simon and Schuster, 1987), pp. 329–74; on ERAP see pp. 184–217.

38. Peter B. Levy, *The New Left and Labor in the 1960s* (Urbana: University of Illinois Press, 1994), pp. 26–45.

39. Morton Horwitz, *The Warren Court and the Pursuit of Justice* (New York: Hill and Wang, 1998).

40. Harold Rome's *Pins and Needles*, featuring Barbra Streisand, 25th anniversary edition (New York: Columbia Records, 1962); and Philip Bezanson, "Homage to Great Americans—for Woodwind Quintet" (1962), commissioned by Radio Station WUOM, University of Michigan Broadcasting Service. The Thomas Paine Elementary Schools of Urbana, Illinois, and Cherry Hill, New Jersey, opened in 1963 and 1968, respectively.

41. Maurice Isserman and Michael Kazin, *America Divided: The Civil War of the 1960s* (New York: Oxford University Press, 2000), pp. 56–57; Michael Harrington, *The Other America* (New York: Macmillan, 1962); Rachel Carson, *Silent Spring* (Boston: Houghton Mifflin, 1962); Betty Friedan, *The Feminine Mystique* (New York: Norton, 1963); and Ralph Nader, *Unsafe at Any Speed* (New York: Grossman, 1965)

42. Miller, *Democracy Is in the Streets*, pp. 35, 73, 74, 136, 144, 164.

43. Todd Gitlin, *The Sixties: Years of Hope, Days of Rage* (New York: Bantam, 1987), pp. 69–70.

44. Todd Gitlin, *Twilight of Common Dreams: Why America Is Wracked by Culture Wars* (New York: Metropolitan Books, 1995), p. 69.

45. Tom Hayden, *Reunion: A Memoir* (New York: Random House, 1988), p. 504; and Todd Gitlin in conversations with the author, Green Bay, Wisconsin, mid-August 2004.

46. Marty Jezer, *Abbie Hoffman, American Rebel* (New Brunswick, N.J.: Rutgers University Press, 1993), pp. 33, 64, 296–97; and Jerry Rubin's remarks in Joan Morrison and Robert K. Morrison, eds., *From Camelot to Kent State: The Sixties Experience in the Words of Those Who Lived It* (New York: Times Books, 1987), p. 283.

47. Paul Foster, *Tom Paine—A Play in Two Parts* (New York: Samuel French, 1967); Bob Dylan, "As I Went Out One Morning," on the album *John Wesley Harding* (New York: Columbia Records, 1968); and Benjamin H. Levin, *To Spit Against the Wind* (New York: Citadel Press, 1970).

48. George McGovern, "Foreign Policy and the Crisis Mentality," *Atlantic Monthly*, January 1967, pp. 55–57.

49. Gitlin, *Sixties*, pp. 261ff.

50. *Work in America: Report of a Special Task Force to the Secretary of Health, Education, and Welfare* (Cambridge, Mass.: MIT Press, 1973).

51. Richard Moser, *The New Winter Soldiers: GI and Veteran Dissent During the Vietnam Era* (New Brunswick, N.J.: Rutgers University Press, 1996), pp. 104, 164–65. VVAW was founded in 1967.

52. Bill Crandell, "Opening Statement," *Winter Soldier Investigation* (1971), The Sixties Project (http://lists.village.virginia.edu/sixties/HTML_docs/Resources/Primary/Winter_Soldier/WS_02_opening.html).

53. Bill Crandell quoted in Gerald Nicosia, *Home to War: A History of the Vietnam Veterans' Movement* (New York: Crown, 2001), p. 79. The VVAW would rename itself the Winter Soldier Organization in 1972.

54. John Kerry, "Testimony to the U.S. Senate Foreign Relations Committee of April 22, 1971," in Marvin Gettleman et al., eds., *Vietnam and America: A Documented History* (New York: Grove Press, 1995), p. 462. Also see Douglas Brinkley, *Tour of Duty: John Kerry and the Vietnam War* (New York: William Morrow, 2004), pp. 1–17, 346–77.

55. Trilateral Commission members included future presidents Jimmy Carter (Democrat) and George H. W. Bush (Republican).

56. Samuel Huntington, "The United States," in Crozier, Huntington, and Watanuki, *Crisis of Democracy*, pp. 59, 102, 113–14 (italics added).

57. John Warner quoted in John Bodnar, *Remaking America: Public Memory, Commemoration, and Patriotism in the Twentieth Century* (Princeton, N.J.: Princeton University Press, 1992), p. 234; and Richard B. Morris quoted in Christopher Capozzola, "It Makes You Want to Believe in the Country: Celebrating the Bicentennial in Age of Limits," in Beth Bailey and David Farber, eds., *America in the Seventies* (Lawrence: University Press of Kansas, 2004), p. 34.

58. "A Prophet Honored," *Time*, May 1975, p. 64; Henry Leland Clarke, *These Are the Times That Try Men's Souls* (New York: Conatus Music Press, 1976); and Steve Allen, *Meeting of Minds—The Complete Scripts* (New York: Crown, 1978), pp. 11–68.

59. Irving Kristol, "The American Revolution as a Successful Revolution" (1975), in Kristol, *Neo-Conservatism: Selected Essays, 1949–1995* (New York: Free Press, 1995), pp. 235–52; and Aram Bakshian, Jr., "A Pamphleteer and a Prince," *National Review*, September 13, 1974, pp. 1051–52.

60. Gerald Ford, "Address Before a Joint Session of the Congress Reporting on the State of the Union" (January 19, 1976), in *Public Papers of the Presidents of the United States: Gerald R. Ford, 1976–77* (Washington. D.C.: Government Printing Office, 1979), pp. 18–19.

61. People's Bicentennial Commission, *America's Birthday: A Planning and Activity Guide for Citizens' Participation During the Bicentennial Years* (1974), quoted in Bodnar, *Remaking America*, p. 235.

62. Ted Howard, *The P.B.C.: A History*, a special issue of the PBC magazine *Common Sense* (Washington, D.C.: People's Bicentennial Commission, 1976), pp. 5–6.

63. Jeremy Rifkin and John Rossen, eds., *How to Commit Revolution American Style* (Secaucus, N.J.: Lyle Stuart, 1973); People's Bicentennial Commission, *Common Sense II* (New York: Bantam Books, 1975); and People's Bicentennial Commission, *Voices of the American Revolution* (New York: Bantam Books, 1975).

64. Senator James O. Eastland, introduction to *The Attempt to Steal the Bicentennial: The People's Bicentennial Commission—Report of the Subcommittee to Investigate the Administration of the Internal Security Act and Other Internal Security Laws of the Committee on the Judiciary, United States Senate, 94th Congress, Second Session* (Washington, D.C.: Government Printing Office, May 1976), p.1.

65. Bernard Bailyn, "Thomas Paine" (1973), in Bailyn, *Faces of Revolution: Personalities and Themes in the Struggle for American Independence* (New York: Alfred A. Knopf, 1990), pp. 67–68, 82, and "Lines of Force in Recent Writings on the American Revolution," in *Proceedings of the Fourth International Congress of Historical Sciences* (San Francisco, 1975), p. 181; David Freeman Hawke, *Paine* (New York: W.W. Norton, 1974); and John Keane, *Tom Paine, A Political Life* (Boston: Little, Brown, 1995), p. xvii. Notably, in the preface to *The Ordeal of Thomas Hutchinson* (Cambridge, Mass.: Harvard University Press, 1974), Bailyn acknowledged the possible influence of student radicalism on his historical thinking. For examples of the work of the radical historians, see the several contributions to Alfred F. Young, ed., *The American Revolution: Explorations in the History of American Radicalism* (DeKalb: Northern Illinois University Press, 1976), as well as Eric Foner, *Tom Paine and Revolutionary America* (New York: Oxford University Press, 1976).

9. IT IS YET TOO SOON TO WRITE THE HISTORY OF THE REVOLUTION

1. Paine, "Constitutional Reform" (1805), in *CW*, p. 2:1006.

2. Paine, "A Serious Address to the People of Pennsylvania on the Present Situation of Their Affairs" (1778), in *CW*, p. 2:281, and *Rights of Man, Part 1* (1791) in *CW*, p. 1:344. For one example of fresh thinking on matters of equality and opportunity, inspired by Paine's arguments in *Agrarian Justice*, see Bruce Ackerman and Anne Alstott, *The Stakeholder Society* (New Haven, Conn.: Yale University Press, 1999).

3. William J. Clinton, "Inaugural Address" (January 20, 1993), in *Public Papers of the Presidents of the United States: William J. Clinton* (Washington, D.C.: Government Printing Office, 1994), p. 1 (italics added). Notably, Senator John Kerry, who had quoted Paine in 1971 when speaking before the Senate Foreign Relations Committee as a leader of Vietnam Veterans Against the War, turned to Paine again in 2004 when accepting the Democratic nomination for president. However—perhaps worried about recalling his involvement in the "Winter Soldiers" movement or worried that his choice of words, "We have it in our power to change the world again," would make it evident that he was echoing Ronald Reagan's 1980 evocation of Paine—Kerry did not actually name Paine when he did so. See John Kerry, "Speech to the 2004 Democratic National Convention," in John Kerry and John Edwards, *Our Plan for America* (New York: Public Affairs, 2004), p. 132.

4. Paine, "To the Citizens of the United States" (1802), in *CW*, p. 2:910, and *Letter to the Abbé Raynal* (1782), in *CW*, p. 2:215.

ACKNOWLEDGMENTS

Thomas Paine wrote in *Common Sense* that "the strength of one man is so unequal to his wants, and his mind so unfitted for perpetual solitude, that he is soon obliged to seek assistance and relief of another." I can vouch for that. I spent many hours alone; but I could never have accomplished this work all by myself.

Fortunately, colleagues and contacts near and far, from diverse disciplines, professions, and political persuasions—some of whom would surely dissent from what I have presented and argued here—were willing to help me with directions, questions, and audits. In particular, I want to thank Al Young, Eric Foner, Elliott Gorn, Jerry Rodesch, Andy Kersten, Paul Buhle, Kim Nielsen, David Wilson, Miriam Brody, Jack Fruchtman, Ken Burchell, Michael Kazin, Christopher Caldwell, Peter Hannaford, Harry V. Jaffa, Jonathan Holloway, Mark Noll, Todd Gitlin, Robin Kelley, Marcus Rediker, Jeremi Suri, Seth Cotlar, Joe Conason, Caleb Crain, Christine Compston, Craig Lockard, Derek Jeffreys, David Voelker, Tony Galt, Bruce Shepard, Tom Perry, David Henley, Jack Frisch, Gary Berton, Andrew Austin, Lynn Walter, David Blake, Allen Ruff, John Jentz, Ronald Collins, Kirsten Fischer, Patrick Carey, David Fitzsimmons, Douglas Egerton, Woody Holton, and Stacey Robertson.

In securing books, pamphlets, and documents from around the country, and in tracking down historical and biographical references, I have depended upon the expert assistance of Mary Naumann, Joan Robb, and Anne Kasuboski at the Cofrin Library of the University of Wisconsin Green Bay. Cherish the librarians! And in that spirit I must not fail to note that I have benefited from the good offices of similar folk from New England to the Hill Country of Texas. Nor should I fail to register how much I have always relied on the talents and enthusiasms of our departmental administrative assistant, Chris Terrien, to keep things running smoothly.

Here I must record as well my gratitude to the National Endowment for the Humanities for granting me a fellowship in 2002–2003 that gave me the time I so desperately needed to pursue this project. But the work took more than time, and in that vein I applaud the talents, skills, and insights of Thomas LeBien, my editor at Hill and

Wang of Farrar, Straus and Giroux. Thomas knows American history and how to get his authors to tell it well, which I hope I have done. It was a pleasure to work with him on this book. I also want to acknowledge Lauren Osborne, who first contracted the volume, and Kristina McGowan for her timely assistance on matters editorial.

Without promising that I will behave any differently in the future, I thank my friends Jerry Rodesch, Dave Jowett, Elliott Gorn, Michael Kazin, Craig Lockard, Cecil Roebuck, Meir Russ, Tony Galt, Derek Jeffreys, Bill Bauman, and Ron Baba for listening to me go on about Paine and the promise of America these past several years. And similarly, but with the greatest affection and warmth, I thank my daughters, Rhiannon and Fiona, my mom, Frances, and most especially, my partner in all things, Lorna, for their support, encouragement, and love. Finally, I dedicate this work to Mum and Dad, Lorna's parents, Ann and Lorimer Stewart.

INDEX

Abbot, Francis Ellingwood, 166
Abel, Darrell, 219–20
abolitionism, 36, 41, 125, 147–51, 153, 155, 203, 244
Act of Union (1707), 19
Adams, Abigail, 11, 17, 52–53
Adams, James Truslow, 210
Adams, John, 3, 11, 17, 40, 50, 89, 93–95, 99, 117, 119, 133, 146–47, 158, 233, 235, 273n4; criticism of *Common Sense* by, 40, 52–56; deism of, 108; elitism of, 31, 92, 260, 268n39; presidency of, 96, 111–15
Adams, John Quincy, 135, 233, 273n4
Adams, Samuel, 17, 51, 203, 235, 255
Address to the Members of the Trade Societies and to the Working Classes Generally (Heighton), 135
Afghanistan, 12
AFL-CIO, 229, 241, 248
African Americans, 11, 37, 122, 174, 157, 212, 216, 227, 248, 267n20; in abolitionist movement, 147–48, 150; in civil rights movement, 222, 237–43; in Communist Party, 216; disenfranchisement of, 181, 227; farming by, 179; labor movement and, 172, 247; militant, 245; oppression of, 163, 204, 234; socialist, 185, 186;

during World War II, 226; *see also* slavery
Age of Reason, The (Paine), 5, 10, 82–84, 86–87, 106, 108–11, 113–14, 120, 123–24, 132, 142–43, 146, 150, 155, 157, 164, 166, 217, 272n42
Agnew, Spiro, 250, 254
Agrarian Justice (Paine), 5, 86–87, 111, 136, 138, 151, 169
Agricultural Adjustment Act, 211
Aitken, Robert, 34, 38
Alien Act (1798), 96, 114
Alien Enemies Act (1798), 114
Alinsky, Saul, 7, 236, 238
Allan, Lewis, 220
Allen, Ethan, 102, 109, 160
Allen, James, 216
Allen, Steve, 254
Altgeld, John, 290n47
Altrusa Women's Club, 220
America First Committee, 294n9
American and Foreign Anti-Slavery Society, 149
American Anti-Slavery Society, 36, 148, 150
American Bible, An (Hubbard), 182, 297n46
American Bible Society, 130
American Colonization Society, 148

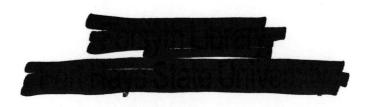